INSIGHT GUIDE

CHINA

Discovery
CHANNEL

APA PUBLICATIONS
Part of the Langenscheidt Publishing Group

ABOUT THIS BOOK

Editorial

Editor
Scott Rutherford
Editorial Director
Brian Bell

Distribution

UK & Ireland
GeoCenter International Ltd
The Viables Centre, Harrow Way
Basingstoke, Hants RG22 4BJ
Fax: (44) 1256-817988

United States
Langenscheidt Publishers, Inc.
46–35 54th Road, Maspeth, NY 11378
Fax: (718) 784-0640

Canada
Prologue Inc.
1650 Lionel Bertrand Blvd., Boisbriand
Québec, Canada J7H 1N7
Tel: (450) 434-0306. Fax: (450) 434-2627

Australia & New Zealand
Hema Maps Pty. Ltd.
24 Allgas Street, Slacks Creek 4127
Brisbane, Australia
Tel: (61) 7 3290 0322. Fax: (61) 7 3290 0478

Worldwide
**Apa Publications GmbH & Co.
Verlag KG (Singapore branch)**
38 Joo Koon Road, Singapore 628990
Tel: (65) 865-1600. Fax: (65) 861-6438

Printing

Insight Print Services (Pte) Ltd
38 Joo Koon Road, Singapore 628990
Tel: (65) 865-1600. Fax: (65) 861-6438

© 2000 Apa Publications GmbH & Co.
Verlag KG (Singapore branch)
*All Rights Reserved
First Edition 1990
Ninth Edition (revised) 2000*

CONTACTING THE EDITORS
Although every effort is made to
provide accurate information, we
live in a fast-changing world and
would appreciate it if readers
would call our attention to any
errors or outdated information
that may occur by writing to:
Insight Guides, P.O. Box 7910,
London SE1 1WE, England.
Fax: (44 20) 7403-0290.
e-mail:
insight@apaguide.demon.co.uk

This guidebook combines the interests and enthusiasms of two of the world's best-known information providers: Insight Guides, whose titles have set the standard for visual travel guides since 1970, and the Discovery Channel, the world's premier source of non-fiction television programming.

The editors of Insight Guides provide both practical advice and general understanding about a place's history, culture, institutions and people, while Discovery Channel and its Web site, www.discovery.com, help millions of viewers explore their world from the comfort of their own home and also encourage them to explore it firsthand.

In this, the eighth edition of *Insight Guide: China*, we travel to the world's oldest continual civilisation. China's ancient cities were thriving long before those of Europe took root, and China's arts, crafts, literature and philosophy inform those of most other Asian cultures today. Its great cities of Beijing, Hong Kong and Shanghai are amongst the world's most dynamic and influential.

point of reference for information on travel, accommodation, restaurants and other practical aspects of the country. Information is located quickly using the index printed on the back-cover flap.

The contributors

This edition was supervised by **Scott Rutherford**, building on the original edition and produced by **Manfred Morgenstern**, who first went to China in the late 1970s.

The history chapters were completely revamped by Beijing-based **Leslie Burgoine**, who has an MA in Chinese history. Also based in Beijing is **Ellen Sheng**, who updated feature essays and wrote the Outside Beijing chapter. **Sharon Owyang**, who was born in Singapore and educated at Harvard, took a sabbatical from Hollywood to travel the Silk Road, Chang Jiang, and to Xi'an. **Lily Tung**, who has lived in Shanghai since the early 1990s, updated the chapter for Shanghai. Beijing-based free-lance writer **Bill Smith** worked on the Beijing chapter.

Jim Goodman, based in Chiang Mai, overhauled the chapters on Yunnan and Guangxi. **Michael Sutherland** in Kunming updated the Sichuan chapter, and **Angie Ching Yuan** in Shanghai updated the Guangzhou chapter. **Ron Glotzer** compiled the Travel Tips. **Bill Cranfield** updated this latest revised edition.

Contributors to earlier editions included **Tim Larimer, Helmut Forster-Latsch, Tom Ots, Marie-Luise Latsch, Elke Wandel, Marie-Luise Beppler-Lie, Karl Grobe-Hagel**, and **Eva Klapproth**.

How to use this book

The book is carefully structured to convey an understanding of China and its culture, and to guide readers through its sights and attractions:

◆ The Features section, with a yellow colour bar, covers the country's history and culture in lively authoritative essays.

◆ The Places section, with a blue bar, provides full details of all the sights and areas worth seeing. The chief places of interest are coordinated by number with specially drawn maps.

◆ The Travel Tips section, with an orange bar and at the back of the book, offers a convenient

Map Legend

— ·· —	International Boundary
— — —	Province
⊖	Border Crossing
— • —	National Park
— — —	Ferry Route
Ⓜ	Metro
✈	Airport
🚌	Bus Station
Ⓟ	Parking
ⓘ	Tourist Information
✉	Post Office
✝ ♁ ♂	Church/Ruins
☽ ♜	Mosque
✡ ♁	Synagogue
♜ ♂	Castle/Ruins
∴	Archaeological Site
∩	Cave
★	Place of Interest

The main places of interest in the Places section are coordinated by number with a full-colour map (e.g. **❶**) and a symbol at the top of every right-hand page tells you where to find the map.

Insight Guide CHINA

CONTENTS

Places

CHINA

After 40 centuries of looking inward, China is now helping to define the world's future, whether we're ready or not.

The name China, as we use it in the West, can presumably be traced back to the Qin dynasty (221–206 BC), when the idea of a unified China became real, and was called Tschin, Tschina or Tzinistan in the Indo-Germanic languages. The Chinese of the Qin dynasty called the country Da Qin, thus giving the new empire a sense of size by preceding *qin* with *da*, which means big or great in size. (In pinyin, the modern transliteration of Chinese pronunciation, *qi* is pronounced *chee*.) While the official name is Zhonghua Renmin Gongheguo – the People's Republic of China – throughout Chinese history this land has always been, simply, Zhongguo – the Middle Kingdom.

China, the third-largest nation in the world in land area and the largest in population, has the world's longest continuously recorded history, and it has given the world some of the most significant scientific and technological inventions.

In Tiantan, the Temple of Heaven in Beijing, a marble altar signifies the centre of the known ancient world, a place that only the emperor was allowed to enter. According to the world-view of ancient China, the Middle Kingdom lay precisely below the centre of the firmament. The farther one was from the emperor's throne, the lower one was in the cosmic hierarchy. The unfortunate people and cultures living on the dark peripheries of the earth, especially to the gloomy north and the arid west, and to Europe beyond, were considered to be barbarians.

Likewise, for centuries Europeans similarly regarded China as equally near the edge of the earth, admittedly an empire of magnificence and cultural interest, but of little importance to the world.

Much later, especially during the 1960s and 1970s, Western analysts and pundits referred to China as a sleeping giant, or if lyrically inclined, a sleeping tiger or even dragon. But it's been a few years since one has heard such expressions about China. No one doubts that China is now wide awake, and increasingly a power that will help define the next millennium. Yet defining the world's history is not something with which China is comfortable or experienced. For most of its existence, it has focused inward, like a *taijiquan* student seeking a centred stability. Consequently, China's emergence as a world power has been clumsy and awkward. China will learn, no doubt, but only if China itself thinks it necessary.

More immediate, perhaps, is China's population. Since the end of World War II, just a little over half a century ago, the country's population has doubled to over a billion people. Only around 10 percent of China's land is suitable for agriculture, but a fifth of the world's people must subsist on that land. Yet experts in China and elsewhere say that China can realistically support only 800 million people.

PRECEDING PAGES: Huang Shan, Anhui; Sani woman, Kunming; Yonghe Gong, Beijing; Victoria Harbour from The Peak. **LEFT:** festival on Cheung Chau, Hong Kong.

Travellers to China's large cities (anyplace with more than 1 million people) will see the result of accommodating the explosive population growth: monochromatic, concrete cities veiled with the smoke of pollution, and legions of men from the countryside looking for work, and perhaps a mate. Travellers will also see increasing affluence and leisure time, and the capitalist signs of people spending money and nurturing a consumer society. Things are getting better in China for the individual. A result of Communism, or the intrusion of capitalism? The question and answer are dialectical.

In the half century since the Communist revolution, the quality of life for the average Chinese has improved significantly. Life expectancy is double that of 1949, and the standard of living and quality of life have improved exponentially. At the same time, Communism has faltered in monumental ways. Misdirected policies created what may have been the world's worst famine in the early 1960s, and the so-called Cultural Revolution, initially nurtured by Mao to increase his stature, spun out of control, destroying much of China's ancient heritage in the process, not to mention China's intellectual and creative talents.

"Seeing is easy, learning is hard" goes an old Chinese proverb. Indeed. The insightful traveller must necessarily realise and acknowledge that China simply is China.

Notes about spellings

For the past century, the most common way to romanise Chinese was the Wade-Giles method. Increasingly, however, *pinyin* is the modern standard, and it is the official system used within the People's Republic. (Taiwan, on the other hand, uses the Wade-Giles system.) This book uses pinyin. Travellers will encounter both forms in Asia, and so must make certain linguistic leaps of recognition at times. China's capital was Peking the old way, Beijing in pinyin. It is now Nanjing, not Nanking. The founder of the Communist Party used to be Mao Tse-tung; now it's Mao Zedong. The goddess of mercy is Kuan Yin in Taiwan, Quanyin in China. The only pinyin transliterations liable to induce indigestion are *qi* (pronounced *chee*), and *xi*, or *shi*. Thus, the Ch'in dynasty is now the Qin dynasty.

Mandarin uses suffixes to indicate many proper nouns, such as river (*-jiang* or *-he*), temple (*-si* or *-ta*), mountain (*-shan*), or street (*-lu* or *-dajie*). In romanised or pinyin form, the suffix is sometimes integral with the root, sometimes not. We have chosen to separate the suffix to clearly identify the subject. Thus, the Tian Mountains are Tian Shan, but never Tian Shan Mountains or Tianshan Mountains. (But one might see them as Tianshan in other publications.) The decision to separate the suffix is primarily one of utility and ease of recognition. Additionally, we use Chinese pronunciations of place names as the primary reference, with English in parentheses.

OPPOSITE: *mahjong*, nearly a national game in China.

Decisive Dates

The Early Empire

Circa 21st–16th centuries BC: Xia dynasty. Some scholars question whether this dynasty existed.
Circa 16th–11th centuries BC: Shang dynasty, the first recorded dynasty. Ancestor worship is ritualised.
Circa 11th cent.–256 BC: Zhou dynasty. Capital established at Chang'an (now Xi'an), later at Luoyang.
770–476 BC: Spring and Autumn Period. Consolidation of aristocratic family-states. Confucius (551–479 BC) stresses moral responsibility of ruler.
403–221 BC: Warring States period.

Qin Dynasty (221–206 BC)

221 BC: Qin Shi Huangdi unifies China to found the first imperial dynasty. Weights and measures, currency, and writing are standardised. Qin Shi Huangdi builds an immense underground tomb, including an army of thousands of terracotta warriors.

Han Dynasty (206 BC–AD 220)

206 BC: Han dynasty founded; capital in Chang'an.
180 BC: Eunuchs appear at imperial court to look after the emperor's wives and concubines.
165 BC: Civil service examinations instituted.
AD 25: Capital moved to Luoyang.
AD 105: Traditional date for the invention of paper. Paper may have already been in use for two centuries.

Commerce between China and Asia/Europe thrives.
2nd century: First Buddhist establishments are founded in China.
AD 220: Abdication of the last Han emperor. Wei, Jin, and Northern and Southern dynasties divide China.

Sui Dynasty (581–618)

581: Following nearly four centuries of division, Sui dynasty reunifies China. New legal code established.
589–610: Repairs of early parts of the Great Wall. Construction of a system of Grand Canals linking northern and southern China.

Tang Dynasty (618–907)

618: Sui dynasty collapses, Tang dynasty proclaimed. Government increasingly bureaucratised. Buddhism influences all sectors of society. Chang'an (Xi'an) grows into one of the world's largest cities by the end of the Tang dynasty.
690–705: Empress Wu (627–705) governs China as its first female ruler. Writing of poetry becomes a requisite in civil service examinations.
907–960: Fall of Tang dynasty. Five Dynasties and Ten Kingdoms partition China. Anarchy in much of China.

Song Dynasty (960–1279)

960: Northern Song dynasty reunites China, capital established at Kaifeng.
1040: Invention of movable type, but not as efficient for printing pages of Chinese characters as wood-block printing. Development of Neo-Confucianism during 11th and 12th centuries.
1127: Beginning of the Southern Song dynasty, as invaders take over northern China and the Song capital is moved to Hangzhou, near Shanghai.

Yuan Dynasty (1279–1368)

1279: After nearly half a century of trying, Mongols led by Kublai Khan, grandson of Ghengis Khan, rout the Song court. Tibet is added to the empire. Trade along the Silk Road flourishes. Beijing is made the capital.

MingDynasty (1368–1644)

1368: Founding of the Ming dynasty after Han Chinese overthrow the Mongols.
1405–33: During the reign of Emperor Yongle, Muslim eunuch Zheng He (1371–circa.1433) commands seven overseas expeditions to Southeast Asia, India, Persia, and East Africa.
1514: The first Portuguese ships anchor off Guangzhou (Canton).
1553: Macau becomes a Portuguese trading port, and the first European settlement in China.

Qing dynasty (1644–1912)

1644: A non-Han Chinese people from Manchuria, the Manchu, seize Beijing, beginning the Qing dynasty.

1661–1722: Reign of Emperor Kangxi.

1736–96: Reign of Emperor Qianlong.

1800: First edict prohibiting the importation and local production of opium.

1838: Lin Zexu, a court official, suspends all trade in opium. The following year, the Qing court terminates all trade between England and China.

1839–42: English forces gather off China's coast. Fighting begins in 1841 in what has been called the First Opium War.

1842: Treaty of Nanjing signed. More Chinese ports are forced open to foreign trade, and Hong Kong island is surrendered to Great Britain "in perpetuity".

1851–64: Taiping Rebellion.

1855–75: Muslim rebellions.

1856–60: Arrow War.

1858: Conflicts arise between European powers, mainly France and England, and China. Treaty of Tianjin signed, opening more ports to foreigners.

1860: British and French troops burn the Summer Palace in Beijing; Kowloon Peninsula ceded to Britain.

1894–95: Sino-Japanese War, which China loses.

1900: Boxer Rebellion seeks to remove foreign influences from China. Boxers take Europeans hostage in Beijing for eight weeks.

1905: Abolishment of the civil service examination

1911: Republican Revolution: representatives from 17 provinces gather in Nanjing to establish a provisional republican government. Sun Yatsen is chosen president, but soon steps down.

1912: Abdication of the last emperor, Puyi.

Post-Imperial China

1916–28: President of the republic, Yuan Shikai, considers declaring himself emperor. Several provinces declare independence, Yuan dies, and China falls apart. Civil war amongst various warlords.

1919: On 4 May in Beijing, a large demonstration demands measures to restore China's sovereignty, thus beginning a nationalist movement.

1921: Founding of the Communist Party in Shanghai.

1925: Sun Yatsen dies, disappointed with the anarchy of China's civil war.

1934–36: The Long March: Communists forced by Nationalists to abandon their stronghold in southern China. 30,000 of the 100,000 who began the march arrive in Yan'an, west of Beijing.

1937: Communists and Nationalists unite to fight the Japanese.

1945: Japan defeated in World War II; full-scale civil war ensues in China.

People's Republic of China

1949: Mao Zdong declares People's Republic in Beijing on 1 October; Nationalist army flees to Taiwan.

1950–1953: Chinese troops support North Korea.

1958–1961: Great Leap Forward results in a mass famine that kills upwards of 30 million Chinese.

1960: Split between China and the Soviet Union.

1964: China explodes an atomic bomb.

1966: Beginning of Cultural Revolution.

1976: Zhou Enlai and Mao Zedong die, the Cultural Revolution ends. Demonstrations in Tiananmen Square.

1978: Deng Xiaoping becomes top leader, instituting a policy of economic reform and opening to the West.

1989: Tiananmen Square demonstrations; military crackdown ends with hundreds of deaths.

1992: Deng restarts economic reforms.

1997: Deng Xiaoping dies in February; Hong Kong reverts to Chinese sovereignty on July 1.

1999: Anti-NATO demonstrations after the accidental bombing of the Chinese embassy in Belgrade. China signs a trade agreement with the US as a prelude to membership of the World Trade Organisation. Macau reverts to Chinese sovereignty in December.

LEFT: Kangxi ruled from 1661 to 1722.

ABOVE: Mao Zedong surrounded by Red Guards.

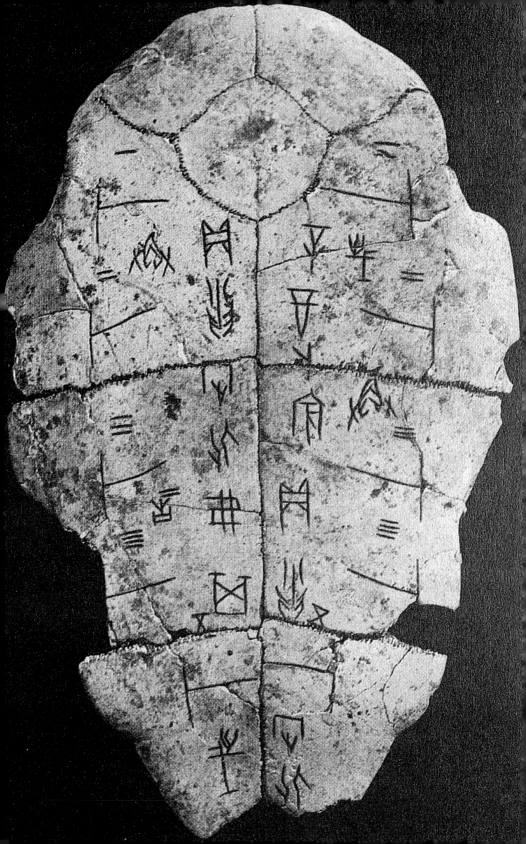

ANCIENT DYNASTIES: XIA TO MING

From the Xia dynasty to the reign of the Ming, which replaced a century of Mongol rule, the record of China's imperial court extends back nearly 4,000 years.

Historical legends remain a powerful symbol of the endurance and unity of Chinese cultural values. During imperial times, emperors claimed to follow the sage kings' examples as rulers; more recently, China's leaders have glorified the length of their history and its early achievements – even while condemning other aspects of the past – to foster unity and nationalism among the people.

Archeological findings indicate that primitive people lived in the territory of today's China one million years ago. In the early decades of the 20th century, archeologists excavated a series of caves, one nearly the size of a football field, near a village just southwest of Beijing. Skulls, teeth, and bones of more than 40 *Homo erectus* were uncovered, along with tens of thousands of stone tools dating from 200,000 to 400,000 years ago. Peking Man and Woman were hunter-fisher-gatherers who lit fires for warmth and for cooking animals like bear, hyena, saber-toothed tiger, and water buffalo.

Human fossils and tools dating from this period continue to be found in widely dispersed sites across China. Discoveries indicate that early Chinese civilisation developed in a number of areas and possessed distinctive local characteristics as well as common features. Archeologists have concluded that fundamental ideas of kinship, authority, religion, and art were already forming in these early cultures.

Neolithic China (12,000–2000 BC) was characterised by the spread of agricultural communities. People hunted and fished for food; they also raised pigs and dogs, and grew hemp to use for fabric. Clustered dwellings suggest kinship

units, and pottery designs featured clan or lineage symbols, as well as pictures and images of animals and plants.

Of the early legendary dynasties – Xia, Shang and Zhou – the actual existence of the Xia remains in doubt by some. However, excavations in 1959 at Erlitou (near present-day Luoyang, in Henan Province) unearthed palaces believed to have been a Xia dynasty capital.

Shang dynasty (16th–11th c. BC)

In 1899, scholars noticed pharmacists selling bones with inscriptions of archaic characters. By the late 1920s, these oracle bones had been traced to Anyang, in Henan Province, where the last Shang capital was excavated. Shamans served the Shang kings and made divinations by applying a hot point to animal shoulder-blade bones to create cracks, which were then interpreted and the results etched onto the bone. Over 100,000 oracle bones have been collected.

Oracle bones and inscriptions on bronze work, the excavation sites themselves, and the written records of the subsequent Zhou dynasty describe the Shang as a remarkably stratified society. The elite hunted for sport and fought in horse-drawn chariots, while the peasantry lived in semi-subterranean dwellings. Ancestor worship was ritualised and royal tombs contained valuable objects as well as animal and even human sacrifices. The mobilisation of mass labour for public works like city walls attested to the authority and power of the Shang aristocracy.

Zhou dynasty (11th c.–256 BC)

The primary structure of the Chinese state is considered to have emerged during the Zhou dynasty. The Zhou clan had long been vassals of the Shang, but eventually grew strong

SILKWORM SECRETS

An achievement of neolithic China was the intricate craft of silk production. This household industry remained a Chinese skill – and secret, under penalty of death – until the 6th century, when silkworms were smuggled to the West.

PRECEDING PAGES: Terracotta warriors, Xi'an, from the Qin dynasty. **LEFT:** early Chinese writing on a tortoise-shell oracle from the Shang dynasty.

enough to defeat them in warfare in the 11th century. Their capital was built at Chang'an (now called Xi'an), and sons of Zhou rulers were dispatched to preside over vassal states in a feudal-like system. A belief in heaven's mandate established a new basis for governing legitimacy. The idea of the mandate of heaven holds that the leader's right to rule is based on his ability to maintain harmony between heaven and earth, himself and his officials, and the officials and the people.

The start of the Eastern Zhou period is marked by the eastward movement of its capital to Luoyang, in 771 BC. In the Spring and

Autumn Period (770–476 BC), aristocratic family-states formed alliances and fought or absorbed each other until there were only seven large states remaining by the era of Warring States (403–221 BC). Despite such political strife, social and economic advances included the introduction of iron, development of infantry armies, circulation of currency, beginning of private land ownership, expansion of cities, and the breakdown of class barriers.

In addition, two components of the later Chinese imperial government began to emerge – military rulers and scholar-teachers. Both focused on ritual and ceremonies to keep human society in accord with the cosmic order. The violence of the age inspired philosophers who hoped for peace and order, proposing their theories for regaining the golden age of the sage-kings who, according to legend, ruled over a peaceful and united China.

The foremost thinkers of the time were Confucius (551–479 BC) and his followers Mencius (circa 370–300 BC) and Xunzi (circa 310–215 BC). These men stressed the maintenance of tradition and the cultivation of personal morality. Confucianism stressed the moral accountability of the ruler toward the people. Peace and abundance were guaranteed if the ruler ruled fairly, preserved the proper relationships in society, and cultivated his own moral values.

Opposed to any of this reformist ideology was Daoism, traditionally attributed to Laozi, who was said by his followers to have been a contemporary of Confucius. Daoists believed in a return to the Way (the *dao*) by following natural feelings and accepting the experience of life without struggle. It was often said that officials were Confucians while in office and Daoists when retired.

Qin dynasty (221–206 BC)

The Qin state grew the most powerful during the Warring States period, ruling by strict laws that supported agriculture and strengthened the state. It finally conquered the other states in 221 BC. The first emperor of the Qin dynasty, Qin Shi Huangdi, is considered to be the first ruler of a united China.

Weights and measures, currency, and, most important, writing were standardised. Highways were constructed, and waterways and canals were dug in the south for water transport. The archives of defeated states were burned and hundreds of scholars critical of Qin rule were murdered. The immensity of his power and ego can still be seen with the discovery near Xi'an of over 7,000 life-sized terracotta warriors created to protect his elaborate tomb. Walls were built during these times, but the legend that the Great Wall was built by Qin Shi Huangdi is not correct. While many dynasties built extensive walls for protection, the Great Wall visible today was mostly built by the Ming dynasty during the 16th century.

Qin Shi Huangdi's ruthless exploitation of people year after year exhausted the populace and China's financial resources, and his empire rapidly fell apart after his death in 210 BC.

Han dynasty (206 BC–AD 220)

While repudiating the harsh rule of the Qin, the Han rulers built upon the established centralised bureaucracy. But the important difference in Han administration was the way in which officials were drafted into service. By the first century BC, it was generally accepted that officials should be men trained in the Confucian classical texts, and so officials now had to reconcile their positions serving the emperor and state with Confucian values of proper behaviour and personal integrity. It was during the Han dynasty that Confucianism became indelibly ingrained in Chinese politics, society, and culture.

who were to play an important role until 1911. Originally, they were hired to look after the emperors' wives and concubines, but they soon became advisors, playing an important part in palace intrigues and power struggles.

The Han dynasty was in its prime under the rule of Han Wudi (140–87 BC). It had always been an important challenge for the Chinese empire to control the nomadic tribes in the north and the west. Wudi succeeded in defeating the Huns, the nomads who had established a strong empire in the north. Now Wudi's empire stretched all the way to the western region, to what is now Xinjiang. During the reign of the

DYNASTY PRIMER

For nearly 4,000 years, China has been ruled by a Son of Heaven. (The Xia dynasty is not recognised by some scholars.) There were occasional periods of chaos, such as the four confusing centuries that separated the Han and Tang dynasties.

Xia	21st–16th centuries BC
Shang	16th–11th centuries BC
Zhou	11th century–221 BC
	Spring and Autumn Period 770–476 BC
	Warring States Period 403–221 BC
Qin	221–206 BC
Han	206 BC–AD 220
Tang	618–907
Song	960–1279
Yuan	1279–1368
Ming	1368–1644
Qing	1644–1911/1912

The stability of the Han enabled China's population to grow to more than 50 million. Trade and industry developed, and communication and transportation systems improved, all of which fostered closer ties among China's diverse regions. Cities attracted the educated and the wealthy from all over the country, becoming important cultural centres. People elsewhere, especially in areas of hardship, migrated to places with more opportunity.

In 180 BC, a new social class appeared at the imperial court for the first time: palace eunuchs,

Han, there were numerous contacts with other cultures through traders coming from afar. From the first century BC, caravans had travelled along the Silk Road, bringing horses and gold in exchange for silk.

Buddhism was introduced to China from India during the late Han period; while Confucianism waned, Buddhist teachings and art made a lasting impression on Chinese culture in the north and the south. Buddhism was permitted to flourish by non-Chinese rulers of northern China, in part because it too came from outside the Chinese establishment that they were subsuming themselves. Buddhist priests could help foster complaisance among the peo-

LEFT: print of Qin Shi Huangdi, Qin dynasty.
RIGHT: old painting of imperial guards.

ple. For the upper classes, Buddhism offered explanations and comfort for the loss of their society. It was intellectually sophisticated and artistically pleasing.

Regionalism and class distinctions grew as the establishment of a strong centralised government was set back during the four centuries of division between the fall of the Han and reunification under the vigorous but short-lived Sui dynasty (581–618). But trade and diplomatic relations with Central Asian peoples were already influential and well-developed before the Sui.

The families who founded the Sui and Tang dynasties had intermarried with northern nomadic groups, who formed the aristocratic families of northwest China. From these herdsmen, the Chinese procured horses for cavalry warfare. When the founder of the Sui took power in 581, he rapidly established a new legal code, organised local governments, and continued a number of institutions begun by earlier kingdoms. Despite the unification and strengthening of the state, the depletion of the country's resources and the visions of grandeur of the second Sui emperor led to the dynasty's downfall.

Tang dynasty (618–907)

The founders of the Tang dynasty inherited the accomplishments of the Sui, including the large capital at Chang'an, now Xi'an. The Chinese bureaucracy continued to develop. During the Sui-Tang era, seven ministries were established – personnel, administration, finance, rites, army, justice, and public works – as was a censorate, an agency responsible for inspecting and reporting on official and even imperial conduct.

Under the second emperor, Tang-dynasty armies expanded west into Korea, south into northern Vietnam, and east into Central Asia. This was the great era of the Silk Road. As trade expanded along this route, contacts with the people and cultures of Central and West Asia increased. Chang'an developed into a great international metropolis. Between AD 600 and 900, no city in the world could compare in size and grandeur. People from Japan, Korea, Vietnam, Persia, and West Asia seeking trade, Buddhist enlightenment, or simply adventure injected their energy into Tang urban life.

The strength of the Tang supported creative vigour in literature and the fine arts. Later periods looked to Tang poetry in particular as a model. That the writing of poetry became a requisite in the civil service exams for higher qualifications and promotion can be credited to China's only female ruler, Empress Wu Zetian, who reigned from around 690 to 705.

Empress Wu's reputation was affected by Confucianism's aversion towards women with authority (though this historical antipathy is not exclusive to China), with tales of murdered officials and other intrigues the most often told. Like many emperors before and after her, she manipulated those around her to gain power. However, she was an intelligent politician, selecting talented scholars who passed the civil

service examinations for key posts. The growing importance of the examinations in the late Tang period served to weaken powerful, aristocratic families of the northwest and presented greater opportunities for those from other areas to be involved in government. Scholar-officials – those who earned their rank through success in the examinations – started to become a minor elite within the imperial bureaucracy. The influence of great families began to correspond to the placement of their members in high office. A powerful family could soon fall apart if two or three generations passed without a member attaining a high position in government.

The height of Tang dynasty splendour was

attained under Emperor Xuanzong, who reigned from 713 until 755. Nevertheless, failings accumulated. Military campaigns became overextended and expensive. Powerful generals meddled in court politics. Officials became involved in factional infighting, and the emperor increasingly turned to court eunuchs for support. In his old age, Xuanzong let his control deteriorate when he fell for a beautiful concubine.

A military rebellion weakened the throne but was put down, Tang rule was restored but its

ALL'S FAIR IN LOVE

Tang emperor Xuanzong fell in love with a concubine, who adopted a favourite general as her son. He, in turn, started a decade-long rebellion against Xuanzong.

called the Five Dynasties and Ten Kingdoms.

The Song dynasty was founded by the palace-guard commander of the last of the Five Dynasties in northern China. While constantly under threat by non-Chinese groups in the north – in fact, the capital was moved from Kaifeng to Hangzhou after invaders took over northern China in 1126 – the Song dynasty is considered one of China's most creative and artistic periods.

Population growth promoted urbanisation, particularly in the

power never fully recovered. In 845, the emperor ordered the repression of Buddhist monasteries that, by this time, had acquired large, tax-exempt estates with glorious temples housing thousands of residents. Buddhism's growth was checked by the court's issuing of ordination certificates for monks.

Song dynasty (960–1279)

Anarchy reigned during the final half century of Tang rule, but eventually regional states emerged out of the political and social chaos

LEFT: bronze image from a tomb of the Tang dynasty.
ABOVE: court ladies in waiting.

capital. Coal and iron industries developed, and foreign trade was a large source of government revenues in the latter Song era, not to be matched again until the 19th century. Foreign trade lessened the land tax and increased the use of paper money, a practice initiated in the Tang dynasty. Chinese ships could carry 500 men on as many as four decks, powered by a dozen sails on four or six masts; in fact, China led the world in nautical expertise.

Paper had been invented in the first or second century BC, and the Song was the first society with printed books, the key to the era's educational development. At first the government tried to control printing, but by the 11th century it was granting land and books to encourage the establishment of schools. The civil service examination system became a huge and elaborate institution crucial to upper-class life, at least until the abolishment of the system in 1905. A majority of officials still gained office by recommendation from a highly-placed relative, but the Song bureaucracy was staffed by more exam graduates than ever before. In theory, nearly any male could take the exams, but of course it was usually only the wealthier families who could afford the time and money on tutors.

The expanding educational system revived the study of Confucianism and fostered its rein-

terpretation by a number of scholars, characterised by its Buddhism-inspired focus on individual self-cultivation.

Yuan dynasty (1279–1368)

The emperors of the Yuan dynasty were the descendants of Mongol leader Ghengis Khan, who had conquered most of central Asia and parts of eastern Europe in the early 1200s. By 1215, a part of northern China was under Mongol control, and in 1279 the Song dynasty finally fell to Ghengis's grandson Kublai Khan, who ruled China from 1271 until 1294.

Yuan officials set up a form of military administration that soon dominated the Chinese-style bureaucracy. Most important posts throughout the empire were filled by Mongols or their non-Chinese allies; few Chinese rose to positions of authority except in cultural affairs. The Mongols were tolerant, however, of differing religions, reflecting the diversity of their multi-ethnic empire. During their rule, Tibet became part of China.

Trade along the Silk Road flourished. The Grand Canal between northern and southern China was repaired, as the new capital in Beijing depended upon grains from the south. Domestic trade flourished, as did maritime trade from West Asia and India.

Ming dynasty (1368–1644)

After a long period of insurrections, the Mongols were overthrown by Han Chinese troops under Zhu Yuanzhang, who became the first emperor of the Ming dynasty in 1386.

Sponsored by Emperor Yongle (1360–1424) and under the command of the Moslem eunuch Zheng He, the Ming naval fleet made seven expeditions between 1405 and 1433 to Southeast Asia, India, the Persian Gulf, and the east coast of Africa.

Although some trade was conducted, the missions were mainly of a diplomatic nature, intended to foster the tribute system whereby China granted large gifts to tributary states who in turn acknowledged China's supremacy and offered tribute (usually smaller gifts than what they received from China). After Yongle's death in 1424, state support of overseas trade and diplomacy ceased. The fleets of immense ships – larger than any European – were dismantled.

During the rule of the Ming, the first Christian missionaries came to China with the arrival at Guangzhou, in 1516, of Portuguese ships. The danger to the Ming emperors' rule, however, continued to come from northern and central Asia. The Great Wall was once again reinforced to protect China from the nomads, and the wars against the Mongols lasted into the 16th century.

Towards the end of the Ming dynasty, intrigues of the palace eunuchs paralysed the court and sometimes its foreign policy, and the secret police suppressed even the slightest signs of opposition.

LEFT: Kublai Khan ruled from 1271 until 1294.
RIGHT: paper and gunpowder were among the many inventions of imperial China.

Inventions

T he concept that the emperor was the Son of Heaven – and that extraordinary celestial and earthly events were the expression of approval or criticism from above – was the cause for the very early development of astronomical observation in China. The imperial court had its own office of astronomy, and in the 13th century, there were 17 different astronomical instruments at the Beijing Observatory. Halley's Comet was first recorded by the Chinese as early as 467 BC. A calendar of 360 days was in use by the 3rd century BC, which suc-

imetly show where a nearby earthquake occurred.

Around 1100, iron foundries in China were already producing quantities of iron and steel that were unmatched in Europe until the 18th century. The use of block and tackle shows that the Chinese understood the laws of mechanics in the 5th century. The so-called Archimedean Screw was used to pump water in the 1st century, and the water wheel in the 4th and 5th centuries. In fact, irrigation, essential for Chinese agriculture, was important in the development of technology.

The written word was always accorded more importance in China than the spoken. This may have been the reason for the early development of

cessive dynasties tried to improve. In the 13th century, they fixed the length of the year as 365.2424 days, nearly the same as modern calculations.

The Clock Tower of Su Song, built in 1088, is an early example of the highly developed art of the clockmaker. Chain-driven and powered by a water wheel, it was fitted with a kind of escapement to regulate the wheels to show astronomical movements very precisely.

Imperial geographers were busy with the deviation of magnetic north from true north even before Europeans were aware that the earth had a magnetic field. The Chinese compass originally consisted of a metal plate with a metal spoon on it, the handle of the spoon pointing to the south. A seismograph of sorts was developed that could approx-

paper. Made of mulberry tree bark around AD 200, and of bamboo some 200 years later, paper is still made today all over the world according to the Chinese method.

Printing, however, was not developed until some eight centuries later. Stone-rubbing and printing with carved stamps seem to have been the more economic methods of reproduction of the written word, especially as the Chinese script consists of thousands of characters and does not lend itself to simple typesetting methods.

In the 9th century, Daoist monks, looking for the elixir of eternal life, mixed charcoal, saltpeter, and sulphur to accidentally make black powder. Later, this was used for fireworks, and by imperial troops in bombs and grenades.

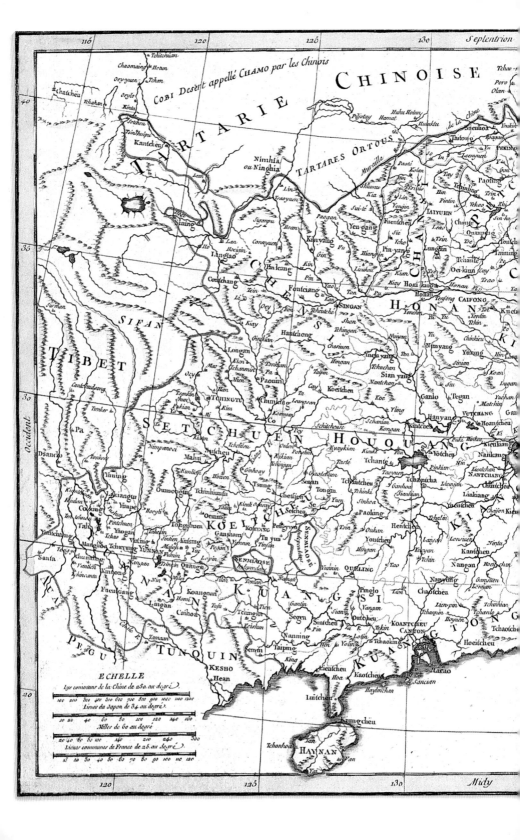

THE QING DYNASTY AND EUROPE

The Qing dynasty – China's last – struggled to embrace or constrain Western missionaries, political ideas, opium, armed troops, and humiliation.

The first recorded account of Europeans in China appears to have been a visit of northern European traders to Kublai Khan's court in 1261. Marco Polo is said to have travelled in China in the 1270s and 1280s, though some scholars now doubt he ever made it (he never mentioned the Great Wall, for example), but instead fabricated his writings from other sources. In any case, his narrative in *The Travels* introduced the splendours of China to medieval Europe, particularly the sophistication of urban life. Early Catholic missionaries made their way to China during the Yuan dynasty (1279–1368).

Large-scale commercial contact between China and Europe did not occur until the 1500s. Portuguese ships dropped anchor off Guangzhou (Canton) in 1514, but the unruly behaviour of the crew onshore offended Chinese officials, who decided to contain them by leasing Macau to Portugal in 1553 as a trading base, from which the Portuguese could conduct business. In the early 1600s, Dutch and English ships also arrived on China's south coast, repeating the rude behaviour of the Portuguese.

China's early encounter with Jesuits, however, was a positive one, as these were educated men who could relate to Chinese scholar-officials on intellectual terms. While the Jesuits condemned Buddhism, they accepted most Confucian precepts, even conceding that the veneration of ancestors was a secular ritual.

Chinese scholars were interested in the Jesuit expertise in astronomy, cartography, European clockworks, and other sciences. Knowledge in astronomy earned Adam Schall von Bell, a Jesuit, his reputation and post in the imperial court. He was requested to begin a foundry for producing cannon in 1636. Despite such an unholy task, he obeyed.

Italian Jesuit Matteo Ricci was probably the most important figure in Jesuit missionary

activity. He arrived in Macau in 1582, where he studied the Chinese language before entering China the next year, where he worked at four new mission posts he helped to open. In 1598 he was introduced at court in Beijing, and a few years later was granted permission to live there on an imperial stipend as a Western scholar. He

also helped other Jesuits gain official status. Ricci impressed his Chinese associates by his mastery of spoken and classical Chinese, devising his own romanisation for Chinese and compiling his own dictionary. His knowledge of mathematics, astronomy, geography, and physics was highly valued by his Chinese colleagues. In addition to their Christian texts, the Jesuits published in Chinese over 100 treatises on Western science and technology. Moreover, political ideas of Renaissance Europe, like those of Voltaire, were influenced by Chinese ideas described by the Jesuits.

The Jesuits in China survived the Ming-to-Qing dynasty transition in the 1600s, but in

Europe dissension arose against the Jesuit order. Rival groups of Catholic missionaries in China, opposed to the Jesuits, regarded Confucian rites of ancestor worship as incompatible with the Christian faith and appealed to the Vatican for a decision against the Jesuits. In 1704, the Vatican decided against the Jesuit position, and relations between Beijing and Jesuit missionaries deteriorated afterwards.

Qing dynasty (1644–1912)

The Qing dynasty was founded by a chieftain of the Manchu, a non-Han Chinese people from Manchuria, the area of northeast China now

appointments in their civil administration, having both Han Chinese and Manchu in important positions and relying on civil service examinations. While the Manchu attempted to maintain their own identity and customs, they also promoted many Chinese traditions. The arts flourished, as did scholarship, and basic literacy was relatively high for that time, even in rural areas.

Maritime challenges

While the Manchu carefully managed the inner frontiers, Western maritime powers were expanding on the sea and continuing to make their way toward East Asia. At the same time,

called Dongbei. The Manchu rulers faced the most serious challenges yet posed by increased contact with Europeans.

The Manchus had long been in contact with the Chinese and the Mongols. Although they were foreign conquerors of China, their rule did not break with Chinese traditions, unlike that of the Mongols in the Yuan dynasty. Instead, they adopted the terms, structure, and ideology of Confucianism to support their political authority. They also promoted the veneration of ancestors and the study of the traditional Chinese classics, and also accepted the Confucian theory that rulers ruled by virtue of their moral uprightness. The Manchu used a system of dual

Chinese seafaring expanded in Southeast Asia and beyond. The Qing court, however, had no interest in protecting the well-being of Chinese mariners and expatriates once they left China, generally considering them to have abandoned the country.

Consequently, Chinese communities that arose overseas lived under different local, official, and social restraints, often becoming entrepreneurs and developing associations to protect their interests in their new homelands.

In China, all legitimate Western trade from 1760 to 1842 was regulated by what was called the Canton system, stipulating that Western traders must conduct all business in Guangzhou

(Canton) under the supervision of Chinese merchants belonging to a guild called the Cohong. Western merchants were restricted to the city's riverbank area, but had to withdraw to the Portuguese settlement on Macau during the off-season. They were discouraged from learning Chinese, and they could not speak directly with government officials, but instead had to communicate through the Cohong.

MACARTNEY'S AXIOM

"Nothing could be more fallacious than to judge of China by any European standard."

The British and Dutch East India companies, established around 1600, were commissioned by their home governments to manage territories overseas and monopolise trade, essentially acting as the counterpart to the Chinese Cohong. The British bought large amounts of tea, silk, and porcelain from China, but the Chinese did not buy much more than woollen textiles from England, and China's low demand for imported goods eventually created a trade imbalance that forced the British to pay for goods in silver, rather than barter.

The British East India Company dispatched James Flint, a Chinese-speaking trader, in 1759 to present complaints to the Qing court about restrictions on trade and on corruption in Guangzhou. Emperor Qianlong at first seemed receptive, agreeing to send a commission of investigation to Guangzhou. Soon, however, he changed his mind and had Flint apprehended and imprisoned for three years, charging him with violating regulations on sailing to northern ports, improperly presenting petitions, and learning Chinese.

In 1792, Lord Macartney was sent by England's King George III to China as a special ambassador to the Qing court. Macartney arrived in Guangzhou in the summer of 1793, and was allowed to continue to Tianjin because he claimed to be honouring Qianlong's 80th birthday. He was accompanied by an entourage of nearly 100 people, including artists and scientists, and two escort vessels loaded with gifts meant to display British manufacturing technology. The gifts were deemed "tribute from England" and once ashore, he was escorted without delay to Beijing.

Macartney requested the abolishment of the

LEFT: Matteo Ricci, an Italian Jesuit, was influential in the court. RIGHT: a Qing emperor and foreign envoys.

Canton system, the right to establish a British diplomatic residence in Beijing, the opening of new ports for trade, and fixed tariffs. Qianlong eventually and firmly dismissed all of the requests.

A growing number of foreign traders continued to arrive in Guangzhou, and the Qing response was to continue to enforce their previously established rules.

British traders, in particular, were becoming exasperated by the trade deficits that compelled them to make huge payments in silver for Chi-

nese tea and luxuries. This trade imbalance motivated the British to ship opium from India to southern Chinese ports. The British East India Company, however, outwardly distanced itself from the opium trade by selling its opium to private merchants (licensed by the company) in India, who then shipped it to smugglers off the southern Chinese coast.

The Opium Wars

As the Chinese consumption of opium grew, so did the outflow of silver from China, distressing Qing officials.

In 1838, a respected court official, Lin Zexu, recommended the strict suppression of the opium trade and the rehabilitation of addicts. He was sent to the south, and upon arrival in Guangzhou, Lin immediately demanded that the foreign merchants hand over all the opium in their possession. In addition, he announced that all foreign merchants would have to sign a bond promising never again to import opium. When the foreigners did not take Lin seriously, he suspended all trade, blockaded foreign factories, and held 350 foreigners hostage, including the British Superintendent of Trade, Capt. Charles Elliot.

COLONIAL PIE

China appeared close at times to being divided up by colonial powers, but treaties left China an "open" nation.

officials persuaded the British to move back to Guangzhou, where further discussions, ultimately unsuccessful, took place. Fighting began around Guangzhou in mid-1841, and after the British captured several coastal cities and the junction of the Grand Canal and the Yangzi river, the Qing agreed to binding negotiations.

The Treaty of Nanjing was signed in 1842. Its provisions included an indemnity to be paid by China to Britain, equal relations between China and Britain, four more ports opened to foreign trade

Elliot commanded all British traders to surrender to him their opium. He issued receipts and took responsibility on behalf of the British government. Elliot then handed over the opium to Lin, who publicly destroyed it. Lin lifted the blockade, permitted the resumption of trade, and released the hostages.

Elliot and the entire British community left Guangzhou, and a Qing imperial edict was issued in 1839 that terminated trade between China and England.

The British government decided that the only recourse to the termination of trade was war. British forces gathered off Macau in 1840 and proceeded north. Skillful negotiating by Qing

with consuls and foreign residency, abolition of the Cohong monopoly, fixed tariffs, and the surrender of Hong Kong to Britain in perpetuity.

Tensions continued between the foreign communities in China and the Qing government. Minor incidents swelled into large-scale conflicts, which led to foreign intervention. Guangzhou was soon overrun by Anglo-French forces, who proceeded north to Tianjin. The Qing court yielded and the Treaties of Tianjin were signed in 1858. Ten new ports were opened, indemnities specified, and diplomatic residences established in Beijing.

Insisting on finalising the treaties in Beijing instead of Shanghai, as the Chinese wanted, the

British sailed north but were repulsed at Dagu. Britain and France sent more forces to China. They soon occupied Beijing, then moved to the Summer Palace and completely destroyed it, forcing the emperor into exile.

The treaty was then reaffirmed, indemnities increased, and the Kowloon Peninsula ceded to Britain. China was now restricted by a series of unequal treaties from which it did not completely free itself until 1943. The treaty effectively rendered China something of a European colony, especially the provision of extraterritoriality under which foreigners were liable to foreign, not Chinese, law.

Missionaries

In addition to foreign merchants, Western missionaries made their mark on Sino-foreign relations in the 19th and early 20th centuries. Some of the more enlightened were appreciative of Chinese culture and conditions, and they secularised their work to promote Western education and ideas to help raise Chinese living standards. Some missionaries founded and maintained schools, libraries, and hospitals. They also played a large role in advancing the education of Chinese women.

LEFT: British representatives negotiating with Chinese counterparts. **ABOVE:** a Boxer rebel is executed.

Many early missionaries, however, conducted themselves with attitudes of self-righteousness, racial superiority, and cultural arrogance. Taking advantage of the privileged positions of foreigners, they flouted local customs and laws, often disrupting communities by harbouring criminals who claimed to have converted and then supporting them in lawsuits against local authorities. In the countryside, Christian missionaries were often seen as the local ideological arm of foreign interference in China, and so were frequently harassed.

Boxer Rebellion

The Boxer Rebellion was a popular protest movement brought about by the combination of Qing misrule and foreign intrusion. In the plains of Shandong Province, where the movement originated, years of floods and drought had left the people desperate. Germany's seizure of Qingdao in 1898 heightened anti-foreign sentiment and unrest.

Shandong peasants turned to secret societies, such as the so-called Boxers, to protect their interests. The Boxers combined martial arts and the practice of spirit possession, and after prescribed rituals, Boxers believed they were impervious to swords and bullets. The movement quickly spread.

The Qing court initially backed the movement in hopes that they might be successful in expelling the foreigners. The Boxers made their way to Beijing, where they killed a number of Christians. They then held missionaries, diplomats, and other foreigners hostage in the Beijing legation quarter for eight weeks until an international army rescued the foreigners.

The Qing court retreated as the foreign troops approached, but it soon worked out an agreement with the foreign powers, who had an interest in maintaining Qing rule – stability was good for foreign trade. So the incident was declared a "Boxer Rebellion," several high officials were executed, and the Qing government was again forced to pay a huge indemnity.

The struggle against foreign intrusion contributed to the downfall of the Qing dynasty, but it was a minor irritation compared to a series of rural rebellions in China's interior. The Taiping Rebellion, a rather diffused rebellion in the rural areas of China, may have killed 30 million people, with numerous other rebellions killing yet millions more people.

EMERGENCE INTO A MODERN NATION

The decades leading up to Mao Zedong's 1949 declaration of the People's Republic of China were of civil war, brutal occupation by the Japanese, and political intrigue.

When Westerners first began to intrude on China's sovereignty in the mid 1800s, China's rulers had to confront outsiders who would not conform to the Chinese view of the world. How to respond to the challenge and make China stronger became a top priority.

By 1901, the Qing court realised reform was unavoidable. The court dispatched two official missions abroad in 1906 to study constitutionalism in England, France, Germany, the United States, and Japan. Japan's prince stressed the importance of the emperor's maintaining ultimate authority, and the delegates returned recommending this approach. They said that a constitution, civil liberties, and public discussion could in fact strengthen the emperor's position, as long as he retained supreme power.

Republican revolution of 1911

Although institutional changes were moving rapidly, dissatisfaction grew more intense, driving the forces of revolution.

Anti-Qing activists came from many quarters. There were Sun Yatsen's anti-Manchu Revolutionary Alliance, secret societies, disaffected military personnel, provincial leaders in government and business, and intellectuals who wavered between advocating a constitutional monarchy and revolution.

In November 1911, representatives from 17 provinces gathered in Nanjing to establish the Provisional Republic Government under Sun Yatsen and a local military commander. To guarantee Manchu abdication, Sun was soon compelled to step down in favour of military strongman Yuan Shikai.

In 1912, Puyi, who had taken the emperor's throne after the death of Cixi in 1908, was forced to sign a declaration of abdication. Puyi continued to live in the Imperial Palace in Beijing until 1924, but the rule of the Sons of Heaven on the Dragon Throne, which had begun 4,000 years earlier, had come to an end.

A number of political parties formed and attempted to make a parliamentary system work, but they were poorly organised and Yuan Shikai was intolerant of their criticism. He periodically dissolved the parliament and had the constitution rewritten, even attempting to make himself emperor in 1915. Yuan died the next year, but the violent opposition he incited helped create the conditions for the warlord period of 1916 through 1928.

May Fourth Movement

The May Fourth Movement was a student protest that took place on 4 May 1919 in response to China's treatment in the Treaty of Versailles, which ended World War I. China had been told by the allies that, upon Germany's defeat in the war, German territorial possessions in Shandong Province would be returned to China. However, during the war, Japan had taken control of Germany's territory in Shandong and, due to the allies' inability to forcibly counter Japan at that time, the Japanese were allowed to retain Shandong. Students took to the streets in indignation.

denounced Confucianism and started socialist study groups, created political journals, travelled to the countryside to educate farmers, and initiated workers' organisations in the cities. Support for Chiang Kaishek's Nationalist Party was revived and interest in Marxism began.

Civil war

The Chinese Communist Party (C.C.P.) was founded in Shanghai in 1921. Chinese intellectuals were attracted to Marxist theory in large part because it provided an explanation for China's hardships – imperialism and exploitation by the upper classes – and prescribed a way

The events of 4 May served to broaden political awareness and participation. The demonstrations of 1919 widened further the belief that protest is an honourable expression of people's concern with political events. It also reinvigorated the discussion of new ideas, as disillusionment with the ability of leaders to govern effectively led to further questioning of the political progress.

Between 1917 and 1923, political and social change, and the conception of modernisation, took on new dimensions. Young intellectuals

to order society that they believed could strengthen the nation. Chiang Kaishek's Nationalist Party (Guomindang) was the Communists' main rival for power. The 1920s through 1940s were years of brutal warfare, first among warlord factions, then between the C.C.P. and Nationalists, and all against invading Japanese.

The epic 10,000-kilometre (6,000 mi) Long March lasted from 1934 to 1936. Under Nationalist attack, C.C.P. troops retreated from south of the Yangzi River, marching to their northern base at Yan'an. Of the 100,000 who set out, fewer than one-tenth survived. During this period, Soviet influence lessened, and Mao emerged as the top leader of the C.C.P.

LEFT: the last emperor of China, Puyi.
ABOVE: Mao Zedong at Yan'an during the civil war.

Modern Leaders

After the fall of the Qing dynasty, **Yuan Shikai**, born in 1859, made a futile attempt to establish himself as emperor. He had a brilliant military career and was a favourite of the emperor's widow, Cixi. She, however, dropped him as he held too many powerful offices. China's last reigning monarch, Puyi, reinstated him in 1911 to save the throne. But Yuan Shikai had understood the signs of the times and joined the republicans, only to betray them shortly afterwards, desiring as he did to become emperor of China. He died in 1916.

Yuan's opponent was **Dr Sun Yatsen** (in Mandarin, **Sun Zhongshan**). Born in 1866 as Sun Wen, Sun lived near Macau, in the district of Guangdong. Influenced by Christian and Western ideas, he plotted the overthrow of the Qing dynasty and founded the republican Guomindang (Nationalist Party). Dismissed by Yuan Shikai, he founded a government in Guangzhou in 1920 that was to rival the military powers in the north, then reorganised the Guomindang with the Soviet Union's help. He died in Beijing in 1925. He is honoured as the father of modern China in both the P.R.C. and Taiwan.

Chiang Kaishek (in Mandarin, **Chiang Zhongzheng**) was Sun's successor. Born in 1887, he underwent military training, then joined the Guomindang and became Sun Yatsen's close friend.

After defeat by the Communists in the civil war, he fled to Taiwan, where his government was able to boost the economy with the help of the U.S. He died in 1975 without achieving his aim: overthrowing the Communists and recapturing the mainland.

The great opponent to Chiang Kaishek, as well as all other Chinese politicians, was **Mao Zedong**. No one else has had such an influence on China in this century. He was born in 1893, the son of a peasant family in the province of Hunan. In 1921, Mao became co-founder of the Chinese Communist Party. During the Long March, he established himself as leader of the Party, and he retained this position until his death in 1976. He led the country out of its postwar economic misery, only to let it sink into chaos during the Great Leap Forward, then again during the Cultural Revolution. A personality cult around Mao emerged during the Cultural Revolution, turning him into a living monument. Mao had unlimited power, governing like an emperor.

The second-most important person after Mao Zedong was **Zhou Enlai**, Mao's closest ally since the Long March in 1925. Zhou was the son of a wealthy family of the gentry, born in Huai'an, province of Jiangsu, in 1898. After studying in Germany and France during the 1920s, Zhou joined the Communist movement and played a leading role soon after his return to China. His special skill, diplomacy, soon became apparent. Some well-planned maneuvers and operations during the Cultural Revolution put him in a secure position. His successes in foreign policy are particularly significant – China emerged from isolation to become a member of the United Nations in 1971. He died in Beijing in 1976, loved and honoured by the people.

Deng Xiaoping, born in 1904, was Zhou Enlai's right-hand man and close friend. Hailing from a peasant family in Sichuan, Deng had an eventful past. In 1920, he first went to France as a student and worked his way through school. After his return, his career in the army and the Party advanced rapidly. He took part in the Long March and was one of the most prominent politicians after 1949. In 1973, he was appointed by Zhou Enlai as deputy prime minister, responsible for opening China's economy to the world.

Despite some setbacks – most notably the suppression of the Tiananmen Square democracy movement in 1989 – Deng displayed finesse by steering China back into the enclaves of the international community. He died in 1997, last of the old leaders. In his last years, China watchers often speculated on just how much he was in charge.

World War II

As early as 1931, Japan had annexed parts of northeastern China, where it founded a puppet state, Manchuguo, headed by Puyi, the last Manchu emperor who had abdicated the imperial throne in 1912. The Japanese planned further conquests in China. Faced by this threat, Chiang Kaishek was unable to use his troops against the Communists. Also, criticism was being expressed within his own party by those wishing to end the civil war and join forces with the Communists

UNIT 731

The Japanese army's Unit 731 murdered at least 4,000 Chinese and Allied prisoners in grisly medical experiments, in Dongbei.

retreated to Chongqing, in the province of Sichuan. The Communists fought a guerrilla war from their bases in the north, while Chiang's troops resisted the Japanese in the south. The Guomindang and Chinese Communists eventually stopped the Japanese advance. In part because of the drain on Japanese resources caused by the war in China, the Allies were able to gain military superiority over the Japanese in the Pacific after 1942.

After Japan surrendered in 1945, the civil war once again

against the Japanese. They even "persuaded" Chiang Kaishek to agree to an alliance with the Communists: two Guomindang, or Nationalist, generals detained Chiang in Xi'an in 1937, and forced him to negotiate with the Communists.

The Japanese provoked an incident at the Marco Polo Bridge outside Beijing in 1937, leading to war between China and Japan. In fact, the incident was choreographed by Japan to justify long-planned aggression in China. Shortly afterwards, Shanghai was bombarded and captured by the Japanese. Chiang Kaishek

continued: Chiang Kaishek, supported by the Americans, fought against Mao Zedong's Red Army, which was fighting mostly on its own and with minimal Soviet support. The four-year civil war was, for the most part, an easy victory for the Communists, because the Guomindang, in the end, lost the support of the people.

After several campaigns, there was a decisive battle on the Chang Jiang, or Yangzi River, and Nationalist troops were weakened to such an extent that they retreated to the island of Taiwan, along with nearly two million refugees. On 1 October 1949 Mao Zedong stood on Tiananmen and pronounced, "The Chinese people have stood up!" And thus, a new nation.

LEFT: Sun Yatsen is admired by both Communists and Nationalists. **ABOVE:** Red Army enters Beijing, 1949.

The People's Republic

The initial public reaction after 1949 was one of euphoria. The C.C.P. army was disciplined and polite, unlike the looting and raping Nationalist troops. Industries were nationalised and government administration taken over.

Land distribution had already taken place in many rural areas in the north before 1949; now it continued in the south. Mao's implementation of class struggle began in the countryside. After individual class status was determined, people were encouraged to "speak bitterness" against their former landlords. As many as one million landlords were not only dispossessed of most of their land and property but were killed.

A new marriage law made women equal to men and divorce possible. The liberation of women, in theory, seemed like true progress, but in reality women had to hold full-time jobs in addition to maintaining the home as before.

By the mid 1950s, Premier Zhou Enlai noted that political pressures had demoralised China's intellectuals and scientists, one cause of the movement named from the ancient adage, "Let one hundred flowers bloom and a hundred schools of thought contend."

For several months in 1957, people were encouraged by statements from Mao and others to criticise the government and its policies. After some hesitation, many vented their dissatisfactions with calls for more freedom of speech, independence of the judiciary, and freer trade unions.

Perhaps shocked by the level of discontent, the C.C.P. reversed its policy of free criticism and the Anti-Rightist campaign ensued. (Some believe Mao's motive for encouraging criticism was to search for enemies, but evidence is unclear.) Limits to free discussion were now specified: any talk and debate must unite the people, benefit socialism, and strengthen the Communist state. Thousands of intellectuals were persecuted and imprisoned, and creativity quenched if not eliminated.

Great Leap Forward

Mao believed that China could be industrialised rapidly, fuelled by ideological motivation and the reorganisation of production. Rural and urban communities were encouraged to use their surplus labour and resources for heavy industries, especially steel production. Communes were established to increase the scale of production, while private enterprise was eliminated. "Backyard furnaces" were built to produce steel, but because of a lack of expertise, most steel produced in these home industries was unusable. Agricultural production was expected to increase, and so local leaders falsely reported astronomical growth to advance their careers and avoid being called politically uncommitted or incorrect.

Between 1959 and 1961, the failure of the policies of the Great Leap Forward combined with three years of bad weather led to this century's greatest famine.

Cultural Revolution

The Cultural Revolution was Mao's attempt to prevent bureaucratic stagnation and the degeneration of the Chinese Revolution. He decided that many of his longtime colleagues needed to be replaced by a younger generation.

Thus, the Cultural Revolution was meant to purge older leaders and replace them with younger ones, whose revolutionary zeal would be amplified by the act of toppling the establishment. Mao saw students as his activists and encouraged them first to turn on their teachers.

The most chaotic phase lasted from May 1966 through late 1967. Students organised "Red Guard" units all over the country. Mao's slogan that "It is right to rebel" propelled their campaigns to destroy remnants of the old society. Brandishing Mao's Little Red Book of quotations, they destroyed temples and historic sites, and broke into private homes to smash and burn books, jewelry, and art. Party leaders and other "counter-revolutionary" forces were denounced, and subject to mass trials.

Many died at the hands of the Red Guard, or, humiliated, committed suicide. Liu Shaoqi, Mao's chosen successor, was one of the first political victims; he was imprisoned and died in jail. The Party Congress in 1969 ended the most extreme phase of the Cultural Revolution, though the end is generally considered to be the arrest of the reactionary "Gang of Four" (including Mao's wife, Jiang Qing) in 1976.

GREAT FAMINE

By the early 1960s, Mao's Great Leap Forward had produced this century's worst famine, with an estimated 30 million dead.

RIGHT: Red Guards marching in Beijing, 1960s.

CONTEMPORARY CHINA

After the death of Mao Zedong in 1976, the People's Republic entered a new era.

Gone was isolationism, replaced by increasing assertiveness and awkwardness.

The tempo and direction of the Chinese society, government, and economy changed dramatically in the late 1970s. Economic development, not political struggle, would define the decade. Although China had turned its back on the Soviet Union and the West during the Cultural Revolution, U.S. President Richard Nixon visited China and met with Mao Zedong in 1972, an historic meeting that signalled fundamental policy changes in China.

Transition to a new era

Zhou Enlai's death in 1976 went unmarked by the Chinese leadership; he had been under indirect criticism from party radicals since 1973. But his death caused widespread grief amongst the people. He was a Politburo member longer than Mao, and had been premier since the P.R.C.'s founding in 1949. During the Cultural Revolution, Zhou had done his best to protect people and the nation from the worst excesses, and he was respected for his modest demeanour and commitment to duties and friends.

Public feeling toward Zhou came forth that spring in Beijing's Tiananmen Square. The Qingming Festival, the traditional day for mourning, fell on 4 April that year. The Monument to the People's Heroes in the centre of the square was adorned with thousands of wreaths and poems in honour of the late premier. Among the flowers were notices supporting Deng Xiaoping, who had been promoted by Zhou and was seen as heir to China's moderation. Also among the flowers were notes denouncing Mao's wife, Jiang Qing.

Overnight, all of the wreaths were removed, sparking a massive demonstration the next day. It was the first genuinely spontaneous demonstration since the founding of the People's Republic in 1949, and it came to be called the 1976 Tiananmen Incident. The crowd of

100,000 clashed with police throughout the day, until the square was cleared early that evening. Deng Xiaoping was dismissed from his posts two days later, and Hua Guofeng became premier and first deputy chairman of the Party.

When Mao Zedong died on 9 September of that same year, Hua Guofeng succeeded him in

key government and party positions. Soon the "Gang of Four" was arrested. This reactionary group included Mao's widow, Jiang Qing, and three radical associates who were the remaining Cultural Revolutionaries in the Politburo from 1973. Accused of a wide variety of crimes, they served as convenient scapegoats for the havoc of the Cultural Revolution.

Rebuilding

The post-Mao era was the era of Deng Xiaoping, even when he was incapacitated, right up until his death in 1997. Although he was purged twice during the Cultural Revolution, he made a final comeback in 1978, acquiring positions and

---

PRECEDING PAGES: queuing for Mao's mausoleum, Tiananmen Square, Beijing. **LEFT:** statues of Mao Zedong remain, but he is no longer idolised as before. **RIGHT:** Red Guard fanaticism faded by the early 1970s.

real power to set the political agenda. Deng began establishing his legitimacy by rehabilitating (or restoring the good reputations of) many of those who had been politically persecuted during the 1950s and 1960s and during the Cultural Revolution.

Within the party and government bureaucracy, many who held prominent and powerful positions had acquired them by demonstrating revolutionary zeal during the Cultural Revolution, not by knowledge or ability. Deng began a reversal of this

TAIWAN DISMISSED

The establishment of diplomatic relations between the U.S. and China in 1979 required that the U.S. cut official ties with Taiwan.

try, national defence, and science and technology – for Chinese development, first proposed by Zhou Enlai some years earlier. Mao had considered politics the key to China's progress. Deng defined China's modernisation to emphasise economic development.

Earlier, during the fall of 1978, wall posters appeared in Beijing calling for a fifth modernisation: democracy. The posters criticised the authoritarianism of Mao's time and appealed for free speech and a range of institutional reforms.

pattern, promoting education and professionalism in the government and party ranks.

The official legacy of Mao Zedong demanded delicate handling. To completely denounce him would mean the discrediting of the entire Communist revolution and the Party's continuing rule. The solution was to divide Mao's history into the good early phase and the bad latter phase. Mao's thinking from his early phase can still be said to guide China's future.

Second revolution

In December 1978, Deng inaugurated what he called a "second revolution". He reiterated the "Four Modernisations" – in agriculture, indus-

Initially tolerated by the leadership, the so-called Democracy Wall Movement was forcibly halted in the spring of 1979.

Relations with the United States were normalised in 1979. Deng travelled to the U.S. a few months later, when he met President Jimmy Carter and congressional and business leaders. Deng's policy of "opening" China to the outside was a recognition that China needed technological expertise and capital from elsewhere. The Chinese political system, however, was not to be influenced by Western political systems or culture. In many ways, this approach paralleled that of the Qing leaders of the late 1800s, who, faced with the superior military might of invading Western powers, wished to study and import Western technology but leave Chinese culture and society unchanged.

To modernise agriculture, Deng disbanded Mao's communes, which had proven over the decades to be a complete disaster. Farmers could now sell excess vegetables, fruit, fish, or poultry in private markets and keep the extra profits. As a result, rural agricultural production increased nearly two and a half times in the 1980s, far outpacing population increase. Deng began reforming industry by upgrading outdated technology and managerial systems, implementing price reforms, advocating foreign trade and investment, revamping the banking system, and encouraging private business. Later, Deng even approved limited stock markets. Promises of private profit for entrepreneurs and other nongovernment workers led to dramatic and sustainable production increases.

Heavy industry had been emphasised during the Mao era, but in 1979 planning strategy shifted to focus on light industrial goods for export. A new responsibility system in industry authorised managers, not party committees as in days past, to make decisions. The opening of foreign trade and investment led to the build-up of coastal cities formerly engaged in foreign trade, especially in the south. Special Economic Zones (SEZ) were set up, beginning with Shenzhen, near Hong Kong.

Relations between ruler and ruled

The media has always had a special function in the People's Republic: to communicate the Party's policy to the people. In addition, the media is used to relay popular attitudes and conditions back to officials, even though much of this information is never published. In theory, these two functions together keep the leaders and average people in touch, and allow the leaders and people to supervise the bureaucracy.

Under Deng Xiaoping , citizens' letters to the editor and investigative reporting were the means for communicating from the bottom up. Some of the problems voiced in letters were addressed, such as cases of official misconduct. The government intended to show that it was straightening things out and righting past wrongs. Another confidence-buiding measure

was the renewal of the local election system. Elections are held at the levels of townships, counties, provinces, and the National People's Congress. Prior to 1979, the voting ballot listed only one name per post, and people simply voted their approval. A new electoral law promulgated in 1979 allowed a choice of candidates on ballots. Few policy issues or larger questions are usually discussed during the brief election campaigns, and candidates and election results must still be approved by party leaders.

A restriction of one child per couple, put into place in the early 1980s, was strongly resisted by many rural families. Forced abortions and

involuntary sterilisations were often carried out. More fundamental to the nation's demographics, the traditional wish to have a son rather than a daughter resulted in female infanticide, a practice that seriously skews the male-to-female ratios, especially in the rural areas.

Protest and demonstrations

In April 1989, Tiananmen Square became the focus of the world's media as university students, later joined by workers, aired their grievances against the government at the largest demonstrations since 1949. Most protesters were angered by widespread corruption, and many demanded democratic reform. Hu

LEFT: posing in old-style uniforms, 1970s. **RIGHT:** Deng Xiaoping during his meeting with Gorbachev, 1989.

Yaobang's recent death had ignited rumours and vanquished the hopes of many that political liberalisation was imminent.

The protests gained momentum and spread to other cities until, on May 19, martial law was imposed. After several attempts by Deng and other leaders to persuade the protestors to leave, the party lost patience. In the early hours of June 4, soldiers fired live rounds and used tanks to force the protesters out of Tiananmen Square. At least 300 people are believed to have died,

ANNIVERSARIES

The violence at Tiananmen Square in 1989 coincided with the 40th anniversary of the People's Republic and the 70th anniversary of the May Fourth Movement.

International issues

Events at Tiananmen in 1989 injected a bit of common sense – if not outright caution – into regional and international communities. It was now clear that China's leadership would not tolerate political changes or challenges. Moreover, it seemed that Beijing cared little about world opinion regarding its internal affairs, or else it was simply naive in how the world would interpret events.

The 1990s would become a decade of tension and awkward-

although the government has never given a full account of what happened. In the following days, similar protests across the country petered out, most peacefully.

A nationwide hunt of the demonstration leaders ensued. Thousands were arrested and some executed. Many dissidents managed to flee the country. Zhao Ziyang and other reformists were ousted from their government positions.

Meanwhile, also in May 1989, the leaders of the two socialist superpowers, Deng Xiaoping and Mikhail Gorbachev, who was pushing reforms in the Soviet Union, met in Beijing in an atmosphere of reconciliation after nearly 30 years of division.

ness between China and other nations, as China grappled with its new influence and responsibilities in the international community.

The governing mechanism of China is anything but transparent, and analysts have tripped over one another trying to rationalise China's increasing assertiveness during the 1990s. Some pundits suggested that the military was asserting itself as the aging Deng Xiaoping lost influence; others suggested that hard-liners, threatened by the collapse of Communism in the former Soviet Union and Eastern Europe, were consolidating their positions and their influence.

Actions by China – or perhaps interpretations of them by others – threatened not only smooth trade relations with neighbours and the world, but regional security as well. China claimed territorial sovereignty, for example, over islands far from its borders and closer to Vietnam, the Philippines, and Indonesia. It offered two arguments: "historical" rights from centuries ago, when imperial ships sailed the South China Sea, and territorial rights, in fact applicable under international law only to true archipelagos like Indonesia and the Philippines. The islands involved – the Paracels and Spratlys, among others – sit on extensive petroleum reserves.

Since 1949, a banner of the Chinese Communist Party has been to reunite Taiwan and China. The Nationalists in Taiwan have carried the same banner, but with differing terms. With the issue of Hong Kong and Macau resolved, (the former was returned by Britain in 1997and the latter by Portugal in 1999), China can focus on Taiwan, which it claims is a renegade province, not an independent state. China's clumsy attempt to influence Taiwan's first direct presidential elections in 1996 – by conducting "missile tests" directly into Taiwan's two primary shipping lanes – cost it considerable political capital. Afterwards, Taiwan's political and commercial contacts increased with several governments.

In September 1999, a major earthquake in Taiwan temporarily halted the growth of cross-straits hostility. In his 50th anniversary (of the People's Republic) speech in Beijing, Jiang reiterated China's determination to push forward "peaceful reunification" with Taiwan. The Chinese government still reserves the right to use force to take back the island.

At the close of the 20th century, relations between China and the United States were again turbulent, partly due to ongoing issues over trade, human rights and Taiwan, and partly due to two particular events in 1999. First came allegations that China had stolen US nuclear weapons technology, which China denies. Then, in April, US planes on a Nato mission in Serbia bombed the Chinese embassy in Belgrade. Though the US claims this was an accident, and President Bill Clinton offered a personal apology, many Chinese remain angry. Demonstrators attacked the embassies of several Nato countries in the week following the bombing.

LEFT: students protesting in Tiananmen Square, 1989.
ABOVE: Hong Kong took to the streets after Tiananmen.

Premier Zhu Rongji called off world trade negotiations for five months after the incident, but, on coming back to the table in November 1999, managed to negotiate a deal for China's entry to the World Trade Organisation. This was no mean feat – it had taken 13 years of negotiation. Despite this, many people believe Vice-President Hu Jintao, whose portfolio expanded, is now the most likely successor to Jiang Zemin.

Domestic changes

No doubt the implosion of Communism in the Soviet Union and Eastern Europe shook the Chinese leadership. It is true that for decades

China and the former Soviet Union had sparred over the true path of Communism – they didn't speak to one another for nearly 30 years, until 1989, when Gorbachev visited Beijing. But for a developing Marxist superpower to see *the* Marxist superpower change its spots must have been unsettling.

During the industrialisation of China in the 1950s and 1960s, the Communist Party was the paramount touchstone in work and society, not only assuring ideological consistency amongst workers, but dictating industrial policy itself. Now, China's blossoming market economy discourages intellectual conformity and rigid industrial policy. And the expanding sector of the economy dominated by non-industrial entities – banks, securities and trading firms, information services – is virtually free of Party influence. Those working in these areas are young, urban, and affluent.

Inevitably, the new freedom has limits. "Social disorder" is the biggest fear of the party, which is determined never to allow a repeat of the 1989 demonstrations. The tenth anniversary of the Tiananmen massacre passed without incident. The Party is far from disappearing. In 1995, 54 percent of new Party members were under 35 years old. In Shanghai, with 14 million people, 1.14 million, or eight percent of the

population, are members of the Communist Party, although out of China's 1.2 billion people, less than five percent are members.

Ideology has been influenced by economic developments, however. In March 1999 the NPC enshrined Deng Xiaoping thought in the constitution, giving him a status equal to Mao. The party publishes several collections of Deng's speeches and reports, and promotes slogans used by him, including "To get rich is glorious" and "Some people must get rich first."

With the exponential rise of personal wealth and the expansion of consumerism in China, crime has mushroomed 10 percent annually since the early 1980s. The government's

response to the problem has been swift and harsh. Between April and July of 1996, for example, in a campaign dubbed Strike Hard, more than 1,000 convicted thieves, murderers, and rapists throughout China were executed.

Minority groups continue to present Beijing with issues that challenge its rule of this immense country. Buddhists in Inner Mongolia and Muslims in Xinjian, not to mention Tibetans, remain under pressure from Beijing not to express their grievances. Civil disturbances in western China during 1997 brought quick retribution. How China handles minority-group activism and human-rights questions in the future may be a barometer of the leadership's self-confidence, and of China's direction.

The future

Chinese history since World War II has been defined, not by quiet progression, but by radical, often unexpected shifts. But China is the world's oldest existing state. Any contemporary civilisation with a written history over 4,000 years old – and with a government bureaucracy of 40 million – necessarily suffers from inertia. Moreover, an undercurrent of Chinese policy this century is that China would never again suffer the colonial humiliation and subjugation. that it did in the 19th century.

Despite Western concerns over human rights and policy towards Taiwan, China seems poised to play a leading role in world economics and politics in the 21st century. The West's policy of engagement based, cynics claim, mainly on economic interests, led to high-profile state visits to China by US President Bill Clinton and by British Prime Minister Tony Blair in 1998. Jiang paid return visits to both countries in 1999. The diplomacy seemed to pay off. In a speech at the end of 1998 to mark the 20th anniversary of economic reform, Jiang promised to uphold the policies introduced by Deng.

International companies continue to beat a path to China's door, and will do so even more, once China has finally entered the World Trade Organisation. Having weathered the financial crisis of 1997, it is China, rather than Japan, that is seen by many as Asia's economic stabiliser in the 21st century. Whatever this century holds for Asia, China will have a major part to play.

LEFT: manufacturing increasingly is a rural industry.
RIGHT: reflective clarity in Hong Kong.

THE LANDS OF CHINA

Words can't begin to describe the diverse lands of China. Photographs help a little, but still fall short. Superlatives include Mt Everest and the Gobi Desert.

For many centuries, China's imposing geographical barriers created a natural border that both protected and isolated the Chinese from foreign contact. To the east and southeast is a coastline of about 18,000 kilometres (11,200 mi), and to the west are the Himalaya and the Tibetan plateau. In the north, contact with "barbarians" from Mongolia spurred the Chinese to build a series of walls over the centuries, collectively called the Great Wall.

As the third-largest country in the world after Russia and Canada, and roughly the same size as the whole of Europe, China covers an area of 9,560,900 square kilometres (3,691,500 sq mi), with a border of 20,000 kilometres (12,500 mi). Its neighbouring countries are North Korea, Mongolia, Russia, Kazakhstan, Kyrgyzstan, Tajikistan, Afghanistan, Pakistan, India, Nepal, Sikkim, Bhutan, Burma (Myanmar), Laos and Vietnam. The distance from the northernmost town of Mohe, located on the northeastern border with Russia, to the Zhengmu Reef on the Nansha Islands in the South China Sea is 5,500 kilometres (3,420 mi). East to west from the eastern border in the Pamir Mountains to the confluence of the Heilong Jiang and the Wusuli Jiang is 5,200 kilometres (3,200 mi).

On the southeastern islands, winter is warm and people enjoy tropical fruits, while at the same time the northeast is paralysed by Siberian frosts and icy winds. Some parts of Tibet endure perpetual frost, while crops grow year-round in Guangdong and southern Yunnan.

Climate

Given the size of China, it is not surprising to find a variety of climatic conditions. The varying elevation from the western mountain ranges to the eastern flatlands affects climate, but the main determining factor of weather is China's position at the edge of the Asian continent on

the vast Pacific Ocean. In winter, cold-air masses form over the high-pressure zones of the Asian continent and then move southward; this results in dry winters. The unpleasant aspect of this is the high dust content in northern China as the air blows the loess in from the Gobi Desert. In summer, the climate is maritime. The

summer monsoons bring the rains from the Pacific, with a rainy season lasting from May until September, with the rain zones moving south to north.

The northeast of China and northern Mongolia have short, warm summers followed by long, cold winters. Immediately to the west lie the desert regions of Inner Mongolia and Xinjiang; they have hot and dry summers with occasional strong winds, and the winters are cold and dry. In the Tibet-Qinghai Plateau, which is, on average, 4,000 metres (13,000 ft) high, the winters are extremely cold and the short summers only moderately warm. In central China, summers are always hot, and rainfall is high. North of the

---

PRECEDING PAGES: the Li Jiang and limestone formations, Guilin; snow-covered peaks in the Himalaya.
LEFT: limestone karst and sun, Guangxi Province.
RIGHT: bamboo groves are found at lower elevations.

Chang Jiang, the main rainfall is in July and August. Here, the agricultural growing season lasts for eight or nine months. In the southern and eastern parts of China, winters are moderate, while summers are hot with high humidity. Typhoons strike coastline areas as far north as the Yangzi in late summer.

Topography

With good reason, China is occasionally called a land of mountains, for two-thirds of its territory is mountainous, hilly or high plateau. Topography falls into three main regions, or geological terraces.

heights averaging between 1,000 and 2,000 metres (3,000–6,500 ft) in central and northwest China. The third terrace is formed by the plains and lowlands on the lower reaches of the large rivers. It rarely rises more than 500 metres (1,600 ft) above sea level and runs along the east coast from the north of China down to the south. More than two-thirds of the population lives along this coastal stretch, and it is China's agricultural and industrial heartland.

This terraced structure is the result of massive tectonic movements beneath the Chinese land mass, which remains unsettled. Earthquakes continue to strike in many regions of China. The

The highest terrace is the Tibet-Qinghai Plateau, which rises 4,000 metres (13,000 ft) above sea level and consists of Tibet, Qinghai and western Sichuan. Although the area is about a quarter of China's total land mass, it is home to less than one percent of the nation's population. All the major rivers of China and Southeast Asia start in the Tibet-Qinghai Plateau. The Huang He (Yellow River) and Chang Jiang (Yangzi River) flow eastward from the plateau, while the Zangbo Jiang (Bramaputra), Nu Jiang (Salween) and Lancang (Mekong) flow south and southeast, coursing their way through some of China's southern neighbouring countries. The second terrace is formed by plateaus of

1976 earthquake in Tangshan, 145 kilometres (90 mi) east of Beijing, claimed an estimated 250,000 to 665,000 lives. In 1996 alone, 26 earthquakes measuring more than 5.0 on the Richter scale hit China, most unnoticed outside of China but causing hundreds of deaths.

Rising above these terraces are the mountains, and China has many of the highest mountains in the world. The Himalaya range, forming the southwest border of the country, is one of the youngest mountain ranges on the planet. The highest mountain in the world is found in the Himalayan range: the well-known Shengmufeng, or Mount Everest, a lofty 8,848 metres (29,028 ft) above sea level.

Running parallel to the Himalaya range farther north are the Kunlun mountains. In summer, the rivers that spring from the Qinghai Plateau are fed with frigid water from its melting glaciers.

Still farther north and again reaching from west to east is the 4,000-metre-high (13,000 ft) Tian Shan range, which means Heavenly Mountains. The Kunlun and Tian Shan ranges enclose China's largest desert, the Taklimakan, and the Tarim Basin, which, protected from polar air, has a seven-month growing season. Lop Nur, a lake

SPLIT SUMMIT

The summit of Mt Everest, or Shengmufeng, is shared by China and Nepal.

This is also China's largest wooded area and thus an important watershed, with considerable influence on the climate. A similarly important climatic divide is the Qinling range, which reaches from the Gansu-Qinghai border all the way to Henan.

In summer, the mountain range acts as a barrier to the heavy masses of humid air caused by the monsoon. In winter, the range stops the cold winds streaming down from the Siberian steppes from entering too far into central China.

in the east of the basin, has long been a favoured location of the Chinese military for conducting nuclear tests.

Running through eastern Tibet, west Sichuan and Yunnan are a group of mountain ranges called the Hengduan, which means "barrier". These ranges have, even in modern times, formed an insurmountable barrier between China and lands lying west of it.

In the northeast, the Greater Xingan range forms a natural border between the Manchurian lowland and the Mongolian steppe.

LEFT: flatness of river and terrain, Xinjiang, in western China. **ABOVE:** the steppes of Inner Mongolia.

Great rivers

In historical terms, Huang He, or the Yellow River, is undoubtedly the most important river in China. The region around the confluence of the Huang and Wei rivers formed the cradle of Chinese civilisation. In prehistoric times, people along these banks were already casting bronze, using the wheel, making silk and writing. Yet, throughout the centuries, the river has also been known as China's sorrow. Given to radical shifts in its course and frequent flooding, the Huang He has been the worry of generations of peasants living by the river.

Rising in the western province of Qinghai, the Huang He makes a sharp bend to the north near

Lanzhou and then farther on, near Baotou in Mongolia, it turns south again, forming the famous Huang He knee. Only as it passes through the Central Chinese Loess Plateau does it fill up with the yellow earth that has suggested the river's name. Due to early deforestation, the land is insufficiently vegetated and erodes very easily. The Huang He transports more than one billion tons of sediment into its lower reaches every year. In fact, the water level in the estuary is so low that there is no shipping route to the sea. As the river bed widens in the lowland plain, the river deposits more than four million tons of silt.

1194 to 1853, it shifted south so that it entered the East China Sea, south of Shandong Peninsula. After some flooding, it shifted its course to flow north of the peninsula. In 1938, Nationalist troops smashed the dikes in Henan to divert the river and slow the advance of Japanese troops. An estimated 900,000 civilian lives were lost as a result. The river was redirected to its present course in 1947.

The longest river in China, and the third-longest in the world, is the 6,300-kilometre-long (3,900-mi) Chang Jiang, more commonly known in the West as the Yangzi River. The Chang Jiang rises in the Tanggula Mountains of

Attempts to control the river go back almost as far as Chinese history itself. In 220 BC, Qin Shi Huangdi ordered dikes built and deepened the river's course. Over the centuries, peasants have built elaborate systems of dikes and levees that require constant maintenance because a breach in even one of the dikes can cause flooding for hundreds of kilometres around. The riverbed continues to grow every year, and in some stretches, the river can be seen flowing 10 metres above the surrounding plain.

The lower channel of the Huang He has radically changed course several times. Between 602 BC and AD 1194, it flowed to the north of its present-day path into the Yellow Sea. From

TERMS OF GEOGRAPHY

In Chinese, a suffix usually follows a name. In this book, most suffixes are separated from the proper name to make recognition easier. For example, we use Huang He (Huang River) rather than Huanghe.

shan: hill, mountain	**lu**: street, road
he, jiang: river	**daqiao**: bridge
pendi: basin	**ta**: pagoda
hu, chi: lake	**si**: temple
xia: gorge	**ling**: tomb
gongyuan: park	**gong**: palace
yuan: garden	**dian**: hall

Qinghai Province. Chang Jiang is the name commonly used for the middle reaches of the river, while the locals call the lower reaches, from Yangzhou to the estuary, the Yangzi. This is the name with which missionaries and colonialists became familiar and which, as a result, became established in Europe.

Along a stretch of 200 kilometres (130 mi), the river passes through Sanxia, the Three Gorges. In the Qutang Gorge, the river is only 100 metres wide, and the difference between deep and shallow water can be 60 metres (200 ft). In the Wu Gorge, mountains rise to a height of 500 to 1,000 metres (1,600 to 3,300 ft).

tall and 2.25 kilometres (1.4 mi) long. Behind the dam will be a reservoir over 640 kilometres (400 mi) long and with an area roughly the size of Los Angeles. While the dam will protect millions of people from flooding and produce as much as one-ninth of China's electrical power, the financial and social costs are high.

Resources

China is a country rich in natural resources. Coal exists in abundant reserves, ranking second in the world, and is used for three-quarters of the country's energy. Chinese oil production easily rates in the world's top ten, with oil fields

While not as partial to massive flooding as its northern neighbour, the Huang He, the Chang Jiang has nonetheless caused considerable flood damage over past centuries. The most notable in recent history is a flood in 1931, in which three million people died. However, China's modern-day monolithic engineering project, the construction of the Three Gorges Dam, will soon control and subdue the mighty river, forever altering the face of the river and lands surrounding it. When completed, the dam will be the largest in the world at 180 metres (600 ft)

located mainly in the north and northwest. Furthermore, in production of gold, tin, mercury, aluminum, tungsten and barite, China is amongst the world's top producers.

Fertile soil is found in the south and east of the country. China is already the world's largest producer of rice, wheat, and yams, yet it must feed a population that has exceeded one billion. This is one of the most serious problems of the Chinese economy: providing enough food for the population without causing ecological damage. Only 40 percent of the country can be used for agriculture or forestry, with only 12 percent of the total land suitable for farming. The remaining 60 percent is barren land.

LEFT: muddy falls on the Huang He.
ABOVE: Geladandong Glacier, autumn on Tian Shan.

THE CHINESE

Over 1.2 billion people – almost a fifth of the planet's population – live in China, and on only one-fifth of the country's land area.

The Chinese consider themselves descendants of the Han dynasty that was a pivotal period in Chinese history. Although over 90 percent of Chinese are ethnically Han, the distinction between Han and other racial groups is not black and white. The notion of being Chinese – Han Chinese – is to some degree a cultural concept, an acceptance of Chinese values. The Han Chinese are, of course, derived from a distinctive racial background, but over the many centuries, the Han have absorbed numerous racial minorities.

The Han Chinese have traditionally populated the eastern part of the country, leaving the empty spaces to the west and north, at least up until modern times, to the minority ethnic groups. Within China, only in Tibet is a minority group actually the majority, with Tibetans making up 98 percent of the population.

Population headaches

Ninety percent of China's population lives on just one-fifth of China's land, mostly in the east and south. In contrast, the vast empty areas in the north and west are sparsely populated and often hardly habitable.

China's population was counted for the first time about 2,000 years ago, in AD 4. By AD 742, during the Tang dynasty, China's population was just over 50 million people. At around the same time as the invasion of Genghis Khan and the Mongols, around AD 1250, the 100 million mark was probably exceeded for the first time. By the middle of the 18th century, the number had doubled; a century later, in 1850, a population of 400 million had been reached.

Shortly after World War II, there were half a billion people in China. Between the mid 1960s and the early 1980s, China's population increased by over 300 million, more than the total population of either the United States or

PRECEDING PAGES: young ballerinas in Hong Kong share a secret. LEFT: long-time companions, Wenzhou, in southern China. RIGHT: department store pitch, in Shenzen, one of the early special economic zones.

the former Soviet Union. China now has more than 1.2 billion people, nearly 20 percent of the world's total population. In recent years, China's population has increased by about 15 million annually.

The governing and administrative challenges of such a huge population are mind-boggling.

Gathering statistics for over a billion people, much less analysing it, defies the imagination. Still, statistics reveal much about China's options. The numbers are chilling, considering that less than 10 percent of the world's agrarian areas are in China. For every 1,000 people, there are 21 births but just six deaths.

The government, in 1978, began a one-child-per-family programme. Opportunities and incentives for those who have only one child are considerable. In urban areas, the programme has been mostly successful. In the countryside, where traditions die hard and larger families are needed for farming, the one-child policy has had limited success.

Skewing all population statistics, however, is the preference for male heirs. In China, family lines are passed on through the male child. Partly because of this, and because male offspring are more likely to support ageing parents, especially in rural areas, sons are preferred to daughters. Female infants in the countryside have fallen victim to infanticide. From 1953 through 1964, the sex ratios at birth were a little under 105 males for every 100 female infants. Ultrasound scanners, which allow the determination of the sex of fetuses, were first introduced to China in 1979. As their use became widespread, especially amongst the middle and upper classes, the ratio climbed (108 males to 100 females in 1982, 114 in 1990, and roughly 119 in 1992), and continues to climb. Doctors are officially banned from disclosing the results of ultrasound scans, but they can usually be persuaded to tell. Also, private businessmen now offer the service.

China's population is increasingly more difficult for the nation to sustain. Most Chinese experts have said China can comfortably support a population of only 800 million, a major reason for the great emphasis China has placed on birth control. Although its original targets have proven excessively optimistic, the one-

TOO MANY PEOPLE, TOO FEW SURNAMES

When Genghis Khan was asked how he would conquer northern China, it is said that he replied, "I will kill everybody called Wang, Li, Zhang, and Liu. The rest will be no problem."

With over one billion people, it is natural to assume that there would be a surplus of surnames to go around in China. Yet of the 12,000 surnames that once existed in China, today there remain just 3,000. Nearly a third of the population shares just five family names. In fact, nearly 90 percent of Chinese use just 100 surnames, with 90 million sharing the name Li, by default the world's most common surname.

In the U.S., by comparison, there are only 2.4 million people with the name Smith, the most common family name in the English-speaking world. It is not surprising, then, that literally thousands of people can share the same full name, leading to frustrating cases of wrong identity. The possibility of a bureaucratic meltdown over the confusion of a limited number of names is not farfetched.

Much of the problem with increasingly fewer surnames began centuries ago when non-Han Chinese, seeking to blend into the dominant culture, abandoned their own surnames and adopted common names of the Han Chinese.

child policy has greatly reduced the rate of population increase. According to a 1993 estimate, the one-child policy had prevented 200 million births by 1993. The average Chinese woman had five or six children in the 1950s, but only around two in the early 1990s.

Yet problems still remain. Thirty percent of births are not planned, despite widespread use of condoms. The State Family Planning Commission, a government agency, suggests several reasons. First, attitudes have not changed in rural areas. To a farmer, sons still provide the only security for old age. Second, sex education is still a taboo topic, especially in conservative

Traditional family values

With so many hopes riding on them, particularly if they are male, children with no siblings are usually spoiled by doting parents and even more by grandparents. These kids have been dubbed "little emperors". A Western equivalent might be "exceedingly spoiled brat". Even the Chinese consider many single children to be rude, unpleasant, and spoiled.

The demographic shift to single-child families may have had profound influences on Chinese society. Parents who grew up during the Cultural Revolution excessively dote on their children amidst a limbo in clear social values.

rural areas where the grandmother educates her grandchildren according to her own beliefs. In the cities, on the other hand, families actually prefer to have one child, as living space is restricted. Because living space in Shanghai or Beijing averages only 3.5 sq. metres (38 sq. ft), population-control measures are accepted.

Given the diverging sex ratio, many males will find themselves without female partners. The government has predicted that, if the current trend continues, there will soon be a 50- to 70-million-strong army of bachelors.

LEFT: tradition makes girls less desirable to a family.
ABOVE: home life in Xiamen.

Still, despite despotic little emperors dominating family life, the family – and traditional Confucian values – remains Chinese society's most important unit. In rural areas, common surnames identify an extended clan.

Land, that icon of family wealth, was passed on equally to a family's sons by the father. Over generations, the amount of land being passed on to each individual grew less and less, until family plots became exceedingly small. Average family wealth decreased.

At the turn of the century, and for the decades until the Communists took control in 1949, conditions for rural families were dismal, with scarce food, minimal health care, and a continuing civil war. Rural conditions stabilised after 1949, with the quality of life gradually improving. In 1949, average life expectancy at birth was 35 years; by 1982, it was more than 65 years. Likewise, annual death rates fell from 23 to 6 for every 1,000 people. Literacy jumped from 20 percent to nearly 80 percent. (This is not to disregard, however, some central government blunders, such as a colossal famine that killed 20 to 40 million people in the early 1960s because of poor planning.)

Although increasingly a rare occurrence in the cities, in a rural family three generations may live together, with responsibility for elders

vative, employers are also concerned that if a woman becomes pregnant, she will be legally entitled to nine months' maternity leave. Adding to the woes of working women is the fact that they are victims of increasing sexual harassment.

Social life

Early mornings in a park in a Chinese city will find men and women seemingly locked in solemn, slow-motion combat with invisible adversaries, swaying and turning and pushing into the air as they work through *taijiquan* routines. Some thrust swords into the air, while others inhale deep breaths and tighten muscles as

falling to the sons. Daughters, on the other hand, become members of their husbands' families after marriage. Families in the cities, however, are increasingly small and self-contained, like most urban families worldwide.

"Women hold up half the sky," proclaimed Mao, but even under his rule, women rarely achieved high positions. The years since have seen further official affirmations of sexual equality, but surveys comparing the real status of women in the world rank China in the bottom third of the rankings. Age-old beliefs are largely to blame. According to Confucius, a woman without talent is virtuous. Besides regarding women as problematic and less inno-

they practice *qongfu*. Old folks may jog by in a soft-shoe shuffle that barely beats a walking pace; they join a group exercise session, gathering in front of an instructor who commands them to bend, twist, and stretch in unison.

Such group activities start young for the Chinese. Before their lessons begin, schoolchildren may "exercise" together. Taped music and a voice blare out from speakers. *Yi er san. One two three.* The children massage their eyes in a routine to counteract eyestrain resulting from too much studying.

Morning streets are crowded with commuters. Armadas of cyclists pour through cycle lanes and scatter across junctions. Buses lurch along the streets, sometimes slowing to a snail's pace as they encounter traffic jams. Buses are always packed – people push their way on into the throng, stand crushed against their neighbours, watch in case a seat becomes free, then push their way out when they reach their destinations. Queuing is an introduced and foreign concept.

As their rich and varied cuisine reflects, the Chinese love to eat, and China's rise in living standards is apparent at meal times. City residents, to whom even pork was once special, now

FOOD WASTE

By one estimate, the Chinese waste enough food, especially at banquets, each year to adequately feed 100 million people.

restaurant in Guangzhou has a banquet that includes a substance most of us do not even think of as food: gold sprinkled on delicacies such as abalone, shark's fin, crocodile, and clam. But whatever the offering, there should always be more food than the diners can eat. Otherwise, the host loses face.

Until recently, dinner was the chief evening event. It may remain so for many people, who, after eating, leave claustrophobic homes for the street outside to meet neighbours or read under street lights. With lit-

regularly consume beef, fish, and shrimp. While meals in the home may be relatively simple affairs with a small selection of dishes from which to choose, restaurant meals can be veritable banquets.

This is especially the case if the meal is charged to entertainment expenses, or is being paid for by a businessman who wants to impress – the Chinese do not usually split the tab. For a banquet to really impress, it should include rare delicacies such as exotic fungi or, sadly and illegally, endangered wildlife such as tiger. One

LEFT: elderly men enjoying an outdoor performance of Beijing opera. ABOVE: Guangzhou disco.

tle or no privacy at home, young couples may head for parks in search of romance. While there are still arranged marriages in China, single people are increasingly free to marry as they please, particularly in urban areas.

China's national and regional television stations are improving, but even though they feature foreign as well as domestic programmes, their efforts rarely grip viewers. "There is too much garbage on television," wrote propaganda *supremo* Li Ruihuan in 1992. "The task of television stations is to liven things up (but) in every respect, television programmes are far too dull and serious; there is not enough action." Because programmes that have proven to be winners with the masses have often drawn flak from ideologues, stations remain cautious, unlikely to rush to follow Li's exhortations to be more "open" and "courageous".

However, increasing numbers of people are no longer limited to watching domestic stations. The masses may be officially banned from receiving foreign satellite television with its Western influences, but state-run factories have been enthusiastically producing the satellite dishes which now dot city rooftops and often serve many households.

risk the attention of the authorities, who may close them down to "eliminate the social evils and purify the air of society". Overwhelmingly, the songs patrons prefer are from Hong Kong and Taiwan; there is also material available from the West.

GOOD RECEPTION?

Satellite dishes bring MTV, Disney Channel and Star TV into Chinese homes – and often in Mandarin.

Working life

"To get rich is glorious", announced Deng Xiaoping in 1978. The people responded with gusto. But despite increases in urban wages, China's current income levels

Outside of Hong Kong, domestically produced films are rare, since, like television, the movie industry is stymied by ideologues. Even so, the Chinese film industry, with directors such as Zhang Yimou, is gaining greater international respect, not to mention audiences. Some films, however, are approved for release in China only after achieving critical acclaim in the West.

Karaoke, that vain Japanese-invented sing-along addiction, has swept China as elsewhere in Asia, joining the discos, bars, and other social venues. Karaoke bars range from the modestly priced to those that are costly even by Western standards. A few are fronts for prostitution and

are still very low compared to those of the West. The figures are, however, deceptive. This is partly because rents for most workers are still heavily subsidised, with apartments costing the equivalent of just a few dollars per month. The cost of living, too, is invariably lower than in the West. Urban life is fast becoming expensive in Beijing, Shanghai, and Guangzhou, and it always has been in Hong Kong.

There was a time – until recently, in fact – when the distinction between rural and urban workers was quite clear and obvious. Rural life meant the farm; urban life, the factory or office. Two-thirds of China's people live in rural areas. Yet they are not all farmers. Increasingly, light industries are peppering the countryside, owned and operated by villages and towns in what the *Washington Post* newspaper called an industrial revolution more profound than that in the coastal urban areas.

Typically called township-and-village enterprises, these small industries blend private-style management with government ownership. For a decade and a half, annual growth rates of these enterprises has exceeded 20 percent, twice as high as China's economic growth. Employing over 100 million people, more than in the notoriously inefficient state-owned industries, town-and-village enterprises are helping to ease the problem of rural people migrating to the cities in search of work.

Moreover, as agriculture becomes mechanised and automated, there are more people available to work in these small industries.

Many of these enterprises began as workshops in the commune system established in the 1960s. After Deng Xiaoping took power in 1978 and liberalised both agriculture and industry, rural incomes rapidly increased, as did buying power. These communal leftovers, at least those that survived, shifted to meet demand. Some are sweatshops, to be sure, and there is a conflict of interest for local governments, who are both owners and regulators of the enterprises.

While these township-and-village enterprises have offered new opportunities for the rural population and thus lessened the burden on cities somewhat, migrant workers seeking employment in the cities remains a city planner's headache.

The problem is especially acute in the south. In Guangzhou, a quarter of the population are migrant workers, the "floating population". It is estimated by the official press that China's floating population may exceed 100 million, nearly equivalent to the population of Japan and greater than that of France.

What drives the floating population are urban incomes that are twice that to be found in the countryside. Moreover, one-third of the rural population is underemployed, if not actually considered unemployed. The "iron rice bowl", as the system of permanent jobs and guaranteed wages was once called, has been proven over the years to be ineffectual, whether in industry

or the civil service (which is the world's largest at nearly 40 million bureaucrats).

Not surprisingly, most state-run firms have proved to be uneconomical and unresponsive to China's increasing demand for commodities and services. China has moved to stem the losses, cutting hundreds of thousands of jobs in state-run companies during the early 1990s, and privatising most of those companies in the late 1990s. But the job cuts have met with resistance; sacked workers have assaulted managers and demonstrated in Sichuan and elsewhere. By contrast, the flourishing private sector is characterised by vitality and vigour.

Nationalities

There are over 50 officially recognised minority groups living in China today, including those in Tibet and Xinjiang. Most of these minority groups live along China's strategic, sometimes troubled and usually sparsely populated international borders.

Thus, when one of the minority groups needles Beijing, such as happens with Tibetans, the central government takes such deviations quite seriously. The minorities have often maintained close relationships with those of their group living on the other side of those borders. As a result, the central government cannot retain absolute control over some frontier peoples.

LEFT: Shanghai rock musicians. **RIGHT:** rural unemployed fill urban centres, such as here in Guangzhou.

The defining elements of a minority are language, homeland, and social values. Perhaps eight percent of China's population is part of a minority group, with the largest being the 12-million-strong Zhuang, in southwestern China.

Out of China's population of 1.2 billion, over 70 million people are non-Han Chinese. The constitution guarantees them certain national rights and privileges.

One of the most important is the right to use their own language. To grant these minorities the right to live according to their own beliefs and traditions is, in the eyes of the Chinese, a sign of goodwill, and the renunciation of the

expansionism of the old regime.

However, spoken and written fluency in standard Mandarin is the only way to become educated and improve social status. Schools for members of national minorities are not found everywhere, and universities teaching a minority language hardly exist.

This reflects an ancient concept, based on historical experience, that there is no other developed culture apart from the Chinese.

In reality, the slow expansion of the Chinese nation from the original area on the Huang He, or Yellow River, and its tributaries up to the South China Sea is linked to an equally slow assimilation of non-Chinese peoples into the Han Chinese society, considered culturally and technically more advanced than the surrounding cultures.

The small minorities that continue to live in less accessible areas (known as "areas one flees to") have resisted the attraction of Chinese culture and civilisation, and so have paid the price of slow progress within their own cultures. At the same time, over the past century, Han Chinese have moved to the outlying regions in great numbers, usually becoming the majority group in urban centres.

In the autonomous region of Xinjiang, Uighurs remain the largest existing ethnic group, but these days make up only 45 percent of the population.

Only when grouped together with the Kazakhs, Kirghiz, and others do Uighurs constitute an Islamic, Turkic-speaking majority. Forty years ago, 80 percent of the population fulfilled these criteria. But now, all the large cities (except for Kashi) have a majority of Han Chinese. Urümqi, a city with over one million people and the capital of Xinjiang, is made up of 80 percent Han Chinese.

The Muslim Hui make up only one-third of the population in their autonomous region of Ningxia, and they usually live in the economically less-privileged parts of the country in the south. Regarding Islam, most Hui can only satisfy the criteria used to classify a Hui (Chinese-speaking Muslim) with great difficulty. One often encounters a Hui to whom the city of Mecca means nothing.

In Inner Mongolia, the Han have predominated for decades and now represent 80 percent of the population. On the other hand, more Mongols live in this region than in the neighbouring country to the north, Mongolia. It is mainly the nomadic population who are Mongolians; almost all settled farmers and people living in towns are Han Chinese whose families immigrated from eastern China.

Although the Zhuang have given their name and the status of an autonomous region to Guangxi, they are nevertheless a minority. In fact, they represent the largest non-Han nationality within modern China today. They are also more assimilated within mainstream society than any of the other minority groups.

LEFT: a woman of the Kazakh, Xinjiang Province.
RIGHT: Hong Kong woman and prized canine.

CHINESE FESTIVALS

Traditional festivals in China have always served as a means of honouring the past. Many are specifically associated with ancestral worship.

Most festivals in China are celebrated according to the Chinese lunar calendar: the first day of the lunar month is determined by when the moon is at its thinnest. These lunar months, of course, don't coincide with those of the Western calendar, so these festivals fall on different dates each year.

THE BIG ONES

The biggest Chinese festival is the **Spring Festival**, or **Lunar New Year**, in either January or February. Forget travelling and forget sightseeing during the Lunar New Year. Among the other better-known traditional Chinese festivals, the **Qingming Festival** on the 12th day of the third lunar month, in April, is an occasion to pay tribute to one's forebears. This festival is marked by visits to the graves of ancestors. Tombs are cleaned, hell money burnt, and food offered in honour of the departed. The **Dragon Boat Festival**, on the fifth day of the fifth lunar month (usually July), commemorates the poet and loyal minister Qu Yuan, who in 278 BC drowned himself in despair and protest over his country's future. It is typically celebrated more in the southern part of China and especially in Hong Kong, where dragon-boat races are held with much international fanfare, and celebrants eat *zong zi,* glutinous rice wrapped in lotus leaf.

The **Mid-Autumn Festival**, also known as the Moon Festival and occurring on the 15th day of the 8th lunar month (September or October), is celebrated today primarily by the eating of mooncakes. During the Yuan dynasty (1279–1368), when China was occupied by the Mongols from the north, the Han Chinese often communicated with each other by hiding messages in mooncakes.

DRAGON-BOAT RACE ▷
More than mere amusement or ritual, dragon-boat races are occasions for intense competition. This race in Hong Kong, for example, has teams from around the world and China competing. Teams spend months training for the event. When not racing, participants share in the *zong zi*, glutinous rice cakes. The festival commemorates the suicide by drowning of Qu Yuan; zong zi were thrown in the river, in Hunan, to keep fishes from eating his body.

CHILDREN'S DAY ▽
Celebrated on 1 June, this is one of several secular holidays in China. Schools let out early, naturally, and children are treated to outings at public parks and amusement theme parks.

◁ DRAGON DANCERS
New Year's celebration with dragon dance and firecrackers. Major Chinese cities have banned firecrackers. The Chinese dragon represents *yang*, a male symbol of the heavens. Although wingless, dragons are a deity of the air, and are among the natural forces found in Daoist philosophy.

BRINGING IN THE LUNAR NEW YEAR

The Chinese celebrate their new year according to the lunar calendar, the actual date in the Gregorian calendar falling usually in January or February.

In China, this festival is more popularly known as *chun jie*, or Spring Festival. It is by far the biggest and most important of Chinese festivals, and it is the only traditional festival to merit a public holiday.

Celebrations, which begin on the eve of the new year with a family reunion dinner, typically last four days, during which much of China shuts down. Tradition holds that the *cai shen* (fortune god) leaves for the heavens on new year's eve to give a report of a family's actions during the past year. He returns on the fifth day of the new year to bestow fortune, so many stores and businesses will reopen on the fifth day. *Hong bao* (red packets) filled with money are usually given to the young and old as people visit relatives and friends to usher in the new.

Nowadays, the festive parades, dragon dances, and fireworks are more in the countryside and in Chinatowns around the world than in large cities in China. In Beijing, people celebrate by attending *miao yue* (temple gatherings), which are really social gatherings in a big park.

◁ **UP ON STILTS IN BEIJING**
Still an art, albeit a dying one, stiltwalking is seen only in parades of major festivals, such as New Year's.

NEW YEAR'S DRAGON ▽
Despite frigid temperatures, most Chinese will not miss the traditional dragon dance celebrating the beginning of a new year in the lunar calendar. In Asia, the dragon is known as a benevolent creature, and it has long been a symbol of the imperial court and emperor.

BELIEFS AND RELIGION

As diverse as the land and people, the beliefs and philosophies found in China
reflect an historical depth and breadth existing nowhere else in the world.

For centuries before the Communists took power, several religious and philosophical beliefs were prominent in China. Two systems that originated in China, Daoism (Taoism) and Confucianism, were not so much religions as ethical and pragmatic standards of behaviour, especially for the educated classes. Buddhism was imported from India in the first century AD.

When the Communists came into power, religion was deemed incompatible with Communism. In recent years, however, religious beliefs have gained wider acceptance, or at least are now more openly tolerated. Confucianism, Daoism, and Buddhism are practised with varying amounts of mixing amongst them. Islam is also practised, especially in the western parts of China, and there is also a small Christian minority. But, of course, no matter what the politics or theology, there are the age-old traditions of lucky numbers, fortune-telling, and geomancy.

Feng shui and lucky numbers

Following a fortune-teller's advice to the letter can involve radical behaviour, such as having your hair shorn off to appease the fortune god, or wearing a bright red belt, no matter what the colour of your outfit. Carrying gold images around may be believed to help bring along good fortune, and also the removing of mirrors from the bedroom, or the eating of more mutton or less beef in the Lunar New Year period.

It is easy for nonbelievers to sneer at these old-fashioned beliefs, dismissing them as superstitions, but many Chinese take them seriously, pointing out that the beliefs go back a long way.

The idea of fate started in the feudal society, when it was believed that "the god" – the emperor – decided one's destiny. When the Yin dynasty was overthrown by rebellions, the myth that the emperor was invulnerable was broken.

Thereafter, people worshiped horses and cows, and realised that the different physical features of animals – such as shape, frame, hair and skin colour – decided their capability, temper and how long they lived. They gradually applied this observation to people.

With the Tang (618–907) and Song (960–1279) dynasties, society became more complicated, people were more concerned about fate, and fortunetelling became a popular profession. *Feng shui* (wind and water) is a set of traditional spiritual laws, or geomancy, used to attract the best luck and prevent bad fortune.

Those who take feng shui seriously consult a geomancer – a master of feng shui – to advise on designs of buildings, dates of important decisions, and layout of one's home and office.

The most important tool of feng shui masters is a compass-like device, which has eight ancient trigrams representing nature and its elements – heaven, fire, thunder, wind, water, hills, and earth. These elements in turn represent eight animals – horse, goat, pheasant, dragon, fowl, swine, dog, and ox.

The feng shui theories are based mainly on the principle of *qi* – life's spirit or breath – which is divided into *yin* and *yang*, the female-passive and male-active elements of life. The concept of *wuxing* also has a prominent standing in Chinese philosophy, medicine, astrology, and superstition. The term can be directly translated as "five elements", in which the five types of energy dominate the universe at different times. Water dominates in winter, wood in spring, fire in summer, metal in autumn, and earth is a transitional period between seasons.

Modern corporations in China often take feng shui seriously. In Hong Kong's Central District, at the site where Hutchison House, Bank of America Tower, and a

BANKER'S HEADACHE

The angular design of the Bank of China tower in Hong Kong is said to fling bad *feng shui* at just about every competing bank.

Most feng shui experts tell fortunes by reading faces and palms, or doing complicated calculations based on a person's name or the time and date of birth. The system of 12 animal signs – rat, bull, tiger, rabbit, dragon, snake, horse, goat, monkey, chicken, dog and pig – was created during the Han dynasty (206 BC–AD 220) by a Chinese philosopher. The theory divides people into the 12 categories according to the year they are born, and also tells their fortune and future by combining philosophy and numbers.

multi-storey carpark now stand, a mass execution was conducted by Japanese troops during World War II. When Hutchison House reached its full height, a Buddhist ceremony was carried out to calm the spirits of the people who had died there.

The feng shui customs have even affected foreign expatriates and business people. Before the Hong Kong Sheraton Hotel opened in 1974, its general manager consulted a feng shui expert about the hotel's opening date, which pleased his local staff.

At the end of every year, dozens of fortunetelling books come out predicting what will happen in the new year. Most of these books have red covers – a colour that traditionally represents happiness, especially during Chinese New Year – and titles in gold colour.

It can only be in Hong Kong that anyone would pay US$641,000 for a license plate number. In 1988, an anonymous businessman did just that in Hong Kong. He thought the number plate "lucky," because in Cantonese the pronunciation of that license number was the same as the written character meaning prosperity.

Usually, the number two stands for easy, three for living or giving birth, six for longevity, eight

LEFT: the *pat kwa* mirror repels evil. **ABOVE:** fortunetellers are ubiquitous; lucky license numbers aren't.

for prosperity, and nine for perpetuity or eternity. But it is the combinations of numbers that make a big difference. For example, 163 means "live forever" or "give birth nonstop". The number 8222 assures that attaining prosperity is extremely easy. The superstition over numbers also applies to street and telephone numbers, not to mention lottery numbers.

Since the license plate auctions started in 1973, the number eight has consistently drawn the highest bid in the lucky-number auctions by the govern-

CHOICE STOREY

An apartment on the 18th storey is preferable to one on the 14th. In Cantonese, 14 means "definitely dies", while 18 means "definitely prospers".

Ancestor worship

The ancestor worship of the Chinese is based upon the assumption that a person has two souls. One of them is created at the time of conception, and when the person has died, the soul stays in the grave with the corpse and lives on the sacrificial offerings. As the corpse decomposes, the strength of the soul dwindles, until it eventually leads a shadow existence by the Yellow Springs in the underworld. However, it will return to earth as an ill-willed spirit and create dam-

ment's transport department. But in Hong Kong, nearly everything is a negotiable instrument, and the trading of lucky numbers had become profitable long before the auctions began; sought-after numbers were freely traded on the open market and numbers were eventually allotted sequentially, and with no restrictions.

Now, all numbers considered lucky in Cantonese, and prestige numbers in single, double, triple and quadruple digits without prefixes, are reserved and available only through auctions. For ordinary car registration, the Hong Kong government has designated a batch of "lucky" numbers and carefully restricts their sale at regularly spaced auctions.

age if no more sacrifices are offered. The second soul only emerges at birth. During its heavenly voyage, it is threatened by evil forces, and is also dependent upon the sacrifices and prayers of the living descendants. If the sacrifices cease, then this soul, too, turns into an evil spirit. But if the descendants continue to make sacrificial offerings and look into the maintenance of graves, the soul of the deceased ancestor may offer them help and protection. Inscriptions on oracle bones from the Shang dynasty (16–11th centuries BC) and inscriptions on bronze, dating from the Zhou period (11th century–256 BC), reveal that there existed in early Chinese history an ancestor worship of high nobility, a cult of a high god called

Di, and an animistic belief in the numerous gods existing in nature.

Originally, ancestor worship had been exclusive to the king. Only later did peasants too begin to honour their ancestors. At first, people believed that the soul of the ancestor would search for a human substitute and create an abode for the soul during the sacrificial ritual. It was usually the grandson of the honoured ancestor who took on the role of substitute.

About 2,000 years ago, genealogical tables were introduced as homes for the soul during sacrificial acts. Up until that time, the king and noblemen had used human sacrifices for ances-

tral worship. Even today, the Chinese worship their ancestors and offer the deities sacrifices of food. This is widely practiced, for example, during the Qingming festival.

The original religion of the people actually focused on the worship of natural forces. Later, the people began to worship the Jade Emperor, a figure from Daoism who became the highest god in the popular religion after the 14th century. Guanyin, the goddess of mercy, originated in Mahayana (Great Wheel) Buddhism. Among the many gods in popular Chinese religion,

LEFT: old photograph depicting ancestor worship.
ABOVE: the Jade Emperor.

there were also earth deities. Every town worshiped its own unique god. Demons of illness, spirits of the house, and even the god of latrines had to be remembered. The deities of streams and rivers were considered to be particularly dangerous and unpredictable. Depending upon one's vocation and location, there were numerous deities to be respected.

Apart from Confucianism, Daoism and Buddhism, there was also a working-class religion known as Daoist Buddhism.

China had long been divided into numerous small states. Only after the Qin dynasty had won over its rivals in 221 BC did the first emperor over a united China come to power. There were many schools of thought, but only Confucianism and Daoism gained wide acceptance.

Daoism

A central concept of Daoism is the *dao*, which basically means way or path, but it also has a secondary meaning of method and principle. Another important premise is *wuwei*, which is sometimes simply defined as passivity, or "swimming with the stream". The concept of *de* (virtue) is closely linked to this, not in the sense of moral honesty, but as a virtue that manifests itself in daily life when dao is put into practice.

The course of events in the world is determined by the forces yang and yin. The masculine, brightness, activity and heaven are considered to be yang forces; the feminine, weak, dark and passive elements are seen as yin forces.

Laozi was the founder of Daoism, living at a time of crises and upheavals. The Daoists were opposed to feudal society, yet they did not fight actively for a new social structure, preferring instead to live in a pre-feudalistic tribal society.

Laozi, it is said, was born in a village in the province of Henan in 604 BC, the son of a distinguished family. For a time, he held the office of archivist in Luoyang, which was then the capital. But he later retreated into solitude and died in his village in 517 BC. According to a famous legend, he wanted to leave China on a black ox when he foresaw the decline of the empire. Experts today are still arguing about Laozi's historical existence. Since the second century, many legends have been told about the figure of Laozi. One of them, for instance, says that he was conceived by a beam of light, and that his mother was pregnant with him for 72 years and then gave birth to him through her left armpit. His hair was white when he was born; he prolonged his life with magic.

The earliest, and also most significant, followers of Laozi were Liezi and Zhuangzi. Liezi (fifth century BC) was particularly concerned with the relativity of experiences, and he strived to comprehend the dao with the help of meditation. Zhuangzi (fourth century BC) is especially noted, if not famous, for his poetic allegories.

The ordinary people were not particularly attracted by the abstract concepts and metaphysical reflections of Daoism. Even at the beginning of the Han period (206 BC–AD 220), there were signs of both a popular and religious

Daoism. As Buddhism also became more and more popular, it borrowed ideas from Daoism, and vice versa, to the point where one might speak of a fusion between the two.

The Daoists and Buddhists both believed that the great paradise was in the far west of China, hence the name, Western Paradise. It was believed to be governed by the queen mother of the West, Xiwangmu, and her husband, the royal count of the East, Dongwanggong. And without making any changes to it, the Daoists also took over the idea of hell from Buddhism.

Religious Daoism developed in various directions and schools. The ascetics retreated to the mountains and devoted all their time to medita-

tion, or else they lived together in monasteries. In the Daoist world, priests had important functions as medicine men and interpreters of oracles. They carried out exorcisms and funeral rites, and read mass for the dead or for sacrificial offerings.

Historical and legendary figures were added to the Daoist pantheon. At the head were the Three Commendables. The highest of the three deities, the heavenly god, is identical to the Jade Emperor, worshiped by the common people. There is hardly a temple without Shouxinggong (the god of longevity), a friendly-looking old man with a long white beard and an extremely elongated, bald head.

There are also the god of wealth (Caishen), the god of fire (Huoshen), the kitchen god (Zaoshen), the god of literature (Wendi), the god of medicine (Huatou) and others. Only the Eight Immortals are truly popular and well-known. Some of them are derived from historical personalities, some are fanciful figures. They are believed to have the ability to make themselves invisible, bring the dead back to life, and do other miraculous deeds.

The classic work of Daoism is the *Daodejing*. It now seems certain that this work was not written by a single author.

Confucianism

While Laozi was active in the south of China, Confucius lived in the north of the country. For him, too, dao and de were central concepts. For more than 2,000 years, the ideas of Confucius (551–479 BC) have influenced Chinese culture, which in turn sculpted the world-view of neighbouring lands such as Korea, Japan and Southeast Asia.

It is debatable whether Confucianism is a religion in the strictest sense. But Confucius was worshiped as a deity, although he was only officially made equal to the heavenly god by an imperial edict in 1906. (Up until 1927, many Chinese offered him sacrifices.)

Mencius, a Confucian scholar, describes the poverty at the time Confucius was born. "There are no wise rulers, the lords of the states are driven by their desires. In their farms are fat animals, in their royal stables fat horses, but the people look hungry and on their fields there are people who are dying of starvation."

Confucius himself came from an impoverished family of the nobility who lived in the state of Lu (near the village of Qufu, in the west of Shandong Province). For years, Confucius – or Kong Fuzi (Master Kong) – tried to gain office with many of the feudal lords, but he was dismissed again and again. So he travelled around with his disciples and instructed them in his ideas. All in all, he is said to have had 3,000 disciples, 72 of them highly-gifted ones who are still worshiped today.

Confucius taught mainly traditional literature, rites, and music, and is thus regarded as the founder of scholarly life in China. The Chinese word *ru*, which as a rule is translated as Confucian, actually means "someone of a gentle

Confucianism is, in a sense, a religion of law and order. Just as the universe is dictated by the world order, and the sun, moon and stars move according to the laws of nature, so a person, too, should live within the framework of world order. This idea, in turn, is based upon the assumption that people can be educated.

Ethical principles were turned into central issues. Confucius was a very conservative reformer, yet he significantly reinterpreted the idea of the *junzi*, a nobleman, to that of a noble man, whose life is morally sound and who is, therefore, legitimately entitled to reign. Confucius believed that he would create an ideal

CONFUCIAN THOUGHTS

It is a pleasure to have friends come to visit you from afar.

It is these things that cause me concern: failure to cultivate virtue, failure to go deeply into what I have learned, inability to move up to what I have heard to be right, and inability to reform myself when I have defects.

A man of humanity, wishing to establish himself, also establishes others, and wishing to enlarge himself, also enlarges others.

He is the sort of man who forgets to eat when he engages himself in vigorous pursuit of learning, who is so full of joy that he forgets his worries, and who does not notice that old age is coming on. (Describing himself.)

nature" – a trait that was attributed to a cultured person. Confucius did not publish his philosophical thoughts in a book. They have had to be reconstructed from fragments of the comments he made on various occasions.

The thoughts of Confucius were collected in the *Lunyu* (Conversations) by his loyal disciples. Some of the classic works on Confucianism are: *Shijing*, the book of songs; *Shujing*, the book of charters; *Liji*, the book of rites; *Chunqiu*, the spring and autumn annals; and *Yijing*, the book of changes.

social order if he reinstated the culture and rites of the early Zhou period (11th century–256 BC). Humanity (*ren*) was a central concept at the time, its basis being the love of children and brotherly love. Accordingly, the rulers would meet success if they governed the whole of society according to these principles. Confucius defined the social positions and hierarchies very precisely. Only if and when every member of society took full responsibility for his or her position would society function smoothly.

Family and social ties – and hierarchy – were considered to be of fundamental importance: between father and son (the son has to obey the father without reservations); man and woman;

LEFT: stone image of Laozi, who founded Daoism.
RIGHT: ink drawing of Kong Fuzi, or Confucius.

older brother and younger brother; and a ruler and subject.

In the 12th century, Zhu Xi (1130–1200 BC) succeeded in combining the metaphysical tendencies of Buddhism and Daoism with the pragmatism of Confucianism. His systematic work includes teachings about the creation of the microcosm and macrocosm, as well as the metaphysical basis of Chinese ethics.

This system, known as Neo-Confucianism, reached canonical status in imperial China; it was the basis of all state civil service examinations, a determining factor for Chinese officialdom until this century.

Buddhism

Today, there are Buddhists among the Han Chinese, Mongols, Tibetans, Manchus, Tu, Qiang and Dai (Hinayana Buddhists) peoples.

The Chinese initially encountered Buddhism at the beginning of the first century, when merchants and monks came to China over the Silk Road. The type of Buddhism that is prevalent in China today is the Mahayana (Great Wheel), which – as opposed to Hinayana (Small Wheel) – promises all creatures redemption through the so-called *bodhisattva* (redemption deities). There were two aspects that were particularly attractive to the Chinese: the teachings of *karma* provided a better explanation for individual

misfortune, and there was a hopeful promise for existence after death. Nevertheless, there was considerable opposition to Buddhism, which contrasted sharply with Confucian ethics and ancestor worship.

At the time of the Three Kingdoms (AD 220–280), the religion spread in each of the three states. Trading towns along the Silk Road as far east as Luoyang became centres of the new religion. After tribes of foreign origin had founded states in the north, and the gentry from the north had sought refuge in the eastern Jin dynasty (317–420), for about two centuries Buddhism developed along very different lines in the north and south of China. During the rule of Emperor Wudi (502–549), rejection and hostility towards Buddhism spread among Confucians. And during the relatively short-lived northern Zhou dynasty (557–581), Buddhism was officially banned (from 574 to 577).

Buddhism was most influential in Chinese history during the Tang dynasty (618–907). Several emperors officially supported the religion; the Tang empress Wu Zetian, in particular, surrounded herself with Buddhist advisors. For three years late in the dynasty, however, Chinese Buddhists experienced the most severe persecutions in their entire history: a total of 40,000 temples and monasteries were destroyed, and Buddhism was blamed for the dynasty's economic decline and moral decay.

In the course of time, 10 Chinese schools of Buddhism emerged, eight of which were essentially philosophical ones that did not influence popular religion. Only two schools have remained influential through today: Chan, or Zen Buddhism, and Amitabha-Buddhism, or Pure Land. The most influential Buddhist school was the so-called School of Meditation, or Chan, which developed under the Tang dynasty. It preached redemption through buddhahood, which anyone is able to reach. It despised knowledge gained from books or dogmas, as well as rites. Liberating shocks or guided meditation were used in order to lead disciples towards the experience of enlightenment. Other techniques used to achieve final insights were long hikes and physical work. The most important method was a dialogue with the master, who asked subtle and paradoxical questions, to which he expected equally paradoxical answers. The masters of Chan considered meditation to be the only path to knowledge.

In Mahayana Buddhism, worship focused on the bodhisattva Avalokiteshvara. Since the seventh century, the ascetic bodhisattva has been a popular female figure in China. She is called Guanyin, a goddess of mercy who represents a central deity for the ordinary people. Guanyin means "the one who listens to complaints".

In Chinese Buddhism, the centre of religious attention is the Sakyamuni Buddha, the founder of Buddhism who was forced into the background in the sixth century by the Maitreya Buddha (who was called Milefo in China, or redeemer of the world). In Chinese monasteries, Sakyamuni greets the faithful as a laughing

arguments. Only the reformer Tsongkhapa (1357–1419) succeeded in rectifying conditions that had become chaotic. He founded the sect of virtue (Gelugpa), which declared absolute celibacy to be a condition and reintroduced strict rules of order. Because the followers of this sect wear yellow caps, this order came to be known as Yellow Hat Buddhism.

Tsongkhapa had predicted to two of his disciples that they would be reborn as heads of the church, anticipating the continuous transfer of powerful positions within the church – for instance, the position of the Dalai Lama and the Panchen Lama. The Dalai Lama represents the

Buddha in the entrance hall. Since the 14th century, the Amitabha school had dominated the life and culture of the Chinese people.

In the seventh century AD, another type of Buddhism, called Tantric Buddhism or Lamaism, was introduced into Tibet from India. With the influence of the monk Padmasambhava, it replaced the indigenous religion, while at the same time taking over some of the elements of this naturalist religion. The monasteries in Tibet developed into centres of intellectual and worldly power, yet there were recurring

incarnation of the bodhisattva of mercy (Avalokiteshvara), who is also worshiped as the patron god of Tibet. The Panchen Lama is higher in the hierarchy of the gods and is the embodiment of Buddha Amitabha. The present 14th Dalai Lama, who was enthroned in 1940, fled to India from Tibet after an uprising in 1959, and has been living in exile since. The Panchen Lama died in Beijing in 1989, at the age of 50, after he came to an understanding with Chinese authorities following the uprising.

In Lamaism, a complex pantheon exists; apart from the Buddhist deities, there are figures from the Brahman and Hindu world of gods and the old Bon religion. Magic, repetitive prayers,

LEFT: golden statue of Buddha Sakyamuni.
ABOVE: burning incense outside of temple.

movements, formulae, symbols and sacrificial rituals are all means for achieving redemption.

In 1949, the year the People's Republic of China was founded, there were approximately 500,000 Buddhist monks and nuns, and 50,000 temples and monasteries. A number of well-known Buddhist temples were classified as historical monuments. By the beginning of the Cultural Revolution in 1966, it seemed as if the Red Guards were intent on completely eradicating Buddhism. Autonomous Tibet was hard-hit by these excesses. Only a few important monasteries and cultural objects could be protected, and completely or only partly preserved.

Islam

Ten of the 56 recognised nationalities in China profess themselves to Islam: Hui, Uzbek, Uighur, Karach, Kirgiz, Tatar, Shi'ite Tadshik, Donxiang, Sala, and Bao'an – a total of 14 million people. The Hui are, as a rule, Han Chinese. Moreover, they are the only group who enjoy the special status of a recognised minority solely because of their religion.

Mohammed was born in Mecca around the year 570 (the exact date is unknown). From the age of 40 onwards, he preached the Koran. Islam soon came to China on two different routes: one was the famous Silk Road, the other from across the sea to the southeastern coast of China. During the Yuan dynasty (1279–1368), Islam finally became permanently established in China. An imperial observatory was built in Beijing, with the Arab astronomer Jamal-al-Din in charge of the observatory.

Many of the policies of the Qing dynasty (1644–1912) were – though it may be oversimplified to say so – hostile to Muslims. In the 18th century, the slaughtering of animals in accordance with Islamic rites was forbidden, and the building of new mosques and pilgrimages to Mecca were not allowed. Marriages between Chinese and Muslims were declared illegal, and relations between the two groups were made difficult.

Some of the Muslim sects were declared illegal during the Qing dynasty. Later, the Cultural Revolution led to many restrictions for religious people. Over the last few years, the People's Republic of China has been attempting to bring socialism and religion closer together and achieve a harmony between them. Believers, irrespective of their religion, are expected to be patriotic and law-abiding, but not to give up their faith. Today, there are approximately 21,000 mosques in China. The Muslims celebrate their festivals, while Chinese-Muslim groups organise pilgrimages to Mecca.

> **ISLAMIC INFLUENCE**
> Islam probably became established in the seventh century, and its influence has been long-lasting.

Christianity

Christianity was first brought to China by the Nestorians, in 635. The followers of Nestorian Christianity disseminated their teachings with the help of a Persian called Alopen, who was their first missionary. The symbol of Nestorianism was a cross with two spheres at the end of all four beams. A stele dating from the Tang dynasty is decorated with such a cross and is on display in the provincial museum of Xi'an.

For a period, in spite of religious persecutions, this religion had spread to all the regions of the empire, and in some parts of the country was practiced until the end of the Mongol Yuan dynasty. At the same time, initial contacts were made between China and the Roman Catholic Church. The first Catholic church in China was probably built by a Franciscan monk from Italy, who arrived in Beijing in 1295. During the Ming period, Catholic missionaries began to be very active in China. A leading figure among the Jesuit missionaries who played an important role was an Italian, Matteo Ricci. When he died, there were 3,000 Christians in China.

The Jesuits had used their excellent knowledge of Western sciences in order to forge links with Chinese scholars. Other Catholic orders were more dogmatic and introduced tensions. The Chinese emperors, fed up with the squabbling, persecuted them all. In the early 1800s, Protestants began missionary activities. The methods used to convert people were not always scrupulous. In any case, the number of people converted was an almost negligible minority.

The Vatican took a strong anti-communist stance after World War II; the Chinese ordered that Catholics in China could no longer be accountable to the Vatican. In addition, the Vatican recognises only the Taiwan government as the government of China.

RIGHT: altar at Man Mo Temple, Hong Kong.

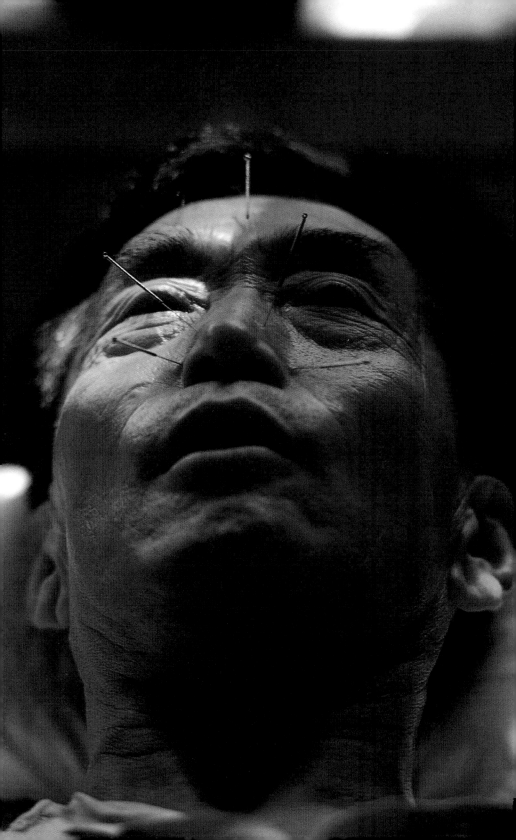

TRADITIONAL MEDICINE

For centuries the old-fashion Chinese methods of caring for and treating the body have worked just fine. A billion people can't be wrong.

The mention of traditional Chinese medicine often conjures up images of magical needles, aromatic herbs, and strange animal parts. Yet, despite its exotic stereotype, traditional Chinese medicine is increasingly gaining respect from both scientists and the general public in the West.

In China, scepticism and debate arose as to the value of traditional Chinese medicine at the beginning of the 20th century. In addition, widespread disapproval of Chinese medicine by intellectual and political groups, such as the Nationalists and Marxists, during the first half of the century harmed the reputation of traditional Chinese medicine.

After the founding of the People's Republic of China, competition between Western and Chinese medicine was eradicated for practical as well as ideological reasons, with an attempt to integrate the two systems.

Today, medical care in China often consists of a mixture of both Western and traditional Chinese medicine, although Western-style medicine, or *xiyi*, tends to be dominant. Large public hospitals (*renmin yiyuan*) in cities across the country offer both traditional Chinese and Western approaches to medical treatment. Hospitals dealing exclusively with traditional Chinese medicine, or *zhongyi*, tend to be smaller, less well-equipped, and harder to find.

The Chinese will usually visit a doctor trained in Western medicine if they feel that they are seriously ill and need to be treated quickly. If the problem is not too serious or urgent, the patient will most likely see a traditional doctor, who can better restore harmony to the body.

Historical roots

Traditional Chinese medicine, as practiced today and in past centuries, is based upon an array of theories and practices from both foreign and native sources. It was during the Zhou period (11th century–AD 256) that many of these

lasting theories first emerged. This stage of Chinese history, marked by fighting and misery, lasted several centuries. Considering the turmoil of the period, it is hardly surprising that people began to search for a solution to the endless strife. Innumerable thinkers, philosophers and social reformers with as many diverse ideas emerged, forming a collection of thought often referred to as the "hundred schools". It was during this time that many ideas took root that were to influence all aspects of life in China for the next 2,000 years – including medicine.

The two most important schools of thought at the time were those of Confucianism and Daoism. Both shared the wish for peace and harmony, but their views on how this was to be achieved differed. These two schools of thought have had the most influence on traditional Chinese medicine. In addition, theories on ancestral healing and "demonic medicine" (a concept about causation of illness by evil spirits) have also been significant factors of influence.

LEFT: acupuncture relies on particular points for effectiveness. **RIGHT:** acupuncture charts and practitioner.

The history of Chinese medicine can be said to go back as far as 5,000 years to the time of Shennong, a divine husbandman credited with the discovery of medicinal herbs. Historical writer Liu Shu reported that "Shennong tasted hundreds of herbs himself . . . some days as many as 70 poisonous herbs in one day." The validity of that statement is surely one to be debated, but *Shennong Bencaojing* (Shennong's Classic on Materia Medica) describes the medicinal effects of some 365 herbs and is the earliest known text of its kind.

Another early text, which continues to be a cornerstone in the Chinese medical canon, is one of the main distinguishing features of traditional Chinese medicine. Whereas Western medicine tends to treat symptoms in a direct fashion, traditional Chinese medicine examines illnesses in the context of a whole.

Yin-yang philosophy and the theory of five elements form a system of categories that explain the complex relationships between parts of the body and the environment. Yin and yang represent two opposite sides in nature such as hot and cold, or light and dark. Each of the different organs is said to have yin or yang characteristics. Balance between the two is vital for maintaining health. The five elements – earth,

Huang Dineijing (The Yellow Emperor's Canon of Interior Medicine). While authorship is unknown, its present-day version is believed to have been compiled between the second century BC and eighth century AD, and later revised during the Song dynasty (960–1279). Over the centuries, volumes upon volumes of commentary have been written about this ancient text. Its influence remains important, as the main principles of Chinese medicine are still based on theories first set forth by it.

Several main concepts are essential to understanding traditional Chinese medicine. Holism, or the concept that parts of a human body form an integral, connected, and inseparable whole,

fire, water, metal, and wood – are categories of characteristics into which all known phenomena can be classified. For example, just as water subdues fire, phenomena associated with water are said to control those classified under fire.

The pharmacy

A traditional Chinese pharmacy has a unique smell made up of thousands of scents emanating from jars and cabinets stocked full of dried plants, seeds, animal parts, and minerals. Among them are the well-known ginseng roots, dried or immersed in alcohol and often looking much like a human figure. In fact, the Chinese word for ginseng contains the character *ren*, which means person. You will also recognise the acupuncture needles and the cupping glasses made of glass or bamboo.

One of the most famous Chinese pharmacies is the legendary Tongrentang pharmacy, in an old part of Beijing south of Tiananmen Square. In business for over 300 years, this pharmacy was once a royal dispensary during the Qing dynasty and still produces all the pills and secret concoctions once used by royalty. The enormous size of this pharmacy is overwhelming, as is the selec-

5,767 SUBSTANCES

The *Encyclopedia of the Traditional Chinese Pharmacopoeia,* published in 1977, has 2,700 pages listing 5,767 substances.

Acupuncture

The increasing popularity of acupuncture outside of China has made it nearly synonymous for many Westerners with all traditional Chinese medicine. Not meant as a cure for everything, acupuncture has nonetheless enjoyed renewed interest in recent decades, and is especially effective in controlling pain.

The practice of acupuncture is based on a theory of channels or meridians by which "influences" flow through the body. The flow of positive influences

tion of remedies: small and large eggs, snakes coiled in spirals, dried monkeys, toads, tortoises, centipedes, grasshoppers, small fish, octopi, stag antlers, rhinoceros horns, and testicles and penises of various unfortunate – and sometimes endangered – animals. And then there are the thousand kinds of dried and preserved herbs, blossoms, roots, berries, mushrooms, and fruits.

Are these supposed to be medicines? Indeed, there are many plant, mineral, and animal substances that can be used as a remedy.

through the body is vital in maintaining health. Unhealthy symptoms are, in fact, manifestations of improper *qi*, the essence of life. The *Huang Dineijing* describes 365 sensitive points used in acupuncture, in addition to 12 main conduits in the human body. Executed properly, acupuncture should be relatively painless.

In some countries, orthodox Western medicine is still somewhat reluctant to accept acupuncture as part of an alternative approach to medicine. However, it is increasingly accepted as a treatment by many Western physicians, particularly for pain relief. While Westerners may rely on drugs to moderate physical pain, the Chinese go to the acupuncturist. Many

LEFT: *A Village Doctor Using Acupuncture*, print from the Song dynasty. **ABOVE:** a traditional pharmacy.

cases of back pain, for example, can be relieved by acupuncture. Chronic problems, however, require a longer healing process.

There is also a system of ear acupuncture, performed without needles. Small, round seed kernels are stuck onto certain points of the ear and massaged by the patient every so often. This method is not only very successful in the treatment of pain, but is also said to relieve some allergies, such as hay fever.

An acupuncture clinic often smells similar to a pharmacy. This is the typical smell of the *moxa* herb, or mugwort. It is considered especially helpful in the treatment of illnesses that,

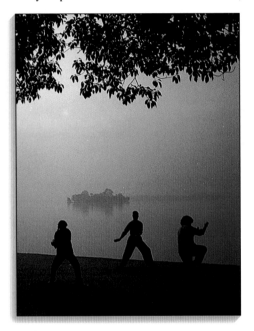

in Chinese medical terminology, are classified as "cold,"; for example, stomach and digestive complaints without fever, certain rheumatic illnesses, chronic pains in the back, and cramped shoulders and neck. The mugwort is formed into small cones and placed on slices of fresh ginger; then it is allowed to grow slowly. The plant is then placed onto the acupuncture point.

Exercise

On any early morning in China, millions of people, most of them old, gather in parks to exercise. There are several types of traditional exercise that are regarded not only as ways to take care of one's body, but also as therapy.

The most common type of exercise is *taijiquan*, the so-called shadow boxing. Another, perhaps less familiar to Westerners, is *qigong*, which is often translated as breathing therapy. With certain exercises, which may or may not involve conscious breathing, the patient learns to control qi – a person's vital energy – and to influence the course of an illness. It is claimed that those who have mastered *qigong* can walk outdoors in subzero temperatures without sufficient clothing but without feeling cold.

Some forms of qigong involve hardly any movement; breathing and "sinking into oneself" are of prime importance. Other forms, like the "wild goose qigong", entail a great deal of movement and are also very aesthetic to watch. The most extreme form is the "crane qigong", which causes violent, sometimes even cathartic emotional outbursts with many people.

During the Cultural Revolution, *qigong* was actually forbidden because it resembled "superstitious" practices too closely. Yet, in 1980, new qigong groups sprang up throughout the country. It was a grassroots movement that soon gained a large following. Today, an estimated 70 million people in China practice qigong on a daily basis. The continued popularity of qigong represents a healthy interest in exercise.

In the diet

For much of China's history, herbalists have attributed medicinal value to various foods; indeed, the distinction between food and treatment is often blurred.

Consider three traditional delicacies: shark's fin, abalone and bird's nest. These are exquisite parts of an extensive cuisine, eaten in part for their sensory delights. Yet each is claimed to have medicinal value. Shark's fin, for example, is said to benefit internal organs, including the heart and kidneys. Abalone calms internal organs. Moreover, it regulates the liver and reduces dizziness and high blood pressure. Bird's nest, usually taken as a soup, cleanses the blood and assures a clear complexion.

Westerners may still remain sceptical about the efficacy of some of the more obscure forms of Chinese medicine, but there are over a billion people who find that it works.

ABOVE: morning *taijiquan* practice, Hangzhou. **RIGHT:** the tiger is killed for its eyeballs (epilepsy), whiskers (toothaches), and bones (rheumatism).

Threatened Wildlife

The use of animal parts for medicine is not new. The Chinese have been using them for well over 1,000 years. The practice spread from China to other countries such as Korea and Japan, as well as throughout the world wherever there are significant East Asian populations.

Increased respect for and patronage of traditional Chinese medicine has helped countless people around the globe treat their ailments. In some cases, traditional medicine is even reputed to be more effective than Western medicine, or at least less harsh on the body.

Yet this renewed interest in alternative medicine has a darker side. Some wildlife, already suffering from the intensive industrial and economic growth of many Asian countries in the past 10 years, is now being pushed to the brink of extinction by the increased demand for their body parts. Unfortunately, the demand in Asia also threatens species in the Americas and Africa.

The demand for tiger parts, for example, is forcing three of the world's five remaining subspecies of tiger ever closer to extinction, threatening the long-term survival of the species as a whole. Various tiger parts are used for traditional medicine: eyeballs are used to treat epilepsy; the tail for various skin diseases; the bile for convulsions in children; whiskers for toothaches; and the brain for laziness and pimples.

Yet of all tiger parts, it is the bones that are most valued. Tiger bone is often used to treat rheumatism, but can also be used for treating weakness, stiffness, or paralysis.

Studies in 1997 estimate that there are only 30 to 80 South China tigers, 150 to 200 Siberian tigers, and 600 to 650 Sumatran tigers left in the wild. In addition, tigers have vanished from many of their habitats worldwide and may now number as few as 5,000. Without radical intervention, tigers may disappear from natural habitats within a decade. And tigers are not the only species suffering from the Asian medicine trade.

Rhinoceros, bear, and even shark populations are also rapidly shrinking. Rhinoceros horn has a reputation for being an aphrodisiac, and the number of rhinoceros in the wild is quickly dropping; only 12,500 rhinos remain in the wild and another 1,000 in captivity. About half of these are white rhinos and the remaining half consisting of about four species. Without assistance, these four species of rhinos could be extinct within a decade or two. Bears are also greatly threatened by Chinese demand. Bears from as far away as North America are valued for their paws, which are believed to have medicinal value.

Shark's fin, though not used exclusively for medicine, is a fancy delicacy. Served most commonly as shark's fin soup, this broth is believed to benefit the internal organs. Sharks are caught and their dorsal fins are sliced off. They are then tossed back into the ocean, alive, to drown. In some areas, the shark population – essential to the ecosystem, as the shark is the top predator – is declining.

In recent years, human populations and expend-

able incomes have increased dramatically in East Asia, along with a resurgence of interest in traditional cures.

Use of traditional medicines is seen as a status symbol, and as a way to hold onto traditional customs amidst rapid social and economic changes. While the effectiveness of these endangered animal products is still disputed, researchers today are confirming the effectiveness of the active ingredients present in many Chinese prescriptions. But as endangered animal populations are rapidly dropping off, the use of their parts to feed an ever-growing demand is no longer sustainable. What is clear is that the trade in endangered animal parts for medicine must stop. This means finding an alternative to alternative medicine.

ARTS AND CRAFTS

With its long history and inward-looking propensities, China has had the patience to develop and refine a resplendent catalogue of fine arts and exquisite crafts.

From very early times, Chinese artisans dazzled the world with technical brilliance and innovation, and today, Chinese arts and crafts are renowned the world over. Since the 1950s, China has attempted to revive the traditional and native arts. Research institutes were established in craft centres to continue the tradition of the crafts, as well as to make further technical advancements. Promising young talent is recruited from around the country for training in specialised schools.

Painting

There has always been a close connection between Chinese painting and calligraphy. Ancient Chinese words started as pictograms, and while each has developed in a separate direction, there has nonetheless remained inextricable ties between the two. As a rule, classical Chinese painters have extensive training in calligraphy, while calligraphers have experience in painting. Both forms are created with the same brushes and are often present together in one piece of work.

In fact, what separated and elevated the status of painting from other crafts was its similarity to calligraphy.

Both calligraphy and painting are considered scholarly pursuits and have grand and esteemed traditions, but calligraphy has been held in higher regard. Literati painters, for example, judged works by their combination of painting, poetry, and calligraphy. Success in all three areas deemed paintings to be art. Under such standards, paintings and other art forms that lacked calligraphy were simply crafts, regardless of their level of technical brilliance.

For the Chinese, the written word is the carrier of culture, and the difficulty of learning written Chinese ensured the high social status of the scholar-gentry class. Mastery of writing

and calligraphy was highly esteemed. Furthermore, despite the numerous spoken dialects in China, Chinese writing has maintained its single standard and style. This nationwide unifying and historically continuous script was therefore always more important than the spoken language.

Writing and painting utensils are referred to in China as the Four Treasures of the Study. They consist of the brush, ink, rubbing stone, and paper – tools held in high esteem by poets, scholars and painters. (There are reliable records of brush and ink already in use during the first century BC.) Brushes are made with bamboo and various kinds of animal hair such as rabbit's fur, horse hair and even mouse whiskers, and come in a wide variety of sizes. Some brush tips are treated with glue to give them a stiff tip.

Ink was already widely used in China during the Han period. It was made from the soot of coniferous resin with the addition of glue. Ink

---

PRECEDING PAGES: detail of ancient art from the Gyangze monastery, in Tibet. **LEFT:** glazed porcelain from the Song dynasty and made in Xi'an. **RIGHT:** a calligrapher at work.

of good quality has perfume added, musk in former days, but cloves are now commonly used. The substance is pressed into the shape of slabs, bars, or prisms. Ink in solid form is used both for writing and painting, although liquid ink is now also available. But using liquid ink removes one of the more contemplative and ritualistic aspects of traditional Chinese painting: making the ink, in which one first drips water onto a rubbing stone, then rubs the ink stick on it. The resulting ink is an intense black, but can be diluted to the lightest of grays as necessary.

Paper is the usual medium on which to paint. Silk was once the standard of professional and

Classical Chinese paintings can be grouped into six general categories: landscapes, portraits, flowers and birds, bamboo and stone, animals, and palaces or other buildings. Art connoisseurs later added four more groups: religious paintings, barbarians and foreign tribes, dragons and fish, and vegetables and fruits.

One of the most favoured painting forms in China since the Tang dynasty (618–907) is landscape painting. Called "mountain water paintings" in Chinese, this style features mountains and water most prominently, accented with clouds, mist and trees. By contrast, human figures are small specks in the landscape and lack

court painters, as it gave better control over graded ink and colour washes, but scholar-painters preferred paper for its immediate response to the brush.

Paper – itself another ancient Chinese invention, developed by Cai Lun and used from the second century AD onwards – is now produced in different qualities, each offering the painter alternative possibilities depending upon absorption and texture.

Painting is learned in much the same way as writing: by copying old masters or textbooks. Once developed, a particular painting style is rarely lost or abandoned, and is preserved in the painting canon.

the detail lavished on the vegetation, water and mountain. These proportions reflect Chinese philosophies on the relationship between individuals and the outside world. Unlike Western paintings, in which humans are central subjects and natural environments are rendered as backdrops, Chinese paintings show people as subservient to or a small part of their surroundings.

Chinese paintings are abstract and do not aim for realism. The best paintings successfully capture the spirit or essence of a subject. Furthermore, a painter is considered a master of his art when the necessary brush strokes for a bird, chrysanthemum, or waterfall flow effortlessly from his hand. Chinese painting values quick execution. Indeed, the nature of the materials and brush techniques do not allow for careful sketching or repainting; mistakes cannot be hidden or painted over.

This strong emphasis on perfection quickly leads to specialisation by painters on particular subjects. In this way, for instance, Xu Beihong (1895–1953) became known as the painter of horses, just as Qi Bai-Shi (1862–1957) was famous for his shrimps.

A feature of the presentation of paintings is the scroll. After

being painted on silk or paper, the painting is backed with stronger paper and mounted on a long roll of silk or brocade. Then a wooden stick is attached at the lower end (or left end, if the scroll is to be displayed horizontally). Typically, the picture was stored away rolled up and brought out only on special occasions, to be slowly unfurled and revealing only parts of a scene that were pieced together in the mind of the observer, subtly drawing him into the picture. Whether vertically or horizontally, pictures were rarely displayed for long.

LEFT: *Quails Among the Chrysanthemums,* from the Song dynasty, 1131. **ABOVE:** modern brushes.

Silk

Calligraphy, painting, poetry, and music are regarded in China as noble arts, the knowledge of which was required of any scholar. By contrast, applied arts such as silk and carving are considered merely honourable crafts, performed by craftsmen and gentlewomen. All the same, in the West these skilled crafts have always held a special fascination.

The cultivation of the silkworm is said to go back to the third century BC. The planting of mulberry trees and raising of silkworms is credited to Fuxi, a legendary figure of prehistoric China. For centuries, silk held the place of currency: civil servants and officers as well as foreign envoys were frequently paid or presented with bales of silk. The precious material was transported to the Middle East and the Roman empire, mostly via the Silk Road.

The Chinese maintained a monopoly on silk until about 200 BC, when the secret of its manufacture became known in Korea and Japan. In the West – in this case the Byzantine empire – such knowledge was acquired only in the sixth century AD. The Chinese had long prohibited the export of silkworm eggs and the dissemination of knowledge of their cultivation, but a monk is said to have succeeded in smuggling – an offense punishable by death – some silkworm eggs to the West.

Today's centres of silk production are in Zhejiang Province around the areas of Hangzhou, Suzhou and Wuxi, where silk can be bought at a lower price. Hangzhou has the largest silk industry in the People's Republic, while in Suzhou, silk embroidery has been brought to the highest artistic level.

Porcelain

The Chinese invented porcelain sometime in the seventh century. The history of Chinese ceramics, however, goes back to neolithic times. Along the Huang He (Yellow River) and Chang Jiang (Yangzi), 7,000- to 8,000-year-old ceramic vessels – red and even black clay with comb and rope patterns – have been found. The Yangshao and Longshan cultures of the fifth to second millennium BC developed new types of vessels in a diversity of patterns in red, black, and brown. Quasi-human masks, stylised fish, and hard, thin-walled stoneware, with kaolin and lime feldspar glazes, were created. Later, light-gray stoneware with green glazes, known as *yue* ware – named after the kilns of the town of Yuezhou – were designs of the Han period (206 BC–AD 220). During the Tang dynasty, Chinese porcelain was known in Europe and the Middle East.

The most widespread form of ancient Chinese porcelain was celadon, a product of a blending of iron oxide with the glaze that resulted, during firing, in a green tone. *Sancai* ceramics, with three-colour glazes from the Tang dynasty, became world-famous. The colours were mostly strong green, yellow, and brown. Sancai ceram-

ics were also found among the tomb figurines of the Tang period in the shape of horses, camels, guardians in animal or human form, ladies of the court, and officials. The Song-period celadons – ranging in colour from pale or moss green, pale blue or pale grey to brown tones – were also technically excellent. As early as the Yuan period, a technique from the Near East was used for underglaze painting in cobalt blue, commonly known as Ming porcelain. Some common themes seen throughout the Ming period were figures, landscapes, and theatrical scenes. At the beginning of the Qing dynasty, blue-and-white porcelain attained its highest level of quality.

Once patronised by imperial courts, Jingdezhen has been the centre of porcelain manufacture since the 14th century. Today, however, relatively inexpensive porcelain can be bought throughout China. Still, antique pieces are still hard to come by, as the sale of articles predating the Opium Wars is prohibited by the Chinese government.

Ivory

The carving of ivory can be traced as far back as the Shang dynasty (16th to 11th centuries BC), during which time elephants were not uncommon in China. Once artisans began to regard elephant tusks as a desirable material with which to make jewellery and containers, the once-large herds of elephants in the south of China eventually shrank to a small remnant, and soon ivory had to be imported. Ming-dynasty carvings exemplified excellent skills, and during Qing times, ivory carving was even further refined, though it was probably not until the 19th century that intricate carvings such as intertwined balls were created.

Today's centres for ivory carving are Beijing, Guangzhou, and Shanghai. All the ivory is imported from Thailand and several African countries. When buying ivory in China, keep in mind that the import of ivory is prohibited in many countries.

Jade

Jade is China's most precious stone and one of the earliest art forms to reach a superior level of achievement. According to a Chinese creation myth, when the god Pan Gu died, his breath became the wind and clouds, his muscles became soil, and the marrow of his bones jade and pearls. Chinese valued the stone for its beauty as well as for attributed magical powers. In early times, jade was used for ritual and religious purposes, but later it came to be used for ornamentation and other aesthetic purposes.

The oldest jades so far discovered come from the neolithic Hemadu culture about 7,000 years ago. The finds are presumed to be ritual objects. Many circular disks called *bi*, given to the dead to take with them, have been found. The round discs represent the harmony between heaven and earth. Even today, many Chinese wear these types of discs.

Jade was believed to have preserving powers and, consequently, burial suits were made with the precious stone. The Han dynasty probably saw an early peak in jade carving. During the Han dynasty, the corpses of high-ranking officials were clothed in suits made of more than 1,000 thin slivers of jade sewn together with gold wire. The History Museum in Beijing displays the jade suit of Prince Liu Xiu, who died in 55 BC. It is said that jade glows with the vitality of the owner. If the owner became ill, for example, the jade would become tarnished. Jade ornaments were believed to impart good health, luck, and offer protection.

Jade is not a precise mineralogical entity, but rather comprises two minerals, jadeite and nephrite. The former is more valuable because of its translucence and hardness, as well as its rarity. Nephrite is quite similar to jadeite, but not quite as hard. Colours vary from white to green, but also black, brown, and red. The Chinese value a clear, emerald-green stone most highly. Jade is an especially difficult material to shape due to its hardness.

In the jade-carving workshops of present-day China, there are thought to be as many as 30 kinds of jade in use. Famous among the jade workshops are those in Qingtian (in Zhejiang Province), Shoushan (Fujian Province), and Luoyang (Hunan Province).

In government shops, jade can be trusted to be genuine. On the open market and in private shops, however, caution is advised. Genuine jade always feels cool and cannot be scratched with a knife. Quality depends on the feel of the stone, its colour, transparency, pattern, and other factors. (If in doubt, a reputable expert should be consulted.)

Lacquerware

The oldest finds of lacquered objects date back to the Warring States period (403–221 BC). At that time, lacquerware was an everyday material: bowls, tins, boxes, vases, and furniture made of various materials (wood, bamboo, wicker, leather, metal, clay, textiles, paper) were often coated with a skin of lacquer. Emperor Qianlong (1735–1796) had a special liking for carved lacquerware; he was buried in a coffin carved and preserved using this technique.

The glossy sheen of lacquerware is not only attractive but also strong and lightweight. The bark of the lacquer tree, which grows in central and southern China, exudes a milky sap when cut, which solidifies in moist air, then dries and turns brown. This dry layer of lacquer is impervious to moisture, acid, and scratches, and is therefore ideal protection for materials such as wood or bamboo.

To make lacquerware, a base coat is applied to a core material, followed by extremely thin layers of the finest lacquer that, after drying in dust-free moist air, are smoothed and polished. If soot or vinegar-soaked iron filings are added to the lacquer, it will dry into a black colour; cinnabar turns it red.

LEFT: porcelain jar from the Qing dynasty.
RIGHT: carved lacquer plate from the 18th century.

CALLIGRAPHIC ART

Although often considered a branch of Chinese painting, Chinese calligraphy is a highly venerated art form in itself.

Writing has always been central to the Chinese, not only as a means of preservation and dissemination of culture, but also as a marker of a person's intelligence and social status. The Chinese characters for calligraphy (*shu fa*) derive from the character for "book" (*shu*). Hence, mastery of calligraphy has always been closely linked with the attainment of knowledge, and it was historically a prerequisite for high office and often part of civil service exams.

The use of brushes in Chinese writing originated in the Shang dynasty (16th–11th cent. BC). By the time of the Han dynasty (206 BC–AD 220), great calligraphic masters had appeared and it was accepted that one could glean the character and personality of the artist by the brushstroke and form demonstrated. The importance of calligraphy and its influence on the rest of Chinese painting was such that by the time of the Yuan dynasty (1279–1368), calligraphic inscriptions – often in the form of poems – had been incorporated as part of the overall painting.

STYLES OF CALLIGRAPHY

In the history of Chinese calligraphy, there are four basic styles of writing. The first is the archaic *xiao chuan* (small-seal script), established in the Qin dynasty (221–206 BC) and which is meticulous and laborious. The square *li shu*, with its clear brushstrokes, was established in the Han dynasty and used in official writing. Many of the inscriptions on steles of ancient Chinese classics are done in this style. *Cao shu* ("grass" or cursive style), in which brushstrokes are often joined together in one continuous flow, was developed as a quicker and simpler alternative to the more formal scripts. More so than any other style, the flamboyance of cao shu is a form of individual expression. Finally, *kai shu* is a combination of the more formal li shu and the more expressive cao shu, and is the basis of today's standard calligraphic script.

Calligraphy is still highly esteemed, practiced by housewives and politicians alike. Even the old masters will claim they are but students of this fine art.

HIRED CALLIGRAPHER ▷
Calligraphers like this one in Xi'an also serve as writers of personal letters and court suits, as well as marriage, divorce, birth, or death announcements.

◁ **ART & SYMBOL**
Combining images and Chinese characters in this stone block, the god of literature, Kuei Xing, has been chiselled as standing atop the sea monster Ao. The image of the god has been created from the symbol of his constellation. Ao's form is derived from the character for fish.

◁ **IN THE SPIRIT OF INK**
It is not unusual to catch calligraphy masters on a warm summer's evening demonstrating their skills outdoors to admirers as they apply brush to paper.

▽ **FOCUSING ON STROKES**
A calligrapher can create lines of different widths merely by adjusting the angle of the brush or the amount of pressure exerted. Even more, a proper state of mind must be present.

FOUR TREASURES OF THE STUDY

A Chinese calligrapher's tools, like those of a painter, are comprised of four basic items that are commonly referred to as the "four treasures of the study". They are the brush, ink, inkstone, and paper.

The brush has a wooden or bamboo handle with bristles from the hair of animals such as goat or deer. The bristles are shaped to a fine point. The black ink is derived from a mixture of oil or pine soot and glue, which is then dried into ink sticks. Mixing the ink with just the right amount of water in a nonporous inkstone is very important, as the consistency of the paint can affect the overall balance and harmony.

Although Chinese artists were painting and writing on silk as early as 400 BC, the use of paper began much later, around AD 300.

The aesthetic excellence of a piece of calligraphy is often determined by brushstroke, which is in turn judged by a set of abstract qualities that includes balance, vitality, strength, and texture. Much more than mere ink on paper, good calligraphy characters should feel alive, organic. The brushstrokes must be applied with skill, finesse, confidence, and speed.

Of course, no work of art – and this includes calligraphy – would be complete without the artist's seal, or chop.

△ **CALLIGRAPHY PAPER**
Commonly called "rice paper", *xuan* paper is actually made from the bark of the plant wingceltis mixed with rice straw. Highly absorbent, it allows for no mistakes or corrections.

◁ **CAO SHU EXAMPLE**
Writings of the monk Huai Su, famed for his cursive style of *cao shu*. (8th cent.)

THE CULTURAL ARTS

Complicated writing makes literature difficult, complex music and motion make Beijing opera challenging. Such are expected after 20 centuries of creativity.

It is not surprising that the written word is more important to the Chinese than the spoken one. Indeed, given the numerous dialects to be found in modern China, the written word – or character, to be precise – is the common means of communication. Chinese characters developed from a pictographic writing system and not only represent sounds, but meaning.

The earliest evidence of the Chinese script was found on the so-called oracle bones – tortoise shells or shoulder blades of animals onto which questions regarding the weather, the yield of crops, or the outcome of battles were carved. They were then thrown into a fire, and the oracle was interpreted according to the cracks that were formed by the heat. This form of writing is more than 4,000 years old and cannot, of course, be described as literature, although they provide information on the development of the Chinese script. Vernacular literature in China took shape as an art form during the Yuan dynasty. Most of the oldest works of literature, however, are from the late Zhou dynasty.

Perhaps the most famous of early writings for Westerners would be the thoughts of Confucius (551–479 BC). Among the compiled works (probably by his students) are the *Spring and Autumn Annals*; the *Book of Changes*, a system of divination; the *Book of Rites*; and a history of Lu, his native state.

Apart from the classic philosophical works of Confucianism and Daoism, there also exists to this day the "monument to the bound language" called *Shijing* (a book of odes, or songs). Legend has it that these songs were collected from the peoples of the different states by a civil servant, Cai Shiguan. The government wished to gain insight into the lives of the people with the help of these songs in order to administer the country more effectively. It is said that more than 3,000 songs were collected. Confucius

selected 300 of them and compiled them in the *Shijing*. The contents of the odes are wide-ranging: love songs, songs about the land, and songs glorifying outstanding personalities or personal qualities. Most of the songs in the *Shijing* originate in the area of the Huang He, known to Westerners as the Yellow River.

Poems in the lyrical or epic style play an extremely important part in Chinese literature. To be able to read and write poetry was part of the elementary education of the higher social classes. Students and civil servants of any rank or age were expected to be able to write a poem for any occasion. Girls and women who knew how to recite poems graciously were ensured the admiration of the opposite sex. The *Chuzi,* another collection of songs, comes from the south of China. Its creation is attributed to the poet Qu Yuan (c. 322–295 BC).

The Tang dynasty (618–907) was the beginning of the golden age for Chinese poetry. No other period in history has enjoyed such a great

---

PRECEDING PAGES: backstage admirer watching preparations for an opera. **LEFT:** Sun Wukong, King of the Apes. **RIGHT:** the ancient poet Qu Yuan, who lived in the fourth century BC.

number of poets, and works of poetry on such a scale and of such quality. *Quan Tangshi*, the large and complete collection of Tang poetry, contains nearly 50,000 poems by 2,200 poets.

One of the most famous poets of the time was Li Bai, or Li Po (699–762), who is said to have written his best-known poems in a state of total inebriation. The story goes that he was quite drunk when he was appointed as an official at the palace. Nevertheless, he immediately wrote a poem at the emperor's request

THE WAY OF WORDS

The oldest Chinese books were written on strips of bamboo, fixed together like a roller blind. This helps explain why traditional writing runs from top to bottom and from right to left.

poet through diligence and practice. He was bold and serious, and greatly concerned about the political and social situation. His lamentations were closely linked to Confucian ideas.

Prose and fiction, which almost always had an educational aspect, were usually considered trivial and not serious forms of literature in ancient China. A status-conscious intellectual would regard it as undignified to concern himself with either of them. This attitude changed, fortunately, in the 20th

that earned him much praise from the public – and, of course, from the emperor.

Du Fu (712–770) must be mentioned together with Li Bai, though his style of poetry is very different. He held office at the court for just a short time, forced to flee due to political upheavals. He then led an unsettled, wandering life for a long time, eventually settling in Chengdu, where one can still visit the straw hut, Du Fu Caotang, that served as his home.

From a contemporary point of view, it is hard to say which of the two poets is more significant. Li Bai was a natural talent, free, open and humourous, devoted to nature and close to the Daoists. Du Fu, on the other hand, became a

century. Nevertheless, there are a number of novels from different epochs that have survived, and which are still read and appreciated by many Chinese today.

Classical fiction

Every child in China knows the novel *Journey to the West* and its famous heroes: the ape king Sun Wukong; a pig, Zhu Bajie; the monk, Sha; and the Buddhist pilgrim and monk, Xuanzang.

The novel describes the adventure of the king of the apes, who, together with the other characters, accompanies the monk Xuanzang from China to the West, or India, in order to collect holy scriptures from that land. The novel mixes

Indian folk stories and legends with Chinese, Buddhist, and Daoist elements.

The *Shuihuzhuan* (The Water Margin) is a novel about robbers dating from the Ming period; its origins are not clear. The story is partly based upon historical facts about the robber Song Jiang and his companions, who wandered through what is now the province of Shandong around the end of the Northern Song dynasty (960–1127). Just like Robin Hood and his merry men, Song Jiang and his men fought injustices according to their code of honour.

They finally submitted to the imperial doctrine and fought against rebels who were threat-

---

A LI BAI SAMPLER

Li Bai, known to appreciate a good stiff drink, was the Tang dynasty's most beloved poet.

Moonlight gleams before my bed,
Like frost on the floor.
Lifting my head I see the bright moon,
Lowering my head I think of my old home.

At Yellow Crane Tower, I said goodbye
to an old friend.
It was the third month, the season of flowers,
when you went down to Yangzhou.
Your solitary sail has become a
distant blue dot, and all I saw was the Yangzi
flowing into the sky.

We are but travellers on the world's horizons.
Meeting thus in a common fate, what does
acquaintance matter?

Jinpingmei portrays people as individual characters and describes the many amorous adventures of its hero, Ximen, in a rather realistic way. Furthermore, this novel conveys a very precise portrayal of social conditions in the 16th century. It describes how upstarts and scroungers who gave themselves up to a totally unrestrained life ran rampant. Among its characters are greedy civil servants and old women who acted as matchmakers. It describes idlers and layabouts curious to find out about the private lives of others, and Buddhist and Daoist priests who took to womanising. All in all, it provides a unique portrayal of life as it was lived by the so-

ening the state system. This novel, too, became extremely popular. It is said to have been Mao Zedong's favourite book, although during the time of the Cultural Revolution, it was considered a negative illustration of capitulation.

Genre novels

The epitome of the genre novel is *Jinpingmei*, or *The Plum Blossom in a Golden Vase*, dating from the Ming dynasty. In contrast to the novels that are heavily influenced by religion and sometimes have almost fanatical tendencies,

called higher echelons of society. It is not clear who the author of *Jinpingmei* was, but in 1617, a second edition was published, of which a few copies have survived. In 1687, Emperor Kangxi banned the book, yet it continued to be read, and in 1708 it was even translated into Manchurian. Emperor Qianlong again banned the book in 1789. It was also banned after 1949.

Hongloumeng, or *Dream of the Red Chamber,* written by Cao Xueqin in the 18th century, is rated the best novel of the Qing dynasty, and many critics consider it China's best novel ever. Its main character is Jia Baoyu, the amorous and sentimental son of a high-ranking official. There are also Lin Daiyu, Xue Baochai and others –

LEFT: noted poets Du Fu, and Li Bai, fond of drink.
ABOVE: image from *Journey to the West*.

Cinema in China

The 1980s film *Red Sorghum*, by Zhang Yimou, drew worldwide attention to Chinese cinema, which for a long time had only been noticed by those interested in martial arts. In contrast, this film allowed the audience to witness a bizarre love story set in China during the 1930s.

The "electric shadow play" has existed in China since the beginning of the 20th century. In the silent-film era, historical, criminal and love films – as well as the first "kung fu" films – were produced mainly in Shanghai, the centre of Chinese cinema developed individual forms of expression. Chen Kaige's debut *Yellow Earth* (1984) describes the failure of people who rebel against tradition and refers symbolically to the failure of China's liberation through communism.

Many of the most successful Chinese films today examine the destruction of people through inhuman methods of power and traditions, thus denoting permanent outrage at those in power in Beijing.

In the meantime, nonetheless, China has produced an internationally recognised cinema, and even an international star, Gong Li, despite state censorship. Collaboration with the Hong Kong film industry, the third-largest in the world, has brought

then. However, socialist realism ousted all unpolitical films from the screen after 1949.

During the Cultural Revolution, film-making came to a standstill for three years. Many film people fell victim to persecution, instigated by a starlet (perhaps with significant connections higher up) from the 1930s; only a few socialist "model operas" were permitted in the early 1970s, and somehow under her directive.

It was not until 1978 that the Beijing Film Academy once again accepted students following a 15-year break. This generation of film-makers was moulded by the experiences of being forced to work in the countryside, and of political terror. While older film directors liked to establish the socialist tradition of the 1950s, these younger directors

significant financial and technical improvements with it. The range of Hong Kong cinema extends from actors like Leslie Cheung (*Farewell My Concubine*) to action star Jackie Chan, now a household name in North America and Europe, and long a familiar name in other parts of the world. Apart from fast action and martial-arts films in the style of Tsui Hark, there are also independent productions such as Wong Kar-wai's *Chungking Express*, which depicted life in the Asian metropolis.

The growing significance of Chinese cinema is also gauged by Hollywood's collaboration with Hong Kong director John Woo (*Broken Arrow*, *Face/Off*), and the Taiwanese Li Ang (*Sense and Sensibility*, *The Ice Storm*). Both directors are now entrenched in Hollywood, as is Hong Kong's Jackie Chan.

twelve girls in all – who are living at the house of the Jia family. The novel describes the rise and decline of the house of Jia. In an imaginative and humourous style, the author has given the male and female members of staff – more than 400 people – individual and distinctive traits, portraying the domestic life of a distinguished Manchu family in all its detail. Because the novel is so popular, it has given rise to specific research into the narrative.

Since the May Fourth Movement of 1919, which amongst other things was aimed at reforming language, prose literature has increasingly been regarded as a means for social change. One of the most outstanding figures in new literature was Lu Xun, a poet, essayist, and novelist who believed China needed to modernise through revolution. In his novel *Ah Q*, he used biting irony to describe the self-destructive and insolent attitude of the underlings who are steeped in tradition and superstition. It was also Lu Xun who, in a brilliant way, introduced the essay form into Chinese literature.

In *The Diary of Sophia*, author Ding Ling describes the lifestyle of her like-minded contemporaries with sceptical distance. Ba Jin wrote critical novels like *The Family* that, following in the tradition of *Hongloumeng*, describe the decline of a civil servant's family at the beginning of this century.

Many writers of this time were sympathetic to the Communist movement, and as this sympathy grew stronger, the direction and content of literature were defined more clearly. After Mao Zedong's speech on art and literature, in Yan'an in 1942, Social Realism was established as the only legitimate form. But other writers were busy singing the praises of workers, peasants, and soldiers, and glorifying their struggles against wicked people such as feudal landlords. In 1956, the "period of the hundred flowers", some writers expressed dissatisfaction with policies. At the end of this period, they were branded as rightists, and their works labelled as "poisonous weeds".

The Cultural Revolution, from 1966 to 1976, virtually halted literary endeavours. Once it was over, however, there was a resurgence of writing. With his story *Scar*, Lu Xinghua gave the name to "wound literature", analysing the trauma caused by the Cultural Revolution. This wound literature was itself part of the so-called New Realism, which typically looked at society's imperfections. But in 1980, the overriding political goals of China's literature were reasserted. Deng Xiaoping wrote that "it is impossible for literature to be independent of politics. Any progressive and revolutionary worker cannot but think of his works' social influence and must consider, therefore, the interests of the nation and the party… The party wishes, without compulsion, that literary workers first consider the public interests."

For decades after 1949, literature in China

was impeded by the dictates of Communism's Social Realism. But the 1980s saw a burst of literary creativity of new writing techniques. Most of the 2,000 novels produced from 1979 to the mid 1990s appeared during this decade.

By comparison, only 320 novels were published between 1949 and 1966, and few or none during the Cultural Revolution. Since the late 1980s, some writers have published little, as they have not wanted to risk criticism for expressing views that might be regarded as supporting bourgeoisie liberalism. Some writers, meanwhile, have found commercial success by writing pop literature, such as sentimental love stories and martial arts sagas.

LEFT: Gong Li in *Raise the Red Lantern*. **ABOVE:** Lu Xun, important 20th-century writer.

Beijing opera

Beijing opera has only existed for about 200 years, although the origins of theatre in China go back much further.

Descriptions of dances dating from the Tang dynasty (618–907) show striking similarities to present-day Beijing opera. During the Ming era (1368–1644), *kunqu* opera, a form of musical drama, was developed. Many elements of the song, dance, and music of Beijing opera can be traced to this form.

In the old days, permanent theatres were a rarity, even in Beijing and the major ports, so Beijing opera was performed on the streets and in works are much better known in China than one might find most literary classics are in the West. But there is also an art to understanding and enjoying this kind of theatre. There is great use of convention, so if you want to enjoy Beijing opera, knowing some of the rules helps.

The four main branches of Beijing opera are song, dialogue, mime, and acrobatics, united categories that are usually separated in European theatre. Sometimes music and song are predominant, sometimes mime. In other pieces, fight scenes dominate and the acrobatics are in the foreground, while in others still, the spoken word gets centre stage.

the market places, a sign of its popularity among ordinary people.

Beijing opera was the only way for commoners to learn anything about life outside the narrow constraints of their own day-to-day existence, and it was probably their main source of Chinese history. There was hardly a single temple festival during which a theatre performance was not given, although the opera performances themselves generally had nothing to do with the religious occasion.

Many Beijing operas go back to popular legends, folk or fairy tales, or to classical literature such as *The Three Kingdoms*, *The Dream of the Red Chamber*, or *Journey to the West*. These

COLOURS OF THE FACE

The tradition of the mask-like make-up, so goes the story, began with Zhuge Liang, a hero from the time of the Three Kingdoms (220–280 AD) who had ɼarticularly fine, feminine features. For this reason, the great strategist had the idea of painting his face with terrifying colours to frighten his enemies, thus inventing the mask. Red shows a loyal, brave character. Black represents someone good and strong, but also coarse. Blue symbolises wildness and courage, and arrogance, while green is a sign of an unstable person. Only gods wear gold.

The main division is between *wenxi* (civilian plays) and *wuxi* (military dramas), but there are also comedies and skits. Wenxi pieces are more like our conception of drama, describing domestic and civilian life. The wuxi, on the other hand, consist mainly of fights, and tell of historical wars and battles by making use of acrobatics.

There are four different types of roles in Beijing opera: *sheng*, or the male lead roles; *dan*, female roles; *jing*, painted-face roles; and *chou*, male or female clowns. Each major group is divided into sub-groups. Then there are also extras, such as guards, soldiers, gadflies, and ladies-in-waiting.

The dan or female role is usually the most important part. There are two historical reasons for this. In most of the dramas – derived from stories and novels that form the bases for the operas – a woman is the focus of interest. Also, the central figure in Chinese dramas has been a woman since the days of the Yuan dynasty (1279–1368).

In general, the dan, who were traditionally played by men, have their faces made up with a white base and various shades of carmine, with a little pale pink around the eyes. They move gracefully with soft, flowing steps. Other characteristics are their half-sung, half-spoken dialogue and a kind of mewing singing. However, for nearly half a century, the training of men to sing female roles has been prohibited. The official reason given is that this practice has led to "sexual perversion".

The costumes are based on court costumes of the Han, Tang, Song, and especially the Ming dynasties (1368–1644), as well as from the era of the Manchu emperors (1644–1912). Old wall paintings and drawings of the period in question were studied when the costumes were designed. The costumes of the Beijing opera, however, are by no means realistic. Their symbolic characteristics are particularly obvious in the beggar costumes: silk with colourful patches.

While the symbolic colours and patterns of stage make-up reveal details of character, colour may also be used purely for aesthetic reasons, creating harmony between costume, face and headdress. The make-up artists can create more than 300 different types of painted-mask faces.

Props are used sparingly. An oar in the hand

of a boatman is enough to make it clear that the scene takes place in a boat. A chair can be just a chair, but it can also be high ground in a landscape. An unlit candle can be the sign that evening is coming on. Every soldier carrying a banner represents a whole regiment. Riders almost always play two parts, for they also have to portray the movement of the horse – rearing, galloping, and trotting – through mime and gesture, thus turning themselves into centaurs.

The style of acting is typical of the "non-reality" of Beijing opera. The aim of the actor is not, as in Western drama, to become the character portrayed. The actor distances him or herself

from the role and tries to quote it, to portray events that are connected to the role. No Beijing opera performers ever end up "beside themselves." The closest parallels in the West to the ritual style of operatic performance with its fixed gestures are to be found in classic mime, in ballet, and among circus clowns.

In China, you never say you're going to see a Beijing opera; rather, you say that you are going to listen to one. Music and song, after all, are the main elements of opera. Indeed, devotees may spend the entire performance with eyes shut, ears open, and mind wandering. Most, however, will also enjoy following the stylised methods of expression.

LEFT: resplendent costume and banners of a female military general. **RIGHT:** gradations of the mask.

CHINESE OPERA

The emphasis in Chinese opera is on Confucian ethics and morality. Stories invariably have endings in which goodness is upheld and evil is punished.

Although Chinese theatre in the form of skits, vaudeville, puppet shows, and shadow plays has existed since the Tang dynasty (618–907), formal music-drama had its origins in the Yuan dynasty (1279–1368), when scholars who were displaced from their government positions by the foreign Mongols turned to writing dramas in which songs often alternated with dialogue. Since then, opera has become one of the most popular forms of mass entertainment in China.

Today, there are more than 300 different styles of Chinese opera. Although rarely performed now, the classical *kunqu* had its origins in the 16th century and was considered by its primary audience, the scholarly gentry, to be too genteel and esoteric for the masses. The flute is the primary instrument and its melodies are wide-ranging. Other styles of regional opera include *chaozhou* (Teochew) opera, the puppet operas of Fujian, and the *bangzi xi* (clapper operas), which are popular in Shaanxi and the northern part of China, and which features as its main accompaniment a datewood clapper struck with a stick.

By far the most popular Chinese opera, however, is the highly stylised *jingxi* (Beijing or Peking opera), which dates from the 1800s. Beijing opera is a composite of different forms: literature, song, dance, mime, and martial arts. Time is marked with the aid of a redwood clapper that produces a high-pitched clicking sound when struck. The accompanying musical instrument in Beijing opera is usually the *huqin,* a Chinese fiddle, although cymbals are sometimes, if not usually, employed in action scenes.

While there are endless variations among the different opera styles, all of them share some general characteristics that are associated with Chinese opera. Plots are based on historical stories or folklore with which audiences are already familiar.

COLOURS OF THE FACE △
Red make-up on a male character indicates bravery and loyalty, while white denotes a powerful villain. Clowns have their own special make-up, often with a white patch on the tip of the nose to indicate wit or playfulness.

WORDS UNDERSTOOD ▷
Whether in soliloquys, spoken verse, songs, or dialogue, the words used in any Chinese opera performance are almost always colloquial. The opera was meant to be watched by the common people. Audiences are usually noisy but appreciative.

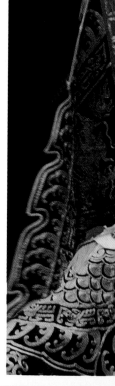

SOCIALIST OPERA △
During the Cultural Revolution, traditional operas were replaced with ideological pieces upholding socialism.

◁ **HELP NEEDED**
It is not uncommon for musicians and assistants to remain on stage throughout the performance to help with prop changes.

THE ART FORM OF OPERA TRAINING

Chinese opera is considered one of the most conventionalised forms of theatre to be found anywhere, requiring years of training to master.

Actors often undergo seven years of training as children, after which they are selected for specific roles such as the male, female, warrior, or clown. Prior to the 1930s, all the roles were required to be played by men.

Mastery of singing, of course, is essential for the male and female roles, while clowns are often required to demonstrate acrobatic prowess. All actors must hone the fine body movements that are the opera's style. An actor's training includes applying the elaborate make-up that identifies the character.

PROPS AND SYMBOLS ▷
Changes in time and place are evoked through speech, action, and ritualised use of props. Walking in a circle is symbolic of a journey, while circling the stage with a whip indicates riding a horse.

SLEEVE ACTING ▽
The long flowing sleeves in certain costumes can be manipulated in more than 100 movements.

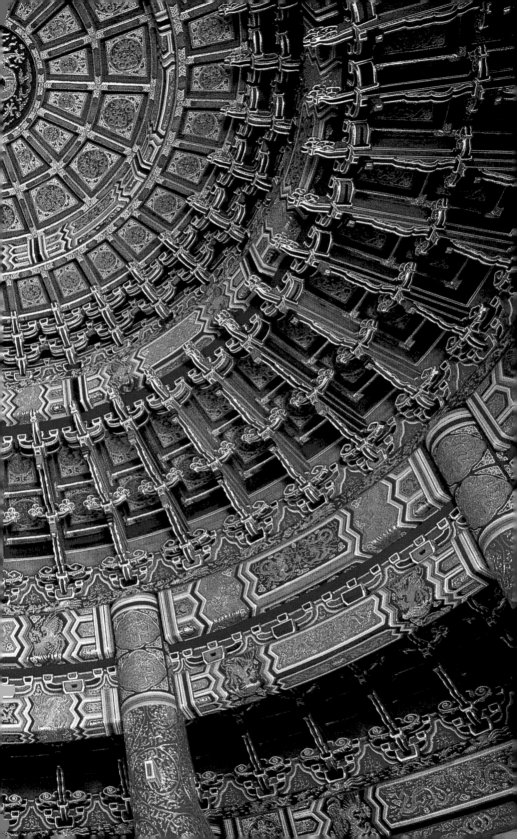

ARCHITECTURE

Chinese architecture and the basic layout of imperial palaces and surrounding environs were dictated by the cosmology defining Heaven and Earth.

Traditional Chinese architecture follows a plan that reflects philosophies of order and authority. Careful layout applies not only to residences and ceremonial buildings, but to entire cities as well. Buildings are preferably oriented on a north–south axis, with the most important structures facing south. Chinese households traditionally centre around courtyards; the higher the rank, the greater the number of courtyards. Therefore, an important official might live in a large residence along with numerous relatives and servants. The home of the head family is situated to the north of the compound and faces south. The side buildings facing the central courtyard might belong to sisters and brothers, while more distant relatives might live around courtyards further south. In more modest homes, a similar layout prevails, with parents living in the main northern quarters facing south and children occupying side quarters facing the courtyard.

Surrounding and enclosing the residence is a wall. Walls are very important to Chinese landscapes, whether as part of a home, palace, temple, town, village, or city. Walls not only provided protection and privacy, but symbolised containment and a group mentality that is an important aspect of Chinese society. Indeed, the longest wall of all, the Great Wall, which once formed the northern boundary of the country, reflects this concept.

The Imperial Palace and the surrounding city layout of Beijing are fine examples of classical Chinese architecture and planning. Designed during the Ming dynasty, the architectural planning reflects the centred power of the emperor

from the heart of the capital, which was the cultural and political heart of the country. Clusters of buildings within the complex reflect the organisation and intricacy of political power. From the central imperial complex, the city radiates outward in orderly fashion and is enclosed by city walls flanked with gates and towers. Today, the walls are no longer in place, but much of the original plan is still apparent. The palace rests nearly in the exact centre of the city with the various highways and expressway ring roads radiating outward in concentric squares.

The design and construction of the imperial complex are in line with classical Chinese planning, only on a very grand and opulent scale. Three basic building types – the hall, tower and pavilion – are unified by common elements in their tile roofs, stone floors, and bays made of wooden posts.

One approaches the imperial complex from the south. Large buildings such as the three great Halls of Harmony in the front part of the palace rise from a terrace. As the most important building of the entire complex, Taihe Dian (Hall of Supreme Harmony) has the largest and most splendid terrace in the whole of the palace grounds. In three raised levels, the entire terrace is framed by a marble balustrade.

Through symmetry and balance, the numerous buildings of the Imperial Palace complex create a pattern according to their function and importance. Their organisation thus symbolised the harmony of the universe maintained by the emperor, the Son of Heaven.

HEAVEN AND EARTH

Beijing's Imperial Palace offers numerous examples of ancient Chinese thinking. The large halls, atop marble terraces, reflect the symbolic and cosmological messages of old texts: "The Heavens cover and the Earth carries." The terraces are the Earth, and the roof, the Heavens.

Architecture and superstition

Very conspicuous on palace roofs are ridge decorations: mythological beasts at the ends of the ridge meant to protect the building from evil spirits. The animals include a lion, dragon, phoenix, flying horse, and unicorn, amongst

PRECEDING PAGES: exquisite ceiling in Tiantan, the Temple of Heaven in Beijing; the dome-like woodwork was created without the use of a single nail.
LEFT: print of the Longhua Pagoda, in Shanghai.

others. One can also spot a man riding a hen – another common figure intended to protect the building and occupants against disaster. Legend has it that this represents a tyrannical prince from the state of Qi (third century BC). After his defeat and death, the inhabitants of Qi are said to have fixed replicas of him riding on a hen to their roofs in order to keep away disaster and stigmatise the tyrant. Tradition has it that the evil tyrant on the hen cannot leave the roof because the hen cannot carry him in flight.

Traditional beliefs are often reflected in Chinese architecture. The so-called ghost wall, for example, was usually put up behind the

entrance of all apartments and palaces to bar the entry of evil spirits, believed to be able to move in a straight path only and not around corners. In large palaces, Jiulongbi, or the splendid Nine Dragons Wall, fulfilled this function.

Pagodas

Majestic and ornate, pagodas have inspired many an imagination and are integral to images associated with the Far East. In fact, pagodas are not indigenous to China and are rather a good example of foreign influence on Chinese architecture. Through many centuries, Chinese pagodas have evolved from an imported concept to one that has incorporated and reflects traditional architectural styles, construction methods, and developments.

Pagodas provide scenic focal points in a landscape, but they are also parts of a whole, segments of a larger harmonious design. In India, where they originated, pagodas were made of brick and used to enshrine sacred objects. During the first centuries AD, Buddhist missionaries spread the teachings of Buddha to China. Many Chinese monks later travelled the same route back to India. In this way, reports of burial rites, religious art, and the impressive monastic and temple architecture filtered into China. In China, however, pagodas slowly lost much of their religious associations and became scenic spots. In Chinese, a pagoda is called *ta*, which earlier was *tappna*, a Chinese rendering of the Indian word *stupa*.

The secularism of Chinese society (and architecture) is also reflected in the temple design of various religious sects. Buddhist temples, for example, have the same architectural design as Daoist and Confucian temples. They are built and designed by the same craftsmen as those who build homes and palaces.

Just as they adapted Buddhism by rapidly mixing the original teachings of Buddha with traditional superstitions and ancestor worship, so did the Chinese invest the genuine style of the Buddhist pagoda with their own forms and building traditions.

The first pagoda structures found in China go back to the third and fifth century AD and were presumably constructed in timber; none of these survive. Songyue Pagoda, the oldest surviving pagoda, is found in the district of Dengfeng, near the old imperial city of Luoyang and close to the famous Shaolin monastery. This 40-metre-high (130 ft), twelve-sided pagoda was built in AD 523. For over 1,400 years, it has withstood the ravages of weather, natural disasters, and revolutions, from the Mongol invasion to the Cultural Revolution.

At the nearby Shaolin monastery, there is another rare sight: Talin, the Forest of Pagodas, a cemetery containing more than 200 stone funerary pagodas and the last resting place of monks. These pagodas are only a few metres high and have a square core to which are

LEFT: roof detail of mythological animals for protection.
RIGHT: Bai Ta, the White Dagoba, in Beijing.
FAR RIGHT: Great Wild Goose Pagoda, Xi'an.

attached memorial tablets or small recesses for offerings. Function and symbolism correspond to the original Indian stupas, but not their architectural style.

Best known for its Imperial Palace complex, Beijing also contains many fine examples of Buddhist-inspired architecture. In Beihai Park, Bai Ta or the White Dagoba rises majestically to the west of the Imperial Palace and above the old imperial city. The white, massive bell-shaped structure is set on a square base in the style of a Tibetan *chorten*. It was built in 1651 by Emperor Shun Zhi to commemorate the first visit of the Dalai Lama to Beijing.

Other ancient structures include what are possibly the best-known pagodas in China: the two Wild Goose pagodas in Xi'an. Dayan Ta, the Great Wild Goose Pagoda, was built at the proposal of and to the design of the monk Xuan Zang, who, in the seventh century AD, undertook an adventurous years-long journey to northern India. His travels are known to today's Chinese as a legend from the literary masterpiece, *Journey to the West*. After his return to China, he had a pagoda constructed to store the manuscripts he brought back with him.

The curious name of this pagoda goes back to a legend supposedly brought from northern

GARDENS OF PHILOSOPHY AND EMPIRES

Chinese gardens strive for a delicate balance between natural and artificial elements, reflecting Daoist principles of harmony with nature. Philosophical concepts such as *yin-yang* as well as literary and painterly subjects were bases of design.

The art of gardens flourished during the Ming and Qing dynasties. Emperors – and the rich and powerful of the times – invested huge amounts of money and labour to build elaborate, private gardens and retreats.

Two main types of gardens dominate: the imperial park and the scholar-official's private retreat. The best-known gardens of the first type are the

Summer Palace and Yuanming Yuan, the old summer palace, as well as Chengde (Jehol). Imperial parks were meant to suggest the riches and diversity of the empire. Chengde, the massive imperial park built by Emperor Qianlong, contains Buddhist-inspired architecture of Tibet that was meant to assert the diversity of China.

The southern cities of Suzhou and Hangzhou, outside of the Shanghai metropolitan area, offer numerous examples of the scholar-officials private garden hideaways, which sought to stir emotions by creating an intense microcosm of the natural world.

India by Xuan Zang. It is said that a large, wild goose fell out of the sky in response to the prayers of starving Buddhist monks. But instead of eating the goose, the monks buried it to show their gratitude. The pagoda in Xi'an is believed to be named after one in India of the same name.

The smaller Xiaoyan Ta, or Little Wild Goose Pagoda, originally had another name but was renamed, in the course of time, because of its similarity to the Great Wild Goose Pagoda. It is of a similar age but appears – because of its slender form and gently-curved topmost point – more graceful than the monumental and somewhat clumsy Great Wild Goose Pagoda.

Chinese construction

From the earliest days, the Chinese favoured timber as a building material. Wood was not only easily transported, but was also more practical. Residences were meant to be rebuilt, not to be permanent monuments.

Brick and stone were used, however, for construction of important structures intended to withstand the elements for a long time, such as imperial tombs and ceremonial buildings, and, occasionally, bridges. As a result of the widespread use of wood, few of the original ancient remnants remain.

Chinese craftsmen developed timber-frame construction into its ultimate form. Traditional

Chinese buildings rest on a floor made of beaten earth, brick, or stone. Posts and beams satisfy structural requirements and are built without the aid of glue or nails. Heavy columns set in stone bases carried the roof and could also be carved for decoration and embellishment.

Roof construction in China differs greatly from that in the West. A Chinese roof is made of beams placed one atop another, gradually diminishing in length. This type of construction made it natural to curve the roof, but might also have been done for aesthetic reasons. Finally, the roof is covered in semicircular tiles.

Colour and construction material varied according to the significance of the building, and social status of the owner. Yellow tiles, for example, were used for imperial buildings, as seen in the sea of golden roofs at the Imperial Palace in Beijing. In addition, different roof shapes were used to denote the importance of a building. The most important buildings had hipped roofs, while unimportant ones had simple gabled roofs.

The roofs of Chinese buildings lend to them an air of weightlessness. The overhanging, upturned eaves cast a shadow upon the walls and appear to float in midair. Yet aesthetic as this may be, the overhanging eaves also serve a very practical purpose: keeping out rain as well as controlling the amount of light entering the building, and keeping out the sun during summer but letting it in during winter.

Traditional Chinese construction provides much flexibility. Partitioning the interior were walls made of light materials that could easily be built up or removed. The function of the walls was not to support the roof, but to separate living space. In summer, the infill panels between the load-bearing columns of simple houses can be easily removed. Windows and doors can be made and changed without any change to the main structure of the building.

The use of brackets also lends itself to standardisation and prefabrication. During the Tang dynasty, prefabrication was already well established. Timber was precut into brackets of several sizes. As soon as a craftsman was told how long a building was to be, he also knew what size brackets were required, how many were needed, and other construction details.

LEFT: Temple of Heaven (Tiantan) dome, Beijing.
RIGHT: ceiling of Summer Palace.

CUISINES OF CHINA

If there's a truly global cuisine, then the nomination of Chinese food is not to be underestimated. Indeed, where in the world can't one buy a Chinese meal?

Few people in the world have a more passionate relationship with food than the Chinese. Food shortages over the many centuries have forced the Chinese to be creative in order to utilise and conserve their food supplies. In addition, the elite have long used food as a way to display wealth and status, boasting numerous cooks and elaborate dishes. China's great geographical variety offers a wealth of different produce and spices.

The Chinese preoccupation with food is reflected in China's philosophy and literature. Indeed, as depicted in numerous historical, literary, and philosophical writings, scholars were also gourmands more often than not. Laozi, the founder of Daoism, said, "Handle a large country with as gentle a touch as you would cook a small fish." Another famous philosopher, Zhuang Zi, wrote a poem in which he advises an emperor to watch his cook: "A good cook needs a new chopper once a year – he cuts. A bad cook needs a new one every month – he hacks." Few will dispute the old saying that "appetite for food and sex is nature." A strong tradition recognising and encouraging the importance of food has helped nurture cuisines that are among the world's best.

Technique

It is said that the four essentials in a Chinese kitchen are a cutting board, knife, wok, and spoon. Historical fuel shortages made a reduced cooking time an early priority, and the proper cutting of ingredients is an important first step. Rapid, even cutting is a required trademark of any good cook. Faithful students of Confucius recorded that "he would not eat meat that was not cut properly, nor that which was served without its proper sauce." His pickiness made sense, since meat and vegetables cut to varying proportions result in unevenly cooked food.

PRECEDING PAGES: *dim sum* is one of those dishes that defines Chinese aesthetics.
LEFT: even the simplest urban meal can be diverse in its dishes. **ABOVE:** sidewalk noodle-maker.

The most common method of cooking is stir-frying in a wok over very high heat. Not only does this save fuel, but it results in both crisp texture and maximum vitamin retention. Deep-frying, steaming, and braising are also popular, while slowly roasted or baked meats are not and are usually produced only in restaurant kitchens.

Chinese cuisines seek a balance of textures, flavours and colours within a meal. Few Chinese dishes feature any one ingredient exclusively. Harmonious blending of ingredients and balance in seasoning is important. The common seasonings are soy sauce, ginger, garlic, vinegar, sesame oil, soybean paste, and scallions.

Ingredients

Rice is the staple food for most Chinese, although those living in the north traditionally eat food created from wheat flour, including noodles, dumplings, and various steamed, deep-fried or griddle-fried breads. Soybean curd, both fresh and dried in either sheets or twists, provides important protein in a country where the majority of arable land is given over to agriculture rather than grazing.

Large animals – cows and sheep, for example – requiring pasture lands are not as common as poultry and the ubiquitous pig. Without doubt, pork is the most popular meat. In addition, both fresh- and saltwater fish are highly prized and usually well prepared.

Vegetables are of supreme importance, but are rarely eaten raw. This stems partly from hygienic considerations, as the typical fertiliser was human waste. The range of vegetables cultivated in China is vast, particularly in the

warmer south, and includes not only those known in the West, but other delights such as a huge range of leafy greens, bamboo shoots, water chestnuts, taro, and lotus root. Some common vegetables such as cabbage and white radish are also salted or dried and used as seasoning, especially during the frigid winter months in the cold north.

The use of monosodium glutamate (MSG) has had a significant effect on 20th-century Chinese cooking. Called *wei jing* in Chinese, this miracle powder was introduced by the Japanese in the 1940s. Cooks discovered that it instantly added a meaty sweetness to the food, which could otherwise only be achieved by simmer-

ing stock for hours. After its mass production, cost was no longer prohibitive and a small revolution in Chinese cooking came about.

Regional differences

Being such a vast land, China encompasses a wide range of terrain, and agricultural produce. Here one can find snow-capped mountains and harsh deserts, mountain gorges slashed by mighty rivers, fertile rice paddies, rich coastal plains and seas teeming with fish. With such climatic and geographic differences, it is not surprising that regional cuisines have developed.

Experts argue endlessly over just how many regional cuisines exist, but it is generally agreed that there are four major styles. These include Cantonese, the food found in the southern province of Guangdong (and in neighbouring Hong Kong); Sichuan, the pungent food of the western region of China, particularly of the cities of Chengdu and Chongqing; Huaiyang, which includes the eastern Chinese cuisines of Shanghai, Jiangsu, and Zhejiang; and Northern cuisine, centred in Beijing but largely inspired by the neighbouring province of Shandong, whose chefs monopolised Beijing's restaurant business in the 19th century.

Cantonese cuisine

Thanks to the large-scale emigration of Chinese from the southern province of Guangdong to elsewhere in the world, this is China's best-known cuisine. Many claim that it is also the finest, and there's no doubt that the fertile south benefits from a benign climate and the widest selection of fresh produce anywhere in China.

Cantonese food is characterised by its great variety, and its delicate seasoning and freshness of ingredients. Cantonese chefs are renowned for their creativity and willingness to incorporate foreign ingredients. Chefs make abundant use of fruit and many types of vegetables, as well as seafood such as prawn, abalone, squid, and crab.

Cantonese cooking methods are lacquer roasting, very quick stir-frying, and steaming. Cantonese roasted chicken and pork are justifiably renowned. Seafood is typically seasoned first and stir-fried in hot oil, or else steamed.

The famous Cantonese array of tidbits known as *dim sum* (or, in Mandarin, *dian xin*) is often served as brunch or a snack. Dim sum portions are usually dainty. Amongst the great variety of treats are dumplings of pork or seafood wrapped in transparent rice-dough wrappers; stuffed mushrooms or chilli peppers; deep-fried yam balls; and tiny spring rolls. Self-serve trolleys arranged with small plates are wheeled through restaurants and teahouses. Although the Chinese do not normally eat dessert, two common offerings at a dim sum spread are custard tarts and cubes of almond-milk jelly.

Sichuan cuisine

After Cantonese, the cuisine of the central province of Sichuan

Some writers claim that the Sichuan love of spicy, pungent food can be attributed to the highly variable climate, which is characterised by humidity throughout much of the year, and to its freezing winters.

There are many excellent Sichuan dishes, including duck smoked over a mixture of camphor and tea leaves, then deep-fried, and beancurd scrambled with minced pork and spicy seasonings. One of the best known Chinese dishes in the world, *mapo tofu* (or *doufu*), comes from Sichuan. Translated as "the

SOUTHERN COOKING

Southerners joke that they will eat anything with four legs but a table, anything that flies but a kite or plane.

(sometimes spelled as Szechuan) is perhaps the best known to Westerners. The food from the province of Sichuan is the most emphatically-flavoured in all of China.

Much of this emphasis comes from chillies, which appear in many guises: dried and fried in chunks, together with other ingredients; ground into a paste with a touch of added oil; as chilli oil; and crushed to a powder. Other ingredients important to Sichuanese cuisine are Sichuan "pepper" (the dried berry of the prickly ash or fagara), garlic, ginger, and fermented soybean.

LEFT: filled dumplings, or *jiaozi*, are popular snacks.
ABOVE: clear oxtail soup.

pockmarked woman's tofu," this dish originated in the 19th century, so the story has been passed along over the years, when Mrs. Chen, the pockmarked woman, created a spicy beancurd dish in a family-owned Sichuan tavern that she owned with her husband.

A typical Sichuan eating experience is hot pot, or *huo guo*. Diners sit around a table with a pot of seasoned broth heated by a gas fire (charcoal was used in the past). Each diner adds bits and pieces of prepared vegetable, meat, fish, and beancurd. The food cooks very quickly and can be fished out of the broth using chopsticks or a special strainer, then dipped in sesame oil, peanut sauce, or a beaten egg.

Huaiyang cuisine

The cuisine of the lower reaches of Chang Jiang (Yangzi River), especially around Huaian and Yangzhou, gave rise to the term *huaiyang* to describe the food of China's eastern seaboard. A fertile area of fish and rice, this region has a wide range of agricultural products, as well as abundant fish, prawns, crab, and eel.

For the most part, the cooking of Shanghai, Jiangsu, and Zhejiang is usually regarded as being part of Huaiyang cuisine. The distinguishing feature of Huaiyang food is the wide variety of quality freshwater and saltwater fish and shellfish; crabs from this region are espe-

Northern cuisine

The cuisine of the north tends to be a rustic, home-style cooking that makes abundant use of onions and garlic, but is lacking in the variety of vegetables characterising the cuisines of China's more fertile regions.

Most northern cuisine stems from Shandong Province, but with some influences from Mongolian and Hebei cooking. Braised meat and poultry cooked in brown sauce, which forms the base of much northern cuisine, are some of the common dishes.

Northerners eat wheat-based foods as a staple, not the rice found elsewhere in China and

cially famed. Aquatic foods are cooked simply, bringing out natural flavours. Huaiyang cooks often steam or gently simmer their food, rather than using the faster deep-frying style. Signature dishes include pork steamed in lotus leaves, Duck with Eight Ingredients, and Lion's Head Meatballs, all of which should be found in any good restaurant around Shanghai.

Huaiyang cuisine places emphasis on soups, which come with every meal. A great many wonderful and imaginative soups originated in this region. In addition, "red cooking" (stewing meat in stock with soy sauce, star anise, and other flavourings) and heavy use of peanut oil and lard are characteristic.

ETIQUETTE PRIMER

The Chinese slurp their soup (to cool it off on the way to the mouth), keep their elbows on the table, and lift their bowls. The proper way to eat a bowl of rice is to hold the bowl up with one hand and shovel the rice into the mouth with chopsticks. Similarly, soup bowls can be held in one hand and the soup either sipped directly from the bowl or with a soup spoon. Careful: don't stick the chopsticks upright into a bowl of rice. This is a very inauspicious sign, and quite rude – it resembles incense sticks burned for funerals or at shrines.

Asia. Indeed, one can find a wide variety of noodles: dumplings that are steamed, pan-fried or boiled; breads (once again, fried or steamed); and deep-fried lengths of dough, excellent with a bowl of sweet or salty soybean milk.

Although the indigenous food is relatively simple, Beijing benefitted from the years when it was the imperial capital, attracting people from throughout China. The emperors sought out the best chefs in the land, and the first among them could count on being given the rank of minister.

It was during these days that the most refined and complex dishes such as Peking Duck, Man-

then the skin painted with a mixture of honey, water and vinegar. The duck is dried, and then roasted in a special oven. The succulent, crisp skin is tucked into fine wheat-flour pancakes, painted with sweet black-sauce and enlivened with spring onions. After this course, diners might enjoy the meat of the duck and complete the experience with a finale of duck soup.

The language of food

For all the attention and significance lavished on food by the Chinese, it is not surprising that Chinese food "language" developed to a level probably unparalleled by any other cuisine.

darin Fish, Phoenix in the Nest, and Thousand-Layer Cake were created. Today, the ordinary citizen of Beijing (and, of course, visiting foreigners) can sample these palace dishes in special, but often expensive, restaurants.

No visitor should leave without a meal of Peking Duck. Proper Peking Duck (or Beijing Duck, if one goes by the *pinyin* transliteration of the Chinese capital) is made from specially bred ducks.

After the duck is slaughtered, air is pumped between the skin and the flesh of the duck, and

Food can be endowed with symbolic meaning, and special occasions such as holidays or birthdays are observed with specific foods.

Chinese New Year is a particularly significant food event. As the most important holiday of the year, much care, planning, and money is spent on celebrating this event with as sumptuous a feast as possible. Oranges and tangerines keep the sweetness of life, ducks represent fidelity and joy, and fish represent prosperity, wealth, and regeneration.

Birthdays are often observed by the serving of noodles, because the lengthy strands are said to represent long life. Another birthday food is steamed buns shaped and coloured to look like

LEFT: flaming stir-fry cuisine.
ABOVE: casual lunch in an old-style *hutong*, Beijing.

peaches, as peaches also represent longevity. Probably the most conspicuous custom of the mid-autumn festival, also known as the Moon Festival, is the eating of heavy, round-shaped pastries called mooncakes. Shaped much like the full moon that can be seen during the festival, these cakes are usually filled with sweet paste and sometimes an egg yolk in the centre.

During the dragon-boat festival, people eat fragrant sticky rice wrapped in bamboo leaves or reeds, a treat called *zong zi.*

The story behind this tradition dates to the time of Confucius, when a disgraced imperial official drowned himself. Townspeople, faith-

ful to his memory, threw zong zi into the river to feed the fish so that the fish would not eat the official's body.

Healthy Eating

For centuries, Chinese have regarded food as curative or preventative medicine. Indeed, at times the relationship between food and medicine can seem quite blurred. In fact, the word for recipe, *fang,* is the same for prescription.

When planning a menu, the chef will want to consider the physical conditions of the diners and external conditions such as the weather. One of the most basic theories behind a balanced Chinese diet is that of "hot" and "cool"

foods. Certain foods are believed to be either *yin* (cooling) or *yang* (warming); the ideal is to seek a balance between the two.

Internal heat is caused by eating "hot" foods such as coffee, meat, and spicy food. Excess internal heat can cause unpleasant symptoms such as heartburn, rashes, cold sores, and bad breath. Not surprisingly, "hot" foods are popular in cold weather. Snake meat, for example, is considered to be fortifying and is therefore a popular winter dish in some parts of the country. On the other hand, "cooling" foods combat excess internal heat. Low-calorie, bland vegetables such as watercress, bitter melon, and white radish, as well as most fruits, are considered "cooling."

Practical matters

Everyday meals are simple affairs. Breakfast might consist of a bowl of *zhou* (rice porridge) with pickled vegetables and bits of meat. For lunch, a noodle soup or a plate of rice with some meat and vegetable is common. A proper family dinner will normally consist of the staple rice or noodles, soup, and three or four freshly prepared hot dishes. The soup is generally served at the end of a meal, except in Guangdong, where it is sipped throughout the meal. Desserts are not usually served, and when they are, the choices are fairly limited.

If you are fortunate enough to be invited to a meal in a Chinese home or to an official function, be well advised to bring a small gift for the hosts, such as alcohol or cigarettes, or even a gift from your home country.

The number of dishes served will depend on the formality of the occasion. A formal meal commences with several cold appetisers. No matter how tempting this is, remember to pace yourself, as you can be sure that there are probably another six or seven courses to follow, including seafood, meat, poultry, vegetables, and soup. No one leaves hungry.

One by one, the prepared dishes of food are placed in the centre of the table. Diners help themselves with a serving spoon, if provided, or with their own chopsticks. It is polite to place choice morsels on your neighbour's plate, but be sure to help yourself only to what is nearest you, rather than reaching across the table.

ABOVE: mooncakes, shaped like a full moon, oddly enough. **RIGHT:** Oriental restaurant in Hong Kong.

PLACES

*A detailed guide to the entire country, with principal sites
cross-referenced by number to the maps.*

The first reports in Europe of a people who lived even farther east than the Scythians were offered by the ancient Greeks, who spoke of a people producing silk, a technique kept secret for centuries by the Chinese under penalty of death. In fact, silk may have been the first commodity of trade between East and West. Exchanges of culture and religion soon followed, with Islam and Buddhism arriving in the Middle Kingdom via the Silk Road. For more than a millennium, in fact, this land route was the only link between Europe and China.

In the early 16th century, new opportunities opened up to mercantile Europeans, as Portuguese ships sailed as far as the southern Chinese coast, trading with the Chinese from a base in Macau. The missionaries who followed and ventured into China drew the first European maps of China (and failed miserably in gaining converts). Only the scale of the coastline is correct on any of these early maps; the further the maps extend into the interior, the more distorted becomes the cartography, or else it remains blank. One might have said the same about European understanding of China as a whole.

There are no blank spaces left in China today. What were once exotic and remote places are now only exotic. Travelling in China is increasingly easier than one might expect, to the chagrin of old-school adventurers. Contemporary travellers will readily see that China is no monolithic culture. The influence of the Han Chinese may seem ubiquitous, but the rich Turkic culture of Xinjiang, the lively colours of Yunnan, or the lofty mantras of Tibet are just as much a part of China. Travellers may also come to recognise northern and southern differences amongst the Han themselves.

The northern part of China extends from Dongbei in the northeast – known to Westerners as Manchuria – across the Gobi Desert and along the Silk Road to Xinjiang, in the far west. The terrain is often less than gracious. In the north's eastern extents, the Huang He, or Yellow River, has nurtured this region for thousands of years, giving rise to civilisation. Anchoring the Huang He's drainage are, of course, the numerous imperial capitals of Chinese civilisation: Xi'an, Luoyang and, finally, Beijing.

The central belt of China follows the grandest of rivers, Chang Jiang, or the Yangzi to Westerners. This river divides China north and south, along the way slicing into the earth to create Sanxia, the Three Gorges, before emptying into the sea near Shanghai.

Southern China is of a distinctly different cast. Along the southeast coast are the feisty, entrepreneurial regions centred around Guangzhou and Hong Kong. Further to the west, the faces, clothes and languages change, until by the time one has reached Tibet, one feels that she or he is in a different country.

PRECEDING PAGES: the Great Wall; limestone formations of Guilin; southern rice fields; Imperial Palace, Beijing. **LEFT:** wall detail of temple.

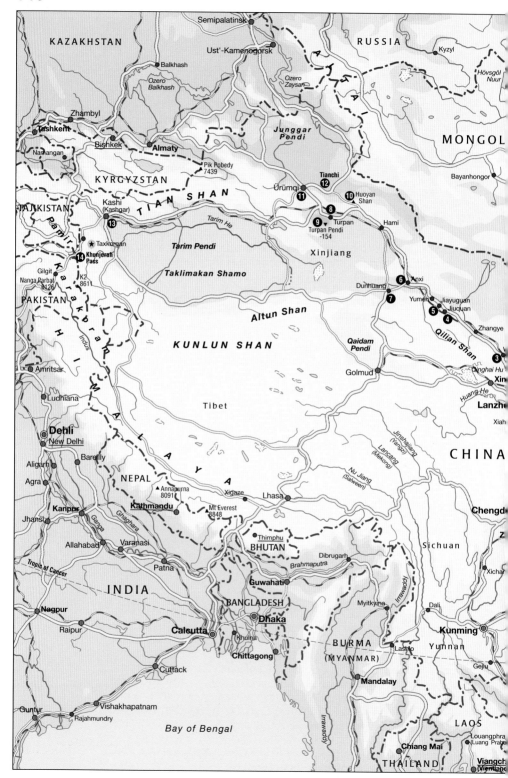

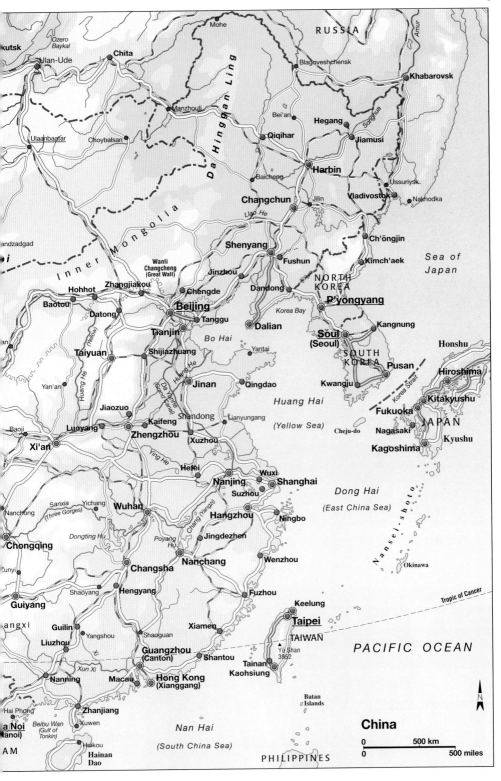

China

0   500 km
0   500 miles

THE NORTH

The north is less than auspicious in Chinese cosmology. But it was here that Chinese civilisation took root and flourished.

Taking the top half of China and collectively – and perhaps naively – calling it "north" leads to the suggestion of a homogeneous quality. Emphatically not. The differences between northwestern China and northeastern China are as significant as between left and right.

Yet there are unifying threads of history, if not culture, winding across northern China. The so-called Silk Road – a German geographer's moniker – extended from east to west, or west to east, if one prefers, linking the mysterious lands of West Asia and Europe, including the waning Roman Empire, with the Chinese court. Its importance faltered after several centuries, however, when the southeastern coast took on nautical and commercial importance.

Along the Silk Road, China exported, yes, silk to the world's shadowy peripheries, and imported Buddhism and Islam. To the west, beyond the Gobi Desert and ancient Buddhist caves, lies a land of superior simplicity and grace, and of Islam. There are also glacier-peppered mountains and waterless basins, and an emptiness that is nevertheless embracing, if not intoxicating.

The capitals of China's ancient rulers were located mainly in the northeast – Xi'an, Luoyang, Beijing. Due west of the Korean peninsula and not all that far from the steppes of Mongolia, a fact not absent from its history, Beijing was the centre of the universe until imperial rule collapsed in 1912. Although not China's largest city, Beijing – the Northern Capital – is best known today for the Imperial Palace, one of the world's architectural wonders, and as seat of China's government.

Northeast of Beijing hovers Dongbei – literally, East-North – but better known to outsiders as Manchuria. Geographically and politically, this area has often been of uncertain mind. In this century alone, Dongbei has been under Japanese, Russian, and Chinese control, and the influences from Korea are considerable and deeply embedded.

Beyond Beijing, whipping westward over the rocky hills and mountains like a restless serpent, is Wanli Changcheng – the Great Wall. An ancient line of defence that lost its usefulness long ago against nomads from the dark edges of the earth, it has retained its timelessness, particularly in sections where the tourists don't flock.

The northeast was also the home of Confucius and the origin of Daoism. More fundamentally, it is home to the source of Chinese civilisation: the Huang He, or Yellow River, which loops through the Mongolian steppes, then southward to Xi'an, from where the first emperor of a unified China, Qin Shi Huangdi, made ancient history.

LEFT: temple guardian deities, Datong.

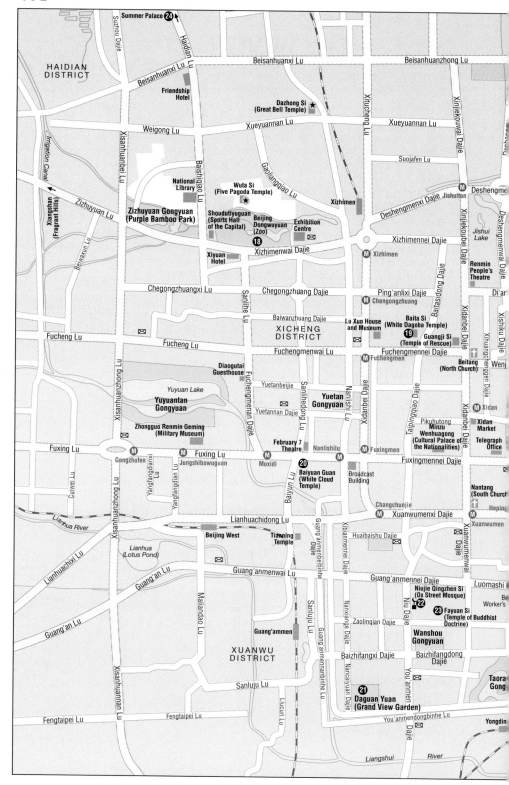

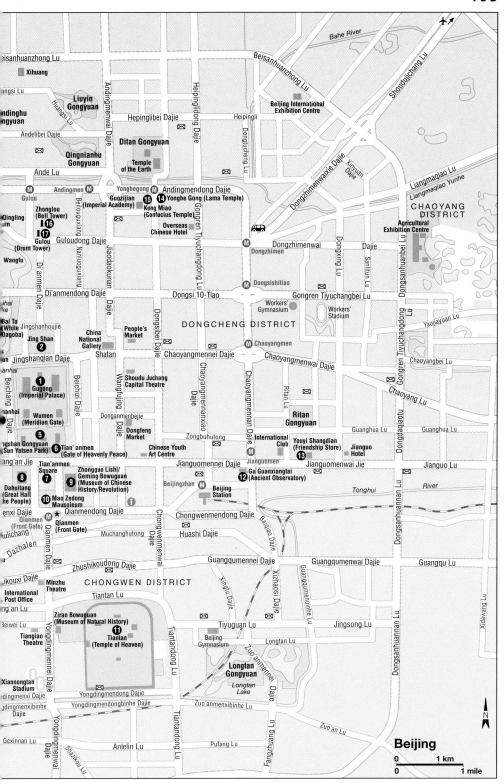

Beisanhuanzhong Lu

Xihuang

Liuyin Gongyuan

ngsi Lu

Huangsi Lu

ndinghu ngyuan

Andelibei Dajie

Qingnianhu Gongyuan

Ande Lu

Zhonglou (Bell Tower)

Gulou (Drum Tower)

Wangfu

Gulou

Qingling um

Qinling

Bai Ta (White Dagoba)

Jing Shan ❷

Di'anmen Dajie

Beichizi Dajie

① Gugong (Imperial Palace)

Wumen (Meridian Gate) ❺

ngshan Gongyuan (Sun Yatsen Park)

Tian'anmen (Gate of Heavenly Peace) ❻

ang'an Jie

❽ Dahuitang (Great Hall of the People)

Tian'anmen Square ❼

Zhongguo Lishi/ Geming Bowuguan (Museum of Chinese History/Revolution) ❾

❿ Mao Zedong Mausoleum

enxi Dajie

Qianmen (Front Gate)

Qianmendong Dajie

Qianmen (Front Gate)

ulichang

Dazhalen

ikouxi Dajie

Minzhu Theatre

International Post Office

ng'an Lu

CHONGWEN DISTRICT

Tiantan Lu

Beiwei Lu

Ziran Bowuguan (Museum of Natural History)

Tiangiao Theatre

Tiantan (Temple of Heaven) ⓫

Xiannongtan Stadium

dingmenxi Dajie

jdingmenxibinhe Dajie

Gexinnan Lu

Beisanhuanzhong Lu

Hepinglibei Dajie

Hepinglidong Dajie

Heipingli

Beijing International Exhibition Centre

Dongzhimenwaixie Dajie

Xinyuan Dajie

Liangmaqiao Lu

Liangmaqiao Yunhe

Shouduijichang Lu

Ditan Gongyuan

Temple of the Earth

Andingmen

Andingmenwai Dajie

Gulou

Beiluoguxiang

Nanluoguxiang

Yonghegong ⓯ Andingmendong Dajie

Guozijian (Imperial Academy)

Kong Miao (Confucius Temple)

Overseas Chinese Hotel

⓮ Yonghe Gong (Lama Temple)

CHAOYANG DISTRICT

Agricultural Exhibition Centre

Dongzhimenwai

Dajie

Dongzhimen

Gongren Tiyuchangdong Lu

Dongsanhuanbei Lu

Guoxixiang

Jiaodaokunan

Guloudong Dajie

Jaodaokunan

Dongsishitiao

Dongsi 10-Tiao

Gongren Tiyuchangbei Lu

Workers' Gymnasium

Workers' Stadium

Yaojiayuan Lu

Di'anmendong Dajie

DONGCHENG DISTRICT

Dongsibei Dajie

Chaoyangmen

Chaoyangbei Lu

Jingshanhoujie

China National Gallery

People's Market

Chaoyangmennei Dajie

Chaoyangmenwai Dajie

Chaoyang Lu

an Jingshanqian Dajie

Shatan

Wangfujing

Shoudu Juchang Capital Theatre

Chaoyangmennanxiao Dajie

Ritan Lu

Ritan Gongyuan

Dongdaqiaotu

Chaoyang Lu

anhai

Beichang

anhai

Dajie

Donganmenbeijie

Dongfeng Market

Zongbuhutong

Chaoyangmennan Dajie

International Club

Youyi Shangdian (Friendship Store) ⓭

Jianguo Hotel

Guanghua Lu

Guanghua Lu

Chinese Youth Art Centre

Jianguomennei Dajie

Jianguomen

Jianguomenwai Jie

Jianguo Lu

Gu Guanxiangtai (Ancient Observatory) ⓬

Beijingzhan

Beijing Station

Tonghui

River

Chongwenmennei

Chongwenmendong Dajie

Huashi Dajie

Baijiao Dajie

Muchanghutong

Dongsanhuannan Lu

Zhushikoudong Dajie

Guanggumennei Dajie

Guanggumenwai Dajie

Guangqu Lu

Xingfu Dajie

Xizhaosi Dajie

Guanggumeninhe Lu

Yongdingmennei Dajie

Tiyuguan Lu

Jingsong Lu

Beijing Gymnasium

Longtan Lu

Dongsanhuannan Lu

Xidawang Lu

Longtan Gongyuan

Longtan Lake

Tiantandong Lu

Zuo'anmennei Dajie

Zuo'anmenxibinhe Lu

Yongdingmendong Dajie

Yongdingmendongbinhe Dajie

Zuo'an Lu

Fangzhuang Lu

Anlelin Lu

Pufang Lu

Shazikou Lu

Tiantandong Lu

Yongdingmenwai Dajie

Beijing

0 _____ 1 km

0 _____ 1 mile

N

BEIJING

Laid out in a grid according to ancient feng shui principles, the Northern Capital and former centre of the world is still anchored by the immense and simply spectacular Imperial Palace.

Map, page 152

Over the past 1,000 years, Beijing has served as the primary residence for three major dynasties. Under the rule of Kublai Khan in the 13th century, the city was known as Khanbaliq – the City of the Khan, and it was a magnificent winter residence for the Yuan dynasty emperor. During the Ming dynasty, which replaced the Yuan, Beijing received the layout that survives today. The Qing emperors lived in the palace until the dynasty collapsed in 1912.

In traditional Chinese thought, the world was not the Ptolemaic disc of the West, but rather a square. It was believed that a city, especially a capital city, should reflect this cosmic order and adhere to its geometrical definition, with a north–south and east–west orientation of roads and buildings. In no other Chinese city was this idea fulfiled as completely as in ancient Beijing. But the history of the area around the capital goes back much further: the discovery of the skull of *Sinanthropus pekinensis* (Peking Man), southwest of Beijing, proved that prehistoric humans settled here more than half a million years ago. Yet little more is known until 5,000 years ago, by which time neolithic agricultural villages had been established.

Nowadays, huge concrete tower blocks have mushroomed and construction sites are everywhere. The best way to see Beijing as a working city is to walk through its fast-disappearing *hutong*, alleys usually flanked by the gates and walls of traditional *siheyuan*, or courtyard houses. Bicycles are still the main form of transport, but the cyclists are segregated from the motorised traffic by road dividers. Taxis, cars, and buses jam the city streets and the multiple-lane ring highways. The local public transport system is underdeveloped and overcrowded, although the limited subway system is faster and tolerable for visitors.

The continental climate brings long, hot summers and cold, dry winters. When sandstorms whirl through the city in spring, Beijing hardly dares to breathe, as the fine dust forces its way through cracks and crevices in badly insulated homes. Vehicle exhaust fumes, dust from construction projects, coal smoke, and industrial emissions have, in fact, turned Beijing into a rather polluted city.

People here make use of every inch of available space. Grassy spots by major highways are used for evening exercises. Kites soar above vast intersections. The broad plazas outside the Imperial Palace are turned into dance floors. Empty concrete expanses in front of office buildings are shared by grandparents and grandchildren on humid summer evenings. And an early morning walk through any park reveals the most enchanting side of Beijing: the sound of a moon fiddle accompanied by an aria from a Beijing opera; the chirping of song birds in bamboo cages hanging from trees; and noiseless *taiji* practitioners.

OPPOSITE: guardian lion, Imperial Palace. **BELOW:** palace wall, 19th century.

Geomantic design

The third Ming emperor, Yongle, is credited with the planning of the capital. In 1421, he moved his government from Nanjing to Beiping (Northern Peace) and renamed it Beijing (Northern Capital). Improperly pronounced in the West, the city became known as Peking, a name that persists in such instances as Peking duck. The plans of Yongle followed the principles of geomancy, the traditional doctrine of *feng shui* (wind and water), that strives to attain harmony between human life and nature. Screened from the north by a semicircle of hills topped by the Great Wall, Beijing lies on a plain that opens to the south, an auspicious direction, as it was toward the south that the generosity and warmth of *yang* was thought to reside. All important buildings in the old city face south, protected from harmful influences from the north – whether winter Siberian winds or enemies from the steppes. South-facing Qianmen – the Front Gate to the city – was the largest, most beautiful, and most sacred gate. The hill of Jing Shan, to the north of the Imperial Palace, was probably also constructed according to geomantic principles.

A north–south axis centred on the Imperial Palace divides the city; important buildings and city features were laid out as mirror images on either side. Ritan (Altar of the Sun), for example, has its equivalent in Yuetan (Altar of the Moon). Equally complementary were Xidan and Dongdan, the eastern and western business quarters, which are still two of the capital's main shopping streets. Some of the most notable landmarks of old Beijing lie on the north–south axis itself, lined up like pearls on a string. From the north: Zhonglou and Gulou (Bell and Drum Towers), Jing Shan (Coal Hill), Gugong (Imperial Palace), Tiananmen (Gate of Heavenly Peace) and Qianmen. In the middle of this chain is the heart of ancient

One of six ancient capitals in China, Greater Beijing today encompasses 16,800 square kilometres and is divided into 10 districts and nine counties.

BELOW: water container once used for fire fighting, Imperial Palace.

China, the Dragon Throne, from which the emperor governed as the ritual mediator between heaven and earth. This was considered the centre of the physical world, perceived like the city as a gigantic grid. The city, and the world, and everything within, were given a clearly defined place in a hierarchy, depending upon how far they were from the centre. This imperial throne remains embedded in a majestic palace, which is also square and surrounded by high red walls on all sides – the so-called Forbidden City. Outside was the imperial city, again square, and crowded around this was a sea of mainly single-storey houses. Curved like the crests of waves, the roofs of the homes of the wealthy and of influential officials in this inner city were not allowed to rise above the height of the Imperial Palace. This part of Beijing is still considered to be the inner city, or old city, but only a few monumental gates of the mighty defensive walls that once surrounded Beijing have survived – Qianmen in the south, and Deshengmen (Victory Gate) in the north.

In the Qing dynasty (1644–1912), the inner city was the domain of the ruling Manchu, the outer city to the south for the Han Chinese. In the Chinese area, the doors of the houses were lower, the hutong (alleys) were narrower, and the rice bowls were less full. Instead of tea, people drank hot water. Instead of satin boots, they wore sandals. Bored Manchu officials and wealthy merchants, and the occasional prince in clever disguise, sometimes left their comfortable surroundings for the Chinese tea and bath houses, brothels, restaurants, and bazaars. Today, the area south of Qianmen remains livelier than other parts of the city. A bustling street running west from the top of Qianmen is **Dazhalan**, a narrow and crowded alley filled with old established shops and businesses of excellent reputation. Dazhalan still attracts crowds from the Beijing suburbs as well as the provinces. Not far away is **Liulichang**, a shopping street restored to its original style for tourists, selling almost everything that China can offer in antiques, art, and kitsch. The busiest shopping districts are Xidan and Wanfujing, both lined with fashionable boutiques and fast-food restaurants.

The imperial city of Ming and Qing times was also a place where the great religions of China competed spiritually, and with their impressive sacred buildings. Unfortunately, many of the Daoist, Buddhist, and Lamaist shrines and temples, as well as mosques and churches, were damaged or destroyed during the Cultural Revolution of the late 1960s, or had been turned into factories, or schools after 1949. But most of Beijing's religious sites have been restored and reopened.

Gugong: Imperial Palace

Five hundred years ago, in the early mornings when the fourth guard watch of the night was proclaimed by powerful beats from Gulou – the Drum Tower – the mandarins in the imperial city would push aside their silk bed curtains, wash, dress, and step into their litters in which porters carried them to their morning audience with the emperor in **Gugong**, the **Imperial Palace ❶** (summer 8.30am–4.30pm; winter 8.30am–3.30pm); entrance fee). A eunuch would show them to their places, arranged according to rank, where they listened to the emperor in respectful silence.

Map, page 152

For Chinese, dragons are friendly creatures with a protective function, and are linked to the east – where the sun rises and rains originate. Since the Han dynasty, dragons symbolised emperors.

BELOW: Dragon Throne.

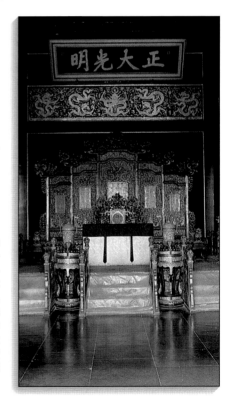

In 1421, after 17 years of construction, the Ming emperor Yongle moved into the new palace. Up until the founding of the republic in 1911, the palace was the imperial residence and centre of the Middle Kingdom during the reign of 24 emperors, from the Ming dynasty (1368–1644) until Puyi, the last emperor of the Qing dynasty, and of China. It has 8,706 rooms in which an estimated 8,000–10,000 people lived, including 3,000 eunuchs, as well as maids and concubines, all within an area of 70 hectares (170 acres).

Behind walls more than 10 metres (30 ft) high, and within the 50-metre-broad (160 ft) moat, life in the Imperial Palace was dictated by complex rules and rituals. Entrance was denied to ordinary people, but today gates lead to a fascinating display of Chinese history in what is probably the best-preserved site of classical Chinese architecture.

Approaching from the south through 35-metre (117 ft) -high **Wumen Ⓐ** (Meridian Gate), one encounters the three great halls and courtyards of the outer area. **Taihe Dian Ⓑ** (Hall of Supreme Harmony), the largest building in the palace, is the first and most impressive of these. In its centre is the ornately carved and golden **Dragon Throne**, from which the emperor ruled. This was the place where the most solemn ceremonies, such as the New Year rites or the enthronement of a new emperor, were held. The outside courtyard could hold 90,000 spectators. Behind Taihe Dian are **Zhonghe Dian** (Hall of Complete Harmony) and **Baohe Dian Ⓒ** (Hall of Preserving Harmony), completing a trinity that reflects the Three Buddhas and the Three Pure Ones of Daoism. To the east of Baohe Dian is the magnificent **Jiulongbi Ⓓ** (Nine Dragons Screen). On the other side of the Outer Court, to the north and separated from it by **Qianqingmen** (Gate of Heavenly Purity), lies a labyrinth of gates, doors, pavilions, gardens and palaces. This is **Qianqing Gong Ⓔ** (Palace of Heavenly Purity), the residence of the imperial family, who were almost all female, as the emperor and eunuchs were the only men permitted to enter. The centre of this private section is formed by three rear halls, **Sanhou Gong**. The politics of state business took place in the interlinked rooms to the left and right of Sanhou Gong. These rooms were the scene of plots and intrigues, and of deaths – natural and unnatural – as the more influential eunuchs and concubines vied for power and influence within the court.

The well in the northeast, just behind **Ningshou Gong Ⓕ** (Palace of Peace and Longevity), was the place of such an episode. In 1900, a concubine of Emperor Guanxu dared to oppose the ambitious Empress Dowager Cixi. As punishment, the concubine was rolled up in a carpet and thrown down into the shaft of the well by the palace eunuchs.

In the smaller halls to the east and west of the main halls are the exhibitions of the Palace Museum. One highlight is the clock and jewellery hall, where the

Emperor Yongle employed 100,000 artisans to work on the Imperial Palace, along with the forced labour of more than one million people.

G Shenwumen (Gate of Divine Prowess)
★ Imperial Garden
Palace of Accumulated Elegance ★
Changchum Palce ★
★ Kunminggong
★ Jiaotaidian
Ⓔ Qianqiun Gong (Palace of Heavenly Purity)
Ningshou Gong Ⓕ (Palace of Peace and Longevity)
Palace of the Culture of the Mind
★ Qianqingmen (Gate of Heavenly Purity)
★ Gate of Peaceful Old Age
Ⓒ Baohe Dian (Hall of Preserving Harmony)
Ⓓ Jiulongbi (Nine Dragons Screen)
★ Zhonghe Dian (Hall of Complete Harmony)
Ⓑ Taihe Dian (Hall of Supreme Harmony)
Gate of Supreme Harmony ★
Goldwater River ★
Ⓐ Wumen (Meridian Gate)

Imperial Palace
0   200 m
0   200 yds
N

exhibits include water clocks and intricate, richly decorated European and Chinese mechanical clocks.

Map, page 152

Across the street from **Shenwumen** ⑥ (Gate of Divine Prowess), the north gate of the Imperial Palace, is **Jing Shan** ❷ (Coal Hill; open daily, 6am–9pm; entrance fee), the best place from which to view the palace complex. This artificial hill was built with the earth dug from the palace moats in the early 15th century. Five pavilions crown the hill. The Drum and Bell Towers stand out to the north, and the White Dagoba dominates the west. The last Ming emperor, Chongzheng, hanged himself from a tree on Jing Shan, in 1644, after fleeing the besieged palace during a rebellion.

To the immediate west of Jing Shan, in the grounds of today's **Beihai Gongyuan** ❸ (North Lake Park; open daily, 6am–9pm; entrance fee), was the winter residence of the Mongol emperor Kublai Khan. Now, only legends remain of his former palace on Qinghuadao (Jade Island), the site of **Bai Ta** (White Dagoba), 35 metres (115 ft) high and a Buddhist shrine from 1651, built in Tibetan style to commemorate the first visit to Beijing by a Dalai Lama.

Bai Ta, the White Dagoba in Beihai Gongyuan.

At the foot of the shrine, on the shores of the lake that fills much of the park, a gourmet restaurant well known to connoisseurs features imperial cuisine. Tuancheng (Round Town), in the southern part of the grounds, was once the administrative centre of the Mongol Yuan dynasty.

From here is a good view of **Zhongnanhai** ❹ (South and Central Lake), the out-of-bounds and guarded site of the Politburo and State Council offices and grounds, known by many as the "New Forbidden City" and strictly closed to the public. Mao Zedong and Zhou Enlai both lived and worked at Zhongnanhai. Its entrance is rather elegant, complete with a ghost wall.

BELOW: Wumen seen from inside the palace grounds.

South of the Imperial Palace

Nestling closely against the southern walls of the palace, to the west between Wumen and Tiananmen, **Zhongshan Gongyuan** ❺ (Sun Yatsen Park; open daily, 6am–8pm; entrance fee) retains impressive imperial architecture and landscaping. The park occupies the site of an old temple honouring the gods of the earth and of fertility. It was renamed after Sun Yatsen (1866–1925), one of the founders of the Chinese republican movement, was buried here. The triumphal arch near the southern entrance was originally set up in a different place in honour of the German ambassador murdered during the Boxer Rebellion.

Just to the east of Tiananmen is the former shrine of the imperial ancestors, now called **Laodong Renmin Wenhua Gong** (Working People's Cultural Palace; open daily, 6am–9pm; entrance fee) and functioning as a college for continuing education and a venue for concerts and art exhibitions. The shrine dates from the Ming dynasty and housed the ancestral tablets of the imperial forebears, which the emperor was required to honour.

On 1 October 1949, Mao Zedong, chairman of the Communist Party, proclaimed the founding of the People's Republic of China from the balcony of **Tiananmen** ❻ (Gate of Heavenly Peace; open daily, 8.30am–4.30pm; entrance fee to climb the tower, free to pass through). Today, Mao gazes south from a huge portrait on the south side of the gate onto **Tiananmen Square** ❼, south of the expansive ceremonial boulevard Chang'an Jie.

The square was quadrupled in size during the 1950s so that it could hold up to a million people. Rallies of Red Guards took place here during the Cultural Revolution; so did the 1989 student demonstrations, which ended when the government used the army to oust the demonstrators, resulting in numerous deaths.

During the early 1960s, Tiananmen Square was enlarged from 11 hectares to 40 hectares, creating room for one million people. Chang'an Jie, once just four metres wide, is now 38 metres wide and serves as Beijing's ceremonial boulevard.

BELOW: Tiananmen Square and Mao's mausoleum.

Map, page 152

In the centre of the square is an obelisk, unveiled in 1958 as a monument to the heroes of the nation and a perfect example of the socialist realist style. Immediately west of the square, **Renmin Dahuitang ❽** (Great Hall of the People; open daily, 8.30am–4pm; entrance fee) opened in 1959. This is an imposing building in the Soviet neoclassical monumental style, where the People's Congress meets and other important conferences and diplomatic meetings take place. A room of the hall is dedicated to each of China's 32 provinces and regions.

The massive facades of the **Zhongguo Lishi Bowuguan** (Museum of Chinese History) and **Zhongguo Geming Bowuguan ❾** (Museum of the Chinese Revolution; both open daily, 8.30am–4pm; entrance fee) border the square to the east. The Museum of Chinese History covers the entire history of China, and has many ancient and unique cultural relics from across the country. The Museum of the Chinese Revolution displays photographs, paintings, documents, and relics from the Communist Revolution in China.

In 1977, one year after Mao's death, the **Mao Zhuxi Jiniantang ❿**, or **Mao Mausoleum** was completed at the southern end of Tiananmen Square. Even today, when the teachings of the Little Red Book of Mao quotations have long gone out of fashion (except amongst tourists who buy them as souvenirs), people from all over China visit his mausoleum, filing respectfully past his embalmed body in its rose-hued, glass enclosure. The mausoleum was closed for renovation work in 1999.

Just outside the mausoleum, visitors get a graphic picture of how socialism is fast becoming mere consumer kitsch as they are ushered through a small bazaar selling Mao busts, bags, badges, and musical lighters playing short renditions of "The East is Red."

The focus of China's national emblem is Beijing's Tiananmen, the gate from which Mao Zedong proclaimed creation of the People's Republic of China.

BELOW: dusk on Tiananmen Square and Qianmen.

Hutongs

In a region formerly protected by the Great Wall, Beijing was also once hidden behind its own city walls. And within the city walls were its citizens, each with a wall built around their own homes and courtyards, or *siheyuan*.

Today, ring roads and walls of high-rise buildings have taken over the function of the city wall, itself a victim of town planning. In the city centre, faceless buildings of the 1950s protect an inner core of a labyrinth of crumbling old grey alleyways, some dating back several centuries. These are the *hutong*. Once the centre of life for Beijingers living outside the Imperial Palace, hutong are now threatened by urban redevelopment.

Hutong history

Beijing is a Mongol city. The nomadic conquerors who made Beijing their capital brought their way of life and language with them. Horses were part of their lifestyle. Wells were dug and horse-troughs, *hut* or *hot*

in Mongolian (as in Hohhot, the capital of the province of Inner Mongolia), were set up. The people of Beijing turned these Mongol wells into the Chinese hutong.

Mongols or no Mongols, Beijingers could hardly leave their houses and homes lying unprotected amid the horse-troughs. All they had to do was close up the small spaces between the houses with a wall and privacy was restored. It was even simpler to build on to the wall of their neighbours, although no one was allowed to build so as to block another householder's route to water. In this way, the tangle of hutong grew, with space just wide enough to let a rider through.

The houses and courtyards, hidden away and boxed in, are themselves closed off with wooden gates that often have carved characters intended to bring good fortune to the house owner and to his trade.

Just inside the gates are the ghost walls. Apparently, a Chinese ghost can only move straight ahead, and the ghost wall bars any further progress beyond the gate.

Courtyard culture

Traditionally, the introverted architecture of these Chinese courtyard tells much about the Chinese family. In a traditional hutong courtyard, there will be a few trees and many flowers and cacti. Three or four single-story buildings overlook the courtyard.

In the siheyuan of families who are higher in the social order, a second and third courtyard may adjoin the first. There may be two small "ear courtyards" to the sides, which contain the kitchens or serve as storage spaces. But this type of housing has become a rarity, as space is needed for the ever-growing population. What were once single-family dwellings have now been adapted for four or five families. Increasingly, many of these hutong courtyards are filled with plywood shanties housing rural migrants.

The names of each hutong tell its story by describing the life it contains. Some indicate professions or crafts: Bowstring Makers' Lane, Cloth Lane, Hat Lane. Some lanes, if mostly populated by a single family, are named after that family.

LEFT: the western districts of Beijing still have a few remaining hutong.

Tiantan

Twice a year during imperial times, the emperor and a magnificent procession of some 1,000 eunuchs, courtiers, and ministers would leave Gugong, the Imperial Palace, for **Tiantan ⓫**, the **Temple of Heaven** (park open, 6am–9pm; entrance fee), 3 km (2 miles) to the south of the palace. Each time he would spend a night of fasting and celibacy in **Zhai Gong** (Palace of Abstinence) prior to the sacrificial rites the next morning. At the winter solstice, he expressed thanks for the previous harvest, and on the 15th day of the first month of the lunar year he begged the gods of sun and moon, clouds and rain, and thunder and lightning to bless the coming harvest.

Set in the middle of a park of 270 hectares (670 acres), Tiantan is an outstanding example of religious architecture, which dates from the Ming dynasty. Destroyed several times, including once by lightning, it was last rebuilt in 1890 and has been open to the public since 1949. The park grounds are square, although the northern edge follows a curve, a symbolic expression of the fact that the emperor, in offering his sacrifices, had to leave the square-shaped earth for the round-roofed heaven.

An exquisite example of Chinese wooden buildings, constructed without the use of a single nail, is the round, 40-metre (130 ft) -high **Qinian Dian** (Hall of Prayer for Good Harvests). Its three levels are covered with deep blue tiles that symbolise the colour of heaven. The roof is supported by 28 pillars: the four largest ones in the centre represent the four seasons, and the double ring of 12 pillars represents the 12 months, as well as the traditional divisions of the Chinese day, each comprising two hours. In the south of the park lies a white, circular marble terrace, **Hianqiutan** (Altar of Heaven), and the **Echo Wall**, famous for its acoustics. The grounds of Tiantan are the best place in Beijing to watch early-morning enthusiasts of taiji, *qongfu*, calligraphy, ballroom dancing, badminton, Beijing opera, and kite-flying.

East of the Palace

Head east from Tiananmen along Jianguomennei Dajie to reach **Gu Guanxiangtai ⓬** (Ancient Observatory; open daily, 9am–5.30pm; entrance fee). Chinese emperors, known as "sons of heaven," were keen patrons of astronomy. An observatory was first built here in 1422, on what was then a tower in the city wall of the imperial capital. Its name changed several times. In the Yuan period it was the Terrace to Bring Down the Heavens, perhaps reflecting the Mongols inclination to conquer. In Ming times it was the Terrace for Watching the Stars. Seventeenth-century astronomical instruments are displayed on the roof of the tower.

Exhibition rooms, set around a quiet garden that makes an excellent resting place for tired visitors, house rare instruments, scientific records, navigational charts and portraits of famous astronomers.

About a kilometre further east from the Ancient Observatory along Jianguomenwai Dajie, near the diplomatic quarter, is the traveller's one-stop shop for everything Chinese, the **Youyi Shangdian ⓭** (Friendship Store; open daily, 9am–9pm) exclusively for foreigners and overseas Chinese. The ground floor offers

Map, page 152

BELOW: Qinian Dian, Tiantan.

foodstuffs, the first floor everything from aspirin to books, and the second floor arts and crafts from throughout China. Other available services include currency exchange, packaging and shipping, and appraisals. Prices are fixed, but they are reasonable and fair.

North of the Palace

The most elaborately-restored sacred building in Beijing is **Yonghe Gong**  (Palace of Eternal Harmony; open Tues–Sun, 9am–4pm; entrance fee), a Lamaist temple in the northeast of the old city. From the Ancient Observatory, head west along Jianguomennei Dajie, then north for about 5 km (3 miles) along Dongdanbei Dajie until it becomes Dongsibei Dajie and eventually Yonghe Gong Dajie. Originally the private residence of Prince Yong, Yonghe Gong was turned into a monastery when Yong became emperor in 1723. According to ancient Chinese custom, the former residence of a Son of Heaven had to be dedicated to religious purposes once he left.

Stone sculpture of Kong Fuzi, known to Westerners as Confucius.

From the mid 1700s, this was a centre of Lamaist (Tibetan Buddhist) religion and art, which at the same time offered the central imperial power welcome opportunities for influencing and controlling Tibetan and Mongolian subjects. The temple belongs to the Yellow Hat sect, whose spiritual leader is the Dalai Lama. In the three-storied central section of Wanfuge (Pavilion of Ten Thousand Happiness) is a statue, 23 metres (75 ft) high, of the Maitreya Buddha carved from a single piece of sandalwood.

BELOW: Yonghe Gong.

Opposite Yonghe Gong, across Yonghegong Dajie, are **Kong Miao**  (Temple of Confucius) and **Guozijian** (Imperial Academy; open daily, 8.30am–5.30pm; entrance fee), tranquil and now largely ignored former cen-

**Map,
page 152**

tres of scholarship. In its glorious past, Kong Miao was where emperors came to offer sacrifices to Confucius for guidance in ruling the empire. Built in 1306 during the Yuan dynasty, the temple's prize possession is a collection of 190 steles inscribed with records of ancient civil service examinations. It is the second-largest Confucian temple in China, after one in Confucius's home town, Qufu.

Now the Capital Library, Guozijian was the highest educational institution in the country. Thousands of students and scholars came here to listen to the emperor expound the Confucian classics. A set of steles commissioned by Emperor Qianlong records 13 Confucian classics. The 800,000 characters were engraved by a single scholar over 12 years.

To the west of Kong Miao, **Zhonglou** ⑯ (Bell Tower) and **Gulou** ⑰ (Drum Tower; open daily, 8.30am–4pm; entrance fee) date from the Yuan dynasty rule of Kublai Khan. The Drum Tower faces towards the Imperial Palace, 3 km (2 miles) due south, and the Bell Tower is immediately north of the Drum Tower. They once marked the northern edge of Beijing, but were in the centre of the Yuan dynasty city. Last rebuilt in 1747, the Bell Tower stands 33 metres (108 ft) high. The Drum Tower once held 24 giant drums that were struck to mark the closing of the city gates and the passing of the night watches. Today, one of the chief attractions of the Drum Tower is the view from the top over the surrounding area of traditional siheyuan courtyard houses.

The Beijing zoo began as an imperial retreat during the Ming dynasty, and later was an imperial park for the Qing emperors. After a few years as an experimental farm, it opened to the public in 1908 – the Garden of 10,000 Animals.

West of the Palace

Known as Wangshengyuan (Ten Thousand Animals Garden) when it was the personal menagerie of Empress Dowager Cixi, **Beijing Dongwuyuan** (Beijing Zoo; open daily, 7.30am–5.30pm; entrance fee) is 7 km (4 miles) west of the

BELOW: Drum Tower.

Drum Tower, near the **Beijing Exhibition Centre**. The animals' living conditions are not as good as those in Western zoos, but the pandas remain popular.

Baita Si ⑲ (White Dagoba Temple; open daily, 8.30am–5.30pm; entrance fee) is 3 km (2 miles) southeast of the zoo. The temple was established in 1096 and extensively rebuilt in Lamaist style in 1271. The white dagoba, from which the temple takes it name, is a Tibetan shrine similar to the one in Beihai Park. The temple also has an exhibition showing the layout of the Yuan dynasty city of Dadu, as Beijing was then known, and the social, economic and political systems under Mongol rule.

Southwest of Baita Si, not far from the showpiece Beijing West Railway Station, lies the serene **Baiyun Guan** ⑳ (White Cloud Temple; open daily, 8.30am–4.30pm; entrance fee), once the greatest Daoist centre of northern China. This former imperial palace was given by Genghis Khan as the headquarters of Qui Chang Chun, a Daoist leader who had promised that "if the conqueror respects Daoism, the Chinese will submit." Today, a small group of monks lives here, but because of the repression of religion during the Cultural Revolution, they are either very old or very young, with an age gap for the period of the upheavals. Headquarters of the China Daoist Association, Baiyun Guan also has a Daoist vegetarian restaurant and holds lively fairs at Lunar New Year.

At the southwest corner of the old city moat, 3 km (2 miles) south of Baiyun Guan, **Daguan Yuan** ㉑ (Grand View Garden; open daily, 8.45am–4.30pm; entrance fee) was constructed in 1984 as the incarnation of the idyllic garden in the novel *Dream of the Red Mansion*, by Cao Xueqin. It is a beautiful example of a classical Chinese landscaped garden, and visitors will see elaborate rockeries, lotus ponds, covered walkways, bridges, and pavilions.

BELOW: Foxiangge, Summer Palace.

Islam reached China during the Tang dynasty (618–907), and Muslims now live in all parts of the country. **Niujie Qingzhen Si** ㉒ (Ox Street Mosque; open daily, 9am–9pm; entrance fee), a 10-minute walk northeast of Daguan Yuan, was built in 966. It has all the usual features of mosques found elsewhere in the world – minaret, prayer hall facing Mecca, Arabic inscriptions – but the buildings themselves are distinctly Chinese. The area surrounding the mosque has one of the main concentrations of Hui Muslims in the capital and excellent Muslim restaurants.

Map,
page 152

A further five-minute walk east is **Fayuan Si** ㉓ (Temple of the Source of Buddhist Doctrine; open daily, 8.30am–11am; 1.30–3pm; entrance fee), completed in 696 during the Tang dynasty to honour soldiers killed in battle. It is the oldest surviving temple in the city, though the current buildings are all from the 18th century. Today, the temple houses the Buddhist Academy, formed in 1956 and devoted to teaching Buddhist novices, who are then sent to monasteries across China. The academy has a library of more than 100,000 precious texts and an exhibition of Buddhist sculpture, some dating from the Han dynasty.

Summer palaces

The great aesthete Emperor Qianlong, who ruled from 1736 to 1795, had a huge masterpiece of landscaping created 16 km(10 miles) northwest of the city centre: **Yuanming Yuan** (open daily, 7am–7pm; entrance fee), now better known to Westerners as the **Old Summer Palace**. Construction followed the most lavish European styles, according to plans by the Italian Jesuit missionary and artist Guiseppe Castiglione and based upon models such as the palace at Versailles. During the Second Opium War (1856–60), the Western

The European-style buildings of the Old Summer Palace were ravaged and destroyed by European troops in the mid 1800s.

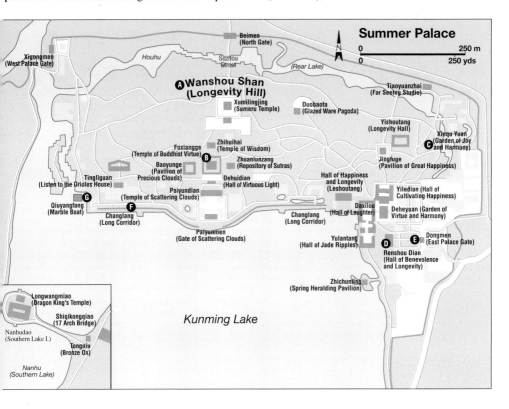

Summer Palace

Map, page 167

Empress Dowager Cixi found the Summer Palace a pleasant enough place for her ego.

OPPOSITE: pagoda of Foxiangge. **BELOW:** landscape near Xiang Shan.

powers, led by British and French troops, pillaged the palace and reduced it to rubble. Amidst the rubble today is a restored brick maze with a central pavilion.

The Qing dynasty built a replacement for the devastated Yuanming Yuan nearby, in the grounds laid out by Qianlong as a place of retirement for his mother. This new summer residence took on special interest for the notorious Empress Dowager Cixi, who fulfiled a wonderful, if rather expensive, dream in 1888. Using money intended for the building of a naval fleet, she constructed **Yiheyuan ㉔**, the Garden of Cultivated Harmony – the **Summer Palace** (open daily, 6.30am–6pm; entrance fee), west of the Old Summer Palace. Originally a concubine of the third rank, Cixi had placed herself on the Dragon Throne after the death of the emperor and ruled in an unscrupulous and self-centred way for 50 years, initially in the name of her young child. By deploying young women and other earthly distractions, she kept him away from matters of government until his death at the age of 18. Bypassing the legal inheritance, she installed her young nephew as emperor and governed from "behind the throne" until he was of age. She then retired to the Summer Palace, but continued to meddle in court politics.

As in every classical Chinese garden, water and mountains (usually represented by rocks) determine the landscape of Yiheyuan. **Kunming Lake** covers three-quarters of the total area of more than 30 sq.km (10 sq miles); on its shore is **Wanshou Shan ⓐ** (Hill of Longevity). Accessible via a series of bridges, stairs, gates and halls is the massive **Foxiangge ⓑ** (Pagoda of the Incense of Buddha), which crowns the top of Wanshou Shan. In the eastern corner is a jewel of classical Chinese garden design, **Xiequ Yuan ⓒ** (Garden of Joy and Harmony), a picturesque copy of a lotus pool from the old city of Wuxi.

To make it more difficult for strangers to spy into the grounds, **Renshou Dian ⓓ** (Hall of Benevolence and Longevity) was built right next to the eastern gate, **Dongmen ⓔ**, now the main gate. Behind it lay the private apartments of Cixi, which today also house a theatrical museum. Here, Cixi used to enjoy operatic performances by her 384-strong ensemble of eunuchs.

Of light wooden construction and decorated with countless painted scenes from Chinese mythology, **Changlang ⓕ** (Long Corridor) runs parallel to the northern shore of the lake, linking the scattered palace buildings. It ends near **Qiuyangfang ⓖ** (Marble Boat), an expensive and useless folly in which Cixi, looking out over the lake, took tea.

Xiang Shan (Fragrant Hill)

One of the most popular destinations for Beijing's day-trippers, particularly when it is in its brilliant autumn colours, is **Xiang Shan**, or Fragrant Hill (open daily, 6am–7pm; entrance fee), 8 km(5 miles) west of the Summer Palace. Mao lived here briefly in 1949 before moving to Zhongnanhai, the Communist Party compound in Beijing. A cable car speeds visitors up the steep climb to the summit of Incense Burner Peak. Some beautiful temples hide in the valleys.

Biyun Si (Temple of the Azure Clouds), with an impressive pavilion and a 35-metre-high (115 ft) *dagoba*, or stupa, lies just to the north of Xiang Shan.

GUGONG: THE IMPERIAL PALACE IN BEIJING

Of paramount importance in Chinese architecture is the consideration of geomancy, or feng shui, which determines position and shapes of buildings.

Chinese court architecture reached its apotheosis with the Imperial Palace, or Gugong, in Beijing. Built during the Ming (1368–1644) and Qing (1644–1912) dynasties, this architectural wonder housed the emperor, empress and imperial concubines, and it served as the seat of government for 500 years. Commonly known to Westerners as the Forbidden City, it was indeed forbidden and strictly off-limits to ordinary Chinese.

The layout of the Imperial Palace, like that of many wealthy traditional Chinese homes and compounds, follows a grid pattern. The most important buildings are laid out on a central north–south axis. These buildings have entrances facing south, which was considered the most auspicious direction – unlike the north, from where came bitter winter winds and barbarians.

Conforming to a basic but distinct pattern, the palace's halls were constructed on elevated stone platforms. Wooden columns rise upwards and, together with a web of cantilevered brackets between the tops of columns and the cross beams, help to support the roofs. The curved roofs were thought to bring good luck.

Imperial buildings have four-sided roofs covered with yellow-glazed tiles. The colour yellow was reserved for the use of royal palaces and imperial temples. Not only was yellow reminiscent of the Yellow River, or the Huang He, where Chinese civilisation is believed to have originated, but it also represented the element of earth that lay at the centre of the universe.

IMPERIAL ROOF TOPS ▷
Within the Imperial Palace, there is a formalised relation of buildings, pavilions and courtyards to one another.

DRAGON BREATH ▽
There are five kinds of dragons: heavenly, spiritual, earthly, one indicating buried treasure, and a five-clawed dragon associated with the emperor, thus the use of "dragon throne" or "dragon robe" to his things.

EMPEROR'S COLOUR △
Imperial buildings are identified by their four-sided roofs covered with yellow-glazed tiles.

◁**ZOOMORPHIC WATCH**
Led by a god riding a phoenix, these mythological creatures atop the Taihe Dian (Hall of Supreme Harmony) protected the building against lightning and fires.

A pair of stone lions is often seen guarding the gates to important structures. On the left, the male is identified by a ball under his paw, symbolising control of the empire; to the right, the female has her paw on a cub, indicating offspring and continuation of empire. Not native to China, lions are associated with power and prestige, and the use of this mythological beast was reserved for the court and officials of high rank. The first use of lions in Chinese architecture dates to the Han dynasty (206 BC–AD 220).

Perhaps even more famous and important than the mythological lion is the dragon, which reigns supreme over all animals. Dragons are believed to rise into the skies in the spring, and later plunge into the waters in autumn.

As a creature between heaven and earth and symbolising the *yang* (male) energy, the dragon came to be identified with the emperor, thought to be the son of heaven.

Together with the mythological phoenix, which represents the *yin* (female) force and is associated with the empress, the dragon appears frequently in decorative designs of imperial buildings. In combination, the dragon and phoenix can also stand for matrimonial harmony.

MARBLE FLAMES ▷
The flame-shaped carvings atop the marble bridges are symbols of illumination.

TORTOISE BURNER ▽
A symbol of longevity, the tortoise in ancient times was also associated with divination. Two bronze tortoise-shaped incense burners were ornamental and functional. Smoke from their mouths added to an occasion's mysticism.

CHINA · Beijing

OUTSIDE BEIJING

The rumble of Beijing challenges the nerves. Outside of the city are several escapes near enough for short trips: the Great Wall, tombs of the Ming emperors, and Chengde, an imperial summer residence.

Wan, the Chinese character representing the number 10,000, is also a synonym for "unimaginable hugeness." Thus Wanli Changcheng, the Chinese name for the Great Wall.

BELOW: Wanli Changcheng, or the Great Wall.

The area surrounding Beijing has some interesting locales that attract visitors hoping to spend time away from the daily chaos of the capital. Transportation by train or bus is readily available and convenient, though for shorter trips such as the Great Wall and Ming Tombs, a hired car might be easiest. Travel agents can arrange tours for short trips outside Beijing.

Wanli Changcheng (Great Wall)

Wanli Changcheng, the Great Wall, winds its way like an endless, slender dragon from the Yellow Sea through five provinces, two autonomous regions, and up into the Gobi Desert. Towers are located at strategic points. The very earliest stages of the building of the wall were in the fifth century BC, but the present course was basically determined around 220 BC by Qin Shi Huangdi, the first Chinese emperor and the founder of the empire. He had smaller, previously constructed sections linked and extended northward to ward off the horse-riding nomads. However, the most impressive portions seen today were built during the Ming dynasty. Soldiers and peasants from all parts of the country were conscripted, spending several years of their lives building this "ten thousand *li* wall" – *wanli changcheng*. Blocks of rock weighing several hundred

kilograms had to be heaved up the steep slopes, and an unknown number of people paid with their lives for this project.

Several Great Wall sites are accessible from Beijing, each fulfiling a different role. From ten in the morning until three in the afternoon, **Badaling ❶**, the section of the wall that is most accessible from Beijing, turns into a true tourist carnival. The avalanche of visitors streams past countless stalls selling tacky souvenirs promoting this great symbol of Chinese civilisation. Then it moves in two different directions, attempting to conquer the steep climb. From the high points are views of the breathtaking scenery, where the mighty wall climbs and descends in a fascinating mountain landscape.

The scenery at **Mutianyu ❷** is imposing as well. This part of the wall, some 120 kilometres (75 mi) to the north of Beijing, was restored a few years ago and is less busy than Badaling. Small parts of the wall here remain as they were – it has not been rebuilt – so visitors have a better sense of its antiquity. The walk is difficult but not treacherous. Cable cars take visitors from the bottom of the hills nearly to the wall itself, though some may prefer to hike up the steep trail.

Simitai is 100 kilometres (60 mi) northeast of Beijing. A cable car is available at the east side of the reservoir. The hike at this site is difficult, as the renovated section quickly turns into steep, dilapidated climbs. However, this area makes for great hiking and camping, with panoramic mountain views. **Jinshanlin**, which has been restored, is a bit kinder and easier to climb. This part is located west of Simitai. **Huanghua Cheng**, 25 kilometres (15 mi) west of Mutianyu, makes for good vigorous hiking. The climb up to the remains of the wall is the most difficult part, though some caution is warranted for hiking on the wall as well, as footing can be a little crumbly.

Map, page 175

Defending the wall. The top part of the Great Wall was designed so that 5 or 6 horsemen could ride side by side. Fortified towers, signal beacon towers, and garrisons completed the defenses.

Ming tombs

A visit to the Great Wall is normally combined with a trip to the Ming tombs at **Shisan Ling ③**. Protected by an auspicious range of hills to the north, east and west, the tombs of 13 of the 16 Ming emperors lie in this geomantically-favourable spot.

Entry from the south on the valley floor passes through numerous gates of honour along Shendao (Soul Path), flanked by the stone guardians of the tombs. The guard of honour of twelve human figures represents civil and military dignitaries and officials; there are also lions, horses, camels, elephants, and mythical creatures.

Two of the 13 tombs are most often visited. The others are unkempt and don't offer much in the way of historical or architectural interest. **Chang Ling** is the final resting place of Emperor Yongle (died 1424), the third emperor of the Ming dynasty. Historians often look at Yongle's reign as ushering in a second phase of the Ming dynasty.

Yongle made significant adjustments to the institutional forms of the state established by the founder of the Ming dynasty, his father. Yongle usurped power from the chosen successor, his nephew, and moved the capital city from Nanjing to Beijing after reconstructing the city.

He was also the one to choose the spot of the present-day Ming tombs to build his own. As he was the first to be buried there, his tomb is the largest and also the most centrally located. Moreover, his tomb has served as the model for the other tombs that followed. The mound of the tomb has not been excavated, and the emperor and the empress still lie within the underground vaults today. Above are the magnificent courtyards and ceremonial halls.

Although Beijing has been the capital for five dynasties, only the Ming tombs are nearby. The Qing tombs are 125km to the northeast, and as the Mongol rulers of the Yuan dynasty had no burial rites, no Yuan tombs survive.

BELOW: stele at the entrance to Ding Ling, tomb of Emperor Zhu Yijun, who died in 1620.

Ding Ling, the tomb of the 13th emperor Zhu Yijun (died 1620), opened to the public in 1959. It is the only Ming tomb to have been excavated. Take the wide staircase down to the entrance of the vaults, the underground palace, located 30 metres (100 ft) below. The emperor's primary wife and one concubine were buried with him, although all you can see down there nowadays are some decorative chests and two stone thrones, placed for the sake of tourists.

The underground palace was sealed with a specially designed lock. The locking stone, which is still on display inside the entrance, fell automatically into place inside the vault when the doors were closed, making it nearly impossible to open them again. But, of course, grave robbers always find a way. When the tombs were finally opened, the vaults were nearly empty, with objects strewn about. The underground palace consists of three main halls. Two exhibition rooms above the vaults showcase rare relics belonging to the royals.

Longer excursions

Tianjin has a population of 7 million and is one of China's major cities. It is 140 kilometres (90 mi) southeast of Beijing and can easily be reached by buses, which depart every 15 minutes, or train.

A walk around Tianjin tells much about its history. If some of the city's architecture and layout seem similar to that of Shanghai, this is because Tianjin had a pros-

Map,
page 175

perous international community during the late 1800s. In 1860, Western powers, wanting to open trade with China, turned Tianjin into a treaty port by landing troops in the city and forcing Beijing to parcel out the city to the various Western interests.

The best-known product from Tianjin is its carpets. Eight large factories produce these renowned carpets, many still made, at least partially, by hand. Visitors may go to some of the factories to observe the process and buy a rug or two. Culture Street, located in downtown Tianjin, is made up of numerous small shops selling books, porcelain, carpets, crafts, and food including the local specialty, *goubuli baozi*, or buns.

Chengde, formerly known as Jehol, was the summer residence of the Qing emperors and, at the same time, a politically important meeting place for the leaders of ethnic minorities. A five-hour train ride northeast from Beijing, Chengde has retreated once again into the sleepy town it was before Qing-dynasty emperor Kangxi started construction on his new summer palace, built there in 1703. His interest in Chengde was strategic, as it strengthened his empire's rule over Mongolians and various frontiers.

In line with this strategy, the architecture found in Chengde exhibits an interesting mix of Han and minority architectural styles. Instead of the ornate carvings and large overhanging eaves that characterise Chinese architecture, the summer palace is relatively simple but elegant.

The temples surrounding the palace also show interesting architectural choices. The remains of seven of the original 11 temples can be seen. The largest of the temples is the **Putuozongcheng**, which is based on the Potala Palace in Lhasa, Tibet. Construction was completed in 1771 under Emperor Qianlong for

Several times I have travelled to the shores of the Yangzi and have seen the lush beauty of the south... In the north I have crossed the Dragon Sands, and in the east I have wandered in the region of the White Mountains, where the peaks and the rivers are mighty... but I have chosen none of them... (Chengde) is the only place in which I desire to live.

— KANGXI, QING EMPEROR

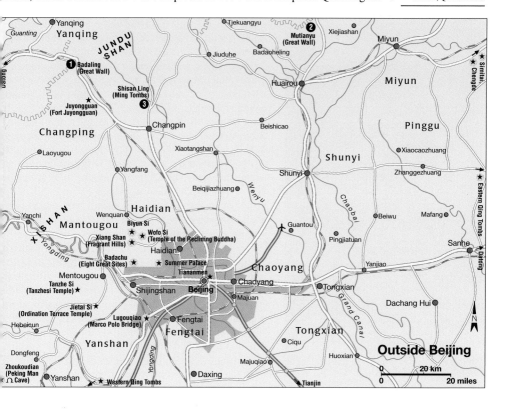

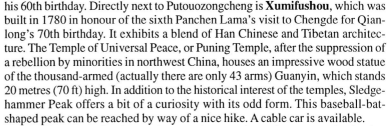

**Map,
page 175**

*Qianlong, the Qing
emperor who built
Putuozongcheng for
his 60th birthday.*

BELOW: Putuo-
zongcheng.
OPPOSITE: the tem-
ple at Xumifushou.

his 60th birthday. Directly next to Putouozongcheng is **Xumifushou**, which was built in 1780 in honour of the sixth Panchen Lama's visit to Chengde for Qian-long's 70th birthday. It exhibits a blend of Han Chinese and Tibetan architecture. The Temple of Universal Peace, or Puning Temple, after the suppression of a rebellion by minorities in northwest China, houses an impressive wood statue of the thousand-armed (actually there are only 43 arms) Guanyin, which stands 20 metres (70 ft) high. In addition to the historical interest of the temples, Sledge-hammer Peak offers a bit of a curiosity with its odd form. This baseball-bat-shaped peak can be reached by way of a nice hike. A cable car is available.

Beidaihe, once a foreigners' hot spot, is now a favourite summer destination of high-level party officials as well as several million tourists every year. The beaches are among the nicest in China and certainly the best in the region. The main strip of beach stretches for 10 kilometres (6 mi). Sumptuous Western-style villas also abound. In 1937, there were a total of 700 villas in the area. Today, many of these belong to party officials.

A common destination for tourists coming from or going to Beijing, **Datong** is best known for its Buddhist caves. Datong is an eight-hour train ride due west from Beijing following the same route that terminates in Inner Mongolia. Now a leading coal producer, this town first gained historic importance from the central Asian people who, in AD 386, founded the Northern Wei dynasty and moved the capital there. Located 16 kilometres west of town, the caves themselves – a total of 53 caves, which open from the south – are centralised in an area that stretches for about one kilometre. Many of the caves have been damaged by the climate, but the site is still grand to see. The Wei rulers were sympathetic to Buddhism and undertook construction of the caves. These were built in various periods leading up to the Tang dynasty. Buddhists who came back to China from pilgrimages in Kabul brought back new architectural techniques that were employed in the carving of the caves into the mountains. There are 21 main caves, each of which exhibit unique qualities. Cave number five houses a 17-metre-high (56 ft) Buddha, and cave six has a 15-metre-high (49 ft) square tower with niches holding small Buddha figures.

In Datong itself there are the Huayan and Shanhua monasteries. Huayan actually has two monasteries. One, first built in 1064, has Qing-dynasty paintings and Ming-dynasty statues in its Great Temple, capped by an interesting roof. The other, first built in 1038, is largely destroyed, save its one magnificent library. Also in the city is Jiulongbi, the nine-dragon wall, which dates from the Ming period. With glazed bricks in five colours, it was once the entrance to a palace.

Nearby **Heng Shan**, 70 kilometres (45 mi) south of Datong, is one of the five sacred mountains in China and home to 18 temples. Five kilometres (3 mi) outside the town of **Hunyuan**, the 1,400-year-old Xuankong Si nestles against an enormous rock supported by extra support poles. **Wutai Shan**, further south from Heng Shan, was once the location of over 300 monasteries during the Ming dynasty. Today, only a few remain, including an octangular pagoda called Foguang Si (Temple of the Light of Buddha), the oldest wood structure in China.

DONGBEI

Map, page 183

More commonly known to Westerners as Manchuria, the northeast-ern provinces of Dongbei have long been at the centre of regional politics and conflict involving China, Russia, Japan, and Korea.

North of Beijing lies a cold and mostly industrial region of three provinces: Liaoning, Jilin, and Heilongjiang. With a blend of Chinese, Korean and Russian influences and peoples, the area sometimes takes on a muddled cultural identity. It has also been an area of conflict and power struggles, including border skirmishes between the former Soviet Union and China. Before that, the area was brutally occupied by the Japanese in World War II, and later was a staging area for fierce battles in the Korean War in the early 1950s.

The Chinese call this area **Dongbei**, which literally means East-North. To the west, the northeastern provinces border the Mongolian steppes, and to the east, the Korean peninsula. The old name of Manchuria, still in use outside China, goes back to the fact that this was once the territory of the Manchu, rulers of the Qing dynasty.

The Manchu had prohibited the settlement of Han Chinese in this region, and it was not until the middle of the last century that a major settlement of Han Chinese was permitted, under the pressure of an expanding population and the confusions of the Taiping Rebellion in the mid 1800s. Up until the end of the 1970s, the Manchu were considered to have been completely assimilated with the Han Chinese; in recent years, however, the special customs and traditions of the Manchu are once more being emphasised. During World War II, the Japanese attempted to separate this region from China by setting up the puppet state of Manchuguo, under the rule of the former, and last, Chinese emperor, Puyi. Today, about 100 million people live in this northeastern region.

PRECEDING PAGES: autumn's light on northern street. LEFT: winter leisure in Dongbei. BELOW: traditional clothing, Shenyang.

A rail journey from Beijing to the region takes about 12 hours, travelling for long stretches along the coast. Apart from the seaside resort of Beidaihe, it also passes the town of Xingcheng, which dates from the Ming period, has many interesting sights and is a popular resort. A good time to travel to Shenyang and northeast China in general is summer, as the winters are bitterly – and famously – cold.

Shenyang

An important meeting point of several transport routes in the northeast, **Shenyang ❶** is also one of the most important industrial cities in China. With a population of nearly 6 million people, Shenyang is sometimes known by its Manchurian name of Mukden.

Although Shenyang's history and that of the entire province of Liaoning can be traced a long way back into history, the city did not gain any importance until the Song dynasty, when it became a centre of trade for nomadic livestock breeders. Its rise to prominence came during the Qing dynasty; Liaoning was, and still is, the home of the Manchu, the Qing emperors. Today, more

than half of the Manchu ethnic minority live in this province. In Liaonin Province itself, there are several autonomous regions inhabited mainly b Manchu. Displays of traditional Manchu culture are put on for foreigners.

In Shenyang, the greatest building from the time of the Manchu Qing dynast is the **Gugong**, or **Imperial Palace**, the most complete and best-preserve palace complex after the Imperial Palace in Beijing. It was built in 1625, after th Manchu had declared Shenyang to be their capital, and it contains more tha 300 buildings in an area covering more than 60,000 square metres (650,000 s ft). This palace, which was maintained after the Qing emperors later moved t the capital of Beijing, was the residence of Nurhachi, the founder of the Qin dynasty, and his successor Abahai (Hong Taiji in Chinese). The main building – an amalgamation of Chinese, Manchu, and Mongol architecture – are th Chongzheng, Qingning Palace, Dazheng, and Wensu Pavilion.

Of the three imperial Qing tombs in Liaoning Province, two are in Shenyang the Northern Imperial Tomb, **Bei Ling** – built in 1643 for Nurhachi's son Aba hai and now in the middle of a park in the north of Shenyang – and the Easter Imperial Tomb, **Dong Ling**, the final resting place of Nurhachi, 8 kilometres (mi) outside of the city. The third tomb, Yong Ling, built by Nurhachi for hi ancestors, is in the Xinbin district. Also worth seeing in Shenyang is **Shishe Si**, a Lamaist temple dating from the 17th century and located in the wester part of the city.

In the middle of the 1980s, Dalian became China's first certifiably rat-free city after an intensive effort to rid the entire city of the rodents.

To the south and east

From Shenyang, the train leaves the main line and goes southward toward **Anshan**, some 80 kilometres (50 mi) from Shenyang. Anshan is a city of mil lions, and perhaps the largest iron-and-steel works ir China is here, producing 20 percent of the nation's steel Anshan is a jumping-off point for a pleasant visit to the scenic **Qian Shan**, a mountain blanketed with ancien pines, pavilions, temples, and monasteries dating from the Ming and Qing periods. Temple markets are held here every April.

BELOW: beach near Dalian, in summer.

From Anshan, the journey continues south through broad fields of millet and soybean to the tip of the peninsula, where the port of **Dalian ❷** lies. The ice-free harbour is one of the most important in China in the north, a fact reflected in its conquest by Japan during World War II and the Soviet Union's takeover of it after- wards. It was returned to China in the 1950s.

The city, surrounded by greenery in the summer, is also a popular place for holidays and excursions, not least because of the extensive beaches and the mild mar- itime climate. The main impression of the city, which lies in a bay, is of a busy port with broad streets and big squares planted with greenery. Don't miss the opportu- nity to visit one of the fish restaurants here. The nature park of Laohutan, right by the sea, is worth a visit.

Southeast from Shenyang via Benxi, or northeast from Dalian, are **Dandong ❸**, near the North Korean border, and the mountainous vistas of **Dagu Shan**. From Dandong, the railway carries on into North Korea as far as its capital, Pyongyang. For those who want to say they've nearly set foot in North Korea, boats carry isitors to within only a few metres of the North Korean side of the **Yalu Jiang**. The main route from Shenyang runs east at first, to the nearby industrial town f **Fushun**, where there is a prison for war criminals, and where the last emperor, uyi, was imprisoned until 1950. Outside of Fushun is one of the world's biggest pen-pit coal mines.

To the east of Fushun and an overnight journey by train is **Tonghua** ❹, a ine-producing town in the southeast of Jilin Province. Sights include a onastery, the mausoleum of Yangjingchu, and a wine cellar.

From Tonghua, **Ji'an** is accessible by train or bus. Ji'an lies on the Chinese-Korean border, on the upper course of the Yalu and was once the capital of the Korean kingdom of Koguryo. There are numerous tombs in the vicinity, but nly some of them are open to the public. Ji'an lies in the middle of an utonomous region of China's Korean minority. There are about 2 million ethic Koreans living in China, and more than 60 percent live in the region.

The capital of this autonomous region – there are two such regions in Jilin – **Yanji** ❺, where the Koreans also have their own university. At Ji'an, the border river Yalu is only some 30 metres (100 ft) wide, and life here is quite idyllic. n the summer, women chat across the border while doing their laundry, and hildren from both sides swim in the river together, although swimming to the pposite bank is not officially permitted.

The Korean influence is not restricted to this area alone. Some parts of henyang, Changchun, Jilin, and Mudanjiang, too, feel rather Korean – people ear Korean clothing, signs are written in Korean, and Korean is the primary anguage of commerce. (In Shenyang, there is a cemetery dedicated to the memry of the Chinese who died in the Korean War.)

Map,
page 183

TIP

Live dangerously. Take one of the daily boats from Dandong that goes out onto the Yalu River, the international border between North Korea and China, and comes within 10 metres of the North Korean side.

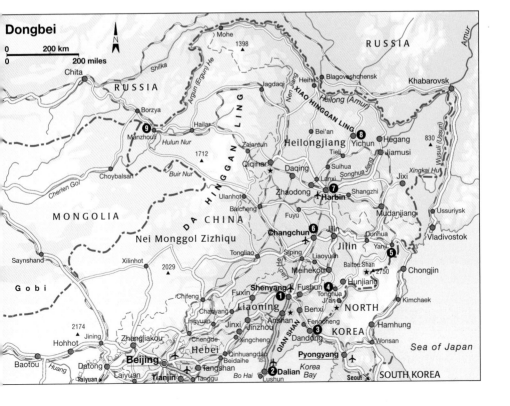

North of Yanji and surrounded by beautiful scenery is the town of **Mudan jiang**. The most famous peak along the Chinese-Korean border is **Baitou Shan** (White Head Mountain), with its beautiful crater lake. In its clear waters, crea tures like the Loch Ness monster have reportedly been seen. The last sighting was in 1981. Nearby is a waterfall, one of the sources of the Sungari River Baitou Shan is considered sacred by Koreans and the Manchu, and it lies in the centre of the **Changbai Shan nature reserve**, covering 2,000 square kilome tres (770 sq mi). It is China's largest natural reserve.

On **Changbai Shan** (Ever White Mountains), along the Chinese-Korean bor der, many animals that have become extinct elsewhere have survived – sables snow leopards, tigers, and bears. Excellent ginseng grows here, too. Like many other mountain ranges in China, Changbai Shan has its own Tianchi (Lake o Heaven), a volcanic crater lake that is about 15 kilometres in circumference.

To the north

From Fushun onwards, the railway turns north until it reaches the provincia capital of Jilin, **Changchun ❻**. On its way, the train runs through huge fields o grain. Here in the northeast, there are still enormous farms owned by the state and from the train old villages with their mud huts can be seen. The town o Changchun did not become important until the end of the 19th century, when i was the terminus of the Manchurian railway, built by skilled Russian labour. In 1932, the town, then known as Xinjing, became the seat of the government of the Japanese puppet state of Manchuguo.

Today, the town still shows signs of Japanese urban planning in its ruler-straight boulevards. Changchun, an industrial and university town, is also well-

BELOW: Ice Lantern Festival, Harbin.

Map,
page 183

known for its car-manufacturing works. Because of its large parks, Changchun is often also known as the "town of woodland". The palace of Puyi has once more been restored to its old form.

Many films are produced here in one of the biggest film studios of the People's Republic. Most films that are internationally-known, however, are produced in Xi'an or in the large coastal cities.

From Changchun, the journey continues via the Trans-Siberian Railway to **Harbin** ❼, the capital of Heilongjiang Province, with a population of over 3 million. The distance from Beijing to this point is almost 1,400 kilometres (900 mi), and the train covers it in 18 hours. Harbin (Place for Drying Fish Nets) can also be reached by plane from Changchun and Beijing.

The city lies along the Songhua Jiang, which joins Heilong Jiang, which defines China's border with Russia to the north. The impression of this city is one of industrial sites and newly built apartment houses that all look alike and are a familiar sight throughout China. In contrast are the older, sometimes almost European-looking residential areas.

Many anticommunist Russians fled from Russia to this city after the Russian Revolution of 1917, forming the majority of the inhabitants together with those Russians already living here. After World War II, most of them went back to what was then the Soviet Union.

In the early 1930s, Puyi, the last emperor of China, was made an emperor again by the Japanese, who had taken control of Manchuria and established a puppet empire called Manchuguo. He remained in Changchun for the next decade.

Some districts of Harbin are still reminiscent of Russian cities today. Russian influences can be detected in the architectural style of many of the buildings, not least in the old churches with their unmistakable onion domes. There are over a dozen Christian churches in Harbin, many of them built in neo-Gothic style. Another of the city's few interesting sights is Jile Si, a temple built in 1924 in the Nangang district.

Here, too, were the gruesome and inhumane medical experiments of the Japanese army's Unit 731, which the Japanese government denied for decades after World War II. The unit's existence was only recently acknowledged by Japan, after a Japanese scholar uncovered documented proof. Over 4,000 prisoners of war – Chinese and Allies – died from "medical" experiments involving cold, heat, chemicals, injections of viruses and plague, and live dissection.

The winters are very cold, and temperatures can fall as low as minus 38°C (−36°F). It is no surprise that ice-sailing is one of the most popular sports in Harbin. Every winter, there are also large exhibitions of ice sculpture in the city; human figures, pavilions, and entire palaces are hacked out of ice.

Near **Yichun** ❽, to the north of Harbin, there is an ancient forest along the Tangwang Jiang composed mainly of Korean pines. This has now been declared a nature reserve and is a perfect place for long hikes.

The train from Harbin runs on to the northwest towards the Russian border. After three hours of travel is **Daqing**, China's biggest oil field.

About 260 kilometres (160 mi) from Harbin, to the northwest in the swamps around Lake Zhalong, is a nature reserve where rare red-crowned and white-naped cranes live.

Not far to the west of Qiqihar, the train route towards the Russian border crosses into **Nei Monggol Zizhiqu**, or **Inner Mongolia**, passing through Da Hinggan Ling, or the Greater Xingan range. The first town in Inner Mongolia is Hailar, in the middle of the Mongolian steppe and with a Siberian atmosphere.

On the Chinese side, the journey ends in **Manzhouli** ❾, where you can begin the train journey, which lasts several days, to Moscow and eventually onwards to Europe and Berlin. Beyond Inner Mongolia is Mongolia itself, an independent nation that has, in the past couple of years, found itself embracing both democracy and capitalism, and doing rather well.

LOWER HUANG HE: SHANDONG AND HENAN

Map, page 191

The Huang He – Yellow River – was the source of civilisation in China. Too, it has been a river of sorrow. Most importantly, perhaps, it has been the source of philosophical ponderings.

I n a country famed for its rich cultural heritage, the lower stretches of the **Huang He** (**Yellow River**), comprising Shandong and Henan provinces, is home to some of China's greatest historical and religious sites, and to the three most revered philosophers of ancient China: Confucius, Laozi, and Mencius. The fertile valleys of Shandong and Henan have been cultivated for at least 5,000 years, and several of the earliest states of ancient China developed here. The great river and its tributaries irrigated the land, but regular floods and changes of course forced people to work in close cooperation. Over the centuries, the Huang He has changed course numerous times, disrupting life and agriculture. Not until 1933 did it find its present outflow to the ocean.

Henan has many of the oldest Buddhist sites in China, including the world-famous Shaolin temple, the original home of Zen Buddhism, now better known for its martial arts. Shandong was the location of the early important ancient states of Qi and Lu. Tai Shan, in Shandong, and Song Shan, in Henan, are two of the country's five sacred Daoist mountains. Shandong's Liang Shan mountain was the hiding place of the legendary heroes of the Chinese classic *Outlaws of the Marsh*, who, in the same spirit as England's Robin Hood, stole from the rich and gave to the poor. The secret Society for Peace and Justice, known in English as the Boxers – of the Boxer Rebellion – originated in Shandong at the end of the 19th century.

Today, Shandong and Henan provinces each have around 80 million inhabitants, making them two of China's three most populous provinces. Although the Shandong peninsula is among China's most developed areas, the inland part of the province, along with most of Henan, is occupied by relatively poor farming families.

PREVIOUS PAGES: Qingdao and Bay of Jiaozhou. **OPPOSITE:** one of many temples on Tai Shan. **BELOW:** Qingdao promenade.

Qingdao

At the end of the 19th century, Germany was still looking for a place in China to plant its colonial ambitions. In 1897, two German Catholic priests were killed by Boxers, which provided an excuse for the emperor, Wilhelm II, to establish a colony at **Qingdao ❶** (Green Island), 320 kilometres (200 mi) from Jinan, the Shandong provincial capital, and 800 kilometres (500 mi) from Beijing. German military superiority quickly forced the Chinese into an agreement to lease the surrounding Bay of Jiaozhou to Germany.

Earlier, before the first German frigate moored in the bay, Qingdao was a simple fishing village. But German officers, sailors, and traders were soon promenading up and down the Kaiser Wilhelm Ufer and dining in the seafront Prinz Heinrich Hotel. They drank beer from

the Germania brewery, which later achieved fame in many parts of the world under the name Tsingtao (the old Wade-Giles system of spelling Qingdao). The success of **Qingdao Pijiuchang** (Tsingtao Brewery, 56 Dengzhou Lu; open daily, for groups only; free), the brewery guides tell visitors, is due not only to German expertise but also to the spring water of Lao Shan, a nearby mountain with beautiful scenery and several Daoist temples.

The modern city retains much evidence of its colonial past, with many 19th-century, neo-Gothic style buildings. Red-tiled roofs, half-timbered facades, sloping gables, triangular attic windows, the tall towers of **Tianzhu Jiaotang** (Catholic Cathedral, Zhongshan Lu; open daily, 7.30am-5.30pm; free), and the former governor's residence, which has the air of a Prussian hunting lodge, create a distinctly German flavour. The German presence lasted until 1914 – the beginning of World War I – when Japan conquered the colony. It was liberated by the Chinese in 1922, but reoccupied briefly by the Japanese in 1938. Although the city is now an important port and industrial centre with sprawling concrete suburbs, the old town has preserved its character, keeping Qingdao as one of China's most popular seaside resorts. Indeed, strolling through the old German area and along the beaches is the principal pleasure here.

Tai Shan

China's most sacred Daoist mountain, **Tai Shan** ❷, lies 300 kilometres (200 mi) west of Qingdao and 80 kilometres (50 mi) south of Jinan. Popular Chinese religion treats mountains as living beings. The stabilising power of mountains perpetuates the cosmic order, and mountains create the clouds and rain. In ancient mythology, Tai Shan rose from the head of Pangu, the creator of the world. Shamans, and later emperors, performed sacred rituals here for as long as 4,000 years.

At the foot of the mountain, in the centre of the quiet tourist town of **Tai'an**, stands the magnificent **Dai Miao** (open daily, 7.20am-6.30pm; entrance fee), honouring the god of Tai Shan. This temple complex of more than 600 buildings was the venue for elaborate sacrifices and provided quarters for the emperor before he ascended Tai Shan. **Tiangong Dian** (Hall of Heavenly Gifts), one of the largest classical temple halls in China, contains a fresco more than 60 metres (200 ft) long.

A few hundred metres north of the temple, **Daizong Fang** (Gate of the God) marks the starting point of a stone stairway to the 1,545-metre-high (5,070 ft) summit. In earlier years, emperors and mandarins were carried up the 6,293 steps in litters. Modern pilgrims and travellers need a whole day for the round trip, or they can ride to a halfway point by minibus, then ascend by cable car almost as far as the summit. But those who take the quick way miss the splendid variety of this open-air museum: temples, pavilions, shrines, stone steles, inscriptions, and waterfalls. A little way off the main path, the text of a sutra has been engraved in a huge block of stone. The 1,050 characters, each 50 centimetres (20 in) high, are considered a masterpiece of calligraphy. A more recent addition to the mountain's calligraphic works is Mao's "the most creative people are the people now," penned in 1969.

Over the last 2,000 years, the Huang He has had 26 major changes in its course. It has also flooded at least 1,500 times in the same period, causing millions of deaths.

Below: Nantian-men, Tai Shan.

Once past **Zhongtianmen** (Middle Gate of Heaven), the ascent becomes steeper. Passing **Wudaifu Song** (Pines of the Fifth Order of Officials), which, according to legend, were given this title by Qin Shi Huangdi after they sheltered the emperor from a thunderstorm, the path leads to **Nantianmen** (Southern Gate of Heaven). This is the entrance to the "realm of the immortals" on the summit, but first one must negotiate the earthly delights of **Tian Jie** (Heaven Street), a Qing-dynasty parade of shops and restaurants. Overnight climbers rest here wrapped in padded cotton overcoats, hoping to see the famous sunrise.

Map, page 191

Qufu

In 1919, Kong Linyu, a descendant of China's greatest philosopher, Kong Fuzi (Master Kong in English, Confucius in its latinised form), died at the age of 76 during a visit to Beijing. According to tradition, Kong Linyu's two daughters could not continue the family line. All was not lost, as his concubine was in the fifth month of her pregnancy. Rival factions of the Kong clan posted guards outside the chamber of the pregnant woman, but the doors of the house remained open, to make it easier for the "wise ancestor" to find his way back for rebirth. In February 1920, Kong Decheng was born, representing the 77th generation after Confucius. Succession was assured, and the "first family under heaven" celebrated. But 17 days later, Kong Linyu's first – and childless – wife poisoned her rival, the mother of the heir.

The scene of this family drama was **Kong Fu**, or **Kong Family Mansion** (open daily, 8.30am–5.30pm; entrance fee), in **Qufu ❸**, the home town of Confucius (551–479 BC) south of Tai Shan. Confucian ideology was given imperial status in the Han dynasty by Emperor Wudi, and subsequent emperors

Out of the 600,000 people who live in or near Qufu, 130,000 of them are named Kong.

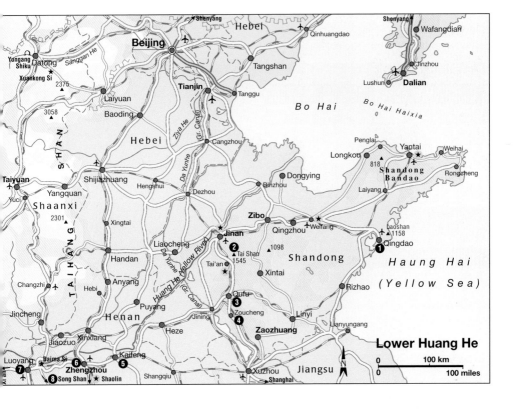

Lower Huang He

granted the descendants of Confucius lavish titles and property. Originally built in the 16th century during the Ming dynasty, the family mansion was home to the Kongs until 1948, when, with the Communist victory imminent, the last of the line left for exile in Taiwan. The outside of the residence looks rather plain, but the residence has around 500 rooms. Towards the end of the last century, the successor of the great sage was one of the wealthiest property owners in the country, presiding over his own judicial system and a private army. Several hundred servants were employed in the front part of the mansion, the Yamen, which consists of administrative buildings and audience halls. In the rear part, which could only be entered by a few selected servants and ladies' maids, were the living quarters of the ducal Kong family. Inside many rooms are valuable works of art, calligraphy, articles of clothing, and extensive archival material.

Confucius was buried under a simple grass-covered mound in **Kong Lin** (Confucius Forest; open daily, 7.30am–sunset; entrance fee), the Kong family cemetery a few kilometres north of town. The way to the mound is lined with human and animal figures in stone, a custom otherwise reserved for emperors. In fact, during imperial times Qufu was the sacred town of China.

Reflecting this former glory is the size and splendour of **Kong Miao**, the Confucian temple (open daily, 7.50am–4.30pm; entrance fee) in the centre of Qufu. A temple is supposed to have been built on this site as early as 478 BC, one year after the death of Confucius. The view on the walk north, past ancient cypress trees and stone steles, is dominated by the triple-roofed, 23-metre-high (75 ft) Kuiwenge (Pavilion of the Constellation of Scholars), first built in the 11th century. Passing the 13 pavilions in which steles with imperial inscriptions are kept, the path leads to the 18th-century Dacheng Dian (Hall of Great Achievements),

According to one popular account, Confucius was born in a cave near Qufu. He taught in the area for many years, travelling to neighbouring states to try and influence everyday politics with his moral doctrines.

BELOW: sunrise on Tai Shan.

the main hall of the temple and once the venue for sacrificial rites in honour of Confucius. The 28 stone pillars supporting the roof of the hall have a total of 1,296 dragons carved on them. The yellow roof on the main hall – yellow was a colour reserved for temples and imperial buildings – again emphasises the traditional importance of the great philosopher.

"It is a pleasure to have friends come to you from afar" is one of the most frequently quoted sayings of Confucius. In recent years, Qufu has taken this to heart by developing more and more tourist facilities. One of the latest and most expensive is the **Kongzi Liu Hua Cheng** (Confucius Six Arts City; open daily, 9am–4.30pm; entrance fee), a small theme park celebrating six arts promoted by Confucius: rites, calligraphy, music, archery, charioteering, and math.

Outside Qufu are many other historical sites. **Zoucheng ❹**, 25 kilometres (16 mi) south, is the home of the most famous follower of Confucius, Mengzi, or Mencius. It has Meng Fu (the Meng family home), Meng Lin (Mencius Forest) and Meng Miao (Mencius Temple). An unusual 6-metre-high (20 ft), pyramid-shaped tomb faced with grey stone, 4 kilometres (2.5 mi) east of Qufu, is **Shao Hao Ling**, said to be the burial place of a legendary emperor, Shao Hao, who ruled this part of China 4,000 years ago.

Kaifeng

Beyond western Shandong and in Henan Province, the ancient Chinese capital of **Kaifeng ❺**, visited by Marco Polo, is 240 kilometres (150 mi) west of Qufu. From the time of the Warring States (403–221 BC), the town served as a capital for seven dynasties, reaching its pinnacle in the Song dynasty. The 12-metre-long (40 ft) scroll painting *Upriver to the Qingming Festival*, dating from the

Map, page 191

BELOW: Kong Miao ceremony, main hall, and a tomb of a descendent of Confucius, in Qufu.

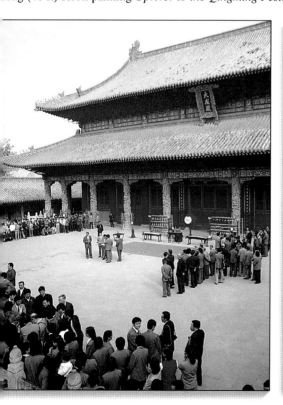

Song period and now stored in the Imperial Palace in Beijing, describes life in this flourishing commercial town. The town declined to a low point in 1644, when in the final year of the Ming dynasty, the dikes of the Huang He were opened to stop advancing Manchu soldiers. It was not a perfect defence, and more than 300,000 people lost their lives in the flood.

In the 20th century, industrial development often passed Kaifeng by, so it still has the look of an old Chinese town, although specific tourist sites are few. Most of the pounded-earth town wall survives. In northeast Kaifeng, just inside the old wall, is **Tie Ta** (Iron Pagoda; open daily, 8.30am–4.30pm; entrance fee), originally erected in the Song dynasty. With 13 stories and over 50 metres (160 ft) high, its name comes from the dark-brown glazed tiles, which from a distance look like cast iron. The oldest, best-preserved building in the town is **Po Ta** (Fan Pagoda; open daily, 8.30am–4.30pm; entrance fee), three storeys high and decorated with numerous carved Buddha figures in niches. Po Ta is outside the town wall to the southeast of the railway station.

Other sights in Kaifeng are Yuwangtai (Old Music Terrace), Longting (Dragon Pavilion) and **Xiangguo Si** (Prime Minister's Temple; Ziyou Lu; open daily, 8.30am–5pm; entrance fee), in the town centre. Built in 555, for many centuries Xiangguo Si was a centre of Buddhism in China. It was destroyed in the intentional flood of 1644, but was rebuilt. The highlights of the monastery are an octagonal pavilion with a remarkable wooden ceiling, and a gold-plated statue of Guanyin made from gingko wood.

Kaifeng once had a sizeable settlement of Jews, a fact recorded by Marco Polo during his alleged travels. A few Jewish people remain, but their synagogue was closed in 1850. A stele at a supermarket marks its site.

BELOW: abacus store and dealer.

Zhengzhou

An important railway junction on the Shanghai–Xi'an and Beijing–Guangzhou lines, **Zhengzhou ❻**, the capital of Henan Province, is 65 kilometres (40 mi) west of Kaifeng and 20 kilometres (13 mi) south of the Huang He (Yellow River). Although it was already populated during the Shang dynasty, the town did not attain great significance until the construction of the railway lines at the end of the 1800s. Due to its strategic significance, it was attacked several times by the Japanese during World War II. The Guomindang (Nationalist) troops blew up the dikes of the Huang He as a defence against the Japanese, in a tragic repeat of the Ming army's action at Kaifeng nearly 300 years earlier. Hundreds of thousands of people died in the flooding around Zhengzhou. The breaches in the dikes were repaired only in 1947, with American assistance. In the 1950s, Zhengzhou, badly damaged during the fighting of 1948–1949, was turned into an industrial and manufacturing area. Today, Zhengzhou is not a major tourist city, but it makes a useful stopover.

Ancient relics from around Henan form the most interesting exhibits at **Henan Sheng Bowuguan** (Henan Provincial Museum; 11 Renmin Lu; open daily, 8am–5pm; entrance fee), particularly those from the ancient Shang-dynasty city found in the eastern suburbs of modern Zhengzhou. These include some of the earliest forms of writing: characters inscribed on bones and tortoise shells.

Luoyang

The emperors of the Eastern Han dynasty (AD 25–220) moved the capital from Xi'an to **Luoyang ❼**, a state capital for 10 dynasties, and which flourished during the Tang and Song periods, then gradually lost its importance to the increas-

Map, page 191

A new dam, China's largest after the Three Gorges Dam, is being built on the Huang He. Designed to control 93 percent of the river's drainage, it is said to have the world's most complex system in a dam to regulate the accumulation of silt.

BELOW: Longmen Shiku.

Map, page 191

Between Zhengzhou and Luoyang are numerous homes burrowed in cliffs of dry loess, which is yellowish and somewhat soft, and is an ideal building material. Though dark inside, cave houses can be warmer in winter and cooler in summer than regular freestanding houses.

ingly prosperous coastal towns. Just prior to the Communist victory over the Nationalists in 1949, the 3,000-year-old town, 105 kilometres (65 mi) west of Zhengzhou, had just 30,000 residents. Industrialisation brought many factories, along with the grey concrete residential districts typical of most of China's industrial cities. **Luoyang Bowuguan** (Luoyang Museum; open daily, 8.30am–6.30pm; entrance fee) houses four special collections of bronzeware, ceramics, gold and silver artefacts, and jadeware, offering an overview of the development of the area from the neolithic period to the Tang dynasty. Some items date back to the Xia dynasty, around 4,000 years ago.

Founded in AD 68 and probably the oldest Buddhist temple in China, **Baima Si** (White Horse Temple; open daily, 8.30am–5pm; entrance fee) is 13 kilometres (8 mi) east of Luoyang. The name of the temple reflects an old legend about two monks who carried Buddhist scriptures from India on the back of a white horse. The texts became the first to be translated from Sanskrit into Chinese.

The most spectacular cultural site outside Luoyang is **Longmen Shiku** (Dragon Gate Caves; open daily, 8am–5pm; entrance fee), 13 kilometres (8 mi) south of town and along both banks of the Yi Jiang. These Buddhist caves were created between the 5th and 7th centuries, with most of the figures and grottoes sponsored by noblemen of the time. There are over 1,300 grottoes and 700 niches containing 40 pagodas, 2,780 inscriptions and more than 100,000 statues and images. Many of the most beautiful sculptures were stolen or beheaded around the start of the 20th century and are now in museums in the West. Despite this, the Longmen caves, like those at Datong and Dunhuang, provide a record of Buddhist art, reflecting different styles from the northern Wei dynasty to the Tang dynasty. The biggest statue is more than 17 metres (56 ft) tall, and the smallest one, less than 2 centimetres. The most striking part of the site is **Fengxian Si** (Temple for Worshipping Ancestors), with an exposed 17-metre-tall (56 ft) central Buddha statue surrounded by *bodhisattva* and heavenly guards. The ears of the Buddha are 2 metres long. Completed in 676 during the reign of the Tang emperor Gaozong, the statue's face is said to be that of empress Wu Zetian.

Song Shan and Shaolin

Known worldwide as the cradle of Chinese martial arts, **Shaolin Si** (Temple of the Small Forest; open daily, 8.30am–5.30pm; entrance fee) is 80 kilometres (50 mi) southeast of Luoyang at the western edge of **Song Shan ❽**, the central of China's four sacred Daoist peaks. It can be reached in 3 hours on a country road through farming villages. But fame has brought change. Far from a remote and romantic retreat where the wisdom of the ages is passed from master to novice, it is a major tourist area, as well as a place of pilgrimage for monks and lay Buddhists. Expect to encounter tour buses, hawkers, louts, and a 360-degree cinema. A training hall, where many foreign enthusiasts come to study, has been built next to the monastery. The founder of the monastery, the Indian monk Bodhidharma, reportedly sat facing the back wall of a cave and meditated for nine years. His silhouette is said to have been imprinted on the rock. Imperial sanction ensured the growth of Shaolin's reputation as a martial arts centre.

After being ransacked by Red Guards during the Cultural Revolution and closed for years, it was restored and now houses 70 monks. One of its greatest treasures are the 18 *arhat* frescoes, painted in 1828, depicting ancient monks in classic fighting poses that today's novices still emulate. In **Qianfo Dian** (Thousand Buddha Hall), depressions in the stone floor of this main hall of the temple serve as reminders of the tough combat exercises performed by the monks. Southwest of the monastery is **Talin** (Stupa Forest) and its 230 stupas and burial mounds, the oldest of which dates from the Tang dynasty.

Shaolin

The Shaolin monastery, in the Song Shan range near Luoyang, is the home of most Asian martial arts. Be it *qongfu* or karate, taekwondo or judo, they all originated in ancient China as fighting techniques of one individual against another. The bald-headed Shaolin monks, well-known for their inimitable shaolin boxing, recognised the signs of the times a few years back and made the monastery a commercial affair.

The monk who founded the Shaolin monastery came to the heights of Song Shan in 527. He realised that many Buddhist monks were unable to keep up demanding meditation exercises in complete quiet and concentration. Based upon observations of the movements of animals, the monk is said to have developed an exercise that he described as a method of physical training, and this in turn became the origin of shaolin boxing. This type of boxing must surely be one of the most sophisticated Asian martial arts.

Wushu – the art of fighting – is the general term for all self-defence sports, some of which may be carried out with the fists or the legs, or with the help of swords or lances. The mastery of the various techniques once entailed very esoteric knowledge, which would only be passed on within a family or a monastery, or from master to pupil.

For an outsider, the variety of *wushu* styles is rather confusing. One wushu technique is "long boxing" or *changquan*, which depends very much on dexterity and speed, and is particularly popular with children and youngsters. Another technique is imitation boxing, *xingyiquan*, which favours forceful and balanced movements, and is therefore popular with middle-aged people. *Nanquan*, the southern style of boxing, is characterised by small jumps and strong arm movements, often accompanied by loud screaming.

Taijiquan, or shadow boxing, is a gentle method that aims to dispel the opponent without the use of force, and with minimal effort. It is based on the Daoist idea that the principle of softness will ultimately overcome hardness. According to legend, it is also – just like shaolin boxing – derived from the movements of animals, geared to breaking the momentum of the opponent's attack and letting it disappear into thin air. It was originally a method of self-defence, but in China, it is mostly older people who use it for meditating and strengthening the body.

Shadow boxing depends on the application and mastery of the life energy *qi*, which can be directed to all parts of the body with the help of mental training. Qi must flow and circulate freely in the body.

The round movements of taijiquan are derived from this – they can be firm or loose, hard or soft, be directed forwards or backwards, but the movement must always be smooth and flowing. Through consistent practice of taijiquan, one eventually comes very close to the ideal of Daoism, namely the *wuwei* – doing without a purpose.

In a wider sense, qigong (breathing technique) is also part of wushu and dates back 3,000 years. In qigong, techniques for regulating the breathing can bring about concentrated thinking and a state of inner calm.

RIGHT: taiji practice using a sword.

XI'AN

Over 7,000 terracotta warriors found in the tomb of Qin Shi Huangdi, the first Chinese emperor, lure travellers to Xi'an. Beyond is Yan'an, where Mao Zedong strengthened the Communist Party.

Map, page 203

C hinese civilisation anchors itself at the bend of the **Huang He**, or **Yellow River**, in the central provinces of Shaanxi and Henan. Here, in the fertile valleys of the loess-covered landscape, the ancestors of the Han Chinese settled in the third century BC. The rich soil encouraged settlements, with the river irrigating the land. The erratic personality of the river – flooding and changing course with regularity – forced people to work in close cooperation. Eventually, the first and strongest states of China developed in this region.

Xi'an, capital of Shaanxi Province, lies in the protected valley of the river Wei, a few dozen miles west of the Wei's confluence with the Huang He. From this valley, the emperor Qin Shi Huangdi unified China for the first time.

During the Tang dynasty (618–907), Xi'an was the largest city in the world. Chang'an (Heavenly Peace), as it was called back then, was linked to many central Asian regions and Europe via the Silk Road, with thousands of foreign traders living in the city. For more than 1,000 years, Xi'an served as the capital for nearly a dozen imperial dynasties. Following the demise of the Tang dynasty, however, Xi'an's importance began to evaporate.

Hu fu, a tiger figure of the Qin dynasty uncovered in the Xi'an area.

Today, Xi'an is a modern industrial town of 5 million, known for its aviation and textile industries, and for its several universities and research institutes. Xi'an's climate has moderate seasonal variation, with mild winters, though in summer, the temperature can rise to 35°C (95°F). In early spring and autumn, the days are pleasantly cool; the rainy season lasts from July to October.

Old imperial centre

While the centre of Xi'an retains its historical layout from the Tang dynasty, it is largely overwhelmed by modern buildings, heavy traffic, and a persistent haze from the exhaust of cars and buses that leaves residents with reddened eyes and sore throats. Modern Xi'an has many new hotels and shopping centres, but it also has wide, tree-lined avenues that give shade in the hot summers and help distinguish Xi'an from most other provincial capitals in China, which are typically bleak and monochromatic.

Air-raid shelters were dug into Xi'an's ancient city walls as protection against Japanese bombing during World War II.

The metropolis was once surrounded by a large wall. The city itself stretched over 9 km (6 miles) from east to west, and nearly 8 km (5 miles) north to south. All roads in the town itself were laid out in a classic Chinese grid pattern, running straight north–south and east–west, meeting at right angles. While the grid layout remains today, the layout of the ancient city is not quite identical with the modern one. Although the walls built during the Tang dynasty no longer exist here, 14 km (9 miles) of the wall from the Ming dynasty still surround the centre. The city has been rebuilding the 12-metre (40 ft) -thick walls, and the moat outside the wall has also been reconstructed and integrated within a park. In certain places it is possible to climb on top of the walls for a nominal fee. In the city centre, where the city's two main roads intersect, is **Zhonglou ❶** (Bell Tower; open daily 8am–7pm, entrance fee). This renovated 36-metre (118 ft) tower dating from 1384 was moved to its present site in 1582, and today is encircled by downtown's shopping and commercial centre. East from Zhonglou east runs Dong Dajie, with many shops and restaurants. Dong Dajie intersects with Jiefang Lu, which runs to the north and leads to the railway station.

PRECEDING PAGES: some of the more than 7,000 excavated terracotta warriors, Xi'an. **LEFT:** each figure has individual facial features.

A few minutes' walk from Zhonglou to the northwest is **Gulou** ❷ (Drum Tower; open daily 8am–6pm, entrance fee). Resembling the Bell Tower and dating from the 18th century, it was rebuilt after the 1949 Communist revolution. More than 60,000 Hui Muslims live in Xi'an, and the Drum Tower highlights the Muslim quarter to the west. Lined with shops selling souvenirs, peasant paintings, and other local artefacts, alleys winding through the Hui neighbourhoods lead to **Da Qingzhen Si** ❸ (Great Mosque; open daily 8am–7pm). The mosque dates back to the Ming period and has been renovated several times. With its inner courtyards, it bears more resemblance to a Chinese temple. The main prayer hall is accessible only to Muslims. The area around the mosque is one of the most fascinating and diverse quarters to explore. Wander down an alley to get a sense of how the Hui Muslims live. Or happen upon one of the many food stalls selling delicious food, such as mutton-filled sesame rolls, or Xi'an's famous *yangrou paomo*, a delightful concoction of mutton, noodles, and flat bread cooked in a piping-hot broth. Some stalls, especially at the north end of the quarters, stay open to the wee hours of the morning.

Near the south gate of the city wall, **Nanmen**, and in a former Confucian temple is the **Beilin Bowuguan** ❹ (Forest of Steles Museum; open daily, 8.30am–5.30pm; entrance fee), with exhibits in three main buildings. The first building has a chronologically arranged exhibition of ancient Buddhist images from the early period of the Silk Road to the end of the Tang dynasty. The second building, the museum's centrepiece, features a "forest" of steles, or around 1,100 stone tablets on which ancient Chinese classical texts, including those of Confucius and Mencius, are engraved. In the early days when printing was still too expensive, this was a way of recording the classic texts for posterity and for

One stele at the Beilin Bowuguan is from the 8th century, carved in Chinese and Syrian and telling of the opening of a church by the Nestorians, an early Christian sect that came to China via the Silk Road.

BELOW: selling embroideries, and the pagoda of Dayan Ta, Xi'an.

the many scholars who came from far and wide. The third section of the museum houses animal sculptures in stone, Tang-dynasty stone friezes, bronzes, and jewels. The museum regularly holds special exhibitions.

Outside the city walls and about one kilometre from Nanmen, the 43-metre (141 ft)-high **Xiaoyan Ta ❺** (Little Wild Goose Pagoda; open daily, 8am–6.30pm; entrance fee) was built in the eighth century. It was severely damaged during an earthquake eight centuries later and repaired in the late 1970s, only to be damaged again in the early 1990s. It has still not been fully restored.

More noteworthy, however, is the 64-metre (210 ft)-high, seven-story **Dayan Ta ❻** (Great Wild Goose Pagoda; open daily, 8am–6.30pm; entrance fee), anchoring the southwest end of Yanta Lu. It was built at the beginning of the Tang dynasty, in 652, by Crown Prince Li Zhi as a memorial to his deceased mother. A noted monk, Xuanzang, went on a pilgrimage to India in 629, returning in 645 with many Buddhist scriptures, which were stored in the pagoda and translated into Chinese. The pagoda was originally part of a Buddhist temple complex. Although only a few buildings remain of the original temple complex of 13 courtyards and over 300 rooms, a few monks have returned, and the temple itself is now a popular place for locals to come and pray. None of the scriptures remain in the pagoda, having long since been removed to various museums and institutions around the country. The building, renovated in 1997, functions mainly now as a viewing terrace for the city of Xi'an and the surrounding countryside, though the view on many days is obscured by a layer of smog.

Near that pagoda, in the south of the city, is a true gem: the **Shaanxi Lishi Bowuguan ❼** (History Museum; open daily, 8.30am–5.30pm; entrance fee). Opened in 1991, the modern museum is housed in a handsome Chinese-style

Map, page 203

TIP

Except for Beijing, Shanghai and Hong Kong, Xi'an has probably the most five-star luxury hotels, mostly foreign-managed, in the People's Republic.

building with clear and attractive displays arranged in chronological order and labelled in English. Included are terracotta horses and soldiers, Ming and Qing pottery, and bronze cooking vessels that sit on tripods from the Shang and Zhou dynasties, as well as tools and pottery from the Palaeolithic and Neolithic ages.

Terracotta warriors

Museums in the city proper offer but a glimpse of Xi'an's greatest and most important attraction: **Bingmayong** ❽, the underground army of terracotta warriors (open daily, 8am–5.30pm, entrance fee). This vast treasure lies 35 km (20 miles) east of Xi'an, at the foot of Li Shan. In 1974, peasants digging a well uncovered these life-size figures of horses and warriors. Visitors are sometimes invited to meet one of the those farmers, if they are willing to buy a book autographed by the farmer.

The terracotta army is only part of a grand tomb, **Qin Shihuang Ling**, built by the first Chinese emperor, Qin Shi Huangdi. What is believed to be the main tomb of the emperor is about 1.5 km (1mile) to the west of the terracotta warriors. According to historic surveys, a splendid necropolis apparently depicting the whole of China in miniature is centred under the 47-metre-high (154 ft) mound. The necropolis itself is said to be immense in size. In order to open up the entire necropolis, 12 villages and half a dozen factories in the area would have to be relocated.

According to old records, the ceiling is said to be studded with jewels depicting the sky, and mercury was pumped in mechanically to create images of flowing rivers. Trial digs have revealed high contents of mercury in the soil. However, the official entrance to the tomb has yet to be found. Several hundred

BELOW: the sun rises on the terracotta army.

thousand workers spent 36 years building the tomb on the orders of the 13 year old emperor. It is said that workers and supervisors involved in its design and construction were buried alive within the tomb. Some speculation has it that the emperor was so superstitious and fearful that he had the necropolis built as a decoy and is, in fact, buried somewhere else.

In the main vault at Bingmayong, the figures are arranged in typical battle formation in 11 columns comprised of officers, soldiers holding spears and swords (many of them authentic weapons), and others steering horse-drawn chariots. Each figure is about 1.8 metres (5 ft 10 in) tall, and each head has been individually modelled with unique facial expressions. The second and third vaults, discovered in 1976, are significantly smaller in size but feature similar figures in battle formation. Some of the over 7,000 terracotta figures thus far excavated have been restored by archaeologists and are exhibited here. In the main hall of the exhibit building is a model of the entire necropolis (main tomb and other tombs); videos are shown of the excavation work. Scientists continue to dig for more figures, and visitors can watch the work in progress while walking the original site's perimeter. However, visitors are strictly forbidden from taking photographs of the terracotta figures.

Another building, set up as a small museum, contains a sensational exhibit: the miniature model of a bronze chariot, with horses and coachman, from the Qin dynasty. The carriage was discovered in 1980 and is similar to carriages used by Qin Shi Huangdi on his inspection tours, alive and above ground.

Though the place is packed with tour groups of every nationality on any given day, it is well worth the effort to persevere through the crowds and even linger awhile to admire the magnificent displays.

Map, page 203

When the terracotta warriors were first uncovered from their earthen graves, their cheeks were rosy and they wore painted uniforms. Exposure to air turned the statues black.

Map, page 203

Excavations at Banpo revealed artefacts several thousands of years old.

BELOW: good-luck charm, Yan'an.
OPPOSITE: autumn colours over temple roof.

Outside Xi'an

On the way back to the city from Bingmayong is **Huaqing Chi** (Hot Springs o Huaqing), in use for over 3,000 years. There are baths and pavilions in the par area, which would be pleasant enough if not for the throngs of tourists. Durin; the Tang dynasty, this is where the most famous concubine in China, Yan; Guifei, bathed. Farther up in the mountain is the place where Chiang Kaishe was recaptured by two of his own generals during an escape attempt, taken pris oner in 1936, and persuaded to join with the Communists against the Japanese

A visit to the neolithic settlement of **Banpo** ❾, (open daily, 8am–6.30pm) 1(km (6 miles) to the east of Xi'an, is also interesting. Some relics, includin; ceramics, weapons, and even infant burial jars from the Matriarchal Yangsha(culture, are exhibited. The excavated village shows the outlines of houses an(cooking areas, and is part of the museum.

About 50 km (30 miles) northwest of Xi'an is **Xianyang** ❿, which served a the capital during the reign of Qin Shi Huangdi. Xi'an's airport is located her(today. Few traces are left of the palaces said to have been built here. There is museum in a former Confucian temple that contains more than 3,000 artefact from the time of the Warring States era and the Han and Qin dynasties. The col lection of miniature terracotta horses and soldiers from the Han dynasty – eac about 50 cm (20 in) high – is impressive.

About 85 km (50 miles) to the northwest of Xi'an is **Qian Ling** ⓫, the join burial place of the Tang emperor Gaozong and his wife, the empress Wu Zetiar The tomb itself has not been opened. The approach to the tomb is guarded by "ghost avenue" of large stone sculptures of animals and dignitaries. There i also a group of 61 stone sculptures, with their heads missing, apparently repre senting foreign dignitaries. The peasants of the time ar(said to have knocked the heads off during a famine believed to have been caused by the presence of thes(foreigners. The tombs contain exquisite frescoes from the Tang dynasty.

Yan'an

Mao Zedong's Long March during the civil war witl the Nationalists ended in Wuqi, in 1936. The leader then established their base in **Yan'an** and stayed for decade. This small market town of just under 60,00(people is 270 km (170 miles) to the north of Xi'ar where a river cuts through the dry mountains.

During the Cultural Revolution and until the 1970s Yan'an was the national centre of pilgrimage, as wel known to cadres as the Imperial Palace in Beijing. Th(headquarters of the military commission of the Chines(Communist Party, along with the houses of the Com munist leaders Mao Zedong and Zhu De, are still pre served in the Fenghuang mountains north of Yan'ar The Museum of the Revolution contains over 2,00(documents and objects from the Yan'an period, which i still praised by many older functionaries of the Chines(Communist Party as the "golden revolutionary era".

Around Yan'an it is still possible to see the caves tha are typical of this central loess landscape, and whicl were used during World War II by the leaders of th Communist Party and Red Army.

ANCIENT TREASURES FROM THE ROYAL TOMBS

The royal tombs of ancient China offer a fascinating glimpse on the life, wealth, and beliefs of the early emperors and rulers

Almost all our knowledge of ancient China comes from the artifacts found in the tombs of princes and warriors. As early as 3000 BC, neolithic caves were elaborately carved and filled, but it was during the ascendancy of the Shang kings, around 1200 BC, that they were the most dazzling. The dynasty had capitals at Anyang and Zhengzhou, and nothing was spared in the attempt to help Shang royalty reach the afterlife. Sacrifices were on an epic scale. Some 700,000 people laboured to build the tomb of the first emperor, and many of those who worked on the tomb were killed. Others simply died in the process. Courtiers and concubines were slaughtered in the death chambers, and both horses and charioteers perished in order to accompany their master (or mistress) into the underworld. Bureaucrats devoted their careers to overseeing the inventories of the tombs, which they prepared in great detail to present to the officials of the underworld, including deeds to prove the deceased owned the land he or she had been buried on.

BRONZE AND JADE

The Shang tombs were constructed during the Bronze Age, and some remarkable bronze items, many of them showing vivid imagination and skill, have been found in the tombs. Perhaps the most dramatic attire of the deceased was the jade shroud. The mineral is very hard and could not be carved. It had to be abraded, worn down to make the small rectangular squares that were then linked by gold or silver thread to fit the body, and to form plugs for the orifices. Jade suits were used from the mid-western Han to the end of the Eastern Han period (141 BC–AD 220) and around 40 have come to light so far. That of Prince Liu Sheng (154–113 BC) and his consort Princess Dou Wan were discovered in 1968 inside coffins in a palatial underground warren of stables, banquet hall and larders. Some 4,000 burial items were found with them.

◁ JADE SUIT
The jade suit of Liu Sheng, Prince of Zhongshan. Knotted with 1,100g (39oz) of gold wire, it took 10 years to make and has 2,498 jade plaques, which carefully follow this *bon viveur*'s paunch.

▽ BRONZE DRAGON
A fanciful bronze creature from the 5th-6th century BC sticks out its tongue. It may have been a stand for a musical instrument. The dragon had many variants down the centuries.

◁ RITUAL VESSEL
This is a vessel for food offerings, from the tomb of Lady Fu Hao, a warrior queen of around 1200 BC. Her tomb near Anyang contained 250 ritual bronzes.

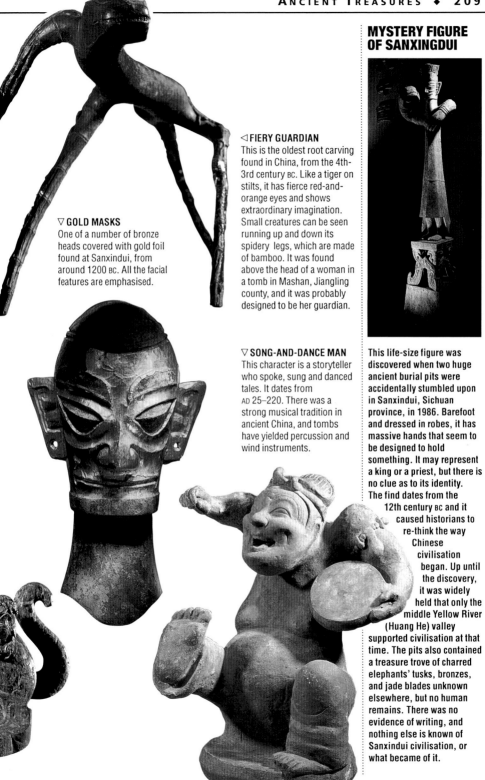

MYSTERY FIGURE OF SANXINGDUI

◁ **FIERY GUARDIAN**
This is the oldest root carving found in China, from the 4th-3rd century BC. Like a tiger on stilts, it has fierce red-and-orange eyes and shows extraordinary imagination. Small creatures can be seen running up and down its spidery legs, which are made of bamboo. It was found above the head of a woman in a tomb in Mashan, Jiangling county, and it was probably designed to be her guardian.

▽ **GOLD MASKS**
One of a number of bronze heads covered with gold foil found at Sanxindui, from around 1200 BC. All the facial features are emphasised.

▽ **SONG-AND-DANCE MAN**
This character is a storyteller who spoke, sung and danced tales. It dates from AD 25–220. There was a strong musical tradition in ancient China, and tombs have yielded percussion and wind instruments.

This life-size figure was discovered when two huge ancient burial pits were accidentally stumbled upon in Sanxindui, Sichuan province, in 1986. Barefoot and dressed in robes, it has massive hands that seem to be designed to hold something. It may represent a king or a priest, but there is no clue as to its identity. The find dates from the 12th century BC and it caused historians to re-think the way Chinese civilisation began. Up until the discovery, it was widely held that only the middle Yellow River (Huang He) valley supported civilisation at that time. The pits also contained a treasure trove of charred elephants' tusks, bronzes, and jade blades unknown elsewhere, but no human remains. There was no evidence of writing, and nothing else is known of Sanxindui civilisation, or what became of it.

THE SILK ROAD

Map, page 148

Who can ignore or dismiss the ancient mystique of the Silk Road? For centuries the main conduit of commerce between Europe and China, it passes through China's most remote areas.

China's vast western region is accessible to travellers along the classic Silk Road, although historically, the trade route was never called such until a German geographer gave it that romantic name in the late 1800s. In AD 200, this transcontinental route linked the Roman Empire in the west with the imperial court of China. Trade along the route was carried on by foreign traders who belonged to neither of the two old empires.

Before the discovery of the sea route to India, the Silk Road was the most important connection between the East and West. It experienced its last great era during the time of the Mongols, when the entire route from China to the Mediterranean was part of the Mongol empire. This ancient trade route starts in the old capitals of Luoyang and Xi'an (then called Chang'an), reaches the Huang He (Yellow River) at Lanzhou, then skirts westward along deserts and mountains before dividing into two routes at the oasis of Dunhuang.

The northern route goes to Hami, another oasis, then winds along Bogda Shan to the oasis of Turpan. It then comes close to Ürümqi, ascends across several mountain passes through the Tian Shan range to Korla and finally finishes at Kashi (Kashgar). The southern route leads from Dunhuang between the river oases on the northern slopes of Kunlun Shan (Altyndagh) and the sand desert of Taklimakan Shamo, in Tarim Pendi (Tarim Basin). The overland link quickly lost is importance as seagoing trade developed. Today, it has been replaced in China with the Lanzhou–Ürümqi railway, the last segment of which was completed in the 1990s.

To the north looms the **Gobi Desert** , one of the world's great deserts, covering around 1.3 million square kilometres (500,000 sq mi). Noted for its vicious sand storms and extreme summers and winters, the Gobi holds important reserves of coal and oil.

The Gobi Desert, the northern extent of China's empire, is felt in Beijing. In winter, cold-air masses form over Russia, then as they move south, they carry fine dust from the Gobi to the streets of Beijing.

Lanzhou

Surrounded on all sides by mountains, present-day **Lanzhou** ❷ is a depressing industrial city, smothered in a layer of thick grey smog. (In an only-in-China turn, the local government began to level the surrounding mountains in 1997 to try and ease the pollution.) There are two places from which to get an overview of the city: **Baita Shan** (White Pagoda Hill), north of the Huang He (Yellow River), is a pleasant park with the White Pagoda Temple on top of the hill; and **Gaolan Shan**, a mountain range to the south of the city, which is accessible by chair lift. A few hours spent at the **Gansu Sheng Bowuguan** (Provincial Museum) is well worth the effort of travelling to the western edge of town. This museum features an impressive exhibition of cultural artifacts from Gansu and the Silk Road, starting from the Dadiwan cultures of 8000 BC up through the Yuan dynasty. Also impressive is a comprehensive map of the various routes used during the height of the Silk Road. In addition, the museum houses a giant fossil of a mammoth, tusks still intact.

Other than the museum and Lanzhou's justifiably acclaimed *niurou lamian* (beef noodles), the city is best used as a base for visiting some fascinating sights around the area. **Bingling Si** (Thousand Buddha Caves, though there are really only 183) is located 140 kilometres (90 mi) west of Lanzhou and comprises

PRECEDING PAGES: ancient wall at Gaochang, near Turpan. **LEFT:** young girl of western China.

Buddhist grottoes carved into a cliff face rising 60 metres (200 ft). The caves contain Buddhist sculptures, frescoes, and statues. The most famous and impressive work is a 27-metre-high (89 ft) statue of Maitreya, the future Buddha. Be warned that entry into the more interesting caves requires significant cost. It is also difficult to get to Bingling Si on one's own, but local travel agencies run day-trips that involve travel by both bus and boat.

Highly recommended is a trip to **Xiahe**, a dusty but quaint town 280 kilometres (175 mi) to the southwest of Lanzhou, by direct bus (8 hours) or by changing buses at Linxia. Chief amongst its attractions is the **Labrang Monastery**, the second-largest of China's six great lamaseries practicing the Yellow Sect (Gelupai) of Tibetan Buddhism. The monastery has more than 2,000 monks in residence and six academic institutes, as well as important Buddhist cultural relics and 10,000 books of Tibetan scripture. The surrounding grasslands and mountains where one can hike amidst Tibetan nomads are another powerful draw.

Lanzhou to Jiuquan

The varied loess landscape and the many contrasts offered by the desert make the overland journey between Lanzhou and Jiuquan, an ancient crossroads and garrison town, truly extraordinary. In the south, the distant snow-covered peaks of **Qilian Shan** flank the railway line. The train reaches a flat, 800-kilometre-long (500 mi) corridor when it arrives at the old administrative and garrison town of **Wuwei** ❸, which became a district capital in 115 BC. The famous Flying Horse, a bronze statue from the Eastern Han period and excavated in 1968, comes from near Wuwei. The original is now in a museum in Beijing; a beautiful replica is in the provincial museum.

TIP

From Lanzhou, trains going west stop at Jiayuguan (17hrs), Liuyuan/Dunhuang (23hrs) and Daheyan/Turpan (34hrs). Trains have three classes, but sleepers are impossible to book at the station. Try a travel agent.

BELOW: monochromes of the western desert.

Zhangye, the capital of the district of the same name, is 140 kilometres (90 mi) to the west. Zhangye, founded in 121 BC as a garrison town, has a bell tower (originally a drum tower) in the town centre. It dates from 1509, with a bell from the Tang period. The wooden pagoda found here also dates from the Tang period. Its first six floors, out of a total of eight, are actually made of brick.

Map, page 148

Jiuquan ❹, a thriving industrial town 200 kilometres (125 mi) further west, was founded in 111 BC as a garrison outpost. Between 127 and 102 BC, the Han emperors relocated nearly a million peasant families to this town, including at least 700,000 victims of a devastating flood in Shandong. Today, the old town quarter around the drum and bell towers is changing; small alleys are being torn down and modern buildings erected. Out in the desert, China's ambitious commercial space program launches Long March rockets into the heavens.

A good 30 kilometres (20 mi) farther to the west is **Jiayuguan** ❺, since 1372 a part of the western end of Wanli Changcheng, or the Great Wall. The fortification, 1,800 metres (5,900 ft) above sea level, was completed four years after the rise of the Ming dynasty. A square inner courtyard is enclosed by walls and two gates. On top of the 10-metre-high (33 ft), 640-metre-long (2,100 ft) wall are 17-metre-high (56 ft) watch towers from the late Ming and the early Qing periods. The wall was first restored around 1507, and again during the Qing period, and then once again in recent years.

Restored fortification on the western stretch of the Great Wall, near Jiayuguan.

At the southern entrance rises an elevated pavilion-like stage. Dignitaries used to watch plays from the pavilion opposite on the right-hand side. The wall, from the Ming period and still intact, stretches southwest to the foothills of Qilian Shan and northward to Bei Shan. The structure, which dominates the landscape, is particularly impressive when approached from the west. A monument with

the inscription "Strongest Fort of the World" has stood outside the western ga￼ since 1809. Superlatives aside, many visitors in recent years have reported bein￼ disappointed with the fort, which can also be viewed from a distance on the tra￼ bound for Liuyuan. Those who insist on seeing the western end of the Gre￼ Wall would do well to spend no more than half a day here.

Weijin Bihua Mu, eight tombs from the Wei (220–265) and the Jin dyna￼ ties (265–420), are 20 kilometres (12 mi) to the northeast of Jiayuguan. The￼ contain wall murals with scenes from daily life, but only one of the eight tomb￼ is open to visitors. Consequently, few foreign tourists make it out here.

At **Liuyuan** and **Anxi** ⑥, the road to Dunhuang turns to the southwest awa￼ from the railway line, crossing the river Shule. About 40 kilometres (25 m￼ before Dunhuang is a well-preserved watchtower dating from 1730, an examp￼ of the type of communications used at that time. By daylight, flag signals wer￼ given from the top platform; at night, fire signals lit the night.

To reach Dunhuang by rail, travel to Liuyuan, which is about 140 kilometre￼ (90 mi) outside of Dunhuang. From there, continue southwest for several hou￼ by bus. After crossing the drained plain of Shule He, remnants of the Great Wa￼ from the eastern Han period are visible. The structure of clay-and-fascine con￼ struction is surprisingly easy to see.

Dunhuang

The oasis town of **Dunhuang** ⑦ lies in an irrigated cotton-producing oasi￼ Between cotton fields and threshing areas at the edge of the town, **Baima T￼** (White Horse Dagoba) is reminiscent of Beijing's White Dagoba. Baima Ta i￼ where the white horse of the famous travelling Indian monk Kumarajiv￼

344–431) is said to have died. The Dunhuang **Xian Bowuguan** (County Museum) has some local finds, visual displays, and models of the oasis, reflecting the historic significance of this settlement, as well as a few manuscripts from the Mogao Caves.

There are 492 caves at the **Mogao Ku**, some 25 kilometres (15 mi) southeast of the town. Of these, around 30 are open to visitors, though a typical morning or afternoon session with a local guide will cover only about a dozen or so grottoes. The first caves are said to have been built by the monk Lezun in 366, the last ones carved out at the time of the Mongolian conquest in 1277. After that, Mogao sunk into oblivion, until the monk Wang Yuanlu settled here at the turn of the 20th century. The first cave he opened is the one now numbered 16. In the adjacent cave, number 17, he found more than 40,000 manuscripts. The Hungarian-British explorer Sir Aurel Stein bought 6,500 manuscripts from Wang between 1907 and 1914; a Frenchman bought a further 6,000 scripts.

The grottoes show an uninterrupted history of Chinese painting, particularly of landscapes, over a period of nearly a thousand years. Visiting them is the high point of travels here. It's difficult to know beforehand which caves will be open. One of the most beautiful caves (#323) shows an Indian Buddha statue made from sandalwood being presented to the reigning emperor. Most impressive is a 35-metre-high (115 ft) statue of Maitreya Buddha carved into the cliff face.

Other tourist attractions in Dunhuang are **Yueyaquan** (Crescent Moon Lake) and **Mingsha Shan** (Singing Sand Mountain), 6 kilometres (4 mi) south of Dunhuang. The lake, hidden in the sand dunes, is a disappointment, but the latter, a mountain range of pure sand, is particularly impressive, etched against a cloudless blue sky. Watching the sunset from the top is an unforgettable experience.

Map, page 148

In the early 1900s, foreign archeologists stripped Mogao Caves of manuscripts, frescoes, and statues. In 1997, the first of these – some 7th-century Buddhist manuscripts – were finally returned by a Japanese business-man, whose father had bought them a decade earlier in a Tokyo bookstore.

BELOW: express train from Beijing to Ürümqi, and Mogao.

Xinjiang region

The population of Xinjiang, an autonomous region and China's largest province is predominantly Islamic. The Uighur people of this autonomous republic speak Turkish and are Muslims, and they constitute approximately 45 percent of the total population. The Han Chinese population has increased from eight percent in 1940 to over 40 percent, living mostly in the larger cities and in new settlements, where the youth from the huge towns of the east, who were "sent to the countryside" after 1958, settled. The smaller oases and nomad areas – and also the agricultural areas in the north of Xinjiang – are still predominantly populated by people of the Uighur and Kazakh minority groups.

Continuing west of Liuyuan, **Turpan** ❽ can also be reached from the regional capital Ürümqi in a half-day bus journey or two-hour train trip. The railway station serving Turpan is at Daheyan, 60 kilometres (40 mi) from the town. The road from Ürümqi leads eastward through the desolate industrial belt of Ürümqi, then through pastures along the northern slope of Tian Shan to Dabancheng, a small industrial town near a pass leading to the richly-forested valley of the Baiyang He (White Poplar River).

At the end of the Baiyang He, the road reaches a stony desert stretching to the edge of **Turpan Pendi** ❾ (Turpan Basin). This oasis, 150 kilometres (90 mi) long from east to west, is a depression 150 metres below sea level, second in the world below sea level only to the Dead Sea. The exact low point is Aydingkol Hu (Moonlight Lake), a salt lake in the basin that is drying up and is 154 metres (505 ft) below sea level. In summer, the temperature in the oasis, bordered in the north by Tian Shan and in the south by Kuruktag, rises to 47°C (117°F).

Only a few old buildings have been preserved in Turpan. **Sugong Ta (Emir**

Several joint Chinese-Japanese expeditions to the Xinjiang region in western China have uncovered important dinosaur fossil fields, especially from the Jurassic era.

BELOW: Sugong Ta.

Minaret), built with clay bricks in 1777 and finished in 1788, and the sparsely furnished mosque next to it are the symbols of the town, and have been designated a historical monument. Sugong Ta's 72 steps leading to the top are now closed to visitors. The mosque, the largest in Turpan, can hold up to 3,000 people and is used only during important Muslim festivals.

In an ancient and fantastic underground irrigation system – the **Karez wells** – melting water from the mountains is channelled to the oasis over long distances underground (to prevent the water from evaporating) using the force of gravity. The subterranean canal system is over 3,000 kilometres (1,800 mi) long.

Towards the east, **Huoyan Shan** ❿ (Fiery Mountains), a range of bare sandstone mountains rising up to 1,800 metres (6,000 ft), stretch for 100 kilometres (60 mi). As a barrier to the search of legendary sutras, the mountain range achieved fame in the novel *The Journey to the West*, which describes the travels of Xuanzang. Born in Luoyang around 602, Xuanzang entered a Buddhist monastery at the age of 13. He departed for India in 629 with the support of the Tang emperor Taizong (627–649), and studied and debated at the Buddhist academy Nalanda, near present-day Patna. He returned after 17 years to China with 557 scrolls and taught in Chang'an (present-day Xi'an), dying there in 664.

Just 45 kilometres (30 mi) to the southeast of Turpan is the ruined city of Gaochang, the ancient Karachotcha or Khocho. The town was founded as a garrison under the Han emperor Wudi (140–86 BC). During its heyday, it had 30,000 inhabitants, over 3,000 monks, and more than 40 Buddhist monasteries. Today, one can see the division of the town into a centre with sacred buildings, and suburbs with bazaars and housing estates.

Six kilometres (4 mi) to the northwest are the **Astana ancient tombs**, a bur-

Map, page 148

BELOW: Gaochang, and Islamic architecture, Xinjiang.

ial ground for Gaochang's dead, with well over 500 tombs. Only three tombs are open to visitors. The first has a wall mural with four figures depicted in earth, gold, jade, and stone, symbolising appropriate Confucian behaviour at different stages of life. The second tomb has a wall mural of everyday life that also contains six types of geese; because the geese are not indigenous to the area, they have come to symbolise the internee's yearning for home. The third tomb contains two mummified bodies.

To the north of Gaochang is the ancient cave monastery of **Bezeklik** (or Qianfodong, Thousand-Buddha Caves). The trip through the canyon leading to Bezeklik begins at a watchtower dating from the Qing period (around 1770) located opposite the cave monastery site Samgin (Murtuq), used from around 450 to the 1200s. The caves of Bezeklik – around 80, of which only five can be visited – have been carved into the cliff face some 80 metres (260 ft) above the western bank of the river.

The plunder of valuable paintings by German and British archaeologists damaged the pictorial representation of the Buddha and *bodhisattva* (redemption deities) in a number of caves. After 1860, Islamic fanatics destroyed most of the facial depictions, and the destruction was near-complete during the Cultural Revolution in the late 1960s. What remains today is hardly interesting, though the caves themselves are still an impressive sight.

Ten kilometres (6 mi) to the west of Turpan, and predating even Gaochang, is the ruined city of **Jiaohe Gucheng** (Old City by Two Rivers), which in the past was called Yariko or Yarkhoto. It was founded in the Han period and served as the centre of a kingdom until the fifth century. Jiaohe lies on a plateau between two rivers, a natural fortification. Civil wars and lack of water at the time of

BELOW: Bezeklik.

Mongol rule in the early 13th century brought the town to ruins. The central sacred site and the remnants of Buddhist monasteries and stupas in the north-west, which are most prominent among the ruins, are still well preserved. The remains of underground dwellings, which offered protection from the summer heat and the freezing winter, are of special interest.

Map,
page 148

Ürümqi

The capital of the Xinjiang autonomous region, **Ürümqi** ⑪, is a huge town 170 kilometres (100 mi) west of Turpan and 900 metres (2,900 ft) above sea level, which has the dubious honour of being the farthest away from the ocean of any large city. About 75 percent of its 1.5 million population are Han Chinese and only 20 percent are Uighur and Hui. The proliferation of industry here has resulted in substantial environmental pollution.

The **Xinjiang Sheng Bowuguan** (Provincial Museum) is worth a visit. Apart from significant archeological finds, it also exhibits life-size models of the houses and tools of the most important nationalities in the region. Also on display are some 3,000-year-old corpses of European and Mongolian ancestry.

In the town, there are numerous small mosques and bazaars full of activity. A pavilion in the style of a Chinese garden lodge and a small pagoda, both symbols of the town, are located on **Hong Shan** (Red Mountain), which also offers a good view of the town. The town itself has modern high-rises and wide, tree-lined streets. Older buildings date from the time of the Soviet presence and influence, and are obvious by their sterile exteriors.

It is worth taking an excursion to the breathtaking **Tianchi** ⑫ (Lake of Heaven), due east some 110 kilometres (70 mi) from Ürümqi and lying 1,900

TIP

The bus between Kashi and Ürümqi takes from 36 hours (straight sleeper) to 72 hours. If taking a sleeper, know beforehand that you'll usually be stuck in the bunk for the entire trip.

BELOW: Tianchi, near Tian Shan.

metres (6,200 ft) high on the slopes of **Tian Shan**, at the foot of the 5,500-metre high (18,000 ft) Bodga range. The road between Ürümqi and Tianchi is no always well-maintained and makes for some bumpy rides, but the journey passes through some scenic landscape. The lake is complete with tourist facilities.

One-hundred-fifty kilometres (90 mi) west of Ürümqi is the Chinese settle ment of **Shihezi**, whose structure and layout go back to its colonisation unde the Qing emperor Qianlong. The town of over 550,000 people is typical of the newer Han Chinese towns in areas with artificial irrigation.

Kashi

Much farther to the west, 1,500 kilometres (900 mi) on the other side of the grea vastness of Tarim Pendi, lies **Kashi**  (Kashgar), on the Tumen river in the middle of an irrigation oasis with cotton and other crops. Kashi is closer to Moscow, Islamabad, Delhi, Kabul, and Teheran than to Beijing, with the borders of Kyrgyzstan, Tajikistan, Afghanistan, and Pakistan nearby.

The climate is extreme: in winter the temperature can fall to minus 24°C (–11°F), and in the summer months it regularly reaches above 40°C (104°F) The frost-free period lasts 220 days each year.

The population of a quarter of a million is predominantly Uighur. Kashi first became Chinese around 200 BC, again during the Tang period, and finally during the period of the Qing emperors Kangxi (1662–1722) and Qianlong (1736–1975).

Aitika Mosque (Id Kah Mosque), in the town centre, has been renovated many times and is China's largest mosque, able to hold 6,000 worshippers Although paint is peeling off its central dome and two flanking minarets, the

BELOW: Aitika Mosque.

Aitika Mosque.

building, dating from 1442, still dominates the town. Behind the gate are open, tree-lined squares for prayer. One hundred metres behind is the Great Prayer Hall, open only for Friday prayer. The steps in front of the side walls are a popular meeting place, particularly for the elderly. On religious feast days, up to 50,000 worshippers come for Friday prayer.

Next to the mosque is **Id Kah Square**, with snack bars, tea houses, craft shops, workshops, and numerous small stores selling everything from flowers to cameras. There has also recently been a proliferation of modern shopping centres smothered by loud Uighur music.

To the north of the mosque and square runs an extremely lively bazaar street of barber shops, book and fur traders, blacksmiths, bakers, tailors, and, directly by the mosque, dentists. The covered bazaar has just about anything for sale.

On the northeastern outskirts of town on Izlati Road is the **Western and Central Asian Market**, another extensive and rambling area where traders from all over have stalls selling fine silk, lace, cotton, knives, hats, and local handicrafts. Prices are very reasonable if you bargain well.

Further afield, about 5 kilometres northeast of town, is **Xiangfei Mu**, the Abakh Hoja mausoleum, dating back to the 16th century and renovated in 1980 and again in 1997. All the buildings of the mausoleum are examples of traditional Uighur architecture.

Abakh Hoja (Aba Hezhuo), who died in 1695, was an outstanding political and Muslim religious leader in Kashi. His sarcophagus, one of 57 in the mausoleum that house 72 of his descendants, lies on an elevated pedestal in the centre of the central building's main hall, which is reminiscent of a mosque (but not facing Mecca), and is flanked by a slightly leaning minaret. In the near left

Map, page 148

TIP

Forget about travelling by ground between Kashi and Lhasa. The route is officially closed, and more than one foreigner has been heavily fined for trying to do so.

BELOW: Uighur children at spice stand.

Map, page 148

corner is the sarcophagus of Xiangfei (Fragrant Concubine), the daughter of the last Hoja, Ali Hoja, and the great-granddaughter of Abakh Hoja, and source of the mausoleum's popular name.

According to legend, Xiangfei is said to have refused to sleep with the emperor Qianlong, who had abducted and taken her to Beijing after the repression of a rebellion here in 1758. Since she would not consummate the relationship, she was forced to commit suicide by the empress dowager, the emperor's mother. Her body was taken back to Kashi in a carriage, the remnants of which are exhibited in the small mosque.

The most important weekly event is the *basha*, or the Sunday market, still held by the banks of the Tumen, which has several bridges over it as well as steps leading to town. Tens of thousands of visitors, buyers, and sellers come to this market, reputedly the biggest in Asia. Nearly all Asian minorities visit the market – Pakistani traders especially – giving it a cosmopolitan atmosphere.

The **mausoleum of Mahmud al Kashgarli** (1008–1105) was built outside of Kashi. The building, which is about 45 kilometres (30 mi) away along the road to Pakistan, towers over a mosque once destroyed in an earthquake.

Mahmud came from the house of the ruling Karachanid family and was one of the most important scholars of his time. Exiled from Xinjiang after the clan's overthrow in 1058, he returned to Kashi shortly before his death. The mausoleum is visited mostly by Turkish travellers, and usually only by foreign tourists on their way back to Kashi from Taxkorgan.

About 20 kilometres (12 mi) north of Kashi, the Buddhist **Sanxian Dong** (Caves of the Three Immortals), on a sheer rock face by the Qiakmak River, are not only less interesting than those of Bezeklik or Dunhuang, but are relatively inaccessible and not worth the effort.

BELOW: dunes of the far western basin. **RIGHT:** sheep on the flanks of Qilian Shan, near Jiayuguan.

Farther to the southwest, 200 kilometres (120 mi) from Kashi at the beginning of the high peaks of the Pamir range, is **Karakul Lake**. The ice-covered peaks of Muztagata (7,550 m/24,800 ft) and Kongur (7,700 m/25,300 ft), the second- and third-highest peaks in the Pamirs, can be seen from Kashi on clear days.

Taxkorgan

About 250 kilometres (150 mi) south of Kashi is **Taxkorgan** (Tashkurgan), 3,600 metres (11,800 ft) above sea level. It is the last outpost in China before Pakistan, and is the capital of an autonomous district of the same name. A majority of Tadzhik people live here. According to accounts by Ptolemy (around AD 140), traders from East and West used to trade their goods here.

Continuing south from Taxkorgan leads to Pakistan's **Karakoram Range** (Black Wall). The 750-kilometre-long (470 mi) track across the 4,700-metre-high (15,400 ft) **Khunjerab Pass** is sometimes difficult due to weather or sometimes to secular unrest; the pass was reopened in 1986 after prolonged disturbances in the area. About 270 kilometres (170 mi) south of the pass is the nearest airport in Pakistan, at Gilgit. Along the mountain road are many wall murals, engravings, and sculptures from the era of the Silk Road. There is also exquisite scenery that is probably unmatched anywhere else in the world.

THE NOMADS OF REMOTE CHINA

Far from China's industrial cities, in the remote reaches of northern and northwestern China, nomads still wander grasslands and deserts.

Comprised mostly of minority groups, China's nomadic peoples are as closely tied to the laws and moods of nature as they are to their own history and customs. Historically, the nomadic tribes of the north and west have always been a problem for China's rulers because of their nomadic tendency to be independent. In the northwest, the Kazakhs, Kirgyzis, and to a lesser extent, Tajiks can be found wandering in different parts of the Xinjiang Autonomous Region, in what is at times an uneasy coexistence with the ruling Han Chinese.

THE KAZAKH WAY

Like their Mongolian brethren, the Kazakhs lead a life of pastoral nomadism based on seasonal migration. Where they continue to exist, tribes still wander together with their grazing stock.

Between April and October, when they are on the move, the Kazakh nomads often pitch their yurts at the foot of Tian Shan, where they graze their herds of sheep, horses, goats, and cattle. In the winter, they retire to the valleys where they live in adobe houses. Muslim Kazakhs live mainly on the meat and dairy products from their herds, with milk tea a popular beverage.

The Kazakhs live in yurts – round tents with a lattice framework that is covered with felt and animal hide. Yurts have a skylight opening in the centre, and they can be easily dismantled and repacked. The inside of the yurts are decorated with colourfully-embroidered cloths, along with beautifully-woven tapestries and carpets.

◁ YURTS AND NOMADS
Easily dismantled, the traditional yurt is well suited to the nomadic lifestyle. The roofs of the yurts of wealthier Kazakhs are often embroidered.

INTERIOR OF YURT △
The interior of a Kazakh yurt near Tianchi lends a homey feeling. Yurts are a source of pride to Kazakhs, and for a given exterior surface area, yurts offer the most efficient use of interior space.

◁ KARAKUL LAKE
In summer, Kirgyzi nomads can often be found wandering the magnificent Pamir Mountains of Xinjiang, in western China.

CARING FOR LAMBS △
Almost all of China's nomadic people herd animals.

GOAT GRABBING ▽
In the Taklimakan desert, Xinjiang, a traditional Kazakh sport tests a person's horsemanship while handling a goat carcass. This "goat grabbing" competition is also an excellent occasion for young Kazakh men and women to socialise.

THE MONGOLIANS OF GENGHIS KHAN

Perhaps the most famous nomads in Chinese history are the Mongolians, who rose from disparate groups of wandering tribes to become the conquerors of the largest empire of land in world history.

In 1206, Genghis Khan united the different warring Mongolian tribes and created an efficient fighting force that began its brutal conquest of Asia and Eastern Europe. The skills forged from years on horseback on the Mongolian plains enabled the Mongols to vanquish armies ten times their size and instill terror wherever they went.

Under the leadership of Genghis Khan's grandson, Kublai Khan, the Yuan dynasty reached its zenith in the late 1200s, stretching from the Yellow Sea to the Caspian Sea.

Today, although some Mongolians have settled in Chinese cities like Hohhot in Inner Mongolia, many still wander the grasslands. For these nomads, the importance of their traditional ways of life can be seen in the celebration of *nadam*, an annual gathering on the grasslands featuring archery, horsemanship, and wrestling that harkens back to the vigorous years of Genghis Khan himself.

THE CENTRE

*Anchored by Shanghai, China's largest city in population,
China's central core is defined by the Chang Jiang.*

While much of ancient China's roots are found in the north-east, much of China's contemporary history – the last two hundred years – arose along the central stretch of its eastern seaboard, and along the corridor etched into the terrain by the Chang Jiang, more commonly known to Westerners as the Yangzi River.

The great city of Shanghai is not known for imperial buildings or court intrigues, nor for its depth of ancient history. Its history of note is recent, starting in the 19th century with the foreign concessions that divided up the city amongst the colonial powers.

Shanghai came into being as a city of commerce, and as with all great centres of commerce, monuments were of little importance. This may be changing, however. China has decided that Shanghai, its largest city with over 14 million people, is to be its cornerstone for the 21st century. No small feat, considering the richness of China's past 40 centuries. But over US$40 billion worth of new infrastructure is being poured, quite literally, over the 19th-century colonial residue, reshaping not only the city's contours, but its personality. Marking the achievement will be a 459-metre-high (1,506 ft) financial centre, the world's tallest building when completed in 2001.

Upriver along the Chang Jiang, the vast eastern region is pock-marked with industrialisation, which has increasingly masked the traditional textures of cities such as Suzhou, Wuxi, and Hangzhou. As the southern terminus for the Grand Canal, or Da Yunhe, which connected northern and southern China, Hangzhou was once one of China's most important urban centres. Farther upriver, but not by much, Nanjing has taken on less of the industrial veneer that now personifies most Chinese cities. Nanjing is a little bit greener, and a little bit more gracious. Perhaps its memorialised reminder of the Japanese rampage of World War II has left it more appreciative.

Farther west is Sanxia, the Three Gorges. A century ago, travel through the gorges was probably the world's most difficult commercial river journey. Now, the gorges are a routine tourist excursion, although with the same exquisite scenery. But the scenery is changing as the new dam, set to be the world's largest, takes shape. By the time it is finished in 2009 and the reservoir filled, the gorges will be 175 metres (575 ft) less deep, and the homes of over one million people will be submerged.

Beyond the gorges is Chongqing, a bit of an odd city for China, as it sits on a rocky promontory, not a flat expanse. In 1997, it became the world's largest municipality in both area and population, taking much of its new wealth from neighbouring Sichuan.

In the centre of China is Sichuan, long protected by mountain ranges on three sides. Sichuan is home to a rather spicy cuisine, and to the few remaining giant pandas in the world.

PRECEDING PAGES: the pedestrianised Nanjing Lu at night. **LEFT:** classical court dance.

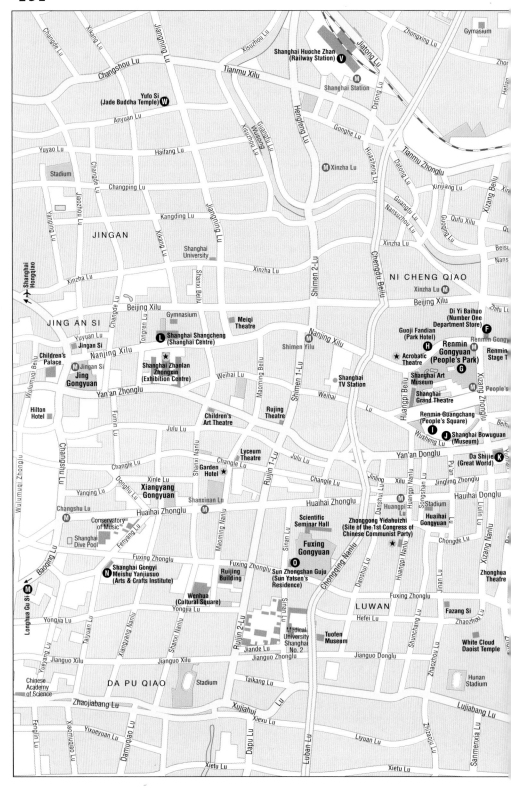

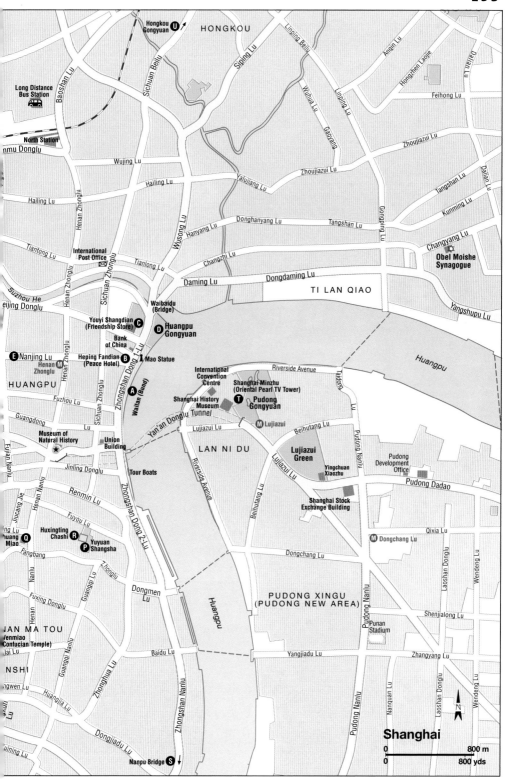

Shanghai

0   800 m

0   800 yds

SHANGHAI

Map, page 232

Back in what some might consider its glamourous colonial days, Shanghai was called the Paris of the East. Today, the government intends it to be the heir to Hong Kong, whatever the cost.

Shanghai sits on the **Huangpu Jiang**, an 80-km (50 mile)-long tributary of Chang Jiang, locally also known as the Yangzi, and which provides Shanghai (lit. upriver to the sea) with ocean access. Once a muddy fishing village, Shanghai today is undergoing an impressive transformation that leaves one breathless. Where there were once neighbourhoods of small houses, there are now high-rises. Where there were once handsome colonial-era buildings, there are now glitzy hotels. Indeed, to visit Shanghai today is to visit a giant public-works project: new highways, new ports, new bridges, new office towers. In fact, in the late 1990s, Shanghai required so many construction cranes that there was a regional shortage in the rest of Asia.

The intent of all this urban revamping is nothing less than to make Shanghai a world-class regional centre of banking and finance. China's former leader Deng Xiaoping himself chose Shanghai as the country's economic spearhead, one that is intended to surpass Hong Kong by 2010. Land that was rice paddies and farmland just a few years ago is suddenly dominated by skyscrapers and instant communities. Marking this ambition is the Shanghai World Financial Centre, which will be the world's tallest building at 459 metres (1,506 ft) high when it is completed around 2001.

Administratively, Shanghai is a metropolis without a province, made up of surrounding rural districts and a dozen city districts. But locals and outsiders agree on one thing: *ren tai duo* – there are too many people in China's largest city. The greater metropolitan area has over 14 million inhabitants. The city proper covers 375 square km (145 sq miles) and has 8 million inhabitants. Whatever the exact number, the population density of Shanghai is one of the highest in the world.

China's most worldly, fashionable, and open people are very individualistic, speaking a dialect that nobody else can understand, eating a different cuisine, and generally considering themselves to be light-years ahead of their nearest competitor, Beijing. Indeed, Shanghai's higher living standard, pulsating night life, and its cosmopolitan air make Beijing seem a bit dowdy in comparison.

For getting away from the central district, the bus routes are somewhat Byzantine, and the buses themselves an exercise in chaos. It's always better to take cabs, which are plentiful and easy to hail. Shanghai recently built an elevated ring road that circles the city, but traffic can still be maddening. However, the ever-expanding subway system is superb.

A cosmopolitan history

Distinctly a city of commerce, the region was already a trading centre in AD 960, flourishing for centuries and

OPPOSITE: the Bund at night. **BELOW:** colonial architecture along the Bund.

becoming an important trading port. Japanese pirates were attracted by this wealth, and after numerous attacks, Shanghai built a protective wall in the 16th century. The wall surrounded the old city centre until 1912, just south of the Bund in a circular area defined by the roads Renmin Lu and Zhonghua Lu. While the wall eventually humbled the Japanese pirates, it failed to impede Western colonial intrusions. As a result of the Opium Wars in the 1840s, the British imposed upon China the Treaty of Nanjing, which, among many things, opened up Shanghai to Westerners.

Foreign concession areas took up most of what is now central Shanghai, save for the old walled Chinese part of the city. Soon Shanghai became the place to be – a city with the best culture, most opulent dance halls, largest volume of business, the tallest buildings. It became a mix of cultures that was always to define its internationalism, even up to present times.

New ideas also allowed for radicalism, a Shanghai tradition. The Communist Party was founded in the city in 1921, and the Cultural Revolution of the 1960s not only began here, but had its headquarters in Shanghai. But despite the enthusiasm of the Red Guards to demolish everything not defined as Socialist Realism – and that included anything foreign, Buddhist, or simply old – many buildings from colonial times have survived in the city. Unfortunately, however, many may not survive China's push to modernise.

On the waterfront

One gets a fine view of this modernisation along Zhongshan Dong Lu, which parallels the western bank of the Huangpu Jiang. Most foreigners know this road as the **Bund** (Waitan) . During Shanghai's heyday, the Bund was occupied

BELOW: Huangpo Jiang.

Map, page 232

by the European, American, and Japanese banks, trading houses, clubs, consulates, and hotels. After liberation, the Communist Party took over the structures for their own use. Today, these neo-classical buildings have been renovated by the government as a sightseeing showcase and are beautifully lit up at night by floodlights. Opposite is a waterfront promenade extending over a kilometre and packed with locals and tourists, hustlers and hawkers alike. In the early morning along the Bund, directly opposite the Peace Hotel, the Shanghai day starts before dawn, with crowds of people practising *taijiquan (ta'i chi chuan)* and other exercises.

Where Nanjing Lu meets the Bund and river is the **Heping Fandian (Peace Hotel) B**, known as the glamorous Cathay Hotel in the old days and Shanghai's most treasured colonial building, with a 1930s atmosphere. Views of the Bund and Shanghai skyline are excellent from its eighth floor. Have breakfast or dinner on old silver plates and meditate on the transforming waterfront. After dinner, have a drink in the first-floor German pub to the sounds of the famous Old Peace Hotel Jazz Band, which has been performing jazz in the city since the early 1920s.

At the northern extent of the Bund, near the **Youyi Shangdian C** (Friendship Store) – a favourite of tourists shopping for arts and crafts, and silk products – and **Huangpu Gongyuan D** (Huangpu Park), the boulevard crosses **Suzhou He** (also called Wusong), a canal that cuts east-west across the city and empties into the river. Huangpu Gongyuan is said to have once had signs prohibiting "dogs and Chinese" from entering the park, although this is unsubstantiated. The old bridge across the canal, **Waibaidu**, has been somewhat overshadowed by a newer parallel bridge. Formerly called Garden Bridge, Waibaidu connected

Once called the Cathay Hotel, the Peace Hotel was <u>the</u> place to stay in the 1930s. It was built by Victor Sassoon, who made millions in the trade of opium, then reinvested it in Shanghai real estate.

BELOW: bird fancier on his way.

the American and British districts until, in 1863, both merged into the International Settlement (Shanghai Zujie), which stretched west and east, with Yan'an Lu its southern border. From 1937 onwards, the bridge defined the border with the Japanese-occupied territory north of the Suzhou. Just at the northern end of the Waibaidu are some examples of old Shanghai architecture, including the Shanghai Mansions hotel, Shanghai Stock Exchange, and the blue-walled consulate of the Russians, the only foreigners who have succeeded in retaining their original consulate building.

Daily river cruises offer views of the Bund and the industry and scenery along the banks of the Huangpu. The one-hour and half-day trips travel from the Bund (the dock is at Jinling Lu) to Wusong and back.

Central Shanghai

The heart of the city is primarily in Huangpu and Jingan districts, making up much of the International Settlement of old Shanghai. **Nanjing Lu** Ⓔ, Shanghai's main thoroughfare, crosses east–west through these two districts. At night neon signs light up the street until the wee morning hours, and in the day, hordes of pedestrians, bicycles, and cars make it what some have called the busiest street in the world. It is often said that Shanghai is nothing but a consumer's paradise, bereft of culture. Street activity along the Bund and Nanjing Lu would certainly enforce Shanghai's reputation as a shopper's paradise – not limited to just clothes, silk, or electronic goods, but also traditional theatre props and musical instruments, art, and even collector's stamps. Old state-owned food stores run alongside the glitzy commercialism of new department stores and the chic fashion of Burberry's, Esprit, and Christian Dior.

BELOW: Nanjing Lu at night.

Halfway down the street from the Bund at the corner of Xizang Lu is the store
that sells everything – the state-owned **Di Yi Baihuo** (Number One Department Store), a typical experience in Chinese domestic shopping. Further west,
wedged between Fuzhou Lu to the south and Nanjing Lu to the north, is **Renmin
Gongyuan** (People's Park). Once a race course of the powerful *taipan* before
1949, it is now the largest, but most unremarkable, park in the city. The **Shanghai Meishuguan** (Shanghai Art Museum; open daily, 9am–5pm; entrance fee)
is currently at 425 Nanjing Lu. It is due to move a short distance east along the
street into the former racecourse club, until recently the Shanghai Library.

North of the park on Nanjing Lu is yet more colonial history. The art-deco
Guoji Fandian (**Park Hotel**) was once the tallest hotel in Asia and almost as
glamourous as the venerable Peace Hotel on the Bund. South of Renmin
Gongyuan is **Renmin Guangchang** (People's Square), a social centre for
the locals and often crowded with families flying kites, kids rollerskating, and
people ballroom dancing and practising martial arts. It is a main stop on the
Shanghai subway.

The new and impressive **Shanghai Bowuguan** (Shanghai Museum; open
daily, 9am–5pm; entrance fee) is also found here at the south end of the park.
This modern and elegant facility, opened in 1996, offers a spectacular collection in a superb setting. Its eleven state-of-the-art galleries house China's first
international-standard exhibits of paintings, bronzes, sculpture, ceramics, calligraphy, jade, Ming and Qing dynasty furniture, coins, seals, and minority art.
The bronze collection is reputedly the best in the world. Information is well presented in English, but the highly informative audio guide is also excellent. This
one socialist project that got it right.

**Map,
page 232**

TIP

The Chinese acrobat is
world-famous. See the
evening show at
Shanghai Zaji Chang,
or the Acrobatics The-
atre, located on Nan-
jing Xilu, a little west of
the Park Hotel.

BELOW: Renmin
Guangchang, with
the Shanghai
Museum in the
background.

Just south of Renmin Guangchang on Xizang Lu is the **Da Shijie** ⓚ (Great World), Old Shanghai's notorious gambling, cabaret, drug, and prostitution den. It has been restored into an entertainment centre offering everything from acrobatic shows to fantasy rides and even a Guinness Book of World Records hall.

Continuing west on Nanjing Lu, Shanghai's commercialisation continues 4 km (2½ miles)to the western extent of the street. The Soviet-built **Shanghai Zhanlan Zhongxin** (Shanghai Exhibition Centre) is at Xikang Lu. Across the street is a foreign business, travel, and social centre, the **Shanghai Shangcheng** ⓛ (Shanghai Centre). This huge complex houses the Ritz-Carlton Hotel, two residential towers, a multinational office building, and a shopping area that includes major airline offices, Western stores, and chain restaurants such as the Hard Rock Café.

To the south

In the south of the city, on the road with the same name, is **Longhua Gu Si** ⓜ a temple and pagoda built in 242 and since destroyed and rebuilt several times. The temple site consists of seven halls that, after the turmoil of the Cultural Revolution, are once again being used for religious purposes. Adjoining the temple, the Longhua Hotel was designed especially for Buddhist travellers and includes a vegetarian restaurant, but it welcomes all visitors.

Considerably closer to central Shanghai, the former French Concession – founded in the 1840s and in the southern part of downtown, south of Yan'an Lu – has kept its own charming character with French-inspired architecture and avenues. Its main road, Huaihai Lu, is perhaps the more pleasant choice for shopping or just strolling. It offers a more relaxed, upscale atmosphere, with many shops, designer boutiques and cafés, but still reflects French and Russian influence. Two hotels – the Jinjiang Hotel (Lao Jinjiang Fandian) and the Garden Hotel (Huayuan Fandian) – on Changle Lu at Maoming Lu (one block north of Huaihai) feature some of old Shanghai's most luxurious architecture.

South of Huaihai on Fenyang Lu is the old French mansion that houses the **Shanghai Gongyi Meishu Yanjiusuo** ⓝ (Shanghai Arts and Crafts Research Institute; open daily, 9am–5pm). Visitors can watch artisans working and purchase a variety of traditional Chinese work. The new **Shanghai Tushuguan** (Shanghai Library; open daily, 9am–5pm), one of the largest in the world, is located further west on Huaihai Lu. Opened in 1996, the library features the most up-to-date information technology. Many foreign consulates are also located in the vicinity.

Sun Zhongshan Guju ⓞ (Sun Yatsen's Residence; open daily, 9am–4.30pm; entrance fee) is on Xiangshan Lu at Sinan Lu, just south of Huaihai, near Fuxing Gongyuan (Fuxing Park). Mao Zedong and Zhou Enlai also lived and worked in this area.

At Xingye Lu and Huangpi Lu is the historical site of the First National Congress of the Communist Party of China (Zhonggong Yidahuizhi). You can enter the original room where the first delegates founded the Party. It remains in its original form, complete with a table set for 13 people at tea.

BELOW: Longhua Si.

The Old City

From the north, paralleling Sichuan Lu, Henan Lu intercepts Renmin Lu, which together with Zhonghua Lu defines a circle outlining the edge of the Old City. The city walls paralleled this small ring road until 1912, when they were knocked down; then the moats were filled in, and the two streets were laid down.

Before 1949, the Old City remained under Chinese law and administration while the rest of central Shanghai was carved up by foreign powers. Most of the residents in these old back alleys were Chinese. Eventually it became notorious as a gangster-and-opium slum. Today, the vices are gone, but the tiny lanes, crowded but quaint neighbourhoods, and small houses still exist.

At the heart of the Old City is **Yuyuan ❿** (Yuyuan Gardens; open daily, 8.30am–4.30pm) and **Chenghuang Miao ❿** (Temple of the Town God). Yuyuan Gardens is one of the few old tourist sights left in the city – and touristy it certainly is. Since the 18th century, the complex, with traditional red walls and upturned tile roofs, has been a marketplace and social centre. The bazaar has been recently renovated, complete with chrome and shiny glass. As befits a bazaar, here one can find both schlock and traditional Chinese trinkets. There is also a basement antique market. Don't be put off by the exterior of the various restaurants. The best one is certainly the **Huxingting Chashi ❿** (Huxingting Teahouse), the city's oldest teahouse in the middle of the small lake, whose famous zigzag bridge leads directly to Yuyuan. The second floor of the teahouse serves some of the best tea in town and is one of the only places in Shanghai that offers a truly tranquil break from the city's chaos. A bit of old China is preserved here, although it also attracts a young clientele. Various musicians meet here nightly to play traditional Chinese music.

Map, page 232

If the old doesn't go, the new won't come.
— CHINESE PROVERB

BELOW: Yuyuan.

Legend has it that Yuyuan's gardens were built in the 16th century by the eccentric and gifted landscape architect Zhang Nanyang, who was commissioned by the Pan family of the Ming court. The traditional rock-and-tree garden is filled with artificial hills, carp-filled ponds, dragon-lined walls, and pavilions connected by zigzagging bridges. One can well imagine how this park served as the home base for the rebels of the Society of Small Swords during the Taiping rebellion. Today, an exhibition about this secret society is located in their former headquarters, the Spring Hall. Just west of Yuyuan at Henan Lu is the Fuyou Lu Sunday antique market. Hawkers come here as early as 4am to set up their goods, usually directly on the ground. The tiny lane is bustling with people by mid morning, by which time the best goods are usually already sold. You'll find an eclectic collection of antiques including old maps of Shanghai, baskets and boxes, porcelain, and old watches, plus some scattered modern goods and Mao paraphernalia.

On the east side

Shanghai harbour is the fourth-largest in the world and an important factor in making Shanghai China's most important industrial base. Across the river from the Bund, on the eastern side, is the special economic zone of **Pudong Xinqu**, or the **Pudong New Area**. But this is not just another urban development project. Pudong is a massive US$40 billion undertaking that will significantly redefine Shanghai. It will have a new container port, an international airport, and acres of new high-rises and skyscrapers, including the future home of the Shanghai Stock Exchange. As work progressed, however, many analysts were beginning to wonder if the Chinese had been too ambitious with Pudong, as many of the high-

BELOW: colonial ambiance in a restaurant.

ses were lacking tenants, and the regional economy was increasingly stagnant. The **Nanpu Bridge** ❺ connects Pudong to western Shanghai. An underwater tunnel for vehicles links the Bund with Pudong, and several more tunnels are planned. (It is hoped that the civil engineers working on it have studied Shanghai's subterranean history: since 1920, when the problem was first noticed, Shanghai has sunk several metres.)

Map, page 232

If for some reason you are unable to locate Pudong from your perch on the Bund, look once more across the river for the impossible-to-miss **Shanghai Minzhu** ❼ (Oriental Pearl TV Tower; open daily, 8am–9.45pm), the huge space-ship-like observation and broadcast spire on the other side of the river, with globes lit up in bright colours at night. High-speed elevators to the top bring visitors to a 360-degree, bird's-eye view of the city. Asia's largest department store can also be found in Pudong. The 10-story mega-mall Yaohan Department Store (Ba Bai Ban) on Zhangyang Lu sells everything from clothing to cars.

The business-minded may want to look further into Pudong to witness its special economic areas – the central financial area of Lujiazui, the Waigaoqiao bonded zone, and the Jinqiao industrial zone. There is a rather unspectacular beach at the eastern edge of Pudong that touches the East China Sea.

North of Suzhou He

From Suzhou He, Sichuan Lu leads northward into Hongkou District, which has retained some of its old southern Chinese charm. As in much of the Old City and the former international and French settlements, laundry is draped from balconies on bamboo canes, and in the side streets, elderly people sit outside on stools to chat, chop vegetables, play cards, or guard the bedding airing out in

Oriental Pearl TV Tower, in the Pudong area.

BELOW: street food.

**Map,
page 232**

Novelist Lu Xun.

OPPOSITE: Nanpu
Bridge to Pudong.
BELOW: Jade
Buddha, Yufo Si.

the street. An evening walk through the streets of Hongkou can be enlighten
ing, although the black, murky canals emit a terrible odour in summer.

At the edge of the northern part of Sichuan Lu is **Hongkou Gongyuan**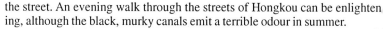
one of the loveliest parks in Shanghai. Within the park is a museum and the
grave of Lu Xun, the most famous Chinese writer of the 20th century. He lived
in Shanghai from 1933 until his death in 1936, and his former home on Dalu
Xincun, a side alley of Shangyin Lu, is just a few minutes' walk east of the park.

Hongkou was already in Japanese hands before the occupation of 1937 and
had the nickname of Little Tokyo. In fact, a large percentage of Shanghai's res
ident 30,000 Japanese lived in Hongkou. Ironically, despite Japan's alliance
with Nazi Germany, Little Tokyo became a haven for Jewish refugees from
Europe. Until 1941, China was one of the last countries open to immigrants,
requiring neither entry visa nor proof of financial means. Although these con
ditions were tightened after 1939, the Jewish community – considered a valuable
asset in Shanghai – gave others assistance with money and job opportunities.
By 1939, 14,000 refugees had reached Shanghai. In 1943, more than 20,000
Jewish refugees lived in the Hongkou ghetto, when the Japanese, meeting
demands from their Nazi allies, forced them into the "Designated Area for State
less Refugees." Today, the **Moxi Huitang** (Ohel Moshe Synagogue), built in
1927 by Hongkou's Jewish residents, still stands on Changyang Lu and now
houses a small museum dedicated to Shanghai's Jewish community.

Due west a few kilometres is the **Shanghai Huoche Zhan** (Shanghai Rail
way Station), which lies in Zhabei District. Here, the day begins even earlier
than in the parks, with crowds of migrants from all over China camping out
either about to leave or having just arrived. The train station has the reputation
of being the dingiest and roughest part of town, but
Shanghai has recently begun efforts to build up the area
by constructing nice hotels, apartment buildings, classy
Western shopping malls and commercial centres.

To the west

West of the train station, on the south side of Suzhou
He on Anyuan Lu, is **Yufo Si** 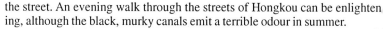 (Jade Buddha Temple,
open daily except Chinese New Year). The temple is
famous for its two Buddha statues made of white jade,
brought back to China from Burma (Myanmar) by the
monk Huigen in 1882. The statues were brought to
Shanghai in 1918, when the temple was completed. One
of the statues, of the Sleeping Buddha representing his
entry into nirvana, is a special rarity. However, the other
white-jade statue of the Seated Buddha – 2 metres (6 ft)
tall, decorated with jewels and weighing 1,000kg (2,200
lbs) – is the more famous. About 70 monks are in resi
dence here, overseeing religious and tourist activities
and operating a public restaurant.

To the southwest is the special commercial zone of
Hongqiao, with a large concentration of Western hotels,
office buildings, and exhibition centres is located here.
The **Shanghai Hongqiao International Airport**
(Shanghai Hongqiao Feijichang) lies at the western end
of Hongqiao Lu. It was once an elite colonial road lined
with glamorous country villas of old Shanghai's expa
triate residents. Some of the homes are still standing.

OUTSIDE SHANGHAI

Escaping the frenzy of Shanghai is not easy. The two easiest escapes, Suzhou and Hangzhou, are themselves top draws for Chinese tourists. Yet there are places worth an excursion.

Map, page 251

In heaven above there is paradise, on earth there are Suzhou and Hangzhou." Repeated like a mantra, this well-known line of poetry is about what are considered to be the garden spots of the country. Small in scale, full of charm, and home to quiet spots tucked away amid fussy cities, even today these towns along **Da Yunhe** , or the Grand Canal, live up to the reputation of the poem by Yang Chaoying, who lived during the Yuan dynasty.

The origins of Da Yunhe go back to the period of the Eastern Zhou dynasty (770–256 BC). Since the end of the 13th century, this waterway has stretched north to south over a distance of more than 1,800 kilometres (1,100 mi). It crosses the provinces of Zhejiang and Jiansu towards Beijing and connects the rivers Qiantang, Chang, Huai, and Huang.

Like the Great Wall, Da Yunhe was assembled from smaller pieces. Preparing for war, the king of the state of Wu had a canal built from Suzhou to Chang Jiang (Yangzi River). It was completed in 495 BC, and was 85 kilometres (50 mi) long. A few years later, the canal was extended to Yangzhou, and the two rivers Chang Jiang and Huai He, in the north, were linked. The emperor's fascination created a link from what was then the capital, Luoyang, to Beijing in the north and to Huai He in the southwest and, subsequently, from Zhenjiang to Hangzhou. As a result, the capital Luoyang was eventually connected with the north and with the economically important southern region by a canal system of 2,700 kilometres (1,700 mi).

The customs tributes that were collected from the canal were transported to the capital. Rare wood and bricks, used for the Imperial Palace in Beijing, were transported on the canal system as well. The Yuan dynasty (1279–1368), which made Beijing the capital, extended the canal system, thus connecting the capital directly with Hangzhou and shortening the distance by 1,000 kilometres (620 mi), to 1,800 kilometres (1,100 mi).

Hangzhou

At the beginning of the 12th century, the Chinese court was defeated in its battle against the "northern barbarians" and fled south. In 1138, the newly formed empire of the Southern Song dynasty took **Hangzhou** as its temporary residence. The town flourished, with officials, writers, and scholars moving there as the dynasty blossomed. It had already been a fortified town since the Tang period, when in the seventh century the building of the Da Yunhe had strengthened its presence, with Hangzhou as the southern terminus for the canal.

The city of Hangzhou was the subject of many poems in the Tang period (618–907), such as in the work of the poet Bai Juyi (772–846), who became governor of the town and had a dam built at Xi Hu (West Lake) that still bears his name, Baidi. Hangzhou became well-known during the Southern Song period. Its population increased from less than half a million to over one million, thus making Hangzhou one of the largest cities in the world at the time. It was nearly destroyed in the second half of the 19th century, during the Taiping rebellion, and not much of antiquity remains now of this town. The city walls and gates have disappeared, and the numerous old canals have been filled in. Today, Hangzhou is the capital of Zhejiang Province, one of the most prosperous

TIP

Nowadays, the Grand Canal is little used for commerce and public transport. Much of it, in fact, is not navigable. But for travellers, parts of it can be an interesting route for a boat trip. However, the sights are not always pleasant, as areas along the canal are often industrialised, and the canal can be tainted with trash and foul smells.

PREVIOUS PAGES: sailors have long adorned the Chang Jiang delta. **OPPOSITE:** Buddha Sakyamuni, Lingyin Si monastery.

regions in China. Its products include silk and Longjingcha (Dragon Well Tea), and its pharmaceutical industry and academy of arts are well-known throughout China. Over a million people live in the city, which covers 430 square kilometres (165 sq mi).

While it is a good walking town, Hangzhou, and particularly Xi Hu, the main attraction, is a tourist trap, with many visitors, especially weekend travellers and honeymooners from nearby Shanghai.

It is said that every Chinese city has a **Xi Hu**, a West Lake. In fact, there are around 30 West Lakes in China; Hangzhou's is perhaps the most famous. Legend has it that Xi Hu was created from a pearl dropped by a phoenix and a dragon. Originally, Xi Hu was only a bay on the river, but since the Tang period, it has been extended into a lake that now covers 5.6 square kilometres. Its eastern shore is close to the town, while the other shores are surrounded by forested mountains often shrouded in mist, which gives the landscape a romantic allure.

The pagoda at **Baochu** to the northeast stands out against the sky, a symbol of the city. It was built in 968, and destroyed and rebuilt several times. The present pagoda dates from 1933 and is 45 meters (150 ft) high.

In the west of the town, at the end of Lingyin Lu, which is easily reached by bus, is the beautifully-situated **Lingyin Si** (Monastery of the Hidden Souls), a popular attraction from where one can see Feilai Feng (Peak that Flew from Afar). The monastery was founded in 326 by the Buddhist Indian Hui Li. He thought he saw in the Peak that Flew from Afar a part of the Gradhrakuta Mountain in India, thus the inspiration for its name.

Since the second half of the 10th century, the rock walls of the mountain have been carved with about 300 sculptures and inscriptions. The earliest figure is

In the southern part of Xi Hu is the island of small seas, Xiaoyingzhou. It was created in 1607 as an artificial coral reef. The island can be reached only by boat.

BELOW: Hangzhou's Xi Hu, or West Lake.

thought to date from 951. A group of three Buddhist deities are at the right hand entrance to the Qinlin cave.

Past these figures is the monastery, one of the ten most famous Buddhist monasteries in China. The most popular figure is at the foot of the mountain: the fat-bellied Buddha from the Song period, one of the most touched and photographed figures anywhere and believed to bring good luck. Up to 3,000 monks used to live in the 18 pavilions and 75 temple halls on the mountain peak. Behind the entrance gate to the temple and two stone columns inscribed with Buddhist texts is Tianwang Dian (Hall of Heavenly Kings), where another statue of the Maitreya Buddha can be seen, guarded by the two Heavenly Kings standing at its side. In Daxiongbao Dian (Precious Hall of the Great Heroes), which lies behind two nine-story pagodas from the tenth century, is the gilded statue of the Buddha Sakyamuni, which is more than nine meters (30 feet) high and made of precious camphor wood. It is the tallest figure made from this material in China.

Towards the northwest is the village of **Longjing** (Dragon Well). Visitors will be hectored constantly in Hangzhou to buy some of the tea from this village, which is somewhat touristy, with obligatory guided tours through shops. For the most part, workers abandoned the tea industry here and returned to private farming some years ago, and the vessels used communally in the past for drying the tea leaves are now set in motion only when the tourist buses arrive.

An excursion to one of the surrounding villages, such as Meijiawu, about 20 minutes by car to the south of Hangzhou, is probably more worthwhile. If fit enough, the trip through the lovely landscape with its famous bamboo grove can be made by bicycle, hired in town. This village also grows tea, and the villagers, who have not yet been overrun by tourists, are very hospitable and will-

Map, page 251

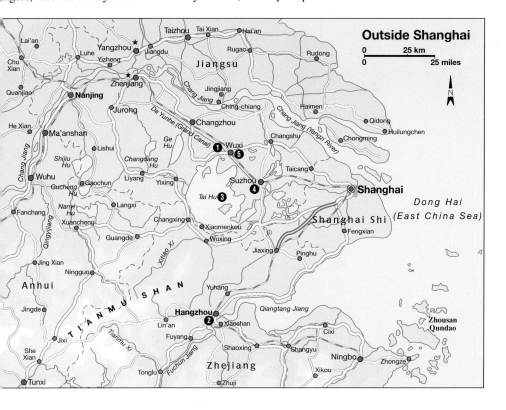

ing to explain tea production. **Shaoxing**, located 60 kilometres (40 mi) to the east of Hangzhou, is accessible directly by train. The town is known throughout the world for its rice wine. Every year the Shaoxing winery produces about 40,000 tons of wine and has been receiving praises for its excellent quality since the seventh century. Shaoxing was once the temporary residence of the emperor, and is linked to Da Yunhe.

Tai Hu

Between the two provinces of Zhejiang and Jiangsu is **Tai Hu** ❸, the third-largest lake in China, covering 2,420 square kilometres (930 sq mi) and peppered with 48 islands. The romantic landscape in green and blue, veiled with fine mist, has made this lake the subject of many poems.

The residents have a more pragmatic view of the lake: it provides them with fish, and they breed ducks and geese as well as grow lotus and water chestnuts on the lake. However, the most important economic factor in the area is the cultivation of mulberry trees.

The largest island, Dongting Xishan, covers 90 square kilometres (35 sq mi). The highest point, Piaomiao Feng (Blurred Peak), reaches 340 meters (1,100 ft). Also of interest is the peninsula Dongting Dongshan, to the south of Piaomiaofeng. The island Dongting Xishan can be reached from Xiaomenkou on the southern bank of Tai Hu, from Wuxi in the north and from Suzhou by boat; there is also a boat connection to the peninsula.

On this island is a cave that is an old sacred Daoist centre lying in the Linwu range. It wasn't until 1985 that it was uncovered from the mud of Tai Hu. A large number of religious artifacts and utensils were discovered, some of which are now exhibited in the provincial museum in Suzhou.

BELOW: moon gates are common in southern Chinese gardens.

Suzhou

Even if Hangzhou has overtaken its sister town as the most popular destination for the Chinese, **Suzhou** ❹ – known as the town of gardens and canals – is at least as charming. While Hangzhou has its large and grand lake, Suzhou is home to small intimate garden spots tucked away behind houses and hidden between narrow streets. Even when it rains, as it often does, the narrow streets and cobblestone walks are given a softened, misty aura that make Suzhou a relaxing, romantic diversion from the chaos of the cities. Be warned, however, that development is overtaking quaintness and tradition.

Suzhou was mentioned in 484 BC, since it was, for a few years, the capital of the state of Wu during the Period of the Warring States (403–221 BC). It flourished as a trading and silk centre in the early sixth century, linked with the capital through Da Yunhe, the Grand Canal. Its most prosperous period was during the Ming and Qing dynasties, when many officials, scholars, and artists settled here and local traders grew rich. This wealth was largely invested in the 150 gardens that make Suzhou so famous today.

The principle of Chinese garden construction – creating an illusion of the universe in a small space – is clearly evident here. Water trickles between unusually-shaped, rocky crags; small islands are connected by

canals and zigzag bridges; winding paths lead to tiny garden spaces with fountains, carefully manicured plants and fish ponds. A walk through the small alleys
in the town, along the canals, and through the gardens has a special charm in
the misty mornings, when the bus loads of tourists haven't yet marched through.

In the northeast of the town is **Zhouzheng Yuan** (Garden of the Foolish Politician), which covers four hectares and is the largest garden in Suzhou. Wang
Xiancheng, a retired court official, had it built in 1513 on the spot where the
poet Lu Guimeng lived during the Tang period. It is said that Wang's son, a gam-
bler, lost the property through gambling. During the Taiping Rebellion, when
Suzhou was substantially destroyed, the Taiping clan made this garden its headquarters from 1860 to 1864. The largest part of the area is covered in ponds,
close to pavilions connected by zigzagging bridges. The ponds are full of lotus
flowers; one pavilion is consequently called Hehua Simian Ting (You See Lotus
Everywhere). Paths wind along shores lined with willow trees.

Farther west on Xibei Lu is **Beisi Ta** (North Temple Pagoda), its current man-
ifestation from the 17th century. The present pagoda dates from the Southern
Song period, although two thorough restorations occurred in the second half of
the 17th century. A splendid view of Suzhou can be seen from the top of the 76-
meter-high (250 ft), nine-story tower, which is built in an octagonal shape. There
is a tea house with refreshments behind the pagoda.

On the western edge of the town, in the street of the same name, is **Liu Yuan**
(Garden for Lingering In). Aptly named, it is a garden with many nooks and
crannies, in which getting lost is a pleasure. A garden was first created here in the
16th century, but the current one was created in 1800 by its proprietors. Liu Yuan
is considered a prime example of a southern Chinese garden of the Qing era

Map, page 251

TIP

For centuries,
Suzhou's gardens –
built for scholars and
officials – have been
considered to be
works of art. If possi-
ble, take time to
savour one, though the
crowds of Chinese
tourists may eventually
overwhelm you.

BELOW: back-alley
canal, Suzhou.

**Map,
page 251**

(1644–1912), and thus belongs to the gardens protected as national cultural monuments. A pond forms the centre of the garden, lined with many paths, halls and pavilions. There are some interesting pieces of furniture and some especially beautiful artifacts in the halls.

Another specialty is a six-meter-high (20 ft) stone from Tai Hu that has been erected in the northeastern courtyard. Opposite Liu Yuan is **Xi Yuan** (West Garden), which together with Liu Yuan once formed a single large area owned by an imperial official.

About one kilometre further to the west, in the village of Fengqiao, is **Hanshan Si** (Monastery of the Cold Mountain), named after the seventh-century monk Han Shan, a Zen Buddhist fond of drink who became famous as an eccentric poet. Thought to have lived in the seventh century, Han Shan's poems have been translated into Western languages and are worth reading. The monastery was built in the sixth century, though the current buildings were rebuilt after being destroyed during the Taiping revolt. In the monastery are statues of the two monks Han Shan and Shi De. Visitors can buy stone rubbings and poems written by the two monks. Hanshan Si is a popular place during the Lunar New Year, and if you like noise and festivities, don't miss it.

The areas around Wuxi are known for silk production. The young worms, spread out on rice-straw mats, are fed juicy mulberry leaves and then put on bundles of rice straw, where they spin a cocoon in less than a week.

OPPOSITE: pagoda near Hangzhou.
BELOW: navigable parts of the Grand Canal are few.

Wuxi

The history of **Wuxi** ❺, reached from Suzhou either by railway in under an hour or by boat on Da Yunhe in about six hours, goes back over 2,000 years, when the town was called Youxi – literally, "there is tin".

The tin reserves must already have been exhausted by the Han dynasty, because since that time it has been called Wuxi, or "there is no tin". Tin or not, Wuxi's importance grew with the completion of Da Yunhe, and its modest wealth was achieved, as in the whole region, through agriculture and extensive silk production. Today, there are nearly a million people living in Wuxi, and tourism plays an increasingly important role for the town, although more as a crossroads and departure point than for any intrinsic interest.

The mild climate, soil, and sufficient water make the region around Wuxi one of the most fertile in China. The town itself offers few sights, but its charming landscape and its close proximity to Tai Hu mean it is a popular destination for excursions and day trips. One special attraction is Da Yunhe, which flows through the town, and the canal's arched bridges. Qingming Bridge, in the town's southeast, is architecturally interesting.

Outside of Wuxi

For almost 1,500 years, the area around Wuxi has produced China's oldest export, silk. Most people living in the Wuxi area now cultivate silkworms, usually as a profitable sideline.

Between April and November, travellers to the region can observe this activity on many farms throughout the area. The silkworm cocoon is washed in silk-spinning mills and then the silk thread is pulled. The thread can sometimes measure more than 1,000 metres (3,300 ft) in length. Several threads are then spun together into a durable yarn that can be woven.

NANJING

One of China's most livable and pleasant cities, Nanjing was the focus of the colonial intrusion into the rule of the Qing court, and the site of Japan's most brutal aggression during World War II.

Map, page 259

Here, in one of the most beautiful cities of China, the struggle between China's rapid development and the preservation of its past can be distilled down to the question of trees. Nanjing's wide avenues are lined with stately sycamore trees, three and four rows deep in some places, that provide a welcome sea of green. But the pressure to accommodate new high-rises, hotels, automobile traffic, and a growing population has meant the trees are starting to disappear. As one elderly resident laments, the trees used to provide a canopy of shade from the harsh summer sun. Now, she says, it is more difficult to find a cool, shady spot. Trees are especially important to Nanjing's residents. Together with Wuhan and Chongqing, Nanjing is considered one of the "three furnaces" of China. In the summer, temperatures rise above 40°C (104°F).

Yet even with a population of one million, Nanjing (Nanking), the former capital of the rich province of Jiangsu, still offers a respite from the frantic, congested pace of nearby Shanghai or Beijing to the north. From the park-like setting of its famous university to the forested Zijin Shan (Purple Mountains) in the east, Nanjing offers an atmosphere that few other Chinese cities can match.

Nanjing can easily be reached by train, boat, or plane. There is an express train, which began running in 1996, that zips from Shanghai in just over three hours, sometimes without any stops in between. Arrival by train from the north crosses China's longest river, the Chang Jiang (Yangzi), via the great **Nanjing Changjiang Daqiao** (Yangzi Bridge), which was opened in l968. The bridge, to the northwest of the city, is a symbol of Chinese independence and national pride. When relations between the former Soviet Union and China were severed in 1960, the Chinese built the bridge – which had been mostly a Soviet project up until then – with their own design and resources. It took 9,000 workers more than eight years to construct the bridge, struggling against the strong currents of the Chang Jiang. Today, the bridge remains an important symbol of progress for Nanjing, as its construction helped spur further development. Nanjing is a centre for shipbuilding and engineering industries, as well as the chemical and petrochemical industry in China.

More interesting for travellers, however, is Nanjing's reputation as a centre for higher learning, making it one of the easiest places to find English-speaking guides or just someone to have a conversation with over a beer.

Historical depth

The region has been populated for more than 5,000 years, and the history of Nanjing itself dates back to the fifth century BC, the beginning of the Warring States Period (403–221 BC). Between the third and sixth centuries AD, Nanjing was the capital of the Southern

OPPOSITE: mausoleum of Dr. Sun Yatsen.
BELOW: one of the few remaining junks on the Chang Jiang.

dynasties at a time when foreigners were ruling in the north of China. After various natural disasters and a peasant rebellion, the new Sui dynasty moved the imperial capital to Xi'an and completely destroyed Nanjing and almost all of its cultural and historical relics. Some animal sculptures and stele outside of Nanjing, and the Buddhist cave grottoes in nearby Qixia, are the few exceptions to the destruction.

Nanjing has been a city of treaties. It was here, following the Opium Wars, that the first of several treaties was signed that opened China to foreigners. The same treaty also ceded Hong Kong island to England.

Nanjing was able to regain national importance at the beginning of the Ming dynasty, whose first emperor set up the seat of government here in the Southern Capital – a literal translation of the name Nanjing – until they later transferred it to Beijing at the beginning of the 15th century. The well-preserved city wall in Nanjing dates from this period, and it is best viewed from the **Zhonghuamen** ❸ (Zhonghua Gate), in the south of the city near the Martyrs Cemetery. Although not terribly symmetrical, the wall had a circumference of over 30 kilometres (20 mi), with an average height of 12 metres (40 ft). The wall took two decades to construct and had 13 gates as defensive ramparts and barracks. Several of the gates remain standing today, including Zhonghuamen, a good reference point for navigating Nanjing, and **Zhongshanmen**, a gate that allows access to the top of the wall. In the city itself, the **Shitoucheng** ❸, a partially-preserved wall to the north of Mochou, is a reminder of Nanjing's turbulent history. There is a secluded, wooded walk that follows the path of the wall, and sections of the stone are still visible. A small park nearby has a military museum and park with models of aircraft and rockets.

BELOW: Nanjing Changjiang Daqiao.

In the same section of town, near Jiangdongmen (Gate on the Eastern Bank of the River), is the sombre **Datusha Jinianguan** ❸ (open daily, 8.30am–5pm) a memorial to the Nanjing massacre and an appropriately simple stone building

with a plain facade. Inside is a quiet, darkened exhibition of photographs, maps, and witness accounts that document the arrival of Japanese troops in December of 1937, and of the brutal rapes, burning and looting of houses and historical relics, and the slaughter of some 300,000 Chinese that occurred over the following six weeks. Over 20,000 cases of rape were reported, including gang rapes followed by execution. Those who survived sometimes ended up as Japanese Imperial Army "comfort women", as the Japanese call Asian and European women held prisoner for sex.

Most silencing is a viewing hall overlooking a mass grave, one of many of the *wan ren keng* (pit of ten thousand corpses) that the Japanese left behind.

Any question about China's lingering resentment over Japanese occupation is answered by this sign in the museum: "We must be on guard against any attempt to distort the history of Japanese aggression or to mollify aggressive war by the forces in Japan." The concern of the Chinese to memorialise the massacre is not one of vanity or self-pity. The Japanese, including government officials, have persistently denied the magnitude of the massacre, if not denying it completely. More people, mostly civilians, died at Nanjing from the Japanese massacre than from the atomic bomb at Hiroshima, yet Japanese textbooks refer to the massacre as a "minor incident". Among those in government denying the massacre have been cabinet ministers – including the foreign, justice, and education ministers – university professors, and the right-wing establishment.

City centre

The **Xinjiekou** ❺ traffic circle marks the modern city centre, packed with people, vehicles of all descriptions, offices, banks, and hotels. Here the Jingling Hotel

Map, page 259

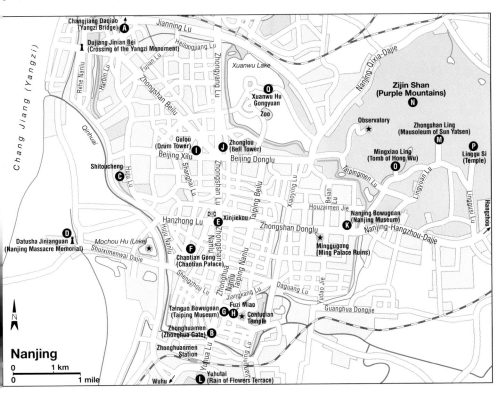

Nanjing

stands out like a beacon, towering above the traffic. To the southwest is Mochou He, a lake named after the Mochou (Lady Without Sorrows), who is said to have lived here in the fifth century. Various Qin pavilions pepper the area.

The **Chaotian Gong ❻** (Chaotian Palace) nearby dates back to the Song dynasty (960–1279), a period know for Confucian revivalism, and is considered one of the area's best-preserved Confucian temples. During the Ming dynasty, the temple was expanded into a school for children of the imperial court. The temple buildings of today are the product of a renovation in 1866, just two years after the Taiping Rebellion was put down. A reminder of the temple's beginnings is the gate of Ling Xing (Spirit Star), a remnant of the Song dynasty and entrance to the complex. Immediately following is a maze of merchants selling brick-a-brack, antiques, and magazines, some from the Cultural Revolution. Operas performed in the Jiangsu provincial tradition are held within the main courtyard. The three halls at the back of the complex contain fossilised human, buffalo, and deer bones from the Neolithic period, as well as a variety of pieces from the Ming and Qing dynasties.

Also in the southern part of the city, near Zhonghuamen, is a Ming-style garden residence housing the **Tainguo Bowuguan ❼** (Taiping Museum). The rise and fall of the "Kingdom of Heaven", popularly know as the Taiping Rebellion, is well documented here in both Mandarin and English. Cannons, guns, swords, and other weapons are displayed alongside photographs and paintings depicting the common man's grievances and advances against the Qing dynasty and the Western colonial powers of the 19th century.

Just two blocks to the west of the Taiping Museum is a lively market area known as **Fuzi Miao ❽**. A carnival atmosphere presides over this labyrinth of

BELOW: slow street-market day, and a trunk seat near the Ming tombs.

alleyways and small squares filled with souvenir and antique shops, and street stalls selling food. At the heart is the site of a Confucian temple and ancient study centre, dating back 1500 years. The temple and surrounding buildings were razed and rebuilt numerous times. The present buildings are Qing dynasty renovations and recent additions built in the Qing traditional style.

To the north of the Xinjiekou traffic circle are two more reminders of the beginnings of the Ming dynasty, **Gulou ❶**, the Drum Tower, and **Zhonglou ❿**, the Bell Tower. The Drum Tower was completed in 1382, just 14 years into the reign of the first Ming emperor. Its purpose was to mark the change in watch and to warn the city of attack. The Bell Tower, completed six years later, was used for ceremonial purposes. On the ground floor of the Drum Tower is a small exhibition hall featuring local artists.

The streets surrounding the leafy campus of **Nanjing University** are filled with lively student cafes, eateries, and bookstores. Students here are well-educated and are often seeking a conversation in English. Nearby is a permanent open market; it is also worth walking from here to **Shanxi Square**, another busy local market. Nearby is a small museum honouring a contemporary leader, former premier Zhou Enlai, who died in 1976 and remains popular today.

In the eastern part of the city, next to Zhongshanmen, is the **Nanjing Bowuguan ⓚ** (Nanjing Museum; open daily, 9am–5pm; fee). It has an extensive collection of ceramics, jade, lacquerware, textiles, bronzes, porcelain, and stone figures from Nanjing and elsewhere in Jiangsu Province. The collection covers 5,000 years of history, with many pieces dating from the Neolithic age. The most important exhibit is a 2,000-year-old shroud from the Eastern Han dynasty (25–220), made from 2,600 green jade rectangles sewn together with

Map, page 259

Drum and bell towers were common in all important imperial cities. Drums in the drum tower would mark the night watches along the city walls, and sometimes alert the city to danger or attack.

BELOW: Zhongshan Ling.

Map, page 259

silver wire. After walking through the various halls, the only way out is by navigating through the well stocked, but over-priced, souvenir and antique shop.

Nanjing, like much of China, is like a living museum where each piece reveals another chapter in China's history. For example, the first Ming emperor, Zhu Yuanzhang, had a wall erected on the foundations of an existing wall that had been built of reddish sandstone in the third century. The second wall is still preserved today. Nearby, to the south of Zhonghuamen, is **Yuhutai ❶** (Rain of Flowers Terrace), where in the fourth century, according to legend, the Buddha made flowers rain from the sky.

Today, there is a memorial in the park to the Communists and their supporters who died in 1927 at the hands of Nationalist troops. And if Zhongshan Lu and its right angle turns at intersections seems confusing, there is a reason. From the docks on the Chang Jiang to the mausoleum, the route taken by the funeral entourage of Sun Yatsen is named after him, and is known reverently by the Chinese as Zhongshan (Middle Mountain).

Outside of Nanjing

For most Chinese, the **Zhongshan Ling ⓜ**, the mausoleum of Sun Yatsen, is Nanjing's main attraction. Known as the father of modern China, he was the founder of the republic in 1911 and wrote many political treatises, which to this day remain required reading in schools in both the People's Republic and Taiwan. A Cantonese, he wanted to find his last resting place here amidst the lovely **Zijin Shan ⓝ** (Purple Mountains).

Dr. Sun Yatsen, known in Mandarin as Sun Zhongshan, plotted to overthrow the Qing dynasty. He is revered in both the People's Republic and Taiwan. He died in Beijing in 1925.

In one of China's largest funerals, Sun Yatsen's last wish was carried out four years after his death in 1925. The massive size of this monument is staggering, covering eight hectares (20 acres). At the end of the tree-lined avenue begins a climb of 392 granite steps leading up to the blue-tiled memorial hall. There are a few places to rest and enjoy the view of Nanjing along the way. The first hall contains a statue of the leader surrounded by walls with inscriptions telling his history and his most influential political theories. Directly in the back of the hall is the entrance to the circular vault room, where the tomb itself may be viewed.

Ruins to the northeast of Nanjing, near Zijin Shan, offer a glimpse of the era of the Ming dynasty (1368–1644). Years before his death, the first Ming emperor, Hongwu (1327–1398), built his tomb known as **Mingxiao Ling ⓞ**. Unfortunately, it was plundered during the Taiping uprising in 1864 and only the yellow walls of the main structure remain. Hung inside of the walls is a short history of the Ming dynasty and some photographs of Ming artifacts. A "sacred path" that has been preserved, however, is lined with stone animals and soldiers and leads directly to the tomb.

To the east of the tomb in Linggu (Valley of the Souls) is **Linggu Si ⓟ**, a temple built at the end of the 14th century. Only the temple site of Wuliang Dian, which has been restored several times and built entirely from stone and without any wooden rafters, remains of the former large structure. The area and its pine trees are popular with Nanjing residents.

Behind Wuliang Dian is the 61-metre-high (200 ft) **Linggu Ta**, a pagoda built in the 1920s in memory of the victims of the civil war between Communists and Nationalists. There is a magnificent view of the surrounding landscape from the top floor. Visible atop the mountain stands an observatory, built in 1934 and extended in 1949. It has a museum with astronomical instruments, old and new. A cable car to the observatory provides a splendid view of Nanjing. The park on **Xuanwu ⓠ**, a lake in the north of Nanjing, offers pavilions and small islands linked to the shore by dams and curved bridges. Understated in its beauty, it is nonetheless a pleasant retreat.

OPPOSITE: rape-seed field in bloom.

CHANG JIANG

Map, page 268

Better known to Westerners as the Yangzi, Chang Jiang slices through central China for over 6,000 kilometres. Along the way it is graced by a series of renowned gorges – visible for now.

The longest river in China is called, appropriately enough, Chang Jiang – Long River. Meandering eastward for approximately 6,300 kilometres (3,900 mi), Chang Jiang begins in the southwestern part of the Qinghai Plateau on Geladandong, the main peak of Tanggula Shan. Its course ends just north of Shanghai, where its eight-mile-wide mouth empties into Huang Hai, the Yellow Sea. Along the way, the river flows across nine provinces, with 700 tributaries draining an area of nearly 2 million square kilometres (700,000 sq mi) – nearly 20 percent of the total geographic area of China, and one-quarter of the country's arable land.

From the delta just north of Shanghai, an area with what is probably China's highest population density, the river is navigable by ocean-going vessels to Wuhan, nearly 1,000 kilometres (600 mi) upstream. The river flows through most of China's important industrialised areas, not to mention centres of silk-weaving, embroidery, lacquer work, and carving. This lower stretch of the river was also known as the Yangzi, its local name changing upriver two more times. When the early colonial powers arrived, they applied this name to the entire river.

The government feels that the river can be even more important to China by accelerating growth in the interior provinces, if they could increase the river's navigability and control disastrous floods. Along the section of the river famed for its gorges, Sanxia, China has begun building a hydroelectric dam at Sandouping, just upstream of Yichang, that will eventually form the world's largest storage reservoir. When completed in 2009, the dam itself will be 2 kilometres wide and 185 metres (600 ft) tall. The new reservoir waters will extend west over 500 kilometres (300 mi) as far as Chongqing, cover 630 square kilometres (240 sq mi), and be up to 175 metres (575 ft) deep. The intent of the dam is in many ways understandable, given that the interior provinces have economically lagged way behind the booming coastal regions. But the dam and reservoir will permanently alter the picturesque landscape by submerging vast sections of the gorges, and forcing over one million people to relocate.

China's longest river, Chang Jiang is the third-longest in the world, after the Nile and Amazon rivers. Traditionally, the river has been known by three local names. Europeans were familiar with the local name – Yangzi – on the lower stretch, and so this became the familiar name in the West.

Wuhan

The industrial and somewhat bland city of **Wuhan ❶**, more or less halfway between Shanghai and Chongqing, has long been accessible by river from the ocean. But the river along this part of the river is not terribly interesting.

Wuhan, which has around 6 million inhabitants, is today known to foreigners and Chinese alike as a starting or finishing point for excursions through Chang Jiang's three famous gorges, Sanxia. This jumping-off point gives Wuhan an attractive position for tourism, but surprisingly, the city has done little to enhance its tourist trade, despite the area's historical importance. Getting around the city has been facilitated by the construction of new bridges and roads, but it is still not a particularly attractive city.

Huanghelou (Yellow Crane Tower) on She Shan (Snake Mountain) in Wuchang district has been carefully restored, and the surrounding buildings have been rebuilt in traditional Chinese style. Some tourists, however, have found the site disappointing and not worth the exorbitant entrance fees. The original Huanghelou is said to have been built in the third century, only to be

PRECEDING PAGES: junks on the Chang Jiang are rarely seen today. **LEFT:** tourist boat on the Chang Jiang.

destroyed and rebuilt numerous times, most recently in 1884. The pagoda-like building holds exhibitions of calligraphy and paintings, and windows on every floor offer different vantage points from which to view **Changjiang Daqiao**, the bridge across the Chang Jiang.

On the eastern edge of town is a large lake area, **Dong Hu** (East Lake), situated in a huge park that has a number of other sights. There is a nice view across the entire lake and park area from Huguangge (Sparkling Lake Pavilion). Despite the crowds of visitors, particularly in the hot summer months when temperatures in Wuhan rise to around 40°C (100°F), it is a pleasantly cool place because of its enormous size.

Wuhan's first five-star hotel, the Lake View Grand Hotel, is painted a rather bright red. Because it is near an old burial ground, a feng shui expert recommended strong measures – and the colour red is one – to ward off bad luck and influences.

Wuhan to Sanxia

Boats travel in both directions along the Chang Jiang. Travelling down-river from Chongqing to Wuhan through the gorges is naturally faster and takes two nights and three days. Upriver takes six days and five nights. Negotiating a boat trip can be confusing. There are upscale cruises with hotel-like accommodations and dining rooms, casinos, and entertainment. At the other end of the scale are local boats in which travellers bunk four or six to a cabin and fend for themselves regarding meals. The boats that leave daily at various times from Wuhan to Chongqing were once called *Dongfanghong* (East is Red) during the days of the Cultural Revolution in the 1960s. Today, they have been renamed after their home ports Chongqing, Hankou, or Shanghai.

The first stop upriver from Wuhan to Chongqing is the town of **Yueyang ❷**, a river port located in Hunan Province on the southern edge of Hubei Province. The best-known sight in this town of 200,000 greets the traveller south of the

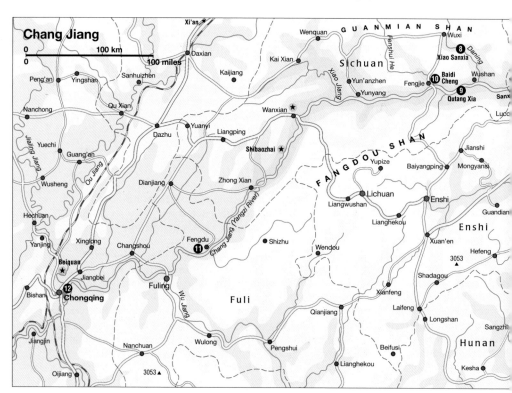

Map,
page 268

iver: **Yueyanglou** (Yueyang Tower), one of the most famous pavilion towers
n the region, if not all of China. Numerous songs have been composed about it
ince the Tang period (618–907), but the restored building currently dates from
he last century. The tower is flanked on both sides by two pavilions, Xianmeit-
ng (Plum Blossom of the Immortal Pavilion) and Sanzuiting (Three Drunks
'avilion). **Dongting Hu**, one of the largest inland lakes in China, is linked to
he Chang Jiang by several rivers, canals, and lakes, and serves as a water reser-
'oir for the river.

During the rainy season, the lake takes up to 40 percent of the waters from
he Chang Jiang. During droughts, it returns its water to the river, when its area
s reduced by almost a third. The lake contains a wealth of fish and is a breeding
·lace for rare waterfowl. In the summer months its shores are covered in the red
.nd green hues of blooming lotus plants.

About 220 kilometres (135 mi) west of Wuhan is **Shashi** ❸ (Sand Town),
till in Hubei Province. This town has few sights to offer. Zhanghua Si was
·ounded in 535, but its present structure dates from the Ming period and con-
·ains two beautifully-worked jade Buddhas. There is also the seven-story-high
·Vanshoubao Ta (Pagoda of Eternal Life). If travelling upriver, some travellers
·pt to embark on their Three Gorges cruise here instead of in Wuhan, thereby
·aving some time and money.

Yichang ❹, the last stop before reaching the gorges, is an industrial town
·hat is fast turning into a large and crowded city, as many people from the sur-
·ounding areas who were displaced by the construction of the new Three Gorges
·lam have relocated here. A four-lane highway now connects Yichang to other
·iver cities. If you have the option of breaking the journey here, enjoy a short

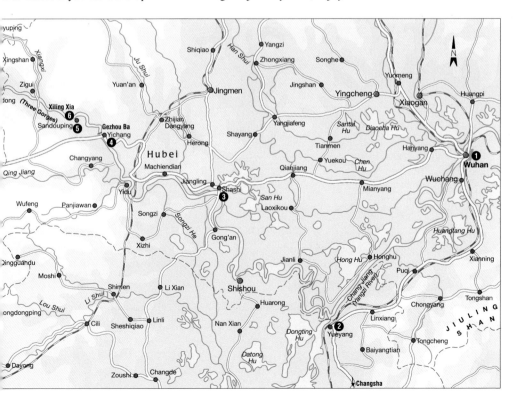

excursion by bus to see how the Chang Jiang emerges from the gorges at the Nanjing Pass, 6 kilometres (4 mi) away.

The famous battle between the state armies of Shu and Wu (AD 221) took place here. The king of Shu and leader of the army, Liu Bei, lost the battle. It is vividly remembered in Chinese history as a victory of a weak army over a numerically much stronger army by the use of tactical skills. After his defeat, Liu Bei was forced to flee through the gorges of the Chang Jiang to Baidichen.

Just behind Yichang, boats enter an enormous lock. In front is **Gezhou Ba**, currently one of the largest dams in China: 2,500 metres (8,200 ft) wide and 47 metres (154 ft) deep. It was completed in 1986 and supplies electricity to the surrounding provinces. The lock of Gezhou Ba lets several boats through at a time, negotiating a height change of up to 30 metres (100 ft).

A new town has grown up in recent years along its banks. However, the dam has raised the water level of the upper course and possibly increased the actual danger of flooding.

West of Yichang, at **Sandouping ❺**, work has begun on what will, when completed, be the world's largest dam. The **Three Gorges Dam** has already proved extremely controversial and enormously costly, with over four million people being relocated due to flood prevention schemes and to make way for the dam itself; this could cause major environmental and ecological problems. The water level through the gorges will be raised 175 metres (575 ft), submerging forever not only whole towns and cities, but historical and archeological relics yet to be uncovered. Also, there are signs that construction work will severely pollute this part of the river. Travellers intending to visit Sanxia should know that the changes due to flooding of the reservoir won't be immediate.

BELOW: damming of the gorges and flood prevention schemes are transforming the muddy landscape.

Sanxia (Three Gorges)

The entire length of **Sanxia**, the Three Gorges, is about 120 kilometres (75 mi). From the dam and upriver towards Chongqing, the three gorges are Xiling Xia, Wu Xia, and Qutang Xia. In 1992, there were over 300,000 foreign visitors to Sanxia. By 1995, only 90,000 foreigners made the trip. But with construction of the new dam, tourism to Sanxia may once again begin to increase, with visitors arriving to see the gorges before the transformation. Markings on the rocky walls of the river indicate the future depth of the water.

The first and longest gorge is **Xiling Xia ⑥**. This 66-kilometre (41 mi) gorge is really made up of several smaller gorges. From the south, the river is overlooked by Huangling Miao (Yellow Hill Temple). The main hall of the temple is said to date from the Han period, while the entrance is from the Qing period. The peculiar shape of the next small gorge earned it the name Niugan Mafei Xia (Horse-Lung and Ox-liver Gorge), though the exotic names refer merely to two small rock outcroppings that are easy to overlook if one is not paying close attention. Behind it is the 120-metre-long (390 ft) abyss of Qingtan (Blue Cliff).

The mouth of Xiangxi He (Fragrant River) on the northern bank, visible by its green waters in contrast to the brown Chang Jiang, signals the end of Xiling Gorge. The boat then passes **Zigui** on the northern bank, the home of the famous poet Qu Yuan (330–295 BC), who, according to legend, drowned himself in despair over the occupation of his home state by the armies of the Qin empire. (The whole of China still celebrates the Dragon Boat Festival in his honour.) Zigui has the dubious honour of being the first town that will be submerged as a result of the construction of the Three Gorges Dam.

Map,
page 268

TIP

Boats on the Chang Jiang don't have uniform classifications amongst the different companies, so for each cruise, it's important to ask exactly what is meant by first-, second-, and third-class berthing.

BELOW: during the rainy season, the river's water turns yellow with silt.

Despite its name, the 45-kilometre-long (28-mi) **Wu Xia** 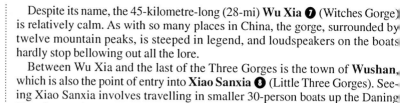 (Witches Gorge) is relatively calm. As with so many places in China, the gorge, surrounded by twelve mountain peaks, is steeped in legend, and loudspeakers on the boats hardly stop bellowing out all the lore.

Between Wu Xia and the last of the Three Gorges is the town of **Wushan**, which is also the point of entry into **Xiao Sanxia** ❽ (Little Three Gorges). Seeing Xiao Sanxia involves travelling in smaller 30-person boats up the Daning He, often against the tributary's strong currents.

But the exquisite scenery to be found here is regarded by many to be the highlight of the entire trip. It's possible to spy wooden coffins tucked into a tiny ledge high up on a mountain. These coffins are said to belong to the Ba people, a lost culture from the Bronze Age that was absorbed by the Qin dynasty. The Ba placed the coffins containing their dead in tiny crevices on remote mountain tops. The Little Three Gorges will be completely submerged when the Three Gorges dam is finished.

Entry into Chang Jiang's third gorge, **Qutang Xia** ❾ (Bellows Gorge), is breathtakingly beautiful. Although it is only 8 kilometres (5 mi) long and thus the shortest of the three, it is probably the most fascinating of the gorges. Perpendicular walls rise up from the river, narrowing it to a width of 100 metres (30 ft) and requiring the helmsman to exert great concentration in steering the vessel through the narrow one-way passage. Swirling brown water reveals that underneath the smooth surface are treacherous maelstroms.

Traveller reports from the 1920s and 1930s offer an exciting account of the journey through the gorges with cargo boats and junks. The boats had to be towed upstream, and the coolies carried out heavy work that could end in death if one of the men lost his footing on the paths hewn into the rock and pulled his mates, chained together, into the abyss. Until this century, this passage was almost the only way to get from eastern China to Sichuan, which is surrounded by nearly impassable mountain ranges.

Sanxia to Chongqing

After exiting Qutang Xia, the boat passes the City of the White Emperor, or **Baidi Cheng** ❿. Legend has it that a ruler of the Eastern Han dynasty (AD 25–220) saw a plume of white smoke in the shape of a dragon emerge from a well outside his palace. He considered it a good omen and henceforth called himself the White Emperor. In the main hall of the local temple, Baidi Miao, are figures of two army generals of Shu from the time of the Three Kingdoms (221–263), Liu Bei and Zhuge Liang. To the west of Baidi Cheng, the boat passes the settlement of **Fengjie**, a bleak industrial town that used to be surrounded by an old city wall with gates that were closed at night. Remnants of the old wall still remain. Both Fengjie and Baidi Cheng are famous for their succulent green oranges.

The next large town is **Wanxian**, for a long time a trading centre and port for ships travelling through the gorges. A steep staircase leads upward to the city near the mooring. All of these steps – with hundreds more leading to a city park – will be submerged after the completion of the dam. The grey concrete buildings that line

TIP

Nearly 20 percent of the complaints that China's tourism authority receives from foreigners are about the Three Gorges, especially about boat operators.

BELOW: stone pagoda along the Chang Jiang.

Map,
page 268

ιe bottom part of the city have all been abandoned as the town, like many oth-
rs along the Chang Jiang, is being relocated to a higher elevation. For the
ιoment, the steps lead to the market, where at almost any time during the day or
ιight traders offer local produce and bamboo goods. Wanxian is particularly
ιmous for its oranges and pomelos.

About five hours from Wanxian, on the northern bank of the river, is
·hibaozhai (Stone Treasure Stronghold). During the reign of emperor Qian-
ɔng (1736–1797), a temple was erected on a rock rising up 30 metres (100 ft)
ɾom the river bank. According to legend, there was a small hole in the temple
ʋall from which enough rice trickled to feed the monks, thus the name, Stone
ʹreasure. However, when the monks became greedy and thought they could get
ʋen more rice if they made the hole bigger, the treasure dried up.

Because the ascent to the temple was very tiring, a pagoda-shaped pavilion
ʋas built against the rock at the time of Emperor Jiaqing in the early 1800s. Its
2 stories reach as far as the temple, so one can easily climb up to the temple
y means of a wooden staircase inside the pavilion. Plans to preserve Shibaozhai
ɾom the rising waters involve building a wall around the pavilion, two-thirds
ɔf which will be submerged.

Fengdu ⓫, which is also on the northern bank of the Chang Jiang, will be
ɔmpletely submerged when the Three Gorges Dam's reservoir fills up. It is
ɾeally called the Ghost or Devil Town, because from the time of the Tang dynasty
ʹ518–907), statues of demons and devils have been housed in numerous tem-
ⅼes. Visitors can take a cable car to several of the temples, which often have
ⅼe feel of a cheap carnival fun-house, with statues of ghosts and demons and
ɾotesque scenes of torture.

Nearly 85 percent of the new reservoir behind the Three Gorges Dam will fall within the city limits of Chongqing.

BELOW: small day-tour boats, and Shibaozhai.

Map, page 268

In 1997, the jurisdiction of Chongqing was considerably extended, making it the world's largest municipality: 30 million people living on 82,400 sq km of land. Much of the new land came from Sichuan Province.

OPPOSITE: smiling street seller. **BELOW:** town to be covered by the Three Gorges Dam.

Chongqing

The journey upriver, which covers nearly 700 kilometres (435 mi), ends i Chongqing ⑫, formerly part of Sichuan Province but now its own municipa ity (as are Beijing, Shanghai, and Tianjin). This city is rare among Chinese citie because it is built on a rocky promontory hugging the river. Actually, it sits rigl at the confluence of two rivers, where the Jialing joins the Chang Jiang, and ha always been an important trading centre.

During the Tang period (618–907), Chongqing was called Yuzhou along th stretch, and it is still called Yu for short. The emperor Zhao Dun, of the Son dynasty (960–1279), renamed it Chongqing, or Twin Fortune, after two luck events: he first became prince of the prefecture, and then later became emperc of China.

"When the sun shines in Sichuan in winter, the dogs bark." This proverb particularly apt for Chongqing, since through most of the winter, from arour October to March when temperatures can fall to 4°C (39°F), the town i shrouded in fog that rises from the rivers, hiding the sun and depressing th spirit. During World War II, when the Japanese occupied parts of the countr and the Nationalist government under Chiang Kaishek fled to Chongqing, th town was bombed for several summers by the Japanese. Then, people wer grateful for the winter fog, since it prevented Japanese reconnaissance plane from flying over the city. Without reconnaissance, no bombers would follow.

Chongqing is not constructed on traditional grid lines. The houses in the ol city centre are typical of the architecture in this region, clinging to the slope with their black roofs resembling swallows nests. The top floor has a door t the street and the lower floors overlook one of the two rivers.

Unfortunately for the aesthetic purist, Chongqing being peppered by an increasing number of ugly higl rises in the city centre. Two cable cars link the rive banks, and a bridge over the Chang Jiang, completed i 1982, has relieved the pressure on the ferries. Anothe bridge, supplementary to the existing two across th Jialing, is intended to further help ease traffic conge: tion in the city.

The old city area around **Jiefangbei** (Liberatic Square) is full of small meandering alleys. Steep step lead from the tip of the peninsula down to the riv banks, studded with moorings. At the tip of the peni sula is a small pavilion, **Chaotianmen** (Door Facir Heaven). The flood level is marked here as a remind of the last big flood in 1982, which covered a large are and caused great devastation.

Not far from Chaotianmen, hidden in a narrow sid street, is a small Buddhist temple, **Luohan Si**. Note for 500 painted terracotta sculptures called *arhat*, it ha been restored in recent years and is worth a quick visi At the northwestern end of the peninsula is the **Da tang**, a convention hall of little interest other than i architecture, which resembles Beijing's Tiantan (Ten ple of Heaven).

In the evening, weather permitting, there are goc views of the city from **Pipa Shan**, and from **Elin Gongyuan** (Eling Park), which is less convenient located on the western end of the peninsula.

SICHUAN

Map, page 281

Long protected from the outside by a ring of mountains, Sichuan is not only the home of one of China's most notable cuisines, it is refuge for the panda. Rockets are launched here, too.

Sichuan is China's most populous province, with approximately 10 percent of the Chinese population – more than 100 million people living in a land area of 570,000 square kilometres (220,000 sq mi). Among this population are 15 recognised ethnic groups, including the Han Chinese, Yi, Tibetans, Miao, Tujia, Hui, and Qiang, mountain dwellers sparsely populating three mountainous autonomous regions of the province. Tibetans in Sichuan have not suffered friction with the Han Chinese to the degree they have in Tibet, due to a long history of peaceful relations with the Chinese and a lack of contention over territorial sovereignty. Historically, the province has not been easily accessible and thus its rich tradition has been preserved. But it has also been at the centre of conflict in efforts to control the region. The two regions of Shu and Ba were part of present-day Sichuan under the first emperor of a united China, Qin Shi Huangdi. These prefixes still appear as abbreviations for Sichuan. Around AD 1000, during the Northern Song dynasty, four districts were created to facilitate administration. They were called Chuan Xia Si Lu (four districts of Chuanxia), and were later abbreviated to the modern name Sichuan.

PRECEDING PAGES: Sichuan rice fields. **OPPOSITE:** bridge across Min Jiang, near Dujiangyan. **BELOW:** well-behaved fowl in Sichuan.

Lay of the land

The lowlands of Sichuan, surrounded by mountains to the east, north, west, and south, have a climate very favourable to agriculture: warm summers and mild winters, with high humidity, allowing cultivation throughout the year. Even during the winter months of January and February, the peasants supply the country's markets with fresh fruit and vegetables. In the countryside, picturesque terraced plots, which can produce up to three harvests in a year, and small, scattered villages cover the land. These small settlements exhibit dramatic differences in character within even one day's walking distance. Unfortunately, the same mountains which moderate the climate for agriculture also trap millions of tons of greenhouse gases and pollutants. This inverted atmosphere gives Sichuan a classic case of the China blues, and the resultant acid rain is ravaging vast areas of forests, which is not as pretty as the blue and gray hues that usually drape the land.

The forests in the western mountainous region are rich in fir and deciduous trees, and in rare animals. Unfortunately, economic exploitation and environmental pollution are visibly affecting these regions. Some areas have been put under special environmental protection to preserve the flora and fauna.

This is the home of the giant panda, which has increasingly been pushed into ever higher mountain regions by human encroachment, and is now threatened with extinction despite efforts to save the species.

The main grain of the region is rice. A large amount of rape seed is also grown which supplies most of the cooking oil used in China. Towards the end of March Sichuan's plains glow yellow with the blooming rape-seed fields. Along the edges of many of the terraced fields are mulberry trees, the food for the silk worm industry that many peasants practice as a lucrative sideline. Other agri cultural products in the relatively wealthy province include oranges, mandarins pomelos, vegetable oil, sugar cane, camphor, raw lacquer, wax, tea, and bam boo, which permeates culture and history with uses from food to furniture, and even festival rockets.

Sichuan is conveniently linked to the rest of China via Chengdu, the centre for air travel, and can be reached quickly and easily from Beijing, Shanghai Wuhan, Guangzhou, Xi'an, Kunming, Lhasa, and Hong Kong. There are numer ous direct railway links between Sichuan and almost all other Chinese provinces and the stretch between Chengdu and Kunming is one of the more beautiful train journeys in the country. The line between Chongqing and Xi'an slithers across hairpin bends, through numerous tunnels and across many bridges, cresting the Qinling range to the north beyond Sichuan. The Chang Jiang (Yangzi River) even after completion of the massive Three Gorges dam project in 2009, will continue to provide an important freight and transportation link with eastern China and the rest of the world.

Chengdu

The capital of the province, **Chengdu ❶**, lies in the centre of the central Sichuan *pendi*, or basin. The city, which is more than 2,000 years old, now has over ? million inhabitants in the city proper, and around 9 million in greater Chengdu

In contrast to some other Chinese urban centres, and despite raging redevelopment, Chengdu has managed to preserve the atmosphere how one might imagine China to have once been sometime in the past.

Chengdu was already the political, economic, and cultural centre of western Sichuan by 400 BC. During the Five Dynasties Period (907–960), Meng Chang, a ruler of the later Shu, had numerous hibiscus trees planted on the city walls, so the town eventually became known as the City of Hibiscus.

Built on flat ground, Chengdu can easily be explored on foot or by bicycle. It has almost a southern aspect with colourful old streets lined by scores of small restaurants and walkways that remain crowded until late with traders, buyers, and people out for a stroll.

One could eat one's way through the region's count less specialties by visiting the snack bars or teahouses which often have free performances of Sichuan opera or other instrumental pieces to entertain guests as they sip their jasmine tea. These teahouses are popular gam ing hangouts, particularly for older men playing *weiqi* (played with black-and-white stones on a 19-by-19 line board), or Chinese chess, which resembles the Western game of chess. Not surprisingly, many teahouses have recently transformed into small cinemas, with recent releases shown from video disks.

Wuhou Si (Temple of the Duke of Wu, open daily entry fee), was built by the king of the Cheng empire in

TIP

Chengdu's teahouses, called *chadian,* have long been centres of activism and free dis-cussion. They were shut down during the Cultural Revolution, but are back again. Try the teahouse in Ren-min Park, but don't expect much elegance.

BELOW: a monk snoozes.

e last years of the Western Jin period (265–316) and named after the Three
Kingdoms military strategist Zhuge Liang. During the Ming period
(368–1644), the temple was merged with the nearby site of Zhaomieliao, a
emple dedicated to the memory of emperor Liu Bei. The temple site as seen
oday was rebuilt in the Kangxi era of the Qing dynasty, in the late 1600s. There
re more than 40 sculptures of famous personalities from the Shu and Han peri-
ds, as well as numerous memorial stones, scrolls, and sacral implements.

On the southwestern outskirts of Chengdu, alongside a stream, is the park
ontaining **Du Fu Caotang** (Hut of the Poet Du Fu; open daily; admission fee).
u Fu, a poet from the Tang dynasty (618–907), fled an official post in Chang'an
now Xi'an) and sought refuge in Chengdu with his family. He built a straw hut
n the property of a helpful friend, then lived there for three years in very mod-
st circumstances. He wrote more than 240 of his popular poems here. The
memorial to Du Fu has been renovated or rebuilt several times during the sub-
quent dynasties, and even today there is an active Chengdu Du Fu study soci-
y. The present site in the park dates from two different periods: the governing
eriod Hongzhi of the Ming dynasty and the governing period Jiaqing of the
ing dynasty. Included at the site are the Shishi Pavilion and the study inside
e hut, next to which is a temple. Handwritten and printed examples of the
oet's works, in various editions, are on display.

Wangjianglou (River Viewing Pavilion Park; open daily; free) stands on the
outhern bank of the Jin Jiang, in the southeastern part of Chengdu. It was built
uring the Qing dynasty in memory of Xue Tao, a famous woman poet of the
ang dynasty. Today, this area is a public park with several towers and pavil-
ns. Most refreshing are the large stands of bamboo. The Chongli Pavilion,

*Poetry of the Tang
dynasty still retains
the sentimental ideol-
ogy of daily life,
reflecting a belief
that simple things
have importance and
passion. Over 50,000
Tang-era poems have
been anthologised.*

Map,
page 281

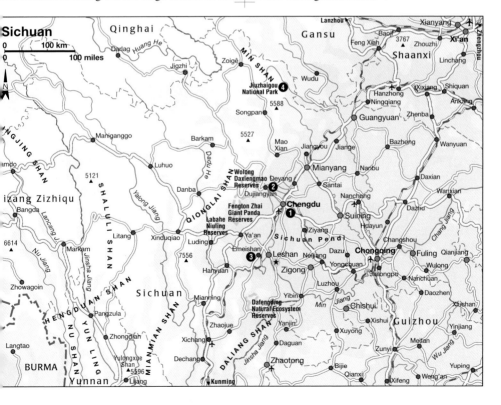

which is 30 metres (100 ft) tall and has four floors, is particularly noticeabl because of its striking ornaments, green-glazed tiles, and red-lacquered columns More than a hundred varieties of bamboo, including such rare varieties as spot ted and square bamboo, have been planted here in honour of Xue Tao, who love bamboo. The poet is said to have fetched water from the well on the site to mak the paper that she used for writing.

The giant panda first came to European notice in the 1860s, when a pelt turned up in France.

It is worth visiting **Wangjian Mu** (Tomb of Wang Jian; open daily; admis sion fee), in the west end of town. Wang Jian was a general during the last day of Tang emperor Lizhu's rule in the early 10th century, and was the first rule of the newly founded state of Shu in present-day Sichuan Province. The build ing, which is 19 metres (62 ft) high, has three burial chambers. The centre cham ber contains a sarcophagus between two rows of stone figures.

If so inclined, one might visit the zoo. Although it is not especially pleasan the Chengdu zoo (open daily; admission fee) has several pandas. However, i giant pandas are your only interest, head north of town for 6 kilometres to th **Giant Panda Breeding Research Facility** (open daily; admission fee; tel: 35 6970), which is much better than the zoo as a natural environment for both th giant and lesser pandas. The research facility was established in 1990 and opene to the public in 1995. There are more than a dozen pandas living here, and th facility has excellent exhibits and a museum. There are plans to enlarge the faci ity, which may be the most natural environment in which to view the pandas.

BELOW: terraces of flooded rice fields.

There are perhaps just 1,000 or so giant pandas still living in the wilds o China, in two or three dozen groups centred in northern Sichuan, and also i Gansu and Shaanxi provinces. Related to both raccoons and bears, the pand lives mainly on bamboo, but is also a meat-eater.

Outside Chengdu

Eighteen kilometres (11 mi) north of Chengdu, in the town of **Xindu**, is the famous Buddhist **Baoguang Si** (Precious Light Monastery; open daily; admission fee). It is thought to have been founded during the Eastern Han dynasty, providing housing for more than 3,000 monks in the 10th and 11th centuries. The site was burned down during the Ming period and then rebuilt in 1670. The oldest building on the monastery site is the 30-metre-tall (100 ft) Sheli Ta, a pagoda in the front courtyard and the only one to have survived the Ming-period fire. The 500 relatively well-preserved *luohan* statues from the Qing dynasty are worth the visit.

Dujiangyan ❷, on the upper course of Min Jiang and 50 kilometres (30 mi) northwest from Chengdu, is an irrigation project over 2,000 years old. Built between 306 to 251 BC, the irrigation network was capable of irrigating 200,000 hectares (500,000 acres) of land shortly after its completion. Today, 240,000 hectares (600,000 acres) of agricultural land are supplied with water from the system. There is a three-metre-tall, 1,900-year-old stone statue of Li Bing, the builder, in Fulongguan (Pavilion of the Dragon's Defeat), erected in the third century to commemorate the success. There is a nice view of the site from here. Erwang Miao (Two Kings Temple) was built in honour of its architects.

Emei Shan

An increasingly popular and commercial area, the Emei mountain range is southwest of the Sichuan basin and 160 kilometres (100 mi) from Chengdu. The town **Emeishan ❸**, at the foot of the mountain range, can be reached either by bus or train from Chengdu. The journey takes about three hours. Alternatively, it's possible to get off the Kunming–Chengdu train at Emeishan. There are minibuses from Emeishan to **Baoguo Si** (Baoguo Monastery), built in the 16th century. The temple is built on a slope and is comprised of four halls, built one above the other. There are also various exhibition halls with artifacts, calligraphy, and paintings. Near Baoguo Si, by a small pond under some trees, is a former rest house for Communist Party cadres, now called Hotel Hongzhushan. Day-trips to the mountain are convenient from here, as are excursions lasting several days. Guest houses have been built next to the hotels, and more are under construction. Baoguo Si is only one of many temples and monasteries – over 150 have been built here over the centuries – scattered throughout the mountain range. Many of the old monasteries fell to decay when they were no longer inhabited, or have been destroyed. Only 20 or so can be visited.

Emei Shan itself was named after its shape: a curved eyebrow. The Daoists began erecting temples here in the second century, but as Buddhism gained popularity from the sixth century onwards, the mountain became a sacred place of Buddhism. In fact, it is one of the five sacred Buddhist mountains in China. There are rare animal and bird species on Emei Shan, and around 200 different types of butterflies. Steps lead from Baoguo Si up to the peak. A road was built some years ago to the Jieyin Dian, a pavilion at an altitude of 2,670 metres (8,760 ft), and now buses go to within 6 kilometres (4

Map, page 281

BELOW: alternative transport up Emei Shan trail.

Map, page 281

TIP

Go ahead and climb Emei Shan. Plan on one day up, one day back down. Be prepared for rain, at times quite heavy. Lodging is simple and cheap at the many monasteries along the way. Most people start at Wannian Si, an option that eliminates much of the leg work at the lower elevations.

OPPOSITE: the traditional look is fading.

mi) of the 3,100-metre-high (10,400 ft) Jinding (Golden Peak). About 20 metre (65 ft) below the summit is **Jinding Si** (Golden Peak Temple), with a 20-metre long (65 ft) bronze hall.

In favourable weather conditions, a remarkable natural phenomenon can b experienced on the peak. If the sun is in the right position, an observer's shado is cast onto the clouds below the peak, and an aura of pastel rainbow colou forms around the silhouette. One can also see this phenomenon from an airplan above the clouds, and in only two other places on earth, including atop Haleaka on Hawaii's Maui. The Buddhist pilgrims, of whom there are still many, interpr it as a special sign when they experience this phenomenon. In the past, som pilgrims would throw themselves from the peak into their shadow, imaginin that this led directly to the longed-for nirvana.

Along the mountain pathways are several monasteries. The larger ones offe food and shelter during the two-and-a-half-day descent. Arrive before 5pm at monastery offering shelter, when it's easier to get a bed in a separate room, rathe than sleeping on the floor in the temple halls with many other hikers.

About 10 kilometres (6 mi) below Jieyin Dian is **Xixiang Chi** (Elephar Bathing Pool), a relatively large temple built against a rock and offering a lovel view of the surroundings. According to legend, this is where the elephant c *bodhisattva* (redemption deity) Samantabhadra took his bath.

Below the Xixiang Chi, the descent divides into a relatively steep but shorte path to Wannian Si or a longer but more beautiful path to Qingyinge. Often o the upper part of the path are a battalion of rude, pushy monkeys demanding toll of peanuts or fruits. If provoked or if they don't get their treats, they ma become aggressive. There have been cases of monkeys grabbing cameras an clothes from people.

Farther along the path is a small gorge, **Yixiantian** (Thread of Sky), throug which winds a stream lined with lush vegetation. **Wannian Si** (Temple of Eter nity) stands at the lower end of the steeper path, at about 1,200 metres (3,90 ft) above sea level. It was built in the fourth century and once consisted of seve halls. Today, only one 16-metre-high (50 ft) hall remains. The square structure with a dome roof and made of bricks without rafters, is typical of Ming-dynast architecture. It contains a bronze figure, of bodhisattva Samantabhadra on white elephant, dating back to around 920.

According to some of the many folk tales relating to this mountain, this bod hisattva came to Emei Shan riding on the white elephant. The northern an southern paths join again at Qingyinge (Pavilion of Pure Sound), where the tw streams Black Dragon and White Dragon also join, the source of the pur sounds. The pavilion is now a rest house that also serves meals.

Northwest

In the northwest of Sichuan and close to the border with Gansu Province, th **Jiuzhaigou Nature Reserve ❹** is open to visitors. Located about 500 kilome tres (300 mi) north of Chengdu, it covers an area of 60,000 hectares (150,00 acres). Apart from development of tourist facilities, this is a real natural won derland. Lush vegetation alternates with grass steppes, lakes, rivers, and water falls, all framed with high, forested mountains and peaks covered with eterna snow. The Tibetan people in the region have a legend about the creation o Jiuzhaigou. An immortal called Dage and a fairy called Wunuosemo lived dee in the mountains. They fell in love. One day, Dage gave Wunuosemo a mirror a a present, which he had polished to a high shine with the wind and the clouds Unfortunately, she dropped the mirror and it broke into 108 pieces, which trans formed into the 108 lakes of the Jiuzhaigou.

THE SOUTH

Historically the most innovative and entrepreneurial regions, the southern provinces still challenge the rest of China.

It was in the south of China, particularly along the southeastern coast, where Deng Xiaoping's economic modernisation program germinated, took root, and prospered. In hindsight, it was both a bold and a necessary experiment, designed to gradually introduce a market economy to China. Not everyone got to participate, especially outside of the select special economic zones, but they could watch the lucky ones prosper. It was learning by example.

The idea of commerce is not an extraordinary notion in southeastern China. Guangzhou was already an international port in the ninth century, and by the 1500s, when the Portuguese arrived in a showy flotilla, the area had replaced the Silk Road as the trade route of choice into China. For over a century, until 1842, Guangzhou held China's international trade monopoly as the only port open to outsiders. Through lazy transliteration, the provincial name of Guangdong somehow ended up coming out of European mouths as Canton.

Southeast China's other port of note has not the historical depth of Guangzhou, but it has an uncanny entrepreneurial depth, unmatched anywhere in the world. A British colony – coerced from China in the 19th century – until 1997, Hong Kong became the definitive capitalist free-market, no-holds-barred port. What happens now as a definitive capitalist free-market port (and maybe still no-holds-barred) in a Communist country is anybody's guess. The power of psychology may be as much a factor as the power of rule.

Inland from the coast, to the west, the land turns more tropical, and the languages and people more distinctive. The terrain in Guangxi, especially Guilin, has seduced poets and artists for centuries. What geologists call limestone karst is actually the romantic blending of misty towers and surreal reality in old Chinese brush paintings.

Yunnan borders Burma, Laos, and Vietnam, and thus it shares the ethnic groups that give this southern region a distinctive feel and ambience. There are no wondrous architectural delights, and no stupendous archeological revelations to be found by travellers in Yunnan. There is just the grace of land and people.

PRECEDING PAGES: trading floor of the Hong Kong stock exchange.
LEFT: hotel bellboy in entrepreneurial Guangzhou.

Baishizhou Splendid China Chegongmao Xiasha Shatouxu Chiwei Huanggang Shatou Ma Tso Lung Jiushixia Zucun Lok Ma Chau Kwu Tun

S h e n z h e n   B a y

Tai Fu Tai San Tin Ponds Mai Po Shek Wu Wai Nam Sha Po Lin Tong Fairview Park Lau Fau Shan Mong Tseng Wai Mai Po Marshes Ngau Tam Mei Kei Kung Leng 572 ▲ Ponds Sha Kong Tsuen Lam Tsuen Co Wang Chau Sha Po Ngau Hom Sha Ha Tsuen Yuen Long Ping Shan ★ ③②

Kat Hing Wai Walled Village ★ Pat Heung Hung Shui Kiu Fui Sha Wai Shui Tau San Tsuen Kam Tin ★ Sh Ha Pak Nai Tuen Tsz Wai Lin Fa Tei Tai Shui Hang Pak Sha Tsuen Yuen Kong Tai Wo Nim Wan Kai Lun Wai Miu-Fat-Buddh.- Kloster Ma On Kong Ching Chung Koon Temple ★ Lam Tei Chung Wong Tei Tai Lam Country Park N e Pei Tu Temple ★ Tai Lam Chung Reservoir Tin Fu Tsai Chi Lung Kwu Tan ▲583 Castle Peak Shek Kok Tsui Tuen Mun Chuk La Yeun Mon Lung Kwu Chau Siu Lang Shui So Kwun Wat Sham Tseng Castle Peak Bay Gordon Hard Siu Lam Tai Lam Chung Ting Kau Sam Pillar Point Pearl Island So Kwun Tan Tuen Mun Rd. Tsing Lung Tau Tsing Yi Tsuer Brothers Point Ma Wan Tsing Ma Bridge Shek Wan Tsi Y Sha Chau Tang Lung Mo To Chau (The Brothers) Siu Mo To Tsing Chau Tsai Chau Nam Wan Tai Mo To Mong Tung Hang

Chek Lap Kok International Airport Sam Pak Penny's Bay Yi Pak Discovery Chek Lap Kok ③⑤ Pak Mong Discovery Bay Peng Chau Siu Kau Yi Chau Kau Yi Chau Sha Lo Wan San Tau Tung Chung Wan Ngau Kwu Long Nim Shue Wan Tsuen Trappist Monastery ★ Tin Hau Temple Sham Shek Tsuen Ma Wan Chung Hung Fa Ngan Tai Shui Hang Tung Chung ③⑥ Tung Chung Pak Ngan Heung Mui Wo ④⓪ Chau Kung To (Sunshine Island) Lantau North Country Park Luk Tei Tong Tai O Po Lin Monastery Lantau Island ③⑨ Ying Hing Monastery③⑧ ③⑦ Ngong Ping ▲869 Sunset Peak Hei Ling Chau Nga Ying Kok Keung Shan 933 ▲Lantau Peak Pui O Tsuen Chi Ma Wan Yi O Lantau South Country Park Man Cheung Po Shek Pik Reservoir Tong Fuk Cheung Sha Chung Hau Yun Shue W Shek Pik Tong Fuk Miu Wan Chi Ma Wan Peninsula Tin Hau T Fan Lau Tai Long Wan Shuihau Ha Keng Pak Tai Temple ★ Fan Lau Fort★ Kau Ling Chung Cha Kwo Chau Cheung Chau Tung Wan Beach ④③ Cheung Chau Shek Kwu Chau Tin Hau Temple

Macau Siu A Chau Soko Islands Ha Tai A Chau

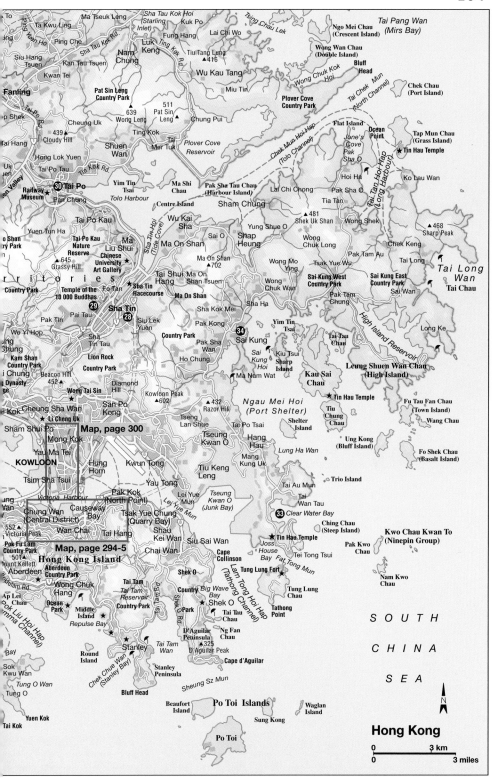

To
Ping Yuen Ho
Ta Kwu Ling
Ma Tseuk Leng
Sha Tau Kok Hoi
(Starling Inlet)
Kuk Po
Fung Hang
Lai Chi Wo
Tsing Chau Lek
Ngo Mei Chau
(Crescent Island)
Tai Pang Wan
(Mirs Bay)

ing
Ping Che
Sha Tau Kok Rd.
Luk Keng
Ting Kok Rd.
Tiu Tang Lung
▲416
Wong Wan Chau
(Double Island)

Siu Hang Tsuen
Kan Tau Tsuen
Nam Chung
Wu Kau Tang
Miu Tin
Wong Chuk Kok Hoi
Bluff Head

Kwan Tei
Tai Chek Mun (North Channel)
Chek Chau
(Port Island)

Fanling
Pat Sin Leng Country Park
511
Pat Sin Leng ▲
Chung Pui
Plover Cove Country Park

p Shek
Tai Po Rd.
Cheung Uk
639
Wong Leng
Chek Mun Hoi Hap (Tolo Channel)
Flat Island
Jone's Cove
Ocean Point
Tap Mun Chau (Grass Island)

439▲
Cloudy Hill
Ting Kok
Tai Mei Tuk
Plover Cove Reservoir
Pak Sha O
★Tin Hau Temple

Tai Hang
Hong Lok Yuen
Shuen Wan

Uk jen
en Valley
Tai Po Tau
Tin Kok Rd.
Yim Tin Tsai
Ma Shi Chau
Pak Sha Tau Chau (Harbour Island)
Lai Chi Chong
Hoi Ha
Pak Sha O
Tai Tan Hoi Hap (Long Harbour)
Ko Lau Wan

Railway Museum
㉚**Tai Po**
Pan Chung
Tolo Harbour
Centre Island
Sham Chung
Tia Tan

Tai Po Kau
Wu Kai Sha
Sai O
Yung Shue O
▲481
Shek Uk Shan
Wong Shek
▲468
Sharp Peak

o Shan
ry Park
Yuen Tun Ha
Tai Po Kau Nature Reserve
Ma Liu Shui
Ma On Shan
Shap Heung
Wong Chuk Long
Chek Keng

▲645
Grassy Hill
Chinese University ★ Art Gallery
Ma On Shan
▲702
Wong Mo Ying
Tsak Yue Wu
Pak Tam Au
Tai Long
Tai Long Wan

Country Park
Temple of the 10 000 Buddhas
Fo Tan
★ Sha Tin Racecourse
Tai Shui Hang
Ma On Shan Tsuen
Wong Chuk Wan
Sai Kung West Country Park
Sai Kung East Country Park
Sai Wan
Tai Chau

㉙
Sha Tin
Ma On Shan
Sha Ha
Pak Tam Chung

Pak Tin
Pai Tau
㉘
Siu Lek Yuen
Sha Kok Mei
Yim Tin Tsai
Long Ke

Wo Yi Hop
ng hung
Sha Tin Tau
Country Park
Pak Kong
㉞
Sai Kung
Kiu Tsui Chau
Tai Tan Chau
High Island Reservoir

Kam Shan Country Park
i Chung
Dynasty
ga
Lion Rock
Country Park
Pak Sha Wan
Ho Chung
Sai Kung Hoi
Sharp Island
Leung Shuen Wan Chau (High Island)

Beacon Hill
452▲
Diamond Hill
Ma Nam Wat
Kau Sai Chau

Wong Tai Sin
San Po Kong
Kowloon Peak
▲602
Tin Hau Temple
Fu Tau Fan Chau (Town Island)

i Kok
Cheung Sha Wan
★ Li Cheng Uk
▲432
Razor Hill
Ngau Mei Hoi (Port Shelter)
Tiu Chung Chau
Wang Chau

Sham Shui Po
Map, page 300
Tseng Lan Shue
Tai Po Tsai
Shelter Island

Mong Kok
Yau Ma Tei
Tseung Kwan O
Hang Hau
Lung Ha Wan
Ung Kong (Bluff Island)
Fo Shek Chau (Basalt Island)

KOWLOON
Hung Hom
Kwun Tong
Tiu Keng Leng
Mang Kung Uk

Tsim Sha Tsui
Yau Tong
Tai Au Mun
Trio Island

ung Van
Victoria Harbour
Lei Yue Mun
Lei Yue Mun
Tseung Kwan O (Junk Bay)
Tai Wan Tau

552▲
Victoria Peak
Chung Wan (Central District)
Causeway Bay
Pak Kok (North Point)
Tsak Yue Chung (Quarry Bay)
㉝ *Clear Water Bay*
Ching Chau (Steep Island)
Kwo Chau Kwan To (Ninepin Group)

Pok Fu Lam Country Park
Wan Chai
Tai Hang
Shau Kei Wan
Siu Sai Wan
★Tin Hau Temple
Pak Kwo Chau

501▲
Mount Kellett
Hong Kong Island
Map, page 294-5
Chai Wan
Cape Collinson
Joss House Bay
Tei Tong Tsui
Nam Kwo Chau

Aberdeen
Aberdeen Country Park
Shek O
Lam Tong Hoi Hap (Tathong Channel)
Tung Lung Fort ★

KFdam Rd
Wong Chuk Hang
Tai Tam
Tai Tam Reservoir
Country Park
Big Wave Bay
Shek O Park
Tung Lung Chau

Ap Lei Chau
Ocean Park
Middle Island
Country Park
Tai Tam Rd.
Tai Tau Chau
Tathong Point

ok Liu Hoi Hap
mma Channel)
Repulse Bay
Tai Tam Wan
D'Aguilar Peninsula
Ng Fan Chau

Bay
Round Island
Stanley
▲325
D'Aguilar Peak
Cape d'Aguilar

Sok Kwu Wan
Chek Chue Wan (Stanley Bay)
Stanley Peninsula
Sheung Sz Mun
SOUTH

Tung O Wan
Tung O
Bluff Head
CHINA

Yuen Kok
Tai Kok
Beaufort Island
Po Toi Islands
Waglan Island
SEA

Sung Kong

Hong Kong

Po Toi

0   3 km
0   3 miles

HONG KONG

Map, page 290

Taken from China during the weak times of the Qing dynasty, Hong Kong – the island of Hong Kong, Kowloon and the New Territories – returned to the dragon's embrace in 1997.

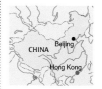

A rchaeological evidence shows Hong Kong has been inhabited since the Stone Age. Han Chinese people began settling here in the Song dynasty (960–1279), but it remained a relatively obscure corner of Guangdong province until British opium merchants recognised the advantages of "annexing" 45 square km (17 sq miles) of the best deep-water harbour in the region. In this they proved more far-sighted than their monarch. "Albert," tutted the Queen, "is so much amused by my having got the island of Hong Kong, and we think Victoria ought to be called Princess of Hong Kong in addition to Princess Royal." And foreign secretary Lord Palmerston has gone down in history as calling it "a barren island with hardly a house upon it".

The former British colony of Hong Kong can be divided into four parts: Hong Kong island, Kowloon, the New Territories, and the numerous outlying islands. Hong Kong island – or simply the Island, as it's popularly known – is 75 square kilometres (29 sq miles) of topsy-turvy real estate. The earliest British settlements were established here, so consequently Queen Victoria's little "joke" is today dominated by great banks and financial houses, enormous futuristic buildings, opulent hotels, splendid residences on Victoria Peak, fine beach resorts, and some of the oldest Chinese communities.

Across Victoria Harbour – just 5 minutes by the underwater Mass Transit Railway, 8 minutes by the venerable Star Ferry and less than 10 minutes by car through the two tunnels – is the city of Kowloon, a commercial-industrial complex packed into 46 square km (18 sq miles). Kowloon and Stonecutters' Island were ceded to the British in 1860, for better defence of the harbour. Most tourists see only the tip of Kowloon, the Tsim Sha Tsui district and its many hotels, bars, and shopping centres. North of Tsim Sha Tsui, along Nathan Road, are the Yau Ma Tei and Mong Kok districts.

Boundary Street marks the demarcation line between the old colony, granted to the British "in perpetuity", and the New Territories, which were leased in 1898 for a 99-year period. All reverted to Chinese sovereignty in July 1997.

Along with the New Territories, England leased 233 outlying islands, only four of which are inhabited by sizeable communities. One of these, Lantau, over twice the size of the Island, is now home to the state-of-the-art international airport. Together with Lamma, Cheung Chau and Peng Chau it serves as a "dormitory" for professionals wanting to escape the rat race.

OPPOSITE: Hong Kong's Central District and the Star Ferry.
BELOW: water transport the old way.

Hong Kong island

Central District: Hong Kong's **Central District** is dominated by its legislative offices, but real power here is held by the banks. Dominating Central is the gleaming

370-metre (1,200 ft) **Bank of China Tower** , designed by famous Chinese-American architect I. M. Pei. The tower's sharp angles point directly at the other banks, which makes for bad (or good, depending which side you're on) *feng shui*. The Hongkong Bank (HSBC) headquarters, designed by British architect Sir Norman Foster, and one of the most expensive buildings in the world, is another central landmark.

The best place to begin a tour is at the **Star Ferry Pier ❷**. The green-and-white Star Ferries have been shunting passengers across the harbour between Hong Kong island and Kowloon since 1898. Right of the terminal is the **Jardine House ❸**, whose distinctive round windows have inspired the Chinese to nickname it the House of a Thousand Orifices. Nearby are the shiny towers of Exchange Square, one of the most modern office complexes in the world and the home of the Hong Kong Stock Exchange, as well as the towering presence of the International Finance Centre.

The colonial **Supreme Court Building** houses the Legislative Council. On the other side of Queen's Road, is the **Government House ❹**, home of former colonial governors. Behind this are the **Zoological and Botanical Gardens** (open daily, 6am–7pm; free), which include a number of red-cheeked gibbons and a good botanical collection. Hong Kong Park includes the **Flagstaff Museum of Teaware** (open Tues–Sun, 10am–5pm; free), and some aviaries. The Anglican **St John's Cathedral ❺**, dating from 1849, is the city's oldest.

Victoria Peak ❻ is Hong Kong's most visited tourist attraction and a prime residential area. Before the opening in 1888, of the funicular railway called **Peak Tramway** (operates daily, 7am–midnight) sedan chairs transported privileged colonials to the top. The best way to see the Peak is by walking around Lugard

TIP

In operation since 1898, the Star Ferry links Tsim Sha Tsui with the Central District and Wan Chai. The crossing takes 7 to 8 minutes, operating from 6.30am to 11.30 pm. Other ferries run to the outlying islands almost every hour.

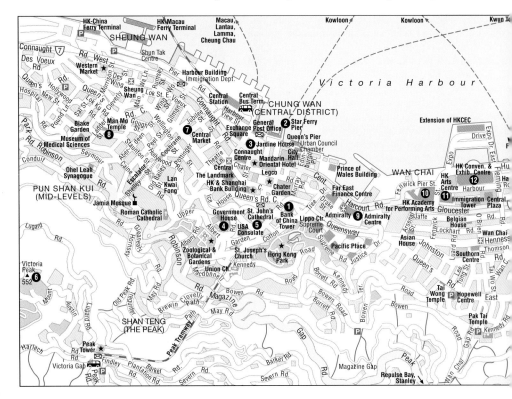

Road, which begins just opposite the Peak Tram's upper terminus at 400 metres (1,300 ft) above sea level. At the top of the Peak are some of the world's finest vistas, all the way to China and Macau.

Western District: As its name suggests, the area is located just to the west of Central, but, although there has been much recent development here, it is still worlds apart from the ultra-modern financial district, offering instead a rare glimpse of the more traditionally Chinese Hong Kong. Western is known as a last refuge of the Hong Kong Chinese artisan, unseen by most visitors, where there are mahjong-makers, herbalists, and craftsmen. The area begins at Possession Street and sprawls west to Kennedy Town, but its atmosphere begins to emerge around the purpose-built **Central Market ❼**. The Central-Mid-Levels Escalator, the world's longest, stretches up to the old city of Victoria. Built in 1993, it runs downhill from 6–10.10am, and uphill from 10.20am–midnight. Take it to the **Man Mo Temple ❽** (open daily, 7am–5pm) built around 1840 on what was a dirt track leading up from Central. Tourists regularly throng through Man Mo, but this doesn't inhibit the temple's regular worshippers from creating thick and redolent clouds with their burning joss offerings. Near the altar are three sedan chairs encased in glass, which were used years ago to parade the icons of the gods Man and Mo through Western on festival days.

In 1841, when the British formally annexed Hong Kong (somewhere around Possession Street), the island extended only as far as Queen's Road. However, land here has been vastly reclaimed over the years. Near the western extent of the island, is **Kennedy Town**, one of Hong Kong's oldest Chinese settlements. Still very crowded, it has a Portuguese-style *praia*, a road that curves along original foot paths bordering Belcher Bay.

Map, page 294

Until the completion of the Peak road in 1924, the tram was the only public transport up the hill. Known as a funicular tram, there are two cars connected by a cable; the downhill car helps pull up the other one with its weight.

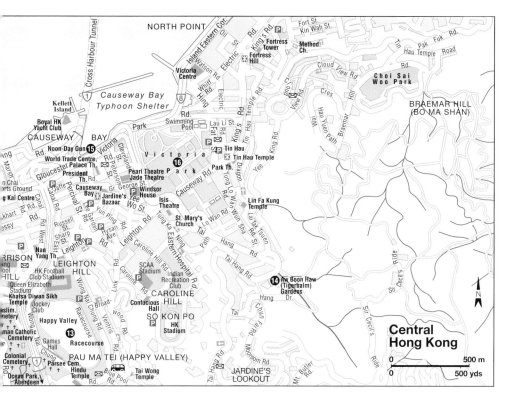

Central Hong Kong

Wan Chai and Causeway Bay: East of Central are the island's liveliest districts for eating, drinking and shopping. Wan Chai and Causeway Bay are among the territory's most crowded and active districts, revealing the authentic flavour of modern Hong Kong. **Admiralty** ❾, once the site of the British naval station, is a combination of gleaming office towers and shopping malls. A few minutes' walk away is **Wan Chai**, the legendary night-life centre of Hong Kong immortalised in the 1960 film *The World of Suzie Wong*, about a Chinese prostitute with a heart of gold. Wan Chai has a completely different personality by day.

Close to the Wan Chai waterfront is the **Academy for Performing Arts** ❿ and the **Hong Kong Arts Centre** ⓫, two of the most popular venues for theatrical and cultural performances in Hong Kong. Right on the harbour is the futuristic **Hong Kong Convention and Exhibition Centre** ⓬, completed just in time for the official handover ceremony in 1997. Nearby is the Central Plaza office tower, Hong Kong's tallest building. Elevated walkways lead south from the convention centre to Lockhart Road, one of the busiest streets in the centre of Wan Chai's night-life district. This western end of Lockhart Road is a lively neighbourhood of bars, restaurants, and old office buildings. To the south of Lockhart Road is a far more "Chinese" part of town, Queen's Road East, which traces Wan Chai's original waterfront. The Hung Shing (Tai Wong) Temple (1860) and the old Wan Chai Post Office (1912) are both on Queens Road East, and the Pak Tai Temple is nearby in Stone Nullah Lane.

Inland is **Happy Valley** ⓭, home of the Hong Kong Jockey Club's Happy Valley Racecourse. During the October–May racing season, it attracts up to 75,000 punters on race nights (Wed). The Hong Kong Racing Museum (open 10am–5pm, 10am–12.30pm on race days, closed Mon; entrance fee) is at the

BELOW: handover ambiance, Central District.

Happy Valley Stand. Opposite are the Colonial and Parsi cemeteries. **Aw Boon Haw Gardens** (open daily, 9.30am–4pm; free) formerly known as the Tiger Balm Gardens is an amusement park resembling a hallucinogenic vision of a Chinese Disneyland. Recently sold, the gardens may soon be redeveloped.

Causeway Bay actually was a bay until the 1950s, when it disappeared into a land reclamation project. The present-day "bay" is occupied by the Royal Hong Kong Yacht Club on Kellett Island (which also was once a real island before land reclamation), and the Typhoon Shelter. Causeway Bay is best known as a busy shopping district, featuring large department stores, mostly Japanese.

Nobody knows for sure why the **Noon-Day Gun** is fired at noon everyday. One story has it that, the tradition began in the mid-1800s when a Jardine opium boat sailed into the harbour and a willing minion gave the boat a 21-gun salute. The Hong Kong governor, incensed that a mere purveyor of "foreign mud" should receive the same greeting as an official figure, ordered that the gun be fired at noon everyday in perpetuity.

Victoria Park , named after Queen Victoria, is one of the few public areas in Hong Kong likely to have its name changed now that Hong Kong has been returned to China. A favoured alternative is to call it Central Park.

South Island: Unlike the northern part of Hong Kong island, the rocky coastline of the south side has changed very little. Fishing villages, beaches, and mountain scenery make this a particularly popular area for visitors to explore.

Aberdeen has a character unlike any other town in Hong Kong, and is famous for its bustling harbour, a natural typhoon shelter crowded with fishing trawlers, houseboats, pleasure junks and tiny sampans, rounded off by three rather theatrical floating seafood restaurants. The old sampan ladies keep an eye out for

The Noon-Day Gun stands by the Typhoon Shelter, across from the Excelsior Hotel. Until 1960, a 6-pounder was used. People found this too loud, so Jardine bought a 3-pounder from the Harbour Police to use.

BELOW: Wan Chai on the night of the handover, 1997.

tourists and are always happy to negotiate a fee for a quick, rather hair-raising spin. A quick bus or taxi ride away is **Ocean Park** (open daily, 10am–6pm, Sunday, 9.30am–6pm; entrance fee), one of Hong Kong's biggest tourist attractions. Offerings include a spectacular cable car ride overlooking the South China Sea, a 3,000 seat marine-mammal theatre, the world's largest reef aquarium, adventure rides, and Middle Kingdom, a recreation of life in ancient China.

Repulse Bay, widened to several times its original size, can get very crowded at weekends. The bay was named after the battleship HMS *Repulse*, which helped to thwart pirates in the early days of settlement in the territory. **Stanley** was the site of the largest indigenous settlement in Hong Kong when the British first set foot here in 1841. The main attraction is Stanley Market, which draws thousands in search of the perfect souvenir or clothing bargain.

Kowloon

Kowloon Peninsula starts at **Tsim Sha Tsui**. The waterfront promenade from the **Star Ferry Pier** ⓱ to Tsim Sha Tsui East offers spectacular views of the harbour and Hong Kong island. The **Railway Clock Tower**, erected in 1915 next to the ferry terminal, is the final vestige of the historic Kowloon–Canton Railway Station, the Asian terminus of the old *Orient Express* to London. Across Salisbury Road is the venerable **Peninsula Hotel** ⓲, built in 1928, where people used to stay before boarding the *Orient Express*. In addition to luxurious hotels, Tsim Sha Tsui has a series of run-down mansion blocks, the most infamous being Chungking Mansions, a labyrinth of guest houses, curry messes, sweat-shops, and sari stores. For budget travellers, the cheap guest houses of Chungking are about the only options left in a city of spiralling rents.

Kowloon was a delightfully peaceful place when I arrived. No lorries, a few small buses... only 12 private cars...Nathan Road was lined on both sides by large trees. Beyond that it continued to Mong Kok through rice fields, not far from the sea.

— MARJORIE BIRD ANGUS

BELOW: Aberdeen.

Near the waterfront, the **Hong Kong Cultural Centre** is a minimalist structure with an impressive concave roof spoilt by ugly tiles. It caused a great deal of controversy in 1984, as it was designed without windows on the prime harbour site in the territory. The Centre stages local and international opera, classical music, theatre, and dance. This complex also houses the **Hong Kong Space Museum** (open Mon, Wed–Friday, 1–9pm, weekends, 10am–9pm, closed Tues; tel: 2734 2722; entrance fee), with daily showings of Omnimax movies on space travel and exhibitions of Chinese astronomical inventions. The **Hong Kong Museum of Art** (open Mon–Sat, 10am–6pm, Sun, 1-6pm, closed Thur; tel: 2721 0116; entrance fee) displays traditional and contemporary calligraphy and painting, and historic photographs and artefacts of Hong Kong and Macau.

Other major museums include the **Hong Kong Museum of History** (open Mon–Thurs & Sat, 10am–8pm, Sun, 1–8pm; entrance fee) in Chatham Road South; and in Science Museum Road, the **Hong Kong Science Museum** (open Tues–Fri, 1–9pm, Sat–Sun, 10am–9pm; entrance fee except Wed).

At the bottom of **Nathan Road** – the start of Hong Kong's famous Golden Mile tourist belt – hundreds of small shops are crammed together: tailor shops, jewellers, and electronics stores. Less than a kilometre north on Nathan Road, in the southeastern corner of Kowloon Park, is the **Kowloon Mosque** ㉑, whose four minarets and large white marble dome gracefully stand out. Built in 1984, it serves the territory's 50,000 Muslims. The previous mosque was built 90 years earlier for the British army's Muslim troops from India.

Continue north on Nathan Road, and left onto Kansu, where the **jade market** ㉒ (open daily, 10am–3.30pm) is packed with stalls selling jade ornaments and jewellery. Dealers offer jade in every sculptable form – from large blocks of

Map, page 300

In the early part of the 20th century, shortly after England leased the New Territories, Gov. Matthew Nathan was mocked for having a road constructed up Kowloon Peninsula, then nearly void of people.

BELOW: Tsim Sha Tsui street, and the Clock Tower.

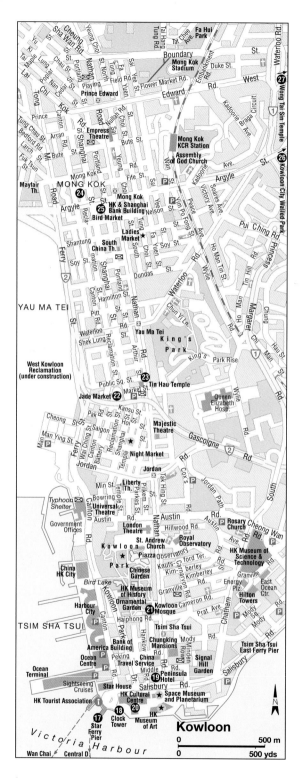

the raw material to tiny, ornately-carved chips. Remember that not everything on offer is genuine.

North from here is **Yau Ma Tei**. Temple Street, originally famous for its temples, is now renowned for its night market (open daily 2pm, but doesn't really get going until 7pm). Here, between Jordan Road and Kansu Street, fake Rolexes, mandarin hats, and other tacky souvenirs are hawked.

The **Tin Hau Temple** ❷ (open daily, 7am–5.30pm) complex stands in Public Square Street, where old men play Chinese chess and cards. Built over 100 years ago, this is one of the oldest and most interesting temples, dedicated to the protector of fisherfolk and seafarers, as befitted its original waterfront location before the days of land reclamation. The second temple on the left was built to honour the local city god and the Ten Judges of the Underworld, depicted with human torsos and animal heads.

If Hong Kong is Earth's most densely populated place, then **Mong Kok** ❷ is certainly one of the most crowded, noisy, and lively districts in the territory. In the early days of British rule, *gweilos* (foreign devils) seldom ventured past Yau Ma Tei, and even today, Mong Kok is notorious for triads, illegal gambling dens, and sleaze. It is also known for several colourful street markets: the **Ladies Market** (open noon–10.30pm) selling a mixture of clothes and souvenirs; the **Goldfish Market** (open 10am–6pm); and the factory outlet shops on Fa Yuen Street offering fashion bargains galore. Further north is Hong Kong's premier **Flower Market** (open 10am–6pm) at the end of which you will find the Yuen Po Street **Bird Market** ❷ (open 7am–8pm), with hundreds of songbirds and beautiful birdcages for sale.

Situated in what's commonly called **New Kowloon**, on the east side of the Peninsula and near the old Kai Tak Airport, Kowloon City and Kowloon Tong are two of the last remaining districts that have evaded redevelopment in recent years. However, the low-rise tenements and family-owned stores of Kowloon

City, and Kowloon Tong's love motels (some of which date back to the 1930s), will soon share the same fate as Kai Tak airport. Now that height restrictions on building development have been removed, the entire area is to be torn down and replaced with tower blocks and shopping malls.

Kowloon City is best seen on foot. Along Junction Road, the **Chinese Christian Cemetery** is a stark reminder of the lack of space in Hong Kong, with graves stacked up like sardines on concrete terraces. An old squatter village lies opposite the cemetery. Next door to the cemetery is the tiny **Hau Wong Temple** (open daily, 8am–5pm) with traditional roof tiles and incense spirals hanging down from the rafters. Built in 1730, the temple is dedicated to Yang Liang Jie, a loyal and courageous general of the exiled Song dynasty's (960–1279) boy emperor, Ping.

Continue east past the temple for 15 minutes, towards **Kowloon City Walled Park ㉖**. Before the British arrived in 1841, the old Walled City was already governed by a Manchu magistrate, and therefore was excluded from the treaty that granted Britain the New Territories on a 99 year lease. At first, Qing dynasty officials continued to be posted in the city, but in 1899 British forces invaded the city, and the Qing officials and troops were expelled.

The area deteriorated into a semi-lawless enclave which was left to its own governance. After World War II, low-rise blocks built without authority and completely lacking proper foundations sprang up on the site, resulting in a multi-storey squatter area with unauthorised electricity and water supplies. By the 1950s, the dank alleyways of the city had become a notorious haven for drug addicts, triad gangs, illegal immigrants, and unlicensed doctors and dentists. In 1987, with China's consent, 35,000 residents were resettled in housing estates,

Map, page 300

Tin Hau, the ubiquitous goddess of the sea in Hong Kong.

BELOW: seductive shopping lights, Tsim Sha Tsui.

and, the entire block was bulldozed to the ground. The park that replaced it, modelled on the Jiangnan garden style of the early Qing dynasty, has exhibits on the Walled City.

Due north, one of Kowloon's most colourful and popular places of worship, the **Wong Tai Sin Temple** ㉗ (open daily, 7am–5.30pm) on Lung Cheung Road, sits opposite an MTR station bearing the same name. Wong Tai Sin, the Daoist god of healing, is said to have discovered the secret of transforming cinnabar (vermillion, a red mercuric sulphide) into an immortal elixir. Backed by the formidable Lion Rock a kilometre away and facing the sea, geomancers agreed that this new site had favourable feng shui. Since Wong Tai Sin is also the god of good fortune, the Chinese, who are too cautious to rely solely on luck, flock to the temple to ask him for advice on all matters, including horseracing.

New Territories

The most logical route for exploring the New Territories is to take the KCR train straight up the middle of the New Territories to within sight of the border with China. As the train pulls out of Kowloon, the city seems to thin out a little before the track is suddenly engulfed by the tunnel under Lion Rock.

Sha Tin ㉘ is one of Hong Kong's fastest growing New Towns, with massive housing projects occupying what were once rice paddies. Sha Tin, directly north of Kowloon, has several places of worship. The **Temple of 10,000 Buddhas** ㉙ (open daily, 9am–5pm) is reached by climbing 431 steps up the hillside above the Sha Tin railway station. A main altar room has 12,800 small Buddha statues on its walls, and the temple is guarded by huge, fierce-looking statues of various gods.

BELOW: Temple of 10,000 Buddhas, Sha Tin.

A further 69 steps up the hill is the **Temple of Man Fat**, the shrine of the monastery's founder. Called Yuet Kai, he was a monk who spent a lifetime studying Buddhism and living a meditative life. His greatest concern was to achieve immortality. After his death, he was buried, but according to Chinese custom, his body was later exhumed to be reburied in its final resting place. However, the body was found to be perfectly preserved and radiating a ghostly yellow glow. Since there was obviously something "supernatural" about Yuet Kai, it was decided to preserve his body in gold leaf.

Another place of interest in Sha Tin is the **Tsang Tai Uk** (literally, Mr Tsang's Big House), a walled village built in the mid-19th century by a wealthy quarrymaster. Most of Tsang's progeny have moved elsewhere, and the fortress is now rented out to more distant relatives of his family. However, this remnant of the former colony's opulent early days has been preserved. The village is rarely visited by tourists, but the people here are hospitable and pleasant, and the complex is less commercial than the more frequently visited Kam Tin walled village.

North of Sha Tin is **Tai Po ㉚**, meaning "buying place": once a small market community, this is now a booming New Town. Two sites worth visiting here are the 19th-century Man Mo Temple and the picturesque Hong Kong Railway Museum (open daily, 9am–5pm).

On the western side of the Kowloon Peninsula, huge reclamation and construction projects are changing the map almost daily for the road and rail links for the new airport on Lantau. The most striking new arrival is the **Tsing Ma Bridge**, the world's longest road and rail suspension bridge, linking Lantau Island to the Kowloon Peninsula. Over 2 km (1 mile) long, its 200-metre (650-ft) twin towers are visible along much of the highway that leads out to Kwai

Map, page 290

TIP

The Kowloon-Canton Railway (KCR) departs Hung Hom station in Kowloon and goes north through the New Territories. The farthest one can go without a China visa is Sheung Shui, this side of the Shenzhen River.

BELOW: shopping mall in Sha Tin.

Chung, an extensive complex of container terminals, and the industrial community of **Tsuen Wan** ❸, another example of Hong Kong's New Towns. It is not certain when Tsuen Wan was first settled, but the recent Chinese presence seems to have begun about the 2nd century AD. The Tsing Ma Bridge Visitors' Centre and Viewing Platform (open daily, except Wed, 10am–5pm) offers a fascinating experience.

Near 580-metre (1,900 ft) **Castle Peak**, adjacent to the light-rail station, is a huge temple called **Ching Chung Koon** which serves as a repository for many Chinese art treasures, including 200 year-old lanterns and a jade seal over 1,000 years old. The library, which holds 4,000 books, documents Dao history.

Just outside of **Yuen Long** ❷ are the walled villages of **Kam Tin**. The most popular for visitors is the Kat Hing Wai village, which stands rather incongruously across the road from a supermarket. There are 400 people living here, all with the same surname: Tang. Built in the 1600s, it is a fortified village with walls 6 metres (19 ft) thick, guard-houses on its four corners, slits for the arrows used in fighting off attackers, and a moat. The authenticity may seem spoiled by some of the commercialism; inside, one street is lined with vendors.

The eastern edge of the New Territories is arguably the most attractive area. In summer, **Clear Water Bay** ❸ is dotted with revellers on corporate junks, and the beach is jam-packed with sunbathers. Branching off Clear Water Bay Road, the highway leads down to **Sai Kung** ❹, a bustling seaside town known for its Chinese seafood restaurants, and a kicking-off point for exploring the natural beauty of Sai Kung Country Park. While the fringes of the town have fallen prey to development, this town still remains very much a fishing community. The most interesting part of the town is hidden behind the Tin Hau temple, off Yi

BELOW: one of the New Territories' walled villages.

hun Street. A maze of narrow alleyways leads past traditional herbalists and ɔodle shops interspersed with ordinary family homes.

utlying islands

ong Kong's new airport – which replaced the one at Kai Tak – opened in 1998 'f **Lantau**'s northern coast on a tiny island called **Chek Lap Kok** ③, with claimed land connecting Chek Lap Kok to Lantau. While this part of the island ıs undergone considerable development, much of Lantau – with twice the area f Hong Kong island – has escaped a lot of the onslaught of development for ɔw, and most of the island remains rural. On the northern side of Lantau, visit ung Chung ③, an old fortress near a bay that curves around the pointed south-n tip of little Chek Lap Kok island. On a hill overlooking this harbour is the old ɔrt built in 1817. The fort's thick ramparts still remain, as do six old cannons, ıuch as they did during the last century when they guarded this town and bay ɔm smugglers and pirates.

Despite the presence of the new airport at Chek Lap Kok (another master-ece by Sir Norman Foster), the large island of Lantau has managed to retain its ʳedominantly rural character. Up on the mountainous central spine is its best-1own attraction, the brightly painted red, orange and gold **Po Lin Monastery** ③. The world's largest outdoor bronze statue of Buddha (24 metres/79ft high), as completed here in 1990. Po Lin's resident monks serve a hearty vegetarian ınch to visitors. West of Po Lin, in the direction of Tung Chung on Lantau's ɔrth coast, is an excellent walking path that traverses mountain ridges and small ınyons en route to Lantau's **Yin Ming Monastery** ③, a haven rich with tra-ɪtional Buddhist paintings and statues.

Map, page 290

BELOW: Buddha, Po Lin Monastery.

**Map,
page 290**

Offshore from Lantau's principle town, **Tai O** , on the west coast, th island's Tanka "boat people" have built rickety homes on stilts over parts of creek, where waters rise during tide changes. Efforts to entice them into ne government-built flats have proved largely unsuccessful.

Lantau is also popular for its many long, smooth, and often empty beache The finest sandy sweeps are on the southeast coastline that arcs from Cheun Sha south of Silvermine Bay to Tong Fuk. The most popular and crowded beac (probably because it is the easiest one to reach, though the water is of dubiou quality) is **Silver Mine Bay Beach** ⓪. Coming by ferry, you will arrive at M Wo, where you can catch buses and taxis to South Lantau Road

The third largest of the outlying islands, and somehow less well-known bot to visitors and to local people, is **Lamma**, associated with some of the earlie settlements in Hong Kong. Although it is just over 13 square km (5 sq miles) i size, Lamma is rich in green hills and beautiful bays and is renowned for i seafood restaurants. Rocky bare hilltops dominate the island's grassy lowe slopes. Lamma is an island devoted to fishing, with a population of aroun 8,000. The town of **Yung Shue Wan** ⓿, at the north end of Lamma, is one c two ferry gateways to the island. This village, popular with expatriates tryin to get away from the noisy crowds of Hong Kong, has streets lined with sma restaurants and bars. Yung Shue Wan's Tin Hau Temple is dedicated to the Quee of Heaven and the Goddess of the Sea. The 100-year-old temple is guarded by pair of stone lions. Inside, behind a red spirit stand (to deflect evil spirits) is th main shrine with images of the beaded, veiled Tin Hau.

The most popular walk on Lamma is a well-maintained pathway runnin much of the length of the island to Yung Shue Wan's sister village of **Sok Kw Wan** ⓬. The well-marked, hilly, concrete-paved trac passes first through neat patches of paddy and an occa sional cluster of brightly-painted houses, then alon Hung Shing Ye, a long and clean beach. The path the leads up and down through hills and valleys. The wal treats hikers to spectacular views out across the sea an back to the soaring skyscraper apartment buildings c Aberdeen and the south side of Hong Kong island. Th walk from one end of Lamma to the other can be com pleted in an unhurried hour and a half.

OPPOSITE: seafood market, Cheung Chau. *BELOW:* temple fortune-telling sticks.

Cheung Chau ⓭ island is much smaller tha Lamma, and it is urbanised in a charming "Old China way. This dumbbell-shaped isle, with hills at either en and a village nestled in the middle is so narrow that yo can walk from Cheung Chau Harbour on its west sid to Tung Wan Harbour on the east in a just a few min utes. Cheung Chau is a fishing island, its curving har bour, filled with boats of all sizes, shapes, and colours including Chinese junks and sampans. They compet for space with the ubiquitous *kaido*, the small boats use as motorised water taxis.

The island was once the haunt of pirates. One of th greatest pirates of all, Cheung Po Chai, used to hide ou on this island when he was in danger and fearing for hi life. His tiny cave retreat can still be explored on a sho walk. There are excellent beaches to be found; they ca be reached by walking on the Peak Road across th island through the little homesteads.

MACAU

Following in the steps of Hong Kong, Macau has become a Special Administrative Region of China, but its Portuguese colonial ambience and the roll of the dice continue to offer a different face.

This elfin Portuguese colony on the South China Sea has always been a pearl facing the outer harbour with wide, banyan tree-covered boulevards winding along the shore. Macau, established in 1557, was the first Western colony on China's shore. On 20 December 1999, it reverted back to the sovereignty of China under a one-country, two-systems policy that guarantees its freedom for 50 years.

The best place to start any foray into Macau is **Largo do Senado Square** Ⓐ the old city's main plaza. Here one will find the main Macau Government Tourist Office, with information and schedules of events.

The pride of the square is the **Leal Senado** Ⓑ (Loyal Senate) building, regarded by most as the best example of Portuguese architecture in the territory. The Leal Senado was dedicated in 1784 and its facade completed in 1876. It was restored in 1939, and more internal restoration was recently completed.

The title "Loyal" was bestowed on Macau's Senate in 1809 by the Portuguese king as a reward for continuing to fly the Portuguese flag when the Spanish monarchy took over the Portuguese throne in the 17th century. It is worth the time to explore the building. The library and council chamber offer Old World woodwork. Around half of the offices on the ground floor create a delightful

BELOW: the facade of St. Paul's.

gallery for visiting exhibitions. From the main road, Avenida de Almeida
Riberio, the square runs up to **São Domingos** (St Dominic's Church); the
church building, in Christian-Oriental motif, stands as one of the oldest and most
famous of Macau's many churches. It's said that there are more churches per
square kilometre here than in Vatican City. St Dominic's dates from the 17th
century, but the Spanish Dominicans had a chapel and convent here as early as
1588. To gain entry, ring the bell to the right of the facade.

From St Dominic's follow the curving pavement on to the ruins of **São Paulo**
D (St Paul's Church). Its towering facade and impressive grand staircase are,
perhaps, the most striking of all Macau's churches. Historians often cite it as
the finest monument to Christianity in the Far East. Unfortunately, the site must
have bad geomancy – what the Chinese call *feng shui*. The first church on the site
was destroyed by fire in 1601, and a new one was begun the following year.

The classical facade you see now was crafted by Japanese Christian artisans
who fled persecution in Nagasaki. In 1835, another fire spread and eventually
destroyed St Paul's. In 1904, efforts were made to rebuild the church, but, as
you can see, little was done. Nonetheless, today the grand facade of St Paul's
remains Macau's most enduring visitor attraction.

Overlooking the facade of St Paul's are the massive stone walls of the **Fort-**
aleza do Monte **E**, simply called **Monte Fort**, built in the early 1620s. When
Dutch ships attacked and invaded Macau in 1622, the then half-completed
fortress was defended by clerics and African slaves. A lucky cannon shot by an
Italian Jesuit hit the powder magazine of the Dutch flag ship and saved the city.
The new Museum of Macau here (open Tues–Sun, 10am–6pm; entrance fee)
showcases Macau's colourful history, popular arts and traditions.

Map,
page 309

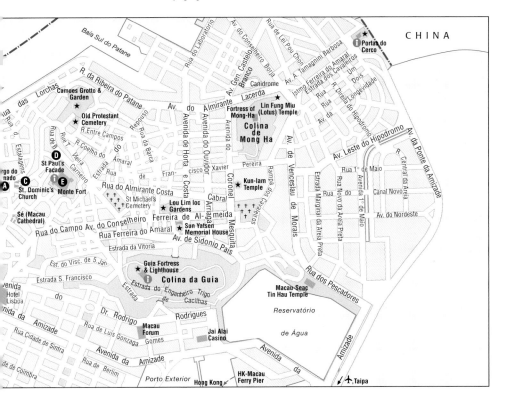

Map, page 309

The historic Hotel Bela Vista ("beautiful view") was closed in early 1999 in order to convert it into the official residence of the Portuguese Consul-General to Macau. Sadly, it is therefore no longer possible to stop for tea on the verandah. The architecture is still impressive, however.

No sojourn to Macau would be complete without a visit to **Temple da Deusa A-Ma ⑥** (A-Ma Temple), beneath Barra Hill at the entrance to Macau's Inner Harbour. It is the oldest temple in the territory, said to date back 600 years to the Ming dynasty. The original temple was said to have been erected by Fujianese fishermen and dedicated to Tin Hau, the patron goddess of fishermen. The oldest surviving part of this temple is a lower pavilion to the right of its entrance. There is a multi-coloured, bas-relief stone carving here said to be a rendering of a junk that carried the goddess A-Ma (Tin Hau in Hong Kong) through typhoon-ravaged seas to Macau, from where she ascended to heaven.

An area often missed by quick tours is the **Camoes Grotto and Garden**, named after Portugal's most famous poet, Luis de Camoes, who lived in the 16th century. The renovated 18th-century building now houses the Orient Foundation, although it was once the residence of the president of the select committee of the East India Company. The **Dom Pedro V Theatre** is a completely restored theatre with 350 seats. In 1985, the Crazy Paris Show, a titillating French strip extravaganza, moved to larger premises after five years of gracing that tired, ancient stage with sexy routines.

Macau's casinos are located in five hotels (Lisboa, Mandarin, Kingsway, Holiday Inn, and Hyatt-Regency on Taipa Island), on a permanently moored floating barge in the Inner Harbour called the Casino de Macau, and a few other locations in the territory. Almost every game known to gamblers can be played

in Macau's temples of money. If gambling, know that the rules in Macau are somewhat unique at times. After placing your bet, a bystander can up the bet and take control of both the bet and the hand.

The "Other Macau" is not on the peninsula that is generally regarded as Macau, but consists of the two outlying islands of Taipa and Coloane. **Taipa ❶** is connected to the mainland by two beautiful arching bridges. Access is as simple as getting into a taxi or climbing aboard a bus. Taipa has a number of high-rises, relieving some of the pressure on congested Macau.

A new international airport, Macau's first, also sits offshore on an artificial island, but both islands are still rural and charming. Towns have Iberian-style buildings around a central plaza, surrounded by typical Chinese farming communities.

Except amongst race fans who frequent Taipa's track, **Coloane ❶** is probably the more popular of these two Macau islands, usually because of the Pousada de Coloane on Cheoc Van Beach and the Westin Resort with the only golf course in the territory (for members and guests only).

Coloane is connected to Taipa by a causeway. At **Hac Sa Beach**, there is a park of the same name with a swimming pool and sports facilities. Cheoc Van Park, also on a beach of the same name, offers pool facilities. Another of Coloane's beaches, Kao Ho, was once a haven for pirates.

GUANGZHOU

Map, page 317

Much of the West's important historical encounters with China focused on Guangzhou and the river known to the West as the Pearl River, and to the Chinese as Zhu Jiang.

At the mouth of the **Zhu Jiang (Pearl River)**, Guangzhou (Canton) was probably founded in 214 BC as an encampment by the armies of the Qin emperor, Qin Shi Huangdi. By the Tang period (618–907), the city was already an international port. In 1514, a Portuguese flotilla reached Guangzhou. After the overthrow of the Ming dynasty by the Manchu in 1644, nationalist ideas survived longer in Guangzhou than in other parts of China. Yet, at the same time, close contact with overseas Chinese (*huaqiao*) ensured the continuation of an openness to the world and a desire for reform in the city. Openness, in turn, would eventually spawn revolutionary zeal. Trade with England increased, particularly the importation of opium. From 1757 to 1842, Guangzhou held a trade monopoly in China, because it was the only Chinese port open to foreigners. Traders were obliged to cooperate with Chinese merchant guilds, a restraint that would later be used by the European powers to intervene in Chinese politics.

In 1839, the Chinese ordered the confiscation of 20,000 chests of opium, leading to military intervention by Great Britain and the First Opium War in the early 1840s. The resulting Treaty of Nanjing led to the opening to foreign trade in Guangzhou, Shanghai, Xiamen, Fuzhou, and Ningbo, and the gift of Hong Kong to England. In 1858, in a reactionary fit by the Chinese, foreign traders were required to limit their base of operations to the island of Shamian, at the mouth of Zhu Jiang. After the Second Opium War (1856–1860), they settled in other parts of Guangzhou and continued trading. After the overthrow of the Qing dynasty in 1912, Guangzhou became the centre of the movement led by Sun Yatsen (Sun Zhongshan) and the headquarters of the Guomindang (Nationalists), the first modern political party in China. During a period of cooperation between the Guomindang and Communists, Mao Zedong worked and taught at Guangzhou's Institute of Peasant Movements, and Zhou Enlai at the military academy.

The modernisation of Guangzhou began in the early 1920s; most of the main streets defining the city today were built then. A feverish sense of urgency in construction – it took only 18 months to build 40 kilometres (25 miles) of road – is evident even today. During that modernisation in the 1920s, the remainder of the old city wall was pulled down. Today, Guangzhou is a city of 5 million people in the greater metropolitan area, with over 2 million within the city proper. Like many of China's cities, Guangzhou's population is probably much higher than official figures indicate. Throughout the city, high-rises, hotels, bridges, and new highways now seemingly materialise overnight.

The personality of Guangzhou differs significantly from that of northern China. Where one can stand in the middle of Tiananmen Square in Beijing and feel the

PRECEDING PAGES: the city's youth increasingly have time and money. **OPPOSITE:** Guangzhou at dusk. **BELOW:** train station.

backbone of Chinese authority, one can easily stand on any street in Guangzhou and feel the lack of order inherent in the traffic and commotion. The language of Guangzhou, Cantonese, is incomprehensible to northern Chinese, who typically speak Mandarin. Cantonese has nine tones, instead of the four tones in the Mandarin dialect.

The area around Guangzhou was overcrowded even 200 years ago, and many peasants from the region emigrated to Southeast Asia, North America and Europe. As a result, Cantonese is the most common dialect amongst overseas Chinese. Likewise, Cantonese cuisine is the most widely-known of all Chinese cuisines, even if it is often mocked by other Chinese. There is a famous Chinese idiom: in Beijing one talks, in Shanghai one shops, and in Guangzhou one eats. Without a doubt, Guangzhou is best known for its eclectic food – from insect omelettes to *dim sum*. Famous for its snack-like form (dumplings, pastries and noodle dishes chosen from carts wheeled around the restaurant), dim sum is ubiquitous in Guangzhou.

The province's name in Cantonese is Guangdong, from which the Portuguese derived Cantáo. From Cantáo came Canton, which came to be the European name for Guangzhou.

Old Guangzhou

In the southwest of the city, the island of **Shamian** **Ⓐ** is a preserved relic of the colonial past. It was originally a sandbar on the north bank of the Zhu Jiang (Pearl River) before it was reclaimed and expanded. The small island was divided in 1859 into several foreign concessions, primarily French and British. A canal was dug around Shamian and late in the evening, Chinese were kept off the island by iron gates and narrow bridges. Today, the island is only one kilometre by half a kilometre in size and feels very much like a resort area, in contrast to the bustle of Guangzhou proper. The former Catholic and Anglican

BELOW: colonial architecture on Shamian.

churches have been reopened for worship, and most of the former trade and consular buildings are now used as local government offices. The buildings, many of which were of French construction and used as consulates, are brightly painted and feature Roman columns. One of Guangzhou's five-star hotels, the White Swan, is located on the southwestern corner of the island, with expensive shops and cafes.

Half way down Shamian, towards the mainland on Qingping Lu, is **Qingping Shichang B**, a market occupying the side alleys around the main roads of Renmin Nan Lu and Nuren Jie. This district has flourished since the economic reforms of 1978 and is always quite crowded with shoppers and those seeking a snack. The whole area has a carnival feel. It was one of the first places to develop under China's gradual adoption of market economics, and for years it was a capitalist oddity. Today, Qingping is notorious for selling every imaginable animal for sustenance, including dogs, cats and owls, as well as a variety of insects. Antique stalls line Dishipu Lu and Daihe Lu selling jade, jewellry, old timepieces, Mao paraphernalia, and some antique porcelain reproductions. To the east is **Wenhua Gongyuan** (Culture Park), with roller-skating rinks, an open-air theatre, theatre halls, art exhibitions, and acrobatic performances.

Opposite the canal that separates Shamian from Guangzhou itself, and where houseboats are occasionally moored, begins the so-called Bund, which continues eastward along the waterfront to **Haizhu C**, the oldest steel bridge across the Zhu Jiang, built in 1933. About 100 metres (300 ft) to the east of **Renmin**, the bridge that connects the eastern end of Shamian with the mainland, is a memorial to Chinese demonstrators who died in a hail of bullets fired by foreign troops guarding the foreign quarters in the mid 1920s.

TIP

Guangzhou is a temperate, subtropical city. The Tropic of Cancer runs a few kilometres to the north. The rainy season parallels the hot summer months, when daily afternoon showers are typical.

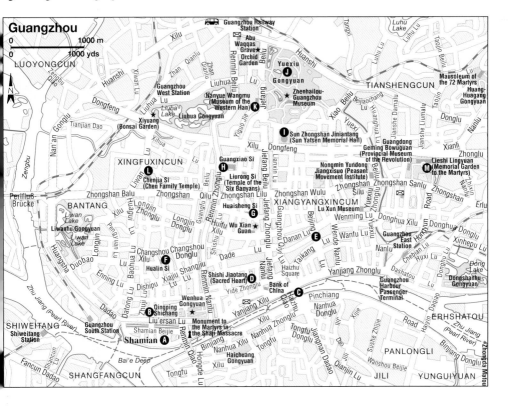

A short distance to the north, many jade and antique shops can be found. About 2 km (1¼ miles) farther east, to the north of Haizhu, the 50-metre-high (160 ft) double towers of **Shishi Jiaotang ⬤** (Sacred Heart Church), the Catholic cathedral, are visible. Built in the early 1860s, the cathedral was left to decay after 1949, particularly during the Cultural Revolution. In the 1980s, it was restored and now holds services under the auspices of the Patriotic Catholic Church, which is officially banned from having contact with the Vatican.

Farther east along the river past Haizhu bridge and heading north begins Guangzhou's main shopping street, **Beijing Lu ⬤**. Guangzhou's proximity to Hong Kong allows for some classy boutiques and fashionable stores one would not find anywhere else in China. Long gone are the solemn grey jackets as an explosion of colourful, at times risqué, fashion has hit the streets of Guangzhou.

Xiajiu Lu leads north to Guangdong, a restaurant. Behind it, in a narrow side alley named Shangxia Jie, is **Hualin Si ⬤**. This temple is said to have been founded by an Indian monk in 526, although the existing buildings date from the Qing period. There are 500 statues of *luohan* – pupils of the Buddha – in the main hall. A statue of Marco Polo with brimmed hat, however, was lost during the Cultural Revolution.

Between Renmin Zhong Lu and Jiefang Zhong Lu, south of Zhong Shan Lu in Guangta Lu, one can spot the onion dome of **Huaisheng Si ⬤**, a mosque dating back to 627 and founded by a trader who was said to be an uncle of the Prophet Mohammed. Arab traders visited China at that time, so the legend may well contain some truth, although it does not give sufficient evidence for an exact date of the mosque's beginnings. The 25-metre (80 ft) minaret, **Guang Ta** (Naked Pagoda), dominates the area, although new high-rises are competing for

BELOW: downtown skyline, Guangzhou.

the skyline. The mosque – the buildings are all of recent construction – is a cultural centre for Guangzhou's 5,000 Muslims.

To the north of Zhongshan Lu, a fairly narrow street leads to **Liurong Si** (Temple of the Six Banyan Trees), and **Hua Ta** (Flower Pagoda), built in 1097 and a symbol of the city. The pagoda appears to be nine storeys in height, each with doorways and encircling balconies, but inside, the pagoda contains 17 levels. Visitors can climb to the top and have a view of Guangzhou's sprawling streets, though some vantage points are a bit marred by skyscrapers.

A few hundred metres northwest is **Guanxiao Si** ❽, a temple preserved during the Cultural Revolution on orders from Zhou Enlai. Local legend has it that the temple is older than the town, dating from around AD 400. Some of the present buildings were, however, built after big fires in 1269, 1629, and most probably after 1832. At the entrance is a brightly painted laughing Buddha, and in the main courtyard, a huge bronze incense burner fills the air. The main hall is noted for its ceiling of red-lacquered timbers, and the back courtyard contains some of the oldest iron pagodas in China.

To the northwest, in a formal garden near Jiefang Bei Lu and Dongfend Lu, **Sun Zhongshan Jiniantang** ❶ (Sun Yatsen Memorial Hall; open daily, 8am–5.30pm) is easy to spot with its blue roof tiles. The hall, built after the death of Sun Yatsen in 1925 and completed in 1931, houses a large theatre and lecture hall of 12,000 square metres (130,000 sq ft) that can seat 5,000 people.

Guangzhou's largest park, **Yuexiu Gongyuan** ❿, due north, is a beautiful example of a landscaped park with three artificial lakes, seven hills, rock sculptures, and lush greenery. It is dominated by **Zhenhailou** (Tower Overlooking the Sea), built in 1380 as a memorial to the seven great sea journeys undertaken

Map, page 317

TIP

Thousands of rural people come to Guangzhou looking for work, often unsuccessfully. As a result, one may encounter more crime, such as pickpocketing, here than elsewhere in China. Be careful near the train station.

BELOW: Sun Zhongshan Jiniantang, and downtown high-rise.

Map, page 317

by the eunuch Zheng He. Between 1405 and 1433, Zheng He travelled to east Africa, the Persian Gulf, and Java. Today, the tower houses a museum on the history of Guangzhou. Nearby is the **Sun Yatsen Monument**, built of marble and granite and sitting on a hill above Sun Yatsen Hall. One can climb to the top for a great view of the city. Yuexiu Gongyuan also features some recreational activities, including a golf driving range, bowling alley, and swimming pool.

To the south along Jiefang Bei Lu is the **Nanyue Wangmu** Ⓚ (Museum of the Western Han; open daily, 8am–5pm; fee), the tomb of the Nanyu emperor. In 1983, when bulldozers were clearing the ground to build the China Hotel, they dug up the tomb of the emperor Wen Di, who ruled southern China from 137 to 122 BC. Today, in its place stands the museum that houses skeletons of the emperor and fifteen courtiers who were buried alive with him, including concubines, guards, cooks, and a musician. The museum recreates the setting of the tomb so that visitors can walk down stairs into the actual chambers. Archeologists found that the tomb walls were built from sandstone carved from Lianhua Shan, about an hour east on the Zhu Jiang. Thousands of funerary objects, from jade armour to bronze music chimes, are displayed in adjoining rooms.

Restored after the Cultural Revolution, **Chenjia Si** Ⓛ (Chen Family Temple; open daily, 8am–5pm) dates from 1894 and lies north of Zhongshan Qi Lu, near the intersection with Liwan Lu. It has six courtyards and a classic layout, and is decorated with friezes. The largest frieze, at 28 metres (90 ft), depicts scenes from the epic *Romance of Three Kingdoms*, with thousands of intricate figures against a backdrop of ornate houses, flourishing gates, and pagodas. The temple features a giant altar of gold-leaf plating and additional wood, brick, and stone friezes along the rooftops. Gardens surround a small lake with row boats, along with tennis courts, swimming pool, and a gym. The family name Chen is one of the most common in Guangdong Province. Families of that name from around the province donated money to build this temple, which is home to the Guangdong Folk Arts Museum. The museum displays Chinese arts.

Eastern districts

In the eastern part of the city, on Zhongshan Lu, is the former **Kongzi Miao** (Confucius Temple). It lost its religious function during the "bourgeois revolution" in 1912. In 1924, the **Peasant Movement Institute** (Nongmin Yundong Jiangxisuo) opened here, in effect the first school of the Chinese Communist Party. The elite of the Communist Party taught here: Mao Zedong (his work and bedroom can be viewed), Zhou Enlai, Qu Qiubai, Deng Zhong, Guo Moruo, and others. This is where Mao developed his theory of peasant revolution.

After the collapse of a workers' uprising in 1927, the Communists were forced to retreat for a time from the cities. A park and memorial, **Lieshi Lingyuan** Ⓜ (Memorial Garden for the Martyrs), was created in 1957 in memory of the uprising and its nearly 6,000 victims. The temple is mostly of Ming-period construction.

Directly east of it is Guangdong Geming Bowuguan (Provincial Museum of the Revolution), a reminder of the role of the Guomindang and its predecessors since the First Opium War.

BELOW: bicyclists in a special lane.
OPPOSITE: monument to Sun Yatsen.

GUANGXI AND GUILIN

Picture-perfect is how artists and photographers have described the landscape near Guilin – limestone spires rising above a smooth river at one of China's most aesthetic destinations.

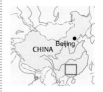

Map, page 327

T he river is like a green silk belt, and the hills are like turquoise jade hairpins." So wrote the Tang dynasty scholar and writer Han Yu (768–94), becoming the first prominent voice to immortalise this bizarre landscape. Ever since, artists have joined the chorus of eulogies in poems and paintings. Nowadays, photographers from all over the world have taken up the aesthetic challenge, aiming for the most evocative possible image. Together with Beijing, Shanghai, and Xi'an, Guilin has become one of China's foremost destinations.

The Guilin area owes its exquisite beauty to geological disruptions over 300 million years ago. Limestone formations pushed through an ancient sea bed, then the wind and rain eroded the hills and peaks into innumerable shapes, leaving behind labyrinthine caves and grottoes within them. With some peaks rounded, and some sharply pointed, with often perpendicular cliffs and trees that sprout from the cracks to bend skyward, this is the surreal landscape geographers call *karst*, which lures travellers to Guangxi and especially to Guilin.

The local people have a more fanciful explanation for the landscape's contours. They say the hills were herded there by the King of All under Heaven, wielding a magic whip made from the hairs left in the brush of a goddess. That deity had assumed the disguise of an old lady, leaving the whip to the workers. But the King of All confiscated it and was driving the hills towards the South Sea in a mad attempt to fill up the oceanic realm of his rival, the Dragon King. But Shark Girl, a loyalist of the latter, contrived to steal the whip and the King of All had to abandon his scheme. Ever since, the hills have remained where they are, enchanting countless generations.

The Zhuang minority is the largest ethnic minority in China, comprising a third of Guangxi's 40 million inhabitants and dominating its eastern half. Another five percent belong to ten other minorities, such as the Yao, Miao, Dong, and Yi, living primarily in the western and northern mountains. The Han Chinese are the predominant group in the urban areas and in the western part of Guangxi.

Because they are far from Beijing to the north, Guilin and Guangxi have a tradition of sheltering refugees. In 1647, the fleeing Ming court established a temporary residence here in their flight from the Manchus. Three centuries later, as the Japanese army swept into China, hundreds of thousands of northerners sought safety in Guilin. In 1949, it was one of the last Guomindang (Nationalist) strongholds to fall to the Communists.

Until the end of the 1970s, this area along the **Li Jiang** (Li River) was a remote and quiet place. But with the development of tourism and the establishment of flight connections with the major cities of China, the city of Guilin has grown up.

PREVIOUS PAGES: autumn in Yunnan's mountains.
LEFT: Li Jiang and limestone spires.
BELOW: cormorant fishing.

Guilin is in the northeastern area of Guangxi Zhuangzu Zizhiqu, an autonomous region that lies in the southern, subtropical part of China, bordering Vietnam to the south. The long summers are hot and humid, and winters often wet, so the best times to visit the province are spring and autumn.

Guilin

Boasting over half a million residents, **Guilin ❶** literally means "cassia tree forest", named for the local cassia trees, whose scent wafts through the city in autumn. Historical records put Guilin's founding at 214 BC, during the reign of Qin Shi Huangdi, the first emperor of a united China, when he ordered the construction of the Ling canal to connect the central plain of China with the south and with Southeast Asia, via the Yangzi, Li, and Zhu rivers. The canal, one of the world's longest, still exists and can be easily seen at Xing'an, 65 kilometres (40 mi) northwest of Guilin.

The plains around Guilin are still mostly agricultural, though the cultivated areas are constantly interrupted by hills and occasional clumps of bamboo. Labour is often by hand, with water buffaloes the beasts of burden. Rice is the main crop. Also grown are sugar cane and *jujube* (the Chinese date), as well as peppers, which go into the piquant local sauce known as *guilinjiang*.

Guilin has no old town left, because the entire city was razed by the Japanese army in 1944. A construction boom only began with the blooming of the tourist business. The city now has the usual characteristics of a modern metropolis – heavy traffic, shopping centres and boutiques, plus the usual scam artists, souvenir stalls and ticket booths that are a part of any popular tourist spot. The most imposing buildings are the fancy new hotels.

BELOW: Ludiyan, or Reed Flute Cave.

On the other hand, it's a clean city with a charming waterfront and ever-changing moods. Hills and parks mottle the urban landscape. A few sights, like Xiangbi Shan (Elephant Trunk Hill), Fubo Shan, and the port area, are illuminated at night. And the many small restaurants offer Li Jiang cuisine, such as fish, eel, frog, turtle, snail, shrimp, and snake.

North of the centrally-located Lijiang Hotel (on Shanhubei Lu) stands **Duxiu Feng**, the Peak of Solitary Beauty. Three hundred steps lead to the top of this 150-metre (500 ft)-high hill, from which one has a splendid panorama of the city. Just below it is **Wang Cheng**, briefly the former capital of the Ming court. Its buildings now house the Guilin Teachers' College.

To the east, at the corner of Binjiang Le and Fengbei Lu, **Fubo Shan** sits on the bank of the Li. This hill is named after the nickname of a Han dynasty general – Restraining the Waves – who saved Guilin from a rebel army. At the foot of Fubo Shan is a two-ton bronze bell, while nearby a huge cooking pot, said to have served 1,000 people, is encased in cement.

Underneath the hill is Returned Pearl Cave, where a dragon used to live, using a magnificent pearl to light his cave. A boy once stole it, but his mother persuaded him to return it to the owner. The grateful dragon richly rewarded them.

At the riverside exit of the cave's tunnel is **Qianfo Yan** (Thousand Buddha Rock), where Tang and Song dynasty devotees have carved hundreds of Buddhist sculptures and left prayers inscribed on plaques. Farther north lies **Diecai Shan** (Piled Brocades Hill), at 220 metres (720 ft) in height, the tallest in the city, with changing hues on the slopes, caves with Buddhist sculptures and calligraphy, and a grand view from the summit.

Map, page 327

On the eastern bank of the Li, just across Jiefang Bridge, lies **Qixing Gongyuan** (Seven Stars Park). It acquired its name from the positions of its seven hills, which suggest the pattern of the Big Dipper constellation. Caves here are also part of the sights, especially Yinlongyan (Hidden Dragon Cave), with its ancient inscriptions. In the park's centre rises Luotou Shan (Camel Hill) and it needs little imagination to notice the almost startling resemblance. Nearby are a bonsai garden and a small zoo.

In the northwest corner of the city, 6 km (4 miles) from the centre, is **Ludiyan** (Reed Flute Cave), which takes its name from the reeds – which were fashioned into flutes – that once grew at the mouth of the cave. Nowadays, a ticket booth and concrete stairway mark that entrance, where guides meet visitors to take them on an illuminated tour 250 metres (800 ft) into the mountain's interior.

The amazing journey passes numerous stalactites and stalagmites in ever-changing, bizarre shapes, suggesting pagodas, mushrooms, lions, waterfalls and icicle chandeliers. The highlight of the descent into the cave is the impressive Crystal Palace of the Dragon King, said to be able to hold 1,000 people at once. In every direction, bizarre rock formations tease the imagination. Most enchanting of all is the subterranean pond at the far end, where the rocks, bathed in soft lights, reflect in the water in a landscape much like that of the best scenery along the Li Jiang.

Cormorant fishing is done mostly for the tourists nowadays.

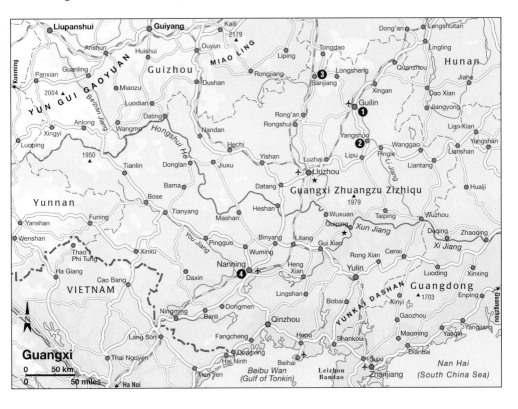

Li Jiang

The boat excursion on the placid waters of the Li Jiang from Guilin to Yang-shuo is a necessary part of any visit to this area. The armada of boats leaves in the morning from the port area between Jiefang Bridge and Xiangbi Shan (Elephant Trunk Hill).

The cruise takes 4–5 hours to reach Yangshuo, 60 km (40 miles) south, and costs over US$50 per person. Much cheaper rides can be arranged from Yang-shuo itself, either north as far as Yangdi (halfway back to Guilin), or east to Fuli, which are some of the best parts of the river. In the drier months, the river is too shallow around Guilin, so the boats start at Yangdi.

The cruise passes through karst landscape, with fascinating spires, many with near-vertical cliffs that shoot up eerily from the flat plains. Poets of the past have dubbed the most striking of them with such names as Expectant Husband, Magic Writing Brush, Mighty Lion Riding a Carp, Mitten Mountain, and Camel Crossing a River. Along the way the timeless rural culture of the river is equally well-developed. Fishermen pole their narrow, three-bamboo rafts along the waters in the evenings, perhaps with a group of cormorants on board for fishing.

Yangshuo ❷ lies within a half-circle of steep hills on the west bank of the Li. A small developed town in which tourism is the main business, Yangshuo fills up in the afternoons when the visitors disembark from the Guilin boats. It mainly caters to low-budget travellers, with a long street lined with restaurants and handicrafts stalls. Amongst the travellers who come here, the most popular pastime is renting bicycles for excursions.

In Yangshuo, the eerie landscapes are closer at hand and superb views can be seen from the hilltop pavilion in the city park, from the port area, and from the

karst *(kärst) n. a limestone region marked by sinks, abrupt ridges, irregular protuberant rocks, caverns, and underground streams.*
— MERRIAM-WEBSTER'S
DICTIONARY

BELOW: Yangshuo.

bridge just south of the settled area. Minibuses take visitors back to Guilin, a two-hour journey past similar plains studded with odd-looking hills.

Map, page 327

Beyond Guilin

To the northwest of Guilin are the counties of **Longsheng** and **Sanjiang** ❸. The former is home to the Dong, Miao, and Yao minorities, the latter to the Dong people. Traditional architecture, terraced hills, and ethnic costumes make this area an excellent introduction to southwest China's minorities. Some Yao, and all Miao groups, are famous for their embroidery skills. Dong architecture features the multi-tiered drum towers, before which important assemblies are held, and the triple-towered, covered "wind and rain bridges", the most outstanding of which is the Chengyang Qiao (165 metres/540 ft long) in Sanjiang.

To Guilin's southwest is the industrial heartland of Guangxi. **Liuzhou**, a city of over half a million residents in the province's centre, has a picturesque river and scattered hill parks, the best at **Dule Yan**, 10 km (6 miles) to the west, also with karst caves. **Guiping**, 260 km (160 miles) southeast of Liuzhou, lies at the confluence of the Qian and Xun rivers. This city has been an important trading town since the 18th century. There is a fast jetfoil service from here to Guangzhou and Hong Kong.

Guangxi's capital of **Nanning** ❹, southwest of Guilin, is an affluent metropolis of 700,000 people. Amongst its attractions are the provincial museum, with its fine bronze drum collection, and the adjoining cultural centre, where architectural examples from the Dong, Miao, Yao and Zhuang minorities have been recreated in an open-air museum. Just 5 km southeast of the city, in Qingxiu Park, stands the highest pagoda in Guangxi.

BELOW: washing produce in the Li Jiang.

YUNNAN

Map, page 333

Skirting the northern part of Southeast Asia, Yunnan straddles temperate and subtropical climates. Asia's great rivers pass through it, and its people are culturally diverse.

China's southwestern province of Yunnan lies at the threshold of Southeast Asia, bordered by Burma (Myanmar) to the west, Laos and Vietnam to the south. Chinese troops first marched into the area from Sichuan in the fourth century BC, but when political reversals cut them off from their homeland, they simply stayed on and created the Kingdom of Dian, near present-day Kunming. The Han dynasty (206 BC–AD 220) later tried to reassert control over Dian to protect newly-established posts on the southern Silk Road.

Over the centuries, Chinese control of Yunnan was intermittent and ephemeral, and Yunnan was, by the Tang dynasty (618–907), divided into several small princedoms. The prince of one of these made the long journey to Chang'an. When the Tang emperor asked from where he came, the prince replied he was from far away to the south, beyond the clouds of rainy southern Sichuan. So the emperor named the prince's homeland *Yunnan*, or South of the Clouds.

In the eighth century one of the princes seized power in central Yunnan and founded the Nanzhao Kingdom, which fought a century-long, three-sided war with Tibet and Tang-dynasty China for control of the southwest. Yunnan remained beyond China's jurisdiction until Kublai Khan conquered Nanzhao's successor, the Kingdom of Dali, in 1253. Even as the Han Chinese finally became a majority of the population, rulers and officials of the imperial court continued to regard it as wild, dangerous, full of barbarians, and culturally deprived – the perfect place to send malcontents, political troublemakers, or villagers of the east forced by natural disasters to start life over as pioneers on the frontier.

OPPOSITE: two sisters of the Mosuo minority group.
BELOW: the village of Lige, Lugu Lake.

The land

No place in China offers the traveller as much diversity, both geographical and cultural, as Yunnan. The heart of the province lies on the elevated Yunnan-Guizhou Plateau, at an average altitude of 2,000 metres (6,500 ft). Mountains comprise a significant part of the landscape, with the ranges in the northwest the highest. The northern half of Yunnan features temperate-zone flora and fauna, with clearly-marked seasons that guarantee spring flowers and bright autumn colours.

In the southern part of the province, tropical vegetation dominates, and the hills are smaller but no less steep, while bamboo, palm, and plantain compete for space with pine and poplar.

Some of the greatest rivers in Asia pass through Yunnan: Chang Jiang (which Yunnanese call the Jinsha Jiang, or River of Golden Sand) in the north; Zhu Jiang (Pearl River) flows to Guangzhou; and the Yuan Jiang (Red River), Nu Jiang (Salween), and Lancang Jiang (Mekong) all twist their way through Yunnan before crossing into Southeast Asia.

Yunnan's ethnic minorities are an even greater draw than its natural attractions. Han Chinese culture exists – temples, gates, and other examples are obvious – but that is not the reason people come to Yunnan.

This fascinating and varying environment is home to 24 recognised minority nationalities. Their lifestyles and local ecosystems vary almost as much as their colourful ethnic costumes. Altogether they form one-third of Yunnan's population and occupy two-thirds of the land.

Since 1979, they have been free to practice their own customs and religion, and have generally enjoyed a cultural renaissance. So long as the visitor acts politely and displays no trace of a superiority complex, the people are quite approachable and eager to meet foreigners.

TIP

A narrow-gauge rail line, built by the French a century ago, connects Kunming with Hanoi via the border crossing at Lao Cai, Vietnam, and Hekou, Yunnan.

BELOW: Bai women.

Kunming

Yunnan's capital, **Kunming ❶**, sits at 2,000 metres (6,500 ft) above sea level off the northern shore of Dian Chi, the province's largest lake and busy with ferries, tour boats, and fishing craft throughout the day. Despite its growing population, already over 3 million, and its development as a business centre for China's burgeoning economic links with Southeast Asia, the city retains much of its old-fashioned charm and atmosphere, with cool summers and mild winters.

Among the oldest structures in the city, dating back to the Tang dynasty, are two 13-tier pagodas, **Dongsi Ta** and **Xisi Ta**, in the southeast quarter. **Yuantong**, in the northern section of town, is a slightly older temple and was greatly expanded in the 14th century to encompass today's ornamental gardens. A short walk from here lies **Cui Hu** (Green Lake), with ornate boats on the water and bright pavilions on its shores. The grounds, along with that of Daguan Park on

the edge of Dian Chi, and the big square at the intersection of Beijing Lu and Dongfeng Lu, fill every morning with Chinese *taiqi* enthusiasts, as well as those practising their ballroom dancing and perhaps arranging an assignation.

Map, page 333

Outside the city are a few temples worth visiting. **Qiongzhu Si** (Bamboo Temple) lies 13 kilometres (8 mi) northwest. The best example of Buddhist art and architecture in the region, Qiongzhu Si is famous for its hall of 500 idiosyncratic statues of the *luohan* (Buddhist saints and disciples), each uniquely sculpted to embody a Buddhist virtue. **Heilongtan** (Black Dragon Pool) lies 11 kilometres (7 mi) north of the city, flanked by a Ming-era Daoist temple and the nearby botanical garden, with its collection of camellias, rhododendrons, and azaleas. And atop Phoenix Song Mountain, 7 kilometres northeast of Kunming, stands **Jin Dian** (Golden Temple), which is actually furnished with walls, columns, rafters, and altars made from copper – about 300 tons of it.

The most popular temple excursion is to the trio at the Western Hills, 26 kilometres (16 mi) west of the city. Pilgrims begin the six-kilometre climb at the temple of **Huating**, at the base of the mountain. Kunming's largest Buddhist temple, it also houses life-sized statues, some in mirth-provoking poses, of the same 500 *luohan* as at Qiongzhu Si. Further up the road, beside a thick forest, is the smaller but prettier temple of **Taihua**. A steep ascent, which occasionally tunnels through the cliff face, ends at Longmen (Dragon Gate) and the Pavilion of Sanqingge (Three Pure Ones).

The entire 40 kilometre (25 mi) length of **Dian Chi** ❷ is visible from the pavilion. The resort of **Baiyukou** and the temple at Guanyinshan lie on the lake's western shore. A park and museum honouring one of Yunnan's most famous native sons – Admiral Zheng He – stands on a hill at **Jinning**, at Dian Chi's

The fleets of Zheng He, a eunuch and native son of land-locked Yunnan, had 300 ships and 28,000 personnel. Each of these "treasure ships" was 120 metres long. Columbus's Santa Maria, by comparison, was 25 metres long.

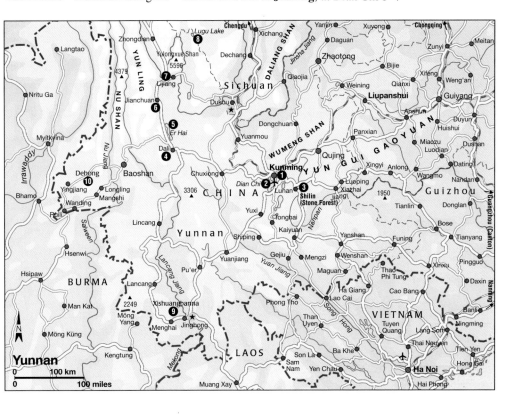

Yunnan

southern end. Mementos and maps of his 15th-century ocean voyages to South-east Asia, India, Africa, and the Middle East are on display. A final attraction in Kunming, especially for those interested in China's minority cultures, is the Minority Nationalities Museum, a few kilometres outside the city. Three buildings with several halls exhibit costumes, tools, implements, jewellery, houses, and anything else to do with the cultures of Yunnan's 24 ethnic minorities.

Visitors to Kunming divide their time between the urban attractions of the city and the wilder, sometimes bizarre landscape of **Lunan** to the east. During the Permian Age 270 million years ago, the area was a lake. But shifts in the earth's crust thrust the limestone bed upwards, and rain and erosion created strangely-shaped karst pillars 5 to 30 metres (16–100 ft) high. While the whole county is replete with small "groves" of such rocks, **Shilin ❸**, or the Stone Forest, 125 kilometres (80 mi) from Kunming, is an 80-hectare (200 acre) concentration of such formations that has become the province's premier tourist site.

Locals have given the stone "trees" some fanciful names. The indigenous Sani people have identified one pillar with their national heroine Ashima, who epitomised all the best qualities of Sani womanhood. A neighbouring ogre of a prince coveted her as a bride for his son. Kidnapped after her refusal, she was rescued by her brother, but when the pair tried to escape, the ogre conjured up a flood that swept her away. Her spirit entered the rock that now bears her name.

Dali

Dali ❹ is an autonomous Bai prefecture 400 kilometres (250 mi) west of Kunming. The high visibility of the brightly-garbed Bai people and their Yi neighbours, a mild climate, stunning mountain scenery, and the beauty of **Er Hai ❺**, Yunnan's second-largest lake, long ago combined to make Dali a favourite stop for foreigners as well as Chinese. A varied range of accommodations, shops, and restaurants with ten-page menus have sprouted in the old city, catering to the strange tastes (pizzas, chocolate pancakes) of foreign travellers.

Most of the historical relics recovered in Yunnan were found in Dali. Many of these date from the Nanzhao Kingdom (738–902), which extended into Burma and east across Yunnan and down into northern Vietnam. An inscribed stele near **Taihe**, Nanzhao's first capital, records the composition of Nanzhao's population, and its organisation, trade, and policies towards Tang-dynasty China.

The best-preserved Nanzhao monuments are **Santa Si**, the famous Three Pagodas just north of Dali city, and the Lone Pagoda near the southern gate. The towering structures (the tallest, and oldest, at Santa Si stands 70 metres, or 230 feet) are all in the close-eaves style, setting the pattern for later pagodas in the province, such as the Snake Bone Pagoda near Xiaguan and the one in Baoshan, 200 kilometres (125 mi) southwest.

The Santa Si pagodas have survived several earthquakes, though the original temple has not. Excavations during a 1979 renovation unearthed a trove of exquisite artifacts – gold Buddhas, silver phoenixes, bronze mirrors, copper utensils – which are housed in a small museum behind the pagodas.

You arrive at the capital city, which is named Yachi (Kunming) and is very great and noble. In it are found merchants and artisans, with a mixed population consisting of idolators, Nestorian Christians, and Saracens...

– MARCO POLO

BELOW: fisherman on Er Hai.

Nanzhao's other great legacy is the collection of cave temples on **Shibao Shan** (Stone Bell Mountain), 130 kilometres (80 mi) north in **Jianchuan** ❻. Sculptures depict not only Buddhist deities but also Nanzhao kings and ministers, commoners, and merchants. A Bai singing festival takes place here every spring.

Internal dissension brought down a Yi kingdom in the area in 902, and when the dust settled 35 years of strife later, a Bai *satrap* seized control and renamed the realm Dali. His descendants held on to it until Kublai Khan arrived in the late 1200s. The Bai still remain the largest community here – the Yi long ago moved to the hills – and live by farming on the plain or fishing in the lake. They are renowned builders, architects, woodcarvers, and marble quarriers.

The word *bai* means white, so the Bai refer to themselves as the White Nationality, descendants of the White King. But the significance of the colour white is unknown, as is their origin and even the name of the White King. Their language is riddled with Chinese loan words, but its grammar is somewhat different, and linguists are unsure exactly how to classify it.

At any rate, white is by no means the dominant colour of the costumes. Bai women favour blue or red, and most still prefer ethnic dress to modern. They wear their distinctive head-dresses even when working in the fields. One of the more assimilated minority groups in China, the Bai observe Han festivals in addition to their own, and their religion is, like the Han, a mixture of Buddhist and Daoist beliefs.

To the northwest: Lijiang

Nestled in the mountains of the northwest, the high plains (2,400 metres/7,800 ft) of **Lijiang** ❼ are dominated by **Yulongxue Shan** (Jade Dragon Snow Moun-

> **Map,**
> **page 333**

In the 19th century, Dali was the headquarters of a Muslim revolt against the Qing government. Mosques and numerous Hui restaurants testify to the continuing Muslim presence.

BELOW: Yulongxue Shan, Lijiang.

tain), 5,600 metres (18,400 ft) in altitude and the best-known massif in the province. First climbed in the 1960s, its 13 peaks are mantled with permanent snow. Yulongxue Shan is home to half of Yunnan's 13,000 plant species, 400 kinds of trees, dozens of flower types, and one-third of China's known species of medicinal herbs and plants. Its many ravines, creeks, cliffs, and meadows all have Naxi names and are settings for the myths and legends of these people, who have made the plain their homeland for a thousand years.

Still heavily forested, the mountain bursts into bloom every spring when the camellias, rhododendrons, and azaleas start flowering. Herders take their cattle, goats, sheep, and yaks to graze on its slopes. In autumn, a portion of the pines turns amber yellow, while the leaves on deciduous trees present patches of orange, bright yellow, mauve, maroon, and scarlet.

Lying only 15 kilometres (9 mi) north of Lijiang, Yulongxue Shan is clearly visible from the city and is best seen in the **Heilong Tan** (Black Dragon Pool), where it is reflected in the water between an arched marble bridge and a three-story Chinese pavilion. Within the park is the **Dongba Research Institute**, where retired Naxi scholars translate the old religious manuscripts. There is also a cultural exhibition hall and the Five Phoenix Tower, which houses a museum and a statue of the Naxi war god, Sanduo.

For closer views of the mountain, travellers can ride north to **Baishui**, or White Water Creek. From there, take a pony ride or cable car up the steep slope to Yunshanping, a delightful meadow at 3,300 metres (11,000 ft). Farther north is the 5,400-metre-high (18,000 ft) Haba towers beside Yulongxue Shan. The 16-kilometre-long (10 mi) narrow valley between them, with the Jinsha Jiang surging below, is Tiger Leaping Gorge, so named because at its narrowest point

BELOW: street in the old part of Lijiang.

leeing tiger is supposed to have escaped a hunter by leaping across the 30-
tre gap to safety.

Besides the scenery, Lijiang's big draw is the 750-year-old Naxi town of
yan. A pair of streams from Black Dragon Pool runs through Dayan, which
ll retains its original layout and traditional architectural style. It is the best
d last of its kind in the country, and so Chinese tourists come here to see the
d of urban environment in which their grandparents grew up. A horrendous
rthquake in 1996 devastated many villages in the region, but fortunately
ected Dayan much less. By the following year, all the damage had been
aired, houses rebuilt, and those buildings within Dayan's boundaries not in
traditional style were razed and replaced with Naxi-style buildings.

The Naxi people migrated to Lijiang long ago from northeastern Tibet. Their
ginal religion, called *dongba* after the name of its ritual specialists, resem-
s the nature worship and other concepts of pre-Buddhist Tibet. It has aroused
interest of the world's scholars, particularly because the dongbas' religious
nuscripts were written with their own pictographic script.

Naxi men have maintained a musical tradition. The first classical Naxi orches-
was founded under Kublai Khan's patronage, and the music and tradition
ve remain unchanged for over seven centuries. Dayan's own orchestra per-
ms nightly in the old town. Naxi women, at least in Lijiang, seem to be
ponsible for all the other work. Naxi women are responsible for the hewing
d hauling, marketing, most of the field work, and managing the family's
ney. Men still retain ownership of the property, however.

The costumes of the women reflect their responsibilities and feature a sheep-
n "seven-starred cape". Frog-shaped, the top is black and the bottom white,

Map, page 333

Naxi dongbas, or ritual spiritualists, long ago invented a pictograph script.

BELOW: barley harvest, Zhongdian.

Map, page 333

The old legends say that the pagoda at Manfeilong, in Damenglong, shelters the wandering Buddha's footprint.

representing night and day, while across the centre seven embroidered circl‹ represent the stars of the Big Dipper. Thus attired, she is ready to "carry the b‹ den of Heaven on her back".

A true matrilineal society exists northeast of Lijiang among the Mosuo, in ‹ area of Lugu Lake and Yongning Basin. There, the house and land pass fr‹ mother to daughter, and all children remain permanently attached to th‹ mother's household. Most Mosuo still practice their "walking marriage" c‹ tom, whereby the man comes to the woman's house only at night and returns his mother's in the morning. Women manage the household, and field work a men are very much in the background.

Lugu Lake ❽ is the most beautiful body of water in Yunnan. At 2,700 met (8,900 ft) above sea level, its 50 square kilometres (20 sq mi) average 40 met (130 ft) in depth. Surrounded by hills, Lugu Lake has wonderful acoustics, ‹ better to hear the distinctive singing of the Mosuo girls while they work in ‹ fields or row their boats. Log cabins are the dominant architecture to be fou along the shore. In the mountains around Lugu live a branch of the Yi peop who are easily recognisable by the women's long, tri-coloured skirts and ‹ black hats.

Beyond the semi-pastoral Yi, the road northwest climbs up onto the Tibe‹ Plateau, at 3,500 metres (11,500 ft). **Zhongdian** exhibits all the traits of typi Tibetan culture: barley cultivation, yaks, lamas, and active monasteries, ch‹ ens, buttered tea, and prayer flags. While this county is relatively flat, **Deqen**, next county north, is very mountainous, with steep ranges rising above the ‹ sha Jiang and, further west, the Lancang Jiang (Upper Mekong), capped by M‹ ixue Shan, near Deqen, at 6,700 metres (22,000 ft) Yunnan's highest pe‹ Beautifully restored monasteries, an often breathtaking landscape, summer fl‹ ers, autumn colours, and the warmth and friendliness of the Khamba Tibetans making Zhongdian increasingly popular amongst visitors.

Xishuangbanna and Dehong

Vast tracts of jungle, tropical vegetation, lush plains, thickly forested mounta‹ – home to rare birds, cats, snakes, elephants, bears and even tigers – characte‹ the prefectures of **Xishuangbanna** ❾, in the deep south, and **Dehong** ❿ the far west at the end of the famous Burma Road. Valuable trees like te‹ mahogany, camphor, and sandalwood abound in these forests. In central Ba‹ (short for Xishuangbanna), a 40-kilometre (25 mi) stretch of virgin fo‹ between Jinuoshan and Menglun has lured researchers from the West.

The Dai are the main inhabitants of the plains of both prefectures. A refi‹ and graceful people, most are Theravadin Buddhists, with a pagoda or monas‹ in nearly every decent-sized village. Other features – the food and fruits, pa‹ lined avenues, bamboo fishing traps, cycle rickshaws, giant multi-rooted ban‹ trees – evoke the mood of Southeast Asia. The Dai have generally kept to t‹ traditional culture in the bamboo and thatch houses of Banna or unbaked b‹ and tile in Dehong. Banna's mountains are home to the Aini (the Akha branc‹ the Hani), Jinuo, Yao, and Yi, while Dehong's mountains harbour mainly Jin‹ (Kachin), with pockets of Achang and De'ang peoples.

Most monuments are Buddhist and are not so striking or richly endowe‹ elsewhere in Southeast Asia. The most outstanding in Xishuangbanna are M‹ **feilong** at Damenglong, 70 kilometres (45 mi) south of Jinghong; the un‹ ally-roofed Jingzhen Baijiaoting, 70 kilometres (45 mi) west of Jinghong; the ochre stupa of Mengzhe, 80 kilometres (50 mi) west. Dehong's best are‹ Yunyan Pagoda near Yingjiang, the Golden Stupa at Jiele, 7 kilometres (4‹ east of Ruili, and the Burmese-style temple of Wuyin Si in Mangshi.

OPPOSITE: a Yi woman in traditional dress.

TIBET

Bumped up against the northern flanks of the Himalaya,
Tibet long eluded the curiosity of outsiders.

Unfortunately, a journey to Tibet no longer has anything in common with the adventures of the past. Instead of a test of strong nerves, energy, and privations, it is now simply an expensive endeavour, and takes about two hours of flying time from Chengdu, in Sichuan. Travellers looking for adventure can go overland from Nepal or elsewhere in China, but expect a ground route to take about a week. Fortunately, however, a journey to Tibet remains as rewarding as ever.

The Tibetans have been nomads for centuries, crossing the highland pastures in the south with their herds of sheep, goats, and yak. In contrast, the north is an uninhabited desert.

The Tibetans are thought to be the descendants of Turan and Tangut tribes from Central Asia, who reached Tibet from the north and mixed with the local population. The Tibetans settled in the Yarlung Zangbo valley, where nature was kind and provided everything necessary for successful agriculture. Today, 2.2 million people live in the autonomous region of Tibet, of whom about 1.7 million are Tibetans. Tibetans also live in Qinghai, Sichuan, and Yunnan provinces, as well as in exile in India and Nepal. The total number of Tibetans is estimated to be 6 million.

The Himalaya are the youngest folded mountains in the world. Before the southern Indian land mass began to shift northward about 40 million years ago, one of the largest oceans in the history of the earth occupied the area. Today, the Tibet-Qinghai Plateau is, at an average altitude of 4,000 metres (13,000 ft), the world's most elevated plateau, covering 25 percent of China. It is closed off on three sides by the highest mountain ranges in the world: to the south, the Himalaya; in the west, the Karakorum; and in the north, the Kunlun and Tanggula ranges.

The Indus and Sutlej rivers have their source in the sparsely populated west, on the sacred mountain of Kailas. The source of the Brahmaputra (Yarlung Zangbo) is to the east. It crosses Tibet in an easterly direction, before flowing through huge gorges southward into the Gulf of Bengal. Further north, in the province of Qinghai, are sources of the two big Chinese rivers: Huang He (Yellow River) and Chang Jiang (Yangzi).

PRECEDING PAGES: Tsangpo River, Tibet; Buddhist monks. **LEFT:** stone image, Sela Si.

Map, page 351

TIBET

To most outsiders, the mention of Tibet suggests idyllic vistas and the life of Shangri-la. In fact, life in Tibet is harsh and often brutal. The high altitude also makes a livelihood challenging.

Known as Xizang in Chinese, Tibet has, for the most part, long been hidden from the rest of the world, historically difficult to reach behind a wall of the world's highest mountains. For centuries, Tibet was the dream of innumerable explorers and adventurers. In past decades, it has been the goal of both backpackers and well-to-do travellers intent on seeing the top of the world.

The 31st king of the Yarlung empire, Namri Songtsen, succeeded in AD 607 in unifying the various Tibetan tribes into the Thufo empire. However, Songtsen Gampo (620–649) is considered historically to have unified the empire, creating a powerful military state, conquering a vast territory, and even threatening the Chinese capital. He eventually transferred his residence from the Yarlung Valley to Lhasa.

Conflicts with the powerful Chinese to the north continued well into the ninth century, when Tibet broke up into numerous small vassals. In 866, the western Tibetan kingdom of Guge was founded. In the 1100s, the abbots of the larger monasteries became powerful rulers, challenging the worldly rulers. In 1207, the first Mongol armies invaded Tibet, and later Kublai Khan gave secular powers to the powerful abbots of the Sa'gya monastery.

In the 1300s and 1400s, the great reformer Tsongkhapa (1357–1416) revived Buddhism and founded new monasteries that became centres of both religious and secular power. He founded the Gelugpa (Virtue) Sect – called Yellow Hat Sect, after the colour of the monks' hats – which was to become the dominant religious and secular power. Indeed, its highest representatives became the Dalai Lama and the Panchen Lama, incarnations of the highest gods of Tibet. The Great Fifth Dalai Lama founded the theocracy of the Yellow Church, supported by the Mongol Khan Gusri, who benevolently governed the Tibetan kings and followers of Tibet's ancient Bon religion.

Han Chinese rule over Tibet began in the 18th century. In 1720, the Qing emperor Kangxi chased the Dsungar invaders out of Tibet and took control. Chinese functionaries, so-called Ambane, headed the local government. Finally, in the late 19th century, the British began to penetrate into the heights of Tibet, and the country quickly became a centre of big-power conflicts. In addition to the British, the Chinese and Czarist Russians also made claims on the country. China, torn by war and revolution in the early 1900s, lost control of Tibet for quite some time, until barely a year after the founding of the People's Republic in 1949. In 1950, the Chinese army entered Tibet and took control.

A Tibetan monk. In Lhasa, Tibet's largest city, there are 100,000 Han Chinese and 140,000 ethnic Tibetans.

The early hopes of Tibetans for a better life and more freedom under the Chinese were quickly crushed. In 1959, a Tibetan uprising was brutally repressed. The Cultural Revolution of the late 1960s and early 1970s resulted in vigorous suppression of religious life, and in the intentional destruction of Tibet's cultural and historical treasures by Red Guards. After China's limited opening of its economic and political system in the early 1980s, demonstrations and violent clashes followed in the late 1980s and into the 1990s.

Lhasa

The capital of the province and centre of Tibetan Buddhism, **Lhasa ❶** lies at an altitude of 3,600 metres (12,000 ft) on the banks of the **Lhasa He**, a river also

PRECEDING PAGES: Potala Palace. **OPPOSITE:** Tibetan woman.

known as Kyichu and a tributary of **Yarlung Zangbo Jiang**. While its name conjures up lofty and romantic images, increasingly Lhasa is taking on the cast of yet another Chinese city, with polluting taxis and trucks crowding the roads, and even exchange-house satellite links to the Shanghai Stock Exchange.

Lhasa can be reached by plane from Chengdu, Xi'an, and Golmud, or via overland routes. The airport is on the southern bank of the Yarlung Zangbo, a two-hour journey south from the city.

The gold-clad roofs of the **Potala Palace** (Budala Gong) greet from afar. A palace built by Songtsen Gampo stood on Marpori, the Red Mountain, in the 7th century. Then after the completion of the Potala Palace in 1645, the Dalai Lamas resided here as religious and secular rulers. The section called **White Palace** was constructed first; half a century later, the **Red Palace** was completed, rising like a huge tower from the sea of white-painted buildings. This is also where the private residence of the Dalai Lama is located. The entire palace covers an area of almost 400 metres (1,300 ft) from east to west, and 350 metres (1,100 ft) from north to south. It rises 120 metres (400 ft) above the Lhasa valley, and the thirteen floors hold almost 1,000 rooms, with ceilings supported by more than 15,000 columns.

In the Red Palace are the great ceremonial halls, 35 small chapels, four meditation halls, and eight vaults for deceased Dalai Lamas. The most splendid and valuable vault is for the fifth Dalai Lama: 15 metres (50 ft) high, and decorated with four tons of gold, and innumerable diamonds, turquoise, corals, and pearls. The vault for the 13th Dalai Lama is about 15 metres (50 ft) long. In the northeastern part of the palace is the chapel of **Avalokiteshvara**, which is considered the oldest part of the structure and said to have been preserved from the original

TIP

Lhasa's altitude is over 3,600 metres, and some of the highway routes to Lhasa cross mountain passes of 5,000 metres. Most travellers experience symptoms – headaches, nausea and vomiting, dizziness – of acute mountain sickness (AMS). Hotels offer pure oxygen for relief.

BELOW: Jokhang.

palace of Songtsen Gampo. The chapel contains a statue of the king Songtsen Gampo with his Chinese wife, Wen Cheng, and his Nepalese wife, Bhrikuti. Look down into the valley and the old city from the roof of the Potala. The holiest temple of all Tibetans is in the city centre. The central building once housed the offices of the Tibetan government administration.

Arrive at the incense-filled temple of **Jokhang** (Dazhao Si) by walking through a prayer hall supported by red columns. The main building of Jokhang, built on a square mandala foundation, dates from the 7th century. The temple was built as a shrine for a Buddha statue that the Chinese princess Wen Cheng brought to Lhasa as a wedding gift from the Chinese emperor. This Buddha, called Jobo in Tibetan, gave the temple its name: Jokhang, the hall of the Jobo Buddha. The centre of the temple is anchored by a courtyard. Four gilded roofs mark the holiest halls: the chapels of the Jobo Buddha, Avalokiteshvara, and Maitreya, and the chapel of Songtsen Gampo.

The golden Jobo statue is richly decorated with jewels and usually covered with brocade and silk bands. At the feet of the Buddha, lamps made of heavy silver and filled with yak oil burn continually. It is not quite certain whether the statue is actually the original from the 7th century, since other artefacts were destroyed during the Cultural Revolution and later replaced with copies.

From the roof of Jokhang is a view of Potala Palace and of the **Barkhor** (Bakuo), the sacred ritual path that surrounds Jokhang and Tsuglagkhang. Numerous pilgrims and traders crowd onto the 800-metre-long (2,600 ft) path. The pilgrims constantly prostrate themselves in the dust and circle in this manner around the Jokhang temple; others continuously turn their prayer hats. On both sides of the path, traders offer their wares. Travelling monks meditate at

Map, page 351

Tibet's natural resources, while difficult to extract, include rich deposits of gold, lithium, and chromium.

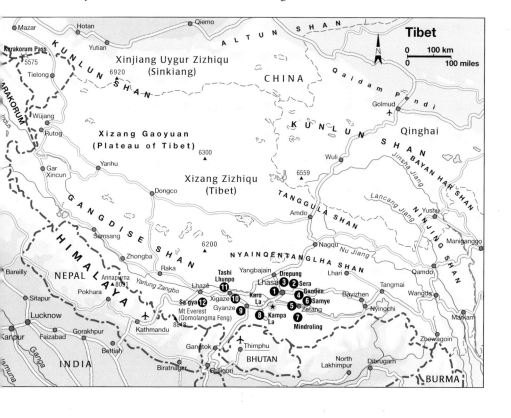

the side of the road and will offer special prayers in return for a donation. There used to be a longer ritual path, the seven-kilometre-long Lingkhor, which surrounded the town, but it has today been broken up by new buildings. In those times, the pilgrims had to measure the path with the length of their bodies before they were allowed to enter the city.

At the entrance of the Jokhang temple, along the Barkhor, a willow tree planted in 1985 marks the spot where, in AD 641, a Chinese princess originally planted another willow as a friendship symbol. A floor tile in front of the temple entrance has an inscription of a Tibetan-Chinese friendship treaty, from 821.

About 7 kilometres (4 mi) from the city centre is **Norbulingka** (Precious Stone Garden), which was built on the orders of the 7th Dalai Lama in the second half of the 18th century. Since then, it has served as a summer residence for the Dalai Lama. The New Summer Palace, which was built for the 14th Dalai Lama and completed in 1956, is the best-preserved of the whole site. On the top floor of the building, which is decorated with numerous wall murals, is an audience hall with paintings from the history of the Tibetan people. Also open are the meditation room and bedroom of the Dalai Lama. There is a throne for the God King in the reception hall, and the wall paintings tell of the various experiences in the life of the 14th Dalai Lama, framed by legends from the lives of the Buddha and Tsongkhapa.

Other buildings in the park include the palaces of the 8th and 13th Dalai Lamas, and the Drunzig Palace, with a library and study.

In the north of the town, near the Barkhor, is **Ramoche**, probably the oldest monastery in Lhasa. It is said to have been constructed in the first half of the 7th century and served as a shrine for a statue brought to Tibet by the Nepalese wife of King Songtsen Gampo. Later, after the arrival of the Chinese princess Wen Cheng, the Jobo Buddha was housed here before it was transferred to Jokhang. The temple was only restored and reopened in 1958, but was later destroyed during the Cultural Revolution and used as a residence. Now, monks reside in it once more.

Three great monasteries near Lhasa are considered important centres of the Yellow Hat sect and pillars of the theocratic state: Sera, Drepung, and Ganden. **Sera Monastery ❷** (Sela Si) was built in 1419 by a pupil of Tsongkhapa, at a place where his great master had spent many years studying and meditating in a small hut. During its most active period, almost 5,000 monks lived in the monastery, which had a brilliant reputation because of its famous academy. Today, around 300 monks live in the monastery, whose main buildings were saved from the destruction of the Cultural Revolution. Sera is 5 kilometres (3 mi) north of Lhasa, at the foot of the mountains dominating the Lhasa valley.

On the way to Drepung Monastery, 10 kilometres (6 mi) west of the town centre, is the small Netschung Monastery, which used to house the Tibetan state oracle. Both monks and lay people could become oracle priests. Before each decision, the oracle was consulted after the priests had put themselves into a trance. The last oracle priest went into exile in India with the Dalai Lama and died there in 1985.

Drepung Monastery ❸ (Zhebang Si), which was built in 1416, also by a pupil of Tsongkhapa, was for a long time the political headquarters of the Yellow Hat sect. Before the Potala Palace was completed, the predecessors of the Great Fifth Dalai Lama resided here before moving to Potala. The tomb stupa of the second, third, and fourth Dalai Lama are housed in Drepung.

Drepung is probably the largest monastery in the world. At the height of its activities, nearly 10,000 monks are said to have lived within its walls. Walking around the cloistered site is somewhat tiring, particularly in the thin air. The

TIP

In 1987, Tibetans rioted in Lhasa. Authorities clamped down on individual foreigners travelling to Tibet until 1992, when restrictions were eased. Still, be prepared for bureaucratic obstacles and costly fees with no apparent purpose.

lower part of the site is occupied by hermitages for the monks, along with numerous storerooms. Further up are the prayer halls and *dukhang*, which contain valuable statues and documents.

Map,
page 351

The third big monastery of the Gelugpa sect is **Gandan** ❹, 40 kilometres (25 mi) northeast of Lhasa. The monastery, which was founded in 1409 by Tsongkhapa, the reformer and founder of the Yellow Hat sect, is one of the most sacred places of Tibetan Buddhism. It was where 5,000 monks once lived, making the almost-total destruction of the site during the Cultural Revolution even more tragic. Hardly any of the monastery's treasures were preserved, and the buildings were torn down to their foundations. Only in 1985 was the rebuilding of the monastery finally completed, and that was limited to the most important buildings, including the mausoleum of Tsongkhapa, recognisable from a distance by its red walls. Since then, however, several hundred monks have returned to the monastery.

Yarlung Valley

A two-hour bus ride in an easterly direction from Lhasa airport south of Lhasa is **Zetang** ❺. This small country town has a few hotels for tourists. From here, one can undertake excursions to the Yarlung Valley and the Tibetan kings' graves, and to the old Samye and Mindroling monasteries. The town of Zetang is said to have been built on the spot where *bodhisattva* Avalokiteshvara descended from heaven in the shape of a monkey and, with the help of a female demon, produced the first Tibetan.

Yama, the god of death, grips the wheel of life.

Seven kilometres (4 mi) south of Zetang, on the road to the Yarlung Valley, is Khrabrug Monastery, one of the first Buddhist monasteries in Tibet and said

BELOW: opening the door to a monastery.

to have been built under the rule of King Songtsen Gampo. After the Cultural Revolution, the site was used as a farm and the buildings for agricultural storage.

Thirty kilometres (20 mi) from Zetang is where the kings of the Yarlung dynasty, who reigned between 627 and 842, were buried. The tombs are only discernible as small mounds of earth. The biggest mound, which has a small temple built upon it, is claimed to be the burial ground of Songtsen Gampo. **Yumbulagang** is said to be one of the few early Tibetan buildings. It looks as if it literally grew out of the peak of a hill. The citadel had already been changed into a chapel in early times. The Cultural Revolution reduced it to a ruin, but the buildings were rebuilt in 1982.

Travellers can visit the oldest monastery of Tibet, **Samye Monastery** ❻, from Zetang. First cross the Yarlung Zangbo in a ferry, which takes less than a couple of hours. On the opposite bank, a lorry or tractor with a trailer carries travellers to the monastery in about 30 minutes. It is said that Samye was founded by the Indian teacher Padmasambhava, around AD 770. He is considered to be the founder of Tibetan Buddhism who, so it is said, succeeded in winning over the demon gods of the Bon religion. Many of the demon gods in the Tibetan monasteries refer back to such Bon gods. The site has been built on a mandala foundation and reflects the cosmic view of Tibetan religion. The main temple stands in the centre and symbolises the mythical Buddhist peak of Mount Meru. Four smaller chapels were erected on the four cardinal points of the compass. The whole site is surrounded by a wall that is still partly preserved.

About 60 kilometres (40 mi) west of Zetang is **Mindroling Monastery** ❼, which can also be visited on an excursion to or from Lhasa. Built in 1676, it is a monastery of Nyingma, the oldest order founded by Padmasambhava.

BELOW: the high-altitude lake of Yamdrok.

The journey from Lhasa, via Gyangze to Xigaze, is a breathtaking experience. First, the route winds along the banks of the Yarlung Zangbo, up to the 4,800-metre (15,700 ft) pass of **Kampa La**. Looking back, the valley of the Yarlung Zangbo is visible below, and in front, a hundred metres or so farther down, are the deep blue-green colours of **Yamdrok**. The road continues for several kilometres along the shores of this lake. Travellers often stop at the lake for a picnic. From the opposite shore, a hairpin road hewn into the steep mountain face leads up to the next pass, the 5,000-metre-high (16,500 ft) **Karo La ⓭**.

The way eastward passes small villages, fertile valleys, cattle herds, and many yaks, the Tibetan oxen that climb up the steepest slopes with surprising skill to graze. **Gyangze ⓮**, which lies by the northern bank of Nyangchu River, 265 kilometres (165 mi) southwest of Lhasa, is, after Lhasa and Xigaze, the third-largest of the old Tibetan towns. The exposed location of the town – on the road from Xigaze to Lhasa and on the trading route to India, Sikkim, and Bhutan – made it one of the most important trading centres. In 1910, an English diplomat compared the market of Gyangze with Oxford Street in London. Apparently, one could buy Scottish whisky and Swiss watches in Gyangze.

Dzong, a fortification on a hill, is visible from quite a distance away. This citadel was attacked and destroyed in 1904 by an English military expedition. The fortification was opened to visitors in 1985.

The most important structure in Gyangze is **Palkhor Tschöde**. The circle-shaped site, which is enclosed by a wall, used to have several monasteries belonging to different sects. The 32-metre-tall (105 ft) Kumbum *dagoba* in the centre of the monastery site is a unique example of Tibetan architectural skill. The layout of this dagoba is in the shape of a three-dimensional mandala and

Map, page 351

Before China invaded Tibet in 1950, Tibet had approximately 2,000 major monasteries with 110,000 Buddhist monks. Now it has around 1,700 monasteries and 64,000 monks.

BELOW: the Kumbum dagoba, Gyangze.

Map, page 351

Tibetan hair ornament made from silver, turquoise and coral.

The number of monks permitted to reside in Tibet's monasteries is regulated by the government "to promote the development of the economy."

symbolises Mount Meru. The central structure at the tip of the dagoba is a chapel for the original Buddha. Again, there are four chapels at the four cardinal points of the compass. Other shrines are located on the four floors, and visitors sometimes walk along it as if in a trance. The path to the centre is thus a symbol of the spiritual path of salvation. The stupa erected in the first half of the 1600s has survived centuries of historical turbulence.

Xigaze ⑩, 360 kilometres (225 mi) west of Lhasa, past Gyangze and on the southern bank of Yarlung Zangbo Jiang, is traditionally the seat of the Panchen Lama, the second head of Tibetan Buddhism. In ancient Tibet, the town, which today has less than 50,000 inhabitants, was the provincial capital of Tsang. The Great Fifth Dalai Lama bestowed the title of Panchen Lama on his teacher from Tashi-Lhunpo Monastery. While the Dalai Lama is said to be an incarnation of the Tibetan deity Avalokiteshvara, the Panchen Lama is worshiped as the reincarnation of the Buddha Amithaba, and is therefore higher up in the heavenly hierarchy. This latent conflict of hierarchy was constantly manipulated by the Russians, British, and Chinese in their colonial rivalries.

The 10th Panchen Lama died in early 1989 in Beijing. In 1993, the Chinese government invited the Dalai Lama to help in the search for the next Panchen Lama, now claimed by the Chinese government to have been found in 1995.

The residence of the Panchen Lama, **Tashi-Lhunpo ⑪**, was founded in 1447 by a pupil of Tsongkhapa. The monastery site was substantially expanded during the 17th and 18th centuries. Nearly 4,000 monks used to live here; today, there are around 600. The most important building is without doubt **Maitreya**, a chapel built in 1914 by the 9th Panchen Lama. A 26-metre-tall (85 ft) golden statue of Maitreya, the Buddha of the Future, is housed in the 30-metre-high (100 ft) red-stone building.

The memorial of the 4th Panchen Lama is also worth seeing. Eleven metres (36 ft) tall and erected in 1662, it is decorated with 85 kilograms (3,000 ounces) of gold, 15 tons of silver, and innumerable precious stones. The gilded roofs of the chapels for the deceased Panchen Lamas tower over the entire site. A high stone wall stands on the slope behind the monastery. On feast days, huge Thangka are revealed there. To the west of the town, in a large park, is the palace of the 7th Panchen Lama. While it was easy to visit in the early 1980s, when it was still a protected building, this has become more difficult in recent years because the palace had been returned to the 10th Panchen Lama, and the resident monks are still not keen on visits from tourists.

About 145 kilometres (90 mi) southwest of Xigaze is **Sa'gya ⑫**. The road to Sa'gya crosses two high mountain passes. On a clear day, one can see the summit of **Mt Everest**. The monastery at Sa'gya has a special place in Tibetan history. Its foundation in 1073 saw the creation of a new order, the Sa'gyapa school. In some ways, the Sa'gya abbots were the predecessors of the Dalai Lamas. Since 1247, when the Mongol Khan Göden made the abbot Pandita of Sa'gya vice-king of Tibet, the Sa'gya Trizin, an incarnation of the bodhisattva Manjusri, ruled over most of the region to the west of Xigaze.

The Sa'gya monastery buildings are striking because of their dark grey colour and the white horizontal stripes under the roof, as well as the red vertical stripes on the corners. While the southern monastery was left alone during the violence of the Cultural Revolution, the northern monastery was almost completely destroyed. Some buildings have since been rebuilt.

On the way back to Lhasa, unless you're planning to leave overland towards Nepal, consider the northern route. There are many pastures here, so you will come across groups of nomads. The route heads across a 5,300-metre-high (17,400 ft) mountain pass, past the glacier-covered summit.

OPPOSITE: Tibetan woman.

INSIGHT GUIDES

Travel Tips

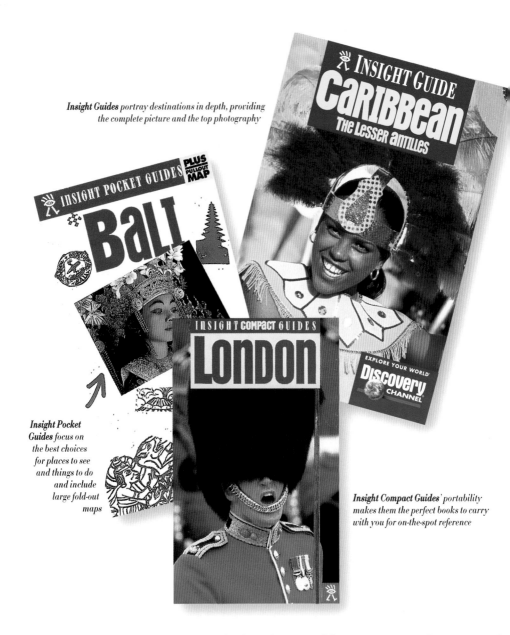

Insight Guides portray destinations in depth, providing the complete picture and the top photography

Insight Pocket Guides focus on the best choices for places to see and things to do and include large fold-out maps

Insight Compact Guides' portability makes them the perfect books to carry with you for on-the-spot reference

Three types of guide for all types of travel

INSIGHT GUIDES Different people need different kinds of information. Some want *background information* to help them prepare for the trip. Others seek *personal recommendations* from someone who knows the destination well. And others look for *compactly presented data* for on-the-spot reference. With three carefully designed series, Insight Guides offer readers the perfect choice. Insight Guides will turn your visit into an experience.

The world's largest collection of visual travel guides

CONTENTS

Getting Acquainted

The Place

Area: 9,560,961 sq. km (3,691,487 sq. miles)
Capital: Beijing
Population: 1.2 billion
Language: Mandarin Chinese (official), Cantonese and a number of local dialects.
Religion: no official religion, but Confucianism, Taoism and Buddhism practised.
Time zone: GMT plus 8 hours adjusted to daylight savings time in summer
Currency: Yuan (RMB)
Weights and Measures: Metric
Electricity: 220 volts
International dialling code: 86

Climate

China covers 35 degrees of latitude, resulting in a great variation of regional climates.The largest area is in a moderate zone with separate seasons. There are distinctive climatic differences resulting from monsoons, the expanse of the land area, and the considerable differences in altitude. While it is generally warm and humid in southeastern and central China, the north and northeast are quite dry. The best times for travelling are spring (May) and autumn (Sept/Oct).

North of the Chang Jiang (Yangzi River), the winter can be extremely cold. The northeast has hot, dry summers and long, cold winters. Summer in the desert regions of Xinjiang and Inner Mongolia is also hot and dry, while winter is cold and dry. In central China, the summers are hot and humid, with a lot of rainfall in the late summer months.

In the low lying regions of the Yangzi, winter is somewhat milder than in the central Chinese mountain regions or in Sichuan, which is surrounded by mountains. In the regions around Beijing, Xi'an and Zhengzhou, there can be sand storms in winter and spring.

Typhoons

Mid-May to September is typhoon season in southern China. In Hong Kong, storm warnings range from 1–10, the former signalling a mild possibility, the latter indicating a head-on, life-threatening storm. Never underestimate a typhoon.
● **To get a storm warning update, tel: 2835-1473 (Hong Kong).**

On the Tibet-Qinghai Plateau (average altitude: 4,000m), summer is short and moderately warm, while winters can get very cold; there is little rainfall throughout the year, and the differences in day and night temperatures are great. A mild climate with warm summers and cool winters generally prevails on the Yunnan-Guizhou High Plateau, with little rainfall, and rare frosts.

Southern China has a sub-tropical climate. Rainfall is distributed around the year; the summers are long, humid and hot, and the winters are short with cooler temperatures. There are frequent typhoons in southeast China during the rainy season, between July and September.

Geography

China is the third-largest country in the world after Russia and Canada. Topographically, the country is made up of 35 percent mountains, 27 percent high plateau, 17 percent basin or desert, 8 percent plains, and 13 percent plains. Only about 11 percent of the land area is actually agriculturally useful. The highest population densities are to be found in the coastal regions of the country.

The People

The People's Republic of China is the world's most populous nation. About 20 percent of the population lives in urban areas. A little over 90 percent are Han Chinese; the remaining percentage, or around 70 million people, includes 55 national minorities who differ fundamentally in their customs, traditions, languages, and culture from the Han Chinese. The minorities have been exempted from China's strict population controls.

Culture & Customs

Although Chinese politeness has always been a formal one that follows strict rules, in some situations Chinese people can seem quite impolite by Western norms. Nevertheless, travellers are advised to remain polite towards their Chinese counterparts, and to refrain from shouting or being insulting. Stay calm in all situations but indicate your problem or inquiry politely and firmly.

Politeness is definitely a foreign word when it comes to public transport. Whether on the underground or the bus, the overcrowded conditions always encourage a struggle. No priority is given to pedestrians on the roads; be careful when crossing – and remember you have no right-of-way.

For Chinese, it is bad to lose face, especially in front of a foreigner. Don't put a Chinese in a position where they might do so. Any criticism should be done discreetly and tactfully.

It is usually not the custom in China to greet people with a handshake, though it is commonly used with foreigners. Moreover, embracing or kissing when greeting or saying good-bye is highly unusual. Generally, Chinese do not show their emotions and feelings in public. Consequently, it is better not to behave in too carefree a manner in public. It is also advisable to be cautious if you get involved in political discussions.

It is very important for the Chinese to make and keep good

connections (*guanxi*); someone who has no connections is only half Chinese, and it is equally important to foreigners on business. One should expect lots of invitations and gifts. *Qingke*, the wining and dining of guests, is an old Chinese tradition and is still used today to thank friends for a favour or to make new business contacts. If invited, you are obliged to return the invitation.

It is considered quite normal in China to eat noisily and belch during a meal. This doesn't mean that a foreign guest must do likewise. An increasing number of Chinese, particularly in the big cities, don't find it very pleasant either. In many simple restaurants, bones and other remnants are thrown on the table or the floor. It is also quite common for people to spit, despite official campaigns to try and restrain this habit. It is important for foreign visitors to know that these things are customary and not at all bad manners.

Government & Economy

The People's Republic of China is a socialist state, founded on 1 October 1949. The country is divided into 23 provinces (including Taiwan), five autonomous regions (Inner Mongolia, Xinjiang, Tibet, Ningxia and Guangxi), and five locally-governed cities (Beijing, Tianjin, Shanghai, Hong Kong and Chongqing, which recently split from the rest of Sichuan and became a separate city state. All provinces and autonomous regions are strictly subordinate to central government.

The **autonomous regions** are mostly populated by members of ethnic minorities who have the right to determine their own affairs – within the framework of a central state policy; they retain their own customs, traditions and language.

The **National People's Congress** is the highest governing body. The people's congresses at the lowest local level are directly elected, although the party retains the right

to propose candidates. The People's Liberation Army, overseas Chinese and the national minorities send representatives to congress.

The **Communist Party**, founded in 1921, has the leading role in state and society. Since the Cultural Revolution the party has been held in low esteem because of bureaucracy and misuse of power and privileges. Mao Zedong led the party from 1935–76; after his death, Hua Guofeng became leader. By 1978, Deng Xiaoping had managed to consolidate his position, and even after officially retiring in the early 1990s he held on as *de facto* leader until his death in 1997. His successor, Jiang Zemin, has continued a policy of economic development and international diplomacy, and is seen as leading a new, more forward-looking China into the new millennium.

The **Four Modernisations**, which are official party policy, refer to agriculture, industry, science & technology, and defence. The Modernisations are an attempt by government to transform the whole of China from a backward agricultural country into an industrialised nation, in which socialist planning will be combined with a market economy.

Names

The family name comes first, the given name second. Mao Zedong's family name is Mao, for example, and the given name is Zedong. Only among family and very good friends is it usual to use given names. Address people by their family name, with an honorific following the family name: *xiansheng* for men, *furen* for women. The same goes for the form of address referring to the person's position, which is sometimes used in China. For instance, Manager Li in Chinese is Li jingli, and Professor Wang is Wang jiaoshou.

Planning the Trip

What to Bring

As with anywhere, it is best to take your usual toilet articles and medicines. Hotel shops will have a limited choice of Western goods. In towns and countryside, items such as tampons or sanitary napkins are still difficult to find. Nowadays, if you are travelling to the major cities of Shanghai, Beijing, or Guangzhou, you will likely be able to find most of your basic items, and then some. But if you are planning to travel outside of these major centres, then by all means bring you own.

Photographic film and batteries, are available, but may be cheaper and fresher if bought before arriving. If you use professional-speed film, bring it with you. It is worth taking a small flashlight, especially for individual travellers who may stay the night in modest hostels. Chinese-made batteries tend not to last long. An electrical adaptor may be useful, too; many of the older hotels have sockets which require a three-pin plug and hotels often only have a limited number of adaptors available.

What to Wear

Simple and appropriate clothing is advisable for visitors. In the summer months, take light cotton clothes that are easily washed and not too delicate. Something warm is useful, even in the hottest season, as the air conditioning in the hotels is often vigorous. Footwear should be comfortable and strong.

Most Chinese wear ordinary clothes to evening performances at the Beijing opera, the theatre or circus. It is best to follow this custom, especially at some of the venues in rural areas: the floor is often of compressed mud, making high-heeled shoes foolish. In contrast, urban discos and clubs call for more formal dress.

Rain gear is useful, especially during the summer months. China's rainy season is from May to August. In the north, winters tend to be very dry and cold. Day temperatures of between −15° to −20°C are common.

Entry Regulations

VISAS & PASSPORTS

All foreigners need an entry visa. If you are part of a group, the tour operator will often obtain it; group visas will usually be issued for groups of at least 10, and the guide accompanying your group will keep the visas. Individual travellers can apply at any Chinese embassy. The procedure is straightforward, taking about a week, although the duration depends on current regulations, and upon your own country's regulations for visiting Chinese citizens. Typical is a 30-day single-entry visa. The passport must be valid for six months after expiration of the entry visa.

Traditionally, it has been quicker and easier to obtain or renew visas (including long-term, multiple-entry visas) in Hong Kong than anywhere else, and this hasn't changed much since the handover.

If your visa expires while you are in China, it can be extended by the local Public Security Bureau (*Gongan Ju*), the ubiquitous police. However, make sure you visit them before it expires, because fines for overstaying can be steep,

Electricty

Electricity in China is 220 volts, 50 cycles AC. Don't forget to take an international adaptor, to accommodate different style plugs. If travelling away from tourist centres, it is worth taking battery-operated equipment.

negotiations long and frustrating and, depending where you are, it may take some time to get the stamp you seek.

There was a time when many areas were off limits to foreigners, or else special travel permits, exceedingly difficult to obtain, were required. Nowadays, most of the country is open to foreigners, except some delicate border areas.

CUSTOMS

On arrival, each traveller must complete a form declaring foreign currency and valuables such as cameras, antiques and jewellery. The declaration must be handed in on departure; if required, the listed objects must be shown to verify that they haven't been sold within China.

Tourists can freely import two bottles of alcoholic beverages and 600 cigarettes, as well as foreign currency and valuables for personal use without restrictions. The import of weapons, ammunition, drugs, and pornographic literature (broadly interpreted, this would probably include The Bible and pictures of the Dalai Lama) is prohibited.

On departure, antiques such as porcelain, paintings, calligraphy, carvings, and old books must carry the red lacquer seal of an official antique shop. Otherwise, they can be confiscated by the customs officials without compensation.

Health

The most frequently reported health problem in eastern Asia is traveller's diarrhoea. The best prevention is to ensure maximum hygiene while travelling, especially in restaurants and roadside snack bars. Never eat raw, uncooked, or partially-cooked food, including salads other than in the top hotels. Animal or human excrement is still frequently used as fertiliser, so that bacteria on uncooked vegetables can easily be ingested. Also suggested if travelling outside of a tour group: acquire chopsticks and a tin bowl with lid for train journeys

and meals in small roadside restaurants. Drink only boiled or bottled water, even though the tap water is drinkable in some places, and reduce exposure to insects as far as possible.

The adjustment to a different climate and different food frequently leads to colds or digestive problems that, although rarely serious, can nevertheless impede one's enjoyment.

Tibet, the northwest, and the tropical province of Yunnan make particularly high demands on the body. Heart disease and high blood pressure can lead to serious problems in Tibet because of high altitude. Temperatures are high and conditions dry along the Silk Road.

If planning to visit areas outside of Beijing, Shanghai, Guangzhou, and Hong Kong, consider carrying emergency evacuation insurance. If injured in the deserts of western China, for example, medical and transportation costs could leave you in serious debt.

Two of the largest emergency evacuation companies are SOS Assistance and Asia Emergency Assistance. They have offices in many major cities worldwide (*see box above for offices in Hong Kong)*

Insect transmitted Illnesses

Malaria
Transmitted to humans by mosquitoes, which are most active from dusk to dawn.

Symptoms: Fever and flu-like symptoms, chills, achiness, and tiredness. Up to one year after returning home, travellers should consult a physician for flu-like illness.

Risk: Little or no risk in urban areas and popular tourist destinations; there is no risk in provinces bordering Mongolia or in Heilongjiang, Ningxia, Qinghai, Hong Kong, or Macau. Risk exists in rural areas not visited by most travellers. In areas of risk, transmission is highest from May to December; in the south, transmission occurs year-round. Whether taking

Evacuation

International SOS Assistance, 507 Kai Tak Commercial Bldg, 317 Des Voeux Road, Central, Hong Kong, Tel: 2541 6483, Fax: 2528 9933.
Asia Emergency Assistance (AEA), Allied Resources Bldg 9F, 32-38 Ice House Street, Central, Hong Kong, Tel: 2810 8898, Fax: 2845 0395. In Beijing: 6462 9100.

preventative drugs or not, travellers in risk areas should reduce exposure to malaria-carrying mosquitoes, which bite mainly during the evening, from dusk until dawn.

Taking drugs to prevent malaria is recommended only for travellers to rural areas and who will have outdoor exposure during evening hours. What medication to take is not as easy as it was a decade ago. There is increasing evidence that mosquitoes in many parts of the world, including in parts of northern Thailand and Burma, are developing resistance to traditional preventive drugs such as choloroquine and Mefloquine (Lariam).

Moreover, some individuals have extreme reactions to many of the more recent preventative drugs. Consult medical authorities or a physician in travel medicine for recommendations.

Yellow fever
Not in China or elsewhere in Asia.

Dengue fever
Primarily an urban — in or around human habitations — viral infection transmitted by mosquitoes. The mosquitoes are most active around dawn and dusk.
Symptoms: sudden onset of high fever, severe headaches, joint and muscle pain, and a rash, which shows up 3 to 4 days after the fever begins.
Risk: Occurs in parts of southern China and Taiwan. The risk is minimal for most travellers. Those who have lived several years in high-risk areas are more susceptible than short-term visitors. There is no vaccine or specific treatment available.

Japanese encephalitis
A mosquito-borne viral disease prevalent in rural areas, often in rice-growing areas.
Symptoms: none, or headache, fever, and other flu-like symptoms. Serious complications can lead to a swelling of the brain (encephalitis).
Risk: Occurs in rural China and Korea, and very rarely in Hong Kong and Taiwan. The mosquito bites in the late afternoon and early evening. Low or minimal risk for most travellers. Transmission is usually seasonal during the rainy season. There is no specific drug for treatment, but there is a preventative vaccine, which should be considered for persons who plan long-term – 4 weeks or more – visits to rural areas.

Contamination

Food and water-borne diseases are the primary cause of illness to travellers. The main one is diarrhoea, which is caused primarily by viruses or bacteria. Transmission is usually through contaminated food or water. The more serious illnesses are:

Hepatitis A
A viral infection of the liver transmitted by fecal-contaminated food or drink, or through direct person-to-person contact.
Symptoms: Fatigue, fever, no appetite, nausea, dark urine and/or jaundice, vomiting, aches. There is no specific treatment, although an effective vaccine is available, especially for those who plan to travel repeatedly or reside in risk areas. Immune globulin is recommended only for short-term protection.

Hepatitis B
All countries in Asia, including China, report high levels of infection. Hepatitis B is a viral infection of the liver transmitted through the exchange of blood or blood-derived fluids, or through sexual activity with an infected person. Unscreened blood and unsterilised needles, or contact with potentially-infected people with open skin lesions, are sources of infection. An effective vaccine is available, which should be started six months prior to travel.

Avoiding Illness

Some diseases are unique to East Asia or the tropics, transmitted by insects, contaminated food and water, or close contact with infected people. Diseases are not restricted to clearly-defined geographical areas. To reduce the risk of infection:
● reduce exposure to insects
● ensure quality of food and water
● be knowledgeable about potential diseases in the visited region

Typhoid fever
A bacterial infection transmitted by contaminated food and/or water, or even directly between people. Travellers to East Asia are susceptible to typhoid fever, particularly in smaller towns or rural areas.
Symptoms: Fever, headaches, tiredness, no appetite, and constipation (rather than diarrhoea). Be cautious in selecting food and water. Bottled or boiled water and eating only well-cooked food lowers the risk of infection. Typhoid fever is treated with antibiotics. Vaccination is recommended for travellers off the tourist routes, especially if staying for six weeks or more. Available vaccines protect 70–90 percent of users.

Cholera
An acute intestinal infection caused by bacteria, most often through contaminated water or food. Although some cases have been occasionally reported in China, the risk is virtually nonexistent.

Symptoms: Abrupt onset of watery diarrhoea, dehydration, vomiting, and muscle cramps. Medical care must be sought quickly when cholera is suspected. The available vaccine is only 50 percent effective, and is not recommended for most travellers.

Schistosomiasis (bilharzia)

An infection from a flatworm larvae that penetrates the skin, including unbroken skin.

Risk: Schistosomiasis is found in some areas of China, including rivers and lakes of southeastern and eastern China, especially along the Chang Jiang (Yangzi River) and tributaries. The risk comes from bathing, wading, or swimming in contaminated freshwater.

There is no easy way to identify infested water. If exposed, immediate and vigorous drying with a towel, or the application of rubbing alcohol to the exposed areas, can reduce risk. Water treated with chlorine or iodine is virtually safe; saltwater poses no risk.

Money Matters

The Chinese currency is called renminbi (people's currency) and is often abbreviated **RMB**. The basic unit is the yuan (colloquially, kuai). Ten jiao (colloquially, mao) make one yuan; ten fen make one jiao. Thus, 100 fen make one yuan. Notes are currently issued for 1, 2, 5, 10, 50 and 100 yuan. Coins come in 1 yuan, 5 jiao, and 1, 2 and 5 fen denominations.

Before China abandoned, in 1994, its dual-currency system of RMBs and FECs (Foreign Exchange Certificates, which foreigners were required to use), there was a reasonably active black market in currency exchange. Since the RMB is not completely convertible on the world markets, a black market still exists, although it is strictly illegal and the black-market exchange rates are laughable and not worth the risk of being short-changed, receiving counterfeit bills, or being arrested.

Most of the world's primary currencies are accepted in banks and hotels. Eurocheques, however, are not accepted anywhere, even branches of European banks.

ATM machines are appearing in all major cities but usually only the Bank of China's ATMs are connected to a global network. Look out for CIRRUS or PLUS. Most banks have agreements with these networks. **Citibank** is also showing a presence in Beijing, Shanghai and Guangzhou and their ATMs usually accommodate lots of different cards. There is a useful Citibank at the Bright China building on Jianguomennei Dajie in Beijing, close to the main railway station.

Increasingly, many places frequented by foreigners take the usual **credit cards** such as American Express, Visa, Diners Club, and MasterCard. Don't expect to use them much outside of the major cities, however. Also, most transport costs (e.g. domestic air and train tickets) are paid in cash.

Cash advances may be obtained from major branches of the Bank of China, including, in Beijing, the head office of the Bank of China, 410 Fuchingmennei Dajie, Tel: 601 6688, or the branch at 19, Dong An Men St, Tel: 6519 9114.

Forget about **wire transfers** of money to China. It'll take about a month and a considerable amount of patience with paperwork.

Getting There

BY AIR

Beijing

Beijing's Capital Airport, 30 km (18 miles) from the centre, connects the city to all parts of China and to the world's major cities. The journey takes 30 minutes if the traffic is light but can take an hour at busier times. Taxis are on the left as you leave the terminal. Make sure the taxi driver uses the meter, unless you have agreed a price in advance (not advised, as you will almost certainly be paying too much). Air China operates coach services to several places in Beijing,

including its offices near Xidan, west of Tiananmen Square; the Lufthansa Centre; and the Beijing International Hotel, close to Beijing Railway Station. Air China coaches have limited luggage space.

Many of the leading hotels offer limousine or minibus services. Passengers from international flights must fill out arrival cards, customs and health declarations.

Capital Airport has connections to around 50 other cities in China. You must check in at least 30 minutes before departure for a domestic flight, although delays are common on many domestic routes, and at least one hour before departure for an international flight. Hotels usually have flight booking services, and most major airlines have offices in Beijing. For shorter journeys within China, the train is generally more enjoyable.

Passengers leaving China by air must pay a 90-yuan airport tax; those on domestic flights must pay 50 yuan.

Chongqing

Chongqing is connected to all the major cities in China by air. The Chinese airlines flying into Chongqing include China Southern, China Eastern, Sichuan Airlines, Shanghai Airlines, Xinhua Airlines, and Wuhan Airlines. Tickets for all flights can be purchased at CAAC's office at 190 Zhongsan Sanlu (Tel: 6386 2813, Fax: 6386 9651) daily from 8am–6pm.

On the international front, Dragonair has direct flights between Chongqing and Hong Kong twice a week. Dragonair's office is located in the Holiday Inn Yangtze, 15 Nan Ping Bei Lu (Tel: 6281 7434). CAAC also offers international flights to Hong Kong (4 times a week) and Macau, and a connection to Singapore via Chengdu.

Chongqing's Jiangbei Airport is 25 km north of the city. CAAC operates shuttle buses every half hour between its offices on Zhongsan Sanlu and the airport. Plan to arrive at CAAC's office two and a half hours before your flight time.

Guangzhou

The major regional airports are in Guangzhou and Shenzhen. Guangzhou's Baiyun Airport is 10 km (6 miles) and a 30-minute drive from the city. The domestic and international terminals are housed in separate buildings. Shenzhen's Fuyong Airport is about 25 km (15 miles) from Shekou, at the western end of Shenzhen, and 55 km (34 miles) from the centre of Shenzhen. Domestic flights operate between Guangzhou and Shenzhen and major cities in China.

Guangzhou is connected via international flights to Bangkok, Hanoi, Ho Chi Minh City, Jakarta, Kuala Lumpur, Manila, Surabaya, Singapore, Sydney and Vientiane. With the exception of Singapore Airlines, MAS, and Garuda, which have offices selling tickets in Guangzhou, tickets for international flights on Chinese and foreign carriers must be purchased from the CAAC main office. Tickets for domestic flights are sold at the offices of the Chinese carriers and also at the CAAC main office. Bear in mind that buying a return ticket on a domestic route is difficult, except to cities like Beijing and Shanghai.

Hong Kong

Hong Kong is a major international air-traffic hub for the region, so there are no shortage of flights in and out of the territory. Hong Kong's new international airport is located at Chek Lap Kok, a small island to the north of Lantau Island and about 34km from Central. Thanks to some remarkable feats of engineering, including the Tsing Ma Bridge, which is the world's longest, single-span suspension

Ticket Prices

Bear in mind that buying a return ticket on a domestic route is difficult, except to cities like Beijing and Shanghai. All pricing discounts have been dropped. Overseas visitors now pay the same fare as Chinese citizens and no discounts are offered for advance bookings.

bridge, the airport can be reached by road or by rail from Hong Kong Island and Kowloon. There are connections via the MTR and bus – the latter is cheaper but not as fast.

The Airport Express is a comfortable 64-seat train that offers the most convenient and cost-effective way to get to and from the airport. The 23-minute journey to Central on Hong Kong island costs HK$70. The fare to Kowloon is HK$40 and to Tsing Yi HK$20. By road, the journey takes about 40 minutes. Flying out, you can check in at the central station 90 minutes before departure.

Kashi (Kashgar)

Xinjiang Airlines has daily flights between Kashgar and Ürümqi, though seats can be incredibly difficult to come by. If you use a travel agent once, let it be this time, from Kashgar to Ürümqi, especially if you have other airline connections in Ürümqi. The flight takes just under 2 hours. The airport is located 11 km north of the city. There is a shuttle bus between the airport and the CAAC office on 95 Jiefang Nanlu (Tel: 282 2113).

Kunming

Kunming's international airport, just 3 km from downtown, is connected with all major Chinese cities and with Rangoon (Yangon), Singapore, Bangkok, Chiang Mai, Vientiane and Hanoi. Check-in times for domestic flights are at least 30 minutes prior and one hour prior for international.

Kunming is also home base for Yunnan Airlines, which flies to most of the major tourist destinations in the province, including daily flights to Dali, Lijiang, and Mangshi and several times daily to Jinghong. In the near future, direct international flights to Jinghong will be available from Vientiane, Laos, and Chiang Rai, Thailand.

Lanzhou

On the domestic front, Lanzhou is connected to all the big cities of China by air. Here, CAAC is known as China Northwest (Xibei Hangkong), and its office is at 46 Donggang Xilu (Tel: 882 1964,

Public Holidays

Traditional festivals, such as the Spring Festival (Lunar New Year), follow the lunar calendar and thus dates vary annually, important official holidays follow the Gregorian calendar. This calender does not apply to Hong Kong or Macau.

1 January: New Year's Day
January – February: Variable. Lunar New Year (Spring Festival)
8 March: International

Women's Day
1 May: International Labour Day
4 May: Youth Day (May 4th Movement)
1 June: Children's Day
1 July: Founding of Communist Party
1 August: Founding of People's Liberation Army
1 October: National Day

Most shops are open on holidays. School holidays in China are between 1 August and 30 September. This also applies to universities.

Don't plan on travel or border crossings during holidays unless reservations have been made and confirmed a long time in advance. It is especially wise not to make any travel plans during the Spring Festival, which is three days long and is the period when everyone is travelling to their hometowns.

8am–9pm). There are no longer any flights between Lanzhou and Hong Kong.

The airport is at Zhongyuan, 85 km north of Lanzhou. CAAC runs an infrequent shuttle bus between its office on Donggang Xilu and the airport. Unfortunately, there are no fixed times for the buses; they vary according to departing and arriving flights on any given day, so be sure to check with the office ahead of time. Taxi drivers charge between 200–300 yuan for the trip. As with most things in China, bargaining is in order. Beware of taxi drivers who mill around the CAAC office and offer to take you to the airport for significantly less. Alternatively, travellers with early morning flights may want to spend the night before at one of the airport hotels, such as the Zhongchuan Hotel (Tel: 841 5926).

Macau

The Macau International Airport (MFM) opened in late 1995. It provides a convenient gateway for travellers to Macau and has scheduled flights to Bangkok, Manila, Singapore and several cities within China. There is a helicopter service to Hong Kong. It is situated on the east side of Taipa Island, and is linked by bridges to the downtown area. It takes less than 30 minutes to get from the airport to anywhere in Macau.

The passenger terminal has shops, restaurants, tourist information and hotel booking counters, bank, post office, and other services. For transportation to and from the airport there are authorised taxis and the regular AP1 bus, which serves major hotels, the Ferry Terminal, and the border gate. Plans are afoot to build an additional ferry terminal at the airport to provide direct transit for passengers to and from the new Hong Kong Airport on Lantau.

There are regularly scheduled flights between Macau and 25 cities in Asia – 12 in China – as well as Lisbon and Brussels. Asian connections include Beijing, Shanghai, Singapore, Manila, Kuala Lumpur, Bangkok, Taipei, and Seoul. Most routes are served by Air Macau, Evergreen Airways (EVA) or Asiana. Passengers on flights to China pay a passenger tax of MOP$80 (MOP$50 for children under 13), and MOP$130 (MOP$80 for children) to other destinations.

If you prefer helicopters, East Asia Airways (in HK, Tel: 2859 3359; in Macau, 727288) operates some 27 round trips daily using helipads on the Macau Ferry Terminal in the Shun Tak Centre in Hong Kong and Macau Ferry Terminal. The fare is HK$1,206 on weekdays, HK$1,310 weekends and holidays, one way. The choppers seat ten and the flight takes 16 minutes.

Shanghai

Shanghai is one of China's main terminuses, connected to a number of foreign destinations and almost all domestic locations, and is set to become even more of a hub due to the opening of the new airport at Pudong in late 1999. International and domestic air traffic into and out of Shanghai comes through either Hongqiao International Airport in western Shanghai, about 15 km from the city centre, or Shanghai International Airport, Pudong.

Call for 24-hour airport information (Tel: 6268 8918).

If leaving on an international flight, you are expected to arrive at the airport two hours before takeoff. Departure tax is 90 yuan. If leaving on a domestic flight, try to arrive at least one hour before departure time. Departure tax is 50 yuan. Domestic connections can be booked through China Eastern Airlines.

It's easy to get to and from the airport to Shanghai's city centre, but it can take anywhere from 30 minutes to an hour. Most hotels have shuttle buses available. Otherwise, plenty of taxis are available at the queues right outside both terminals. Don't hire drivers who tout their services at the terminal entrances. Their cars don't have meters, and they'll try to charge you exorbitant rates. To get into the city, most drivers use the recently opened expressway that connects to the Ring Road. Expect to reimburse the driver for the toll.

Ürümqi

Ürümqi is connected via domestic flights to Beijing, Shanghai, Guangzhou, Changsha, Chengdu, Xi'an, Zhengzhou, Tianjin, Fuzhou, Lanzhou, and Chongqing. Out here, CAAC is known as Xinjiang Airlines. Ürümqi is also connected via international flights to Almaty (Kazakstan), Islamabad (Pakistan), Moscow, and Tashkent. Within Xinjiang, there are flights from Ürümqi to Yining, Tacheng, Kelamayi (Karamai), Kashi (Kashgar), Akesu (Aksu), Hetian (Hotan), Kuche (Kuqa), Kuerle (Korla), Qiemo (Jumo), and Aletai (Altai).

China Northwest has its office at 67 Youhao Nanlu, Tel: 452 5594, 451 2212, and is open daily from 7am–noon. Across the street is the office for Xinjiang Airlines at 62 Youhao Nanlu, Tel: 451 4668. Just outside the Xinjiang Airlines office you can catch shuttle buses to the airport, which is 17 km north of the city. The airport bus also stops by the northern end of Renmin Park. As with most airport shuttles in China, they are infrequent, and are timed to departing and arriving flights.

Xi'an

Xi'an's airport connects it to most of the big cities in China, as well as to Hong Kong, Macau, Nagoya and Hiroshima. In Xi'an, CAAC is known as China Northwest Airlines (Xibei Hangkong). Its ticket office is located at the corner of Laodong Nanlu and Xiguan Zhengjie, 1 km outside the west gate of the old city (Tel: 870 2299, Fax: 862 4068). China Northwest offers 4 flights a week between Xi'an and Hong Kong, while Dragonair offers 2 flights a week. Dragonair's ticket office (Tel: 426 2988) is located in the lobby of the Sheraton Hotel at 12 Feng Gao Road.

The airport is about 40 km northwest of Xi'an at Xianyang.

Most major hotels offer limousine or bus transfers which have to be arranged ahead of time. CAAC runs a shuttle bus between its offices on Laodong Nanlu and the airport and is timed to its arriving and departing flights.

Otherwise you're looking at some hard bargaining with taxi drivers who charge as much as 200 yuan to go into the city. The trip takes around 50 minutes. From the CAAC office you can take a taxi to your hotel. Make sure that the taxi drivers use their meters.

BY RAIL

Beijing

Beijing has two main railway stations: Beijing Station (*Beijing zhan*) and Beijing West (*Xi zhan*). Some trains to other parts of China run from the city's three smaller stations.

If arriving from Europe via the **Trans-Manchurian** or **Trans-Mongolian** railways (often called the Trans-Siberian, which in fact goes to Siberia's Pacific Coast, not China), all the same health and customs procedures apply as if arriving via an international flight.

There is a choice of two routes. The Chinese train – which is better equipped and maintained – takes 5 days via Ulan Bator through Mongolia, entering China via Erlian. The Russian train, which goes through Manchuria, takes a day longer, and enters China at Manzhouli. Both leave once a week from Moscow.

Depending on the type of train, there are two or three classes. Food is not included in the ticket price. Initially, the food seems fairly reasonable, but becomes increasingly monotonous as the journey continues.

If you want to interrupt the train journey in Russia for longer than 24 hours, you need a tourist visa and will have to show a hotel booking.

Tickets and visas are easier to obtain for Beijing-Moscow than for Moscow-Beijing. The Chongwenmen and Beijing International hotels both have international train booking offices. Allow at least a week to obtain Russian and, if necessary, Mongolian and Polish visas in Beijing.

For travel within China, the best place to buy tickets is the foreigners' booking office to the left of the main concourse inside Beijing Station, where you can also buy tickets for trains leaving from Beijing West. Beijing West also has a foreigners' booking office. If you want a sleeper berth, especially in summer, it is best to buy your ticket two or three days in advance. Return tickets can be purchased for Hong Kong-Beijing, but not for other routes.

Chongqing

Chongqing is connected via direct trains to Beijing (33 hr), Shanghai (46 hr), Chengdu (11 hr), Kunming (17 hr), Guangzhou, Zhengzhou, Yangzhou, Wuchang, Guiyang, Nanning, and Zhejiang. Trains also go to nearby Dazu (4 hr). Trains offer 3 classes of service. There is a special ticket window to purchase sleeper tickets, though these can be hard to come by during the peak summer months. The train station is next to the long-distance bus station at the southwestern end of the main peninsula on Nanqu Lu.

Guangzhou

There are trains to most large cities in China. Four daily trains link Guangzhou and the Hunghom station on the Kowloon side of Hong Kong (departure times 8.50am; 12.05pm; 1.23pm and 4.08 pm, with two extra trains added during special festivals, the Guangzhou Fair and other peak periods). Travelling time is 2 hr. There is also a direct train between Foshan and Hong Kong, with a travelling time of 3 hr.

In Guangzhou, most hotels and the CTS office can help get train tickets. In Hong Kong, tickets can be purchased through travel agents, hotels, CTS offices, or at the lobby of the Hunghom railway station (Tel: 2627 4400). A much cheaper alternative, or if tickets to Guangzhou are sold out, is to take the Kowloon-Canton Railway (KCR) to the border terminus of Lo Wu (a 40-minute journey, with three departures an hour from 5.30am–10.19pm). The Shenzhen station is right across the border.

There are approximately two departures every hour on the express trains between Shenzhen and Guangzhou. Travelling time is 1 hour 10 mins. Trains arrive in Guangzhou either at the central station or at Guangzhou East Railway Station (Guangzhou Dong), in Tianhe, a 30-minute taxi ride from the city centre.

All trains between Kowloon and Guangzhou are air-conditioned, but not all between Shenzhen and Guangzhou. Look for the express trains which cost about 60 percent more than the slow trains. Four departures per day are on the new high-speed train imported from Spain. Speeds of up to 200km/125 miles an hour are claimed and travelling time is substantially reduced. Ask for the air-con class when buying a ticket, a small price to pay when temperatures soar in the heat of summer.

In Hong Kong, tickets can be purchased through travel agents, hotels, CTS offices or at the lobby of the Hunghom railway station, tel: 2627-4400.

Kunming

A narrow gauge rail line, built by the French a century ago, connects Kunming with Hanoi, via the border crossing at Lao Cai, Vietnam and Hekou, Yunnan. From Hanoi it is also possible to take the train to Dong Dang and cross into Guangxi, in Pingxiang County, 247 km southeast of Nanning.

Lanzhou

From Lanzhou, there are long-distance trains to Beijing, Shanghai, Xining, Ürümqi, Xi'an, Chengdu, and Golmud. Going west to Ürümqi (38 hr), trains stop at Jiayuguan (17 hr), Liuyuan, the train station serving Dunhuang (23 hr), Daheyan, the station serving Turpan (34 hr).

Trains offer 3 classes of service, though sleepers are incredibly hard to come by if you try to get them yourself at the railway station. You'd do better to go to a travel agency. Also beware of the train station – it's a pickpocket's paradise.

Shanghai

Shanghai has a bustling train station that is connected to many destinations in China by direct and express routes. All trains arrive and depart from the Shanghai Railway Station (303 Moling Lu) in the northern part of the city. There are several trains a day to Suzhou, Hangzhou, Nanjing, and other nearby destinations. The best train to catch to Beijing is the overnight express train that leaves around 7pm and arrives in Beijing the next morning. The new express train to Hong Kong is also running, but you can also get there via Guangzhou and Shenzhen. There are a few daily express trains running to these two destinations.

You can buy train tickets at CITS, but they charge you a service fee. The best place to buy same-day, next-day, and sometimes third-day tickets is the foreigners' ticket office in the Longmen Hotel (777 Hengfeng Lu, Tel: 6317 0000) located just west of the train station. For 24-hour train information, Tel: 6317 9090.

Ürümqi

Ürümqi is the northwestern end point of China's railway line. From here, the domestic trains only go east and south to Beijing, Shanghai, Zhengzhou, Chengdu, and Xi'an, all of which stop at Lanzhou. Only the trains coming from Beijing and Shanghai have air-conditioning.

Between Ürümqi and Lanzhou, the stops include Daheyan (Turpan Railway Station), Hami, Liuyuan (serving Dunhuang), and Jiayuguan. As with rail travel out of Lanzhou, sleepers are difficult to come by. The railway station is located at the southwestern end of town.

Xi'an

There are trains from Xi'an to many large cities in China, including

Beijing (17 hr), Shanghai, (24 hr), Guangzhou, Chengdu, Hefei, Wuhan, Qingdao, and Ürümqi. In Xi'an, most hotels, travel agencies and CITS can help get train tickets with at least 2 days' notice, though some places might be able to wangle tickets in less time. You can try and get your own tickets at the Railway Station on Huancheng Beilu Dongduan just outside the northeast corner of the old city. The foreigners' ticket office is on the second floor, but don't expect to get tickets for sleepers on overnight

Luggage

Take sturdy, strong luggage, which should be lockable; sometimes it won't be transported unless it is locked.

trains on short notice. You'd do better going to a travel agency or hotel booking service and paying the extra if you need to get out in a hurry.

Most overnight trains have three classes of service: soft sleeper, hard sleeper, and hard seat. Not all overnight trains have air-conditioning; not to worry if it's winter.

Overland Routes

Beijing

Long-distance buses connect Beijing with many cities, including Tianjin, Chengde, Beidaihe, Taiyuan, and Hohhot. On some routes buses are faster, but generally less comfortable, than trains.

Sleeper buses operate on longer routes. Buses are recommended for shorter journeys to places such as Tianjin (2 hr) or Chengde (4 hr). Beijing's main long-distance bus stations are at Dongzhimen, Xizhimen, and Yongdingmen. A few long-distance buses, including some to Tianjin, leave from outside Beijing Station.

Chongqing

There are buses connecting Chongqing to many towns in Sichuan Province including Emei,

Haikou, Leshan, Shazhou, Yibing, and Neijiang. Buses to Dazu (3 hr) and Chengdu (4 hr) are frequent. The long-distance bus station is located next to the train station at the southwestern end of the peninsula on Nanqu Lu and is relatively clean and user-friendly.

Kashi (Kashgar)

The long-distance bus station is on Tiannan Lu just south of Renmin Lu. There are daily buses from Kashgar to Korla, Kuqa, Aksu, Hotan, Daheyan, Ürümqi, and Yengisar. The route between Kashi and Lhasa is not only dangerous, but is officially closed to foreigners, which has not stopped some tourists from trying to travel it. Many foreigners have been severely fined for doing just this.

It is also possible, occasionally, to take a bus to Kyrgyzstan through Turgart, but these are infrequent and unreliable.

Lanzhou

Travelling east from Lanzhou, there are long-distance buses going to Xi'an, Yinchuan, and Guyuan. The long-distance bus station serving points east is on Pingliang Lu between Minzhu Lu and Jiuda Lu. Going west, buses serve Linxia, Xiahe, and Hezuo.

The west bus station is at the western edge of town on Xijin Donglu. There are several buses serving Linxia and Hezuo a day, but only one direct bus to Xiahe a day, in the early morning. If you miss that service, you can always take one of the many buses going to Linxia, and change there for one of the many minibuses buses going to Xiahe.

There is a dual pricing system at work when travelling long-distance by bus in Gansu Province. Not only are foreigners charged double the local prices, but they are required to buy travel insurance, without which you will not be allowed on long-distance public buses. You can purchase insurance at PICC, 150 Qingyang Lu (Tel: 841 6421), at travel agencies, or directly at the bus stations.

Shanghai

It's generally more convenient to take a train to Shanghai rather than a bus. But the city is connected to the cities of Suzhou, Nanjing, and Hangzhou by new highways that have made travel much easier. There is a deluxe coach that runs between Shanghai and Nanjing from the terminus at 58 Laochongqing Nan Lu (Tel: 6358 8089). Regular, less comfortable buses arrive and depart from the long-distance bus station on Qiujiang Lu, west of Henan Bei Lu. There are several each day to closer destinations such as Hangzhou and Suzhou. CITS books bus tickets.

Ürümqi

Ürümqi is the hub of bus travel throughout Xinjiang Province, though trying to figure out which station to leave from can be confusing. For most destinations in Xinjiang, buses leave from the long-distance bus station on Heilongjiang Lu. For Turpan, buses leave from the Erdaoqiao Market at the southern end of town. In 1996, heavy flooding washed out the road between Turpan and Ürümqi. Construction on the new freeway, has resulted in a very bumpy, uncomfortable ride which can take anywhere between 4 to 6 hours.

Buses to Kashi leave from the Kashi Bus Station which is just to the east of the railway station at the southwestern end of town. Riding the bus to Kashi (a true test of endurance) now takes anywhere from 36 hours (straight sleepers) to 72 hours. Know beforehand that if you get a sleeper seat, you are confined to the same position for the whole ride. Foreign women travelling alone have reported being harassed on these bus trips.

It is also possible to take a bus between Ürümqi and Almaty in Kazhakstan, for which a visa is needed. Check at the bus station for more information.

Unlike in Gansu Province, it is not official policy here to charge foreigners a different price for bus travel, though many drivers may try to do just that, often at double the

local price. Nor is it necessary to purchase insurance, though should you want to, PICC's telephone is 281 5031.

Xi'an

There are long-distance buses connecting Xi'an with Zhengzhou, Yichang, and Luoyang, as well as to Yan'an and Huashan. However, the majority of foreign travellers appear to prefer taking the train. The long-distance bus station is opposite the railway station in the northeastern corner of the old city.

Xishuangbanna

From Laos, travellers can enter Mengla County, eastern Xishuangbanna, at Boten in Luang Nam Tha Province. Occasionally tours are arranged to go by boat up the Mekong to Jinghong. These are irregular at the moment, but likely to increase in the future. Crossing the Burmese border is still problematic and the brief, over-the-border tours from Xishuangbanna and Dehong are still restricted to Chinese citizens. For up-to-date info, though, check at the Myanmar Consulate in the Camellia Hotel, Kunming.

INTERNATIONAL

Several of China's international borders are open for crossing. Other parts, like the frontier with Bhutan, are restricted areas.

Kazakhstan

There are both a daily bus service and a twice-weekly train service between Urumqi and Almaty, in Kazakhstan.

Myanmar (Burma)

A border crossing with Burma, now officially known as Myanmar, opened in 1996, but the Burmese discourage foreigners from using the border crossing. Visas are obtainable at the consulate in Kunming, although unless one asks specifically, they will include the words "not for overland entry".

Nepal

Crossing via Nepal by bus or taxi has been possible since 1985, with sporadic periods of closed borders. Procure a Chinese visa anywhere else but Nepal, unless you are part of a tour.

It's possible to travel by road between Kathmandu and Lhasa, but it requires considerable time, not only for travel, but for bureaucracy, including mandatory tours of Lhasa upon arrival. Independent travellers should note that transport on the Nepal side is good, but scarce on the Tibetan side. Most travellers must plan on a vehicle hire/share to Lhasa.

Pakistan

Since 1986, it has been possible to travel the Karakorum Highway between Kashi and Islamabad. Visas are required for entering Pakistan and cannot be obtained at the border for either Pakistan or China. Officially the border is open between April and October, though even those dates are weather-dependent. During this time, there are daily buses, weather permitting, going from Kashi to Taxkorgan (5 hr) which is the last outpost in China where immigration and customs checks are performed. The bus stops here overnight. From Taxkorgan, buses go to Pirali (2 hr) where you'll need to change to a local Pakistani bus which will take you over the Khunjerab Pass to Sust where Indian customs is located.

On both the Pakistani and Chinese sides of the border the roads may be blocked by landslides, and you may have to walk a fair distance, carrying your luggage. Accommodation en route is quite modest.

Kazakhstan

There is a daily bus service and a twice-weekly train service between Urumqi and Almaty, in Kazakhstan.

Russia/Mongolia

A journey on the Trans-Mongolian/Trans-Manchurian railways between Moscow and

Beijing was once one of the world's classic train journeys. Things have changed, and the train now carries a larger number of scoundrels and thieves. Service on the Russian train (both China and Russia run trains on the service) is said to have degraded considerably. Nevertheless, it is an adventure worth considering.

Vietnam

In 1995, train services began between Hanoi and Beijing via the Friendship Gate crossing, but they have been plagued by red-tape at the border. Travelling from Vietnam to China requires a special visa. One may also cross the border by foot at Hekou (China) and Lao Cai (Vietnam), and at Friendship Gate (Dong Dang, Vietnam/Pingxiang, China).

Water Transport

Chongqing

One of the most popular ways to arrive or depart Chongqing, of course, is by boat on the Chang Jiang. Sailing downstream from Chongqing to Wuhan takes 3 days and 2 nights and is usually a more popular option for tourists who are pressed for time, though some tourists have regretted not having enough time to savour the exquisite scenery around them. Sailing upstream from Wuhan takes 6 days and 5 nights. Many tourists going upstream actually bypass the first day of sailing, which is devoid of any significant sights, by embarking the boat at Sashi or Yichang instead.

In Chongqing, boats are moored at the Chaotianmen Docks, which are at the tip of the main peninsula that makes up the heart of Chongqing. Given the number of tourists who pass through here daily, it is a wonder that the docks are not better maintained. Steep flights of stairs often strewn with litter lead up from the boats, making the climb for arriving passengers a rather rude and unpleasant end to their cruise. There are any number of waiting

porters, however, who will happily carry your luggage for as much as they can get away with, so be sure to bargain well in advance.

Because there is every variety of boats sailing the Chang Jiang, it is important to know exactly the kind of boat one is buying a ticket for. There are two basic types of vessels plying the Chang Jiang: the first are transport boats that ferry everything from passengers to cargo. These ships usually have cabins ranging from first-class (2 bunks in a room with private shower) to 4th class (communal bunking), with passengers left to fend for themselves at mealtimes and where hygiene and sanitation are poor. These boats may be the only option for passengers on a tight budget, but are devoid of all amenities including any explanation of the sights along the way.

Tickets for these boats can be purchased at the Chaotianmen Chongqing Gang (Chaotianmen Docks) on Shaanxi Lu (Tel: 6384 1342). The ticket offices are open daily from 5am–11.30pm. Officially, foreigners and locals pay the same price for tickets on these boats.

The other alternative, which most tourists prefer, is the luxury cruise ships which cater only and specifically to tourists. But even here, there can be a great deal of difference in the facilities and quality of the ships. So make sure you know in advance the kind of ship you're booking yourself on. Trips booked from outside China are often much more expensive than booking a comparable ship through a local travel agent, but the former often provide the added luxury of amenities ranging from casinos to daily movies to mahjong lessons.

There are innumerable travel agencies around the dock area selling boat tickets, as well as the traditional outfits like CITS, CYTS, and booking offices in many large hotels. Unfortunately, despite lip service to the contrary, the lucrative practice of charging foreigners higher prices is alive and flourishing.

Because of the construction of the Three Gorges Dam and the natural vagaries of the weather leading to unpredictable water conditions, passengers often find their cruise schedule altered on a daily basis, which can often lead to frustration and disappointment. Tourists have also complained about the decrepit condition of some of the smaller sampan boats used to ferry passengers to and from the smaller gorges. Unfortunately, this situation is unlikely to improve at least until 2003, when the first phase of flooding of the smaller gorges is complete and boat operators can then reassess their needs and upgrade accordingly.

Hong Kong

If travelling to China from Hong Kong by boat, the choice of destinations includes Guangzhou, Xiamen, Shantou, and Shanghai.

There used to be an overnight steamer between Hong Kong and Guangzhou, which took 8 hours but, at present, service is suspended with no news of any resumption. There is also a daytime catamaran service, which takes one and a half hours. Ferry journeys from Hong Kong to Shantou take 14 hours; to Xiamen, 20 hours; and to Shanghai, 60 hours. All ferries have restaurants on board and the catamarans have a small canteen serving hot cup noodles and drinks.

Hong Kong is linked by high-speed turbojet with Guangzhou, Shenzen, Huangpu, Guangzhou technological and economic development district, and the delta cities of Lianhua Shan, Nansha, Shekou, Shunde, Zhongshan, and Zhuhai. There are also services between Hong Kong and Shekou. For information on ferry schedules, call 2833 9300 or 2859 3333 in Hong Kong. Most departures are from the Hong Kong-Macau Ferry Terminal at the Shun Tak Centre (200 Connaught Road, Hong Kong) and from the China Ferry Terminal, Canton Road, Tsim Sha Tsui. There are over 100 daily scheduled sailings (catamarans and jetfoils) each way between Hong Kong and Macau; journey time is 55 minutes.

By day, the most impressive trip is the one between Kowloon and the Bogue port of Nansha, sited at the entrance of the Zhu Jiang (Pearl River), aboard a huge modern catamaran travelling at 45 knots. From the Nansha terminal, a free bus shuttle takes travellers to the White Swan Hotel in Guangzhou. Three high-speed catamaran hydrofoils operate daily (1-hour) between Nansha and Hong Kong: 8.30am, 9.15am, 2pm from Hong Kong, and 11.20am, 4pm and 5pm from Nansha. Tickets can be purchased from the China Ferry Terminal (Tel: 2375 0537) in Hong Kong, the Nansha Terminal (Tel: 498 8312) or the basement floor of the White Swan Hotel in Guangzhou.

You can also catch a night boat from Hong Kong and Macau to Guangzhou. They run daily except on the last day of each month, leaving either way at dinner time and arriving at sunrise. The departure from Hong Kong sails through the harbour and the view is especially impressive. The *Xinghu*, sailing from Hong Kong, is the most comfortable boat. Departures are from the China Ferry Terminal in Hong Kong and from the Porto Interior in Macau.

There are numerous cruises from Hong Kong along China's coast. They usually stop at Xiamen, Shanghai, Yantai, Nanjing, Qingdao, and Dalian.

Shanghai

Shanghai is connected to Hong Kong and Japan by boat. The trip to Hong Kong takes two-and-a-half days and departs from Waihongqiao Harbour (1 Taiping Lu). Tickets to both Japan and Hong Kong can be booked through CITS.

Most domestic boats leave from the Shiliupu Dock on Zhongshan Dong Lu just south of the Bund. Shanghai is connected to several destinations on the Chang Jiang (Yangzi River), such as Wuhan, Chongqing, Nanjing, Wuhu, and Jiujiang, as well as to cities on the coast, such as Guangzhou, Qingdao, Dalian, Ningbo, and Fuzhou. Overnight boats to the island of Putuoshan leave every other day; there is also a less convenient, but faster speed boat that departs every day.

The foreigner ticket booth at the Boat Ticket Booking Office (1 Jinling Dong Lu) sells domestic tickets from first to fourth class. CITS also books tickets for a nominal service fee. You can call for river passenger transport information at Tel: 6326 1261.

INTERNATIONAL

Korea

Ferry service is available from Inchon, South Korea, to Weihai, Qingdao, and Tianjin. Between Inchon and Weihai takes about 18 hours, departing twice weekly. Between Inchon and Qingdao takes at least a full 24 hours, departing weekly. Between Inchon and Tianjin takes nearly 30 hours, operating every five days. Fares for all services range from US$100 to US$350, depending upon class.

Japan

There is a weekly deluxe cruise ship between Shanghai and Japan, alternating every week between Yokohama and Shanghai. There is also a weekly boat between Kobe and Tianjin/Tanggu. Trips take two days, and fares run from US$300 to $1,500 or more.

Macau

You will not believe the number of ways you can get from Hong Kong to Macau by sea. Fares for sea crossings vary between services and the class of ticket you purchase, the time of the day and the day of the week you travel. Generally, tickets cost between HK$100 and HK$200. For the most up to date information on fares check with the company providing the service, the Hong Kong offices of the Macau Government Tourist Office (2857 2287), or the Macau Tourist Information Bureau (2540 8180). Also, an embarkation fee is added to the ticket price: HK$26 from Hong Kong and MOP$19 from Macau.

Regardless of when you go, make certain you have your return tickets in your possession, since seats are always fully booked. Baggage is limited to 9 kg (20 lbs), and there is not much space on board for large suitcases.

Just about all the Macau ferry sailings use the Macau Ferry Terminal in the Shun Tak Centre, on the waterfront West of Central District, Hong Kong (Sheung Wan station on the MRT and the A2 Airbus from the airport), with the exception of the catamaran and hoverferries, which use the China Ferry Terminal on the Tsim Sha Tsui waterfront alongside Harbour City, on the Kowloon side.

Jetfoils: Built by Boeing, jetfoils are propelled by water jets and ride above the waves at about 40 knots. They carry the largest percentage of passengers between Hong Kong and Macau in about 55–60 minutes. They carry about 270 passengers per vessel and light refreshments are provided on board, with complimentary newspapers, coffee and tea on the first-class top deck. The newer Norwegian-built Foilcats are two-deck catamarans that carry 400 passengers at 45 knots. Jetfoils and Foilcats depart every 15 minutes from 7am to 5pm, then every 30 minutes to midnight, with several other sailing throughout the night. Contact the Far East Hydrofoil Co., Tel: 2859 3333.

There is also a computer booking service for Jetfoils and Foilcats called Ticketmate. Many of their 11 outlets in Hong Kong are in the major MTR stations. You can buy a passage up to 28 days in advance. Their three outlets in Macau allow you to buy a passage up to 7 days in advance. In Hong Kong, between 7am and 10pm, holders of American Express, Master Card, Visa or Diners Club credit cards can book by phone up to 28 days in advance by dialling 2859 6596 or

2183 8138. (This service is not offered in Macau.)

Catamarans: Swedish-built Jumbocats are single-deck catamarans which carry 300 passengers and have a refreshment counter on board. Turbocats and Tricats are newly developed catamarans which have 250 seats on the main deck and 45 on the upper first-class deck, which includes a 6-seat VIP cabin. All three make the crossing in about one hour. Jumbocats, Turbocats and Tricats make 28 round trips daily, including 6 from Kowloon and 4 at night. They depart every 30 minutes during the day. Contact CTS-Parkview Holdings Ltd., Tel: 2851 3533.

HYF Catamarans (Hong Kong Yaumati Ferry Co., Tel: 2516 9581) carry 433 passengers on two decks, and have on board TV laser disc systems and bar and snack counters. They make the crossing in about 60 minutes. HYF Catamarans make 12 round trips daily from 8.30am to 8pm from the China Ferry Terminal in Kowloon, with 1 night return to Shun Tak Centre.

Special Information

DISABLED

Only in recent years have the needs of disabled people received attention in China. In general, towns, institutions, public transport and sights offer little accessibility for the disabled. Travelling in a group for the disabled certainly reduces these problems considerably. The China National Tourist Offices and CITS have information about special trips for the disabled.

CHILDREN

The Chinese are fond of children, so travelling with family in China is not difficult. If with toddlers or babies, note that disposable nappies and baby food in jars are not readily available. Children travel at reduced cost on trains and planes. Big hotels offer child-care for a fee.

STUDENTS

There are no special rules for foreign students in China. Only the student cards of foreign students studying in China are usually recognised; international student cards are not.

Useful Addresses

PUBLIC SECURITY BUREAU

Beijing: 85 Beichizi Dajie, Tel: 8522-5050/8401-5300. Monday–Friday 8.30am–5pm, Saturday 8.30–11.30am.
Chongqing: 1 Linjiang Lu, Tel: 6383 1830, Monday–Friday 8.30am–noon, 2–6pm.
Guangzhou: 863 Jiefang Beilu, Tel: 8333 1326.
Kaifeng: Sengfu Qianjie, Tel: 55 8899.
Kashi (Kashgar): 67 Renmin Donglu, Tel: 282 2048.
Kunming: 525 Beijinglu, Tel: 312 6191.
Lanzhou: 38 Qingyang Lu, Tel: 882 0961, Monday–Friday 8–noon, 2.30–6.30pm.
Luoyang: Tiyuchang Lu, Tel: 393 8397.
Nanning: Minzudadao, Tel: 20 2431.
Qingdao: Hubei Lu, Tel: 286 1134.
Shanghai: 333 Wusong Lu, Tel: 6357 6666, Monday–Friday, 9–11am, 2–5pm.
Tai'an: Qingnian Lu, Tel: 822 4004.
Ürümqi: 116 Jiefang Beilu, Tel: 281 0452 ext. 3614, Monday– Friday 9.30am– 1.30pm, 4–8pm.
Xi'an: 138 Xida Jie, Tel: 723 4500

ext. 51810, Monday–Friday 8am–noon, 3–6pm.
Zhengzhou: Bei Erqi Lu, Tel: (0371) 622 2023.

VISITOR HOT LINES:

Beijing: Tel: 6513 0828
Shanghai: Tel: 6252-000
Shanghai Visitor Association: Tel: 6275-5880
Guangzhou: Tel: 8667 7422

CHINA NATIONAL TOURISM OFFICE (CNTA)

Australia, Level 19, 44 Market St., Sydney, NSW 2000, Australia, Tel: 299 4057, Fax: 290 1958.
France, Paris, 116, Ave des Champs-Elysees, 75008 Paris, France, Tel: 4421 8282, Fax: 4421 8100.
Germany, China Ilkenhans Strasse 6, D-60433 Frankfurt A.M. Deutschland, Tel: 52 0135, Fax: 52 8490.
Israel, P.O. Box 3281 Tel-Aviv 61030, Israel, Tel: 524 0891, Fax: 522 6281.
Singapore, 1 Shenton Way, #7-05 Robina House, Singapore 068803, Tel: 211 8681, Fax: 221 9267.
Spain, Gran Via 88, Grupo 2, Planta 16-8 28013, Madrid, Espana, Tel: 548 0011, Fax: 548 0597.
United Kingdom, 4 Glentworth St., London NW1 5PG, UK, Tel Info: 09001-600188; office: 020 7935 9787; Fax: 7487 5842.
United States, 350 Fifth Ave, Suite 6413, Empire State Bldg, New York, NY 10118, Tel: 760 9700, Fax: 760 8809.

TOUR OPERATORS

There are countless travel agencies within and outside of China that handle domestic travel arrangements. Prominent among the agencies is **China International Travel Services** (CITS), formerly and virtually the sole agency handling overseas tourists. It has branches throughout China that operate

Important Numbers

Police: 110
Fire: 119
Ambulance: 120
Local directory assistance: 114
Domestic directory assistance: 116
International directory assistance (English): 115
Time: 117
Weather: 121

independently. **China Travel Services (CTS)** is a similar organisation, originally responsible for domestic tourists and overseas Chinese, but now also catering to foreigners. While the efficiency of both organisations can be brutally lacking in some of their offices, some say CTS is slightly better than CITS.

Agencies may also have business interests extending beyond simply arranging tours and bookings; they may own or partly own hotels. An agency that arranges a tour may do so by contacting agencies in places you will visit, and asking them to deal with local bookings. If you go direct to an agency in the area you are visiting, savings may be possible.

Sometimes agencies such as CITS may hold tickets for rail journeys, operas, acrobatic performances, and concerts, even when such tickets are sold out at the stations or venues. Prices will be high, however.

There are also small-scale, unlicensed tour operators. Reportedly, some of these use unroadworthy vehicles, take their customers to shops and restaurants that give the guides "backhanders" (though perhaps this can also happen with licensed operators), and demand mark-ups of 100 percent or more for tickets to tourist sites. Others may be trustworthy, and cheap.

It is also quite possible nowadays – and increasingly common amongst the adventurous – to travel in China without the services of any agency. Note that within China, agencies have nothing to do with visa extensions or other passport matters. Visit the police for these.

CITS OFFICES

Beijing, branches at: Beijing Tourist Building, tel: 6515-8562; 28 Jianguomenwai, China World Hotel, Tel: 6607 1575, 6608 7124. Open Monday–Saturday 8am–8pm, Sunday 8am–noon.
Chengdu, 65, Sec 2, Renmin Nan Lu, tel: 667-5578.
Chongqing, 63 Zaozilanya Zhenglu, Tel: 6385 1098. Open Monday–Friday 8.30am–noon, 2–5.30pm; (CYTS) 125 Renmin Lu, Tel: 6385 7015. Open Monday–Friday 9am–6pm.
Dalian, 1 Changtong St, Tel: 364 0273.
Guangzhou, No. 1, Shihan Rd, Tel: 8515 2888 Ext. 256. Open Monday–Saturday 8.30am–5pm.
Guilin, 41 Binjiang Lu, tel: 282-8017.
Hangzhou, 1 Shihan Lu, Tel: 515 2888, Ext. 256.
Hong Kong, 6th Fl, Tower 2, South Seas Centre 75, Mody Rd, Tsim Sha-Tsui, Kowloon, Tel: 732 5888, Fax: 2721 7454.
Kashi (Kashgar), Qinibagh Hotel, 93 Seman Road, Tel: 282 5390. Open daily 9.30am–1.30pm, 4–8pm.
Kunming, 285 Huan Cheng Nan Lu, Tel: 313 2895.
Lanzhou, 361 Tianshui Lu (the entrance is actually on Nongmin Xiang), Tel: 841 6638 ext. 6763.
Luoyang, Xiyuan Lu, Tel: 491 3701.
Nanjing, 202-1 N Zhong Shan Lu, Tel: 342 1125. Open Monday–Saturday 9am–5pm.
Ningbo, East Seaport Hotel, No. 52 Caihong North Rd, Tel: 737 5751. Open Monday–Saturday 8.30am–5pm.
Qingdao, Huiquan Dynasty Hotel, 9 Nanhai Lu, Tel: 287 0830.
Shanghai, Beijing Xi Lu 1277, tel: (021) 6321-7200.
Suzhou, 115 Shiquan Lu, tel: 522-3783.
Tianjin, 22 You Yi Rd, Tel: 835 5309. Open Monday–Friday 9am–5pm; Saturday 9am–noon.
Ürümqi, 51 Xinhua Beilu, Tel: 282 6719. Open Monday–Friday 9.30am–1.30pm, 4–8pm; (CYTS), 9 Jianshe Lu (Main Branch), Tel: 283 4969; and Ground Floor, Hongshan Hotel, 108 Xinhua Beilu, Tel: 281 6017, 281 8447, Fax: 281 7078
Wuhan, Rm 303, 1365 Zhongshan Daiie, Hankou, Tel: 284 2331. Open Monday–Friday 8.30–11.30am, 2–5pm.
Wuxi, 7 Xing Sheng Rd, Tel: 20 4420. Open Monday–Saturday 9am–5pm.
Xiamen, No. 2 Zhongshan Lu, Tel: 203 1781 or 202 5277. Open daily 8am–5.30pm.
Xi'an, 48 (N) Changan Lu, tel: (029) 524-1864; Bell Tower Hotel, tel: (029) 727-9200, Ext 2842. Open Monday–Friday 8.30am–noon, 2.30–5.30pm.

The **Macau Government Tourist Office** is at 9 Largo do Senado, Macau. tel: 315566, fax: 510104. Their website is at www.macautourism.gov.mo

AMERICAN EXPRESS

Beijing, Room 2101, L115D West Wing Bldg., China World Trade Centre. Beijing 100004, Tel: 6505 2888. Open Monday–Friday 9am–5pm, Saturday 9am–noon.
Guangzhou, 339 Huan Shi Dong Lu, Guangzhou 510060, Tel: 8331 1771. Open Monday–Friday 9am–5pm, Saturday 9am–noon.
Shanghai, 206 East Tower, Shanghai Centre. 1376 Nanjing Rd West, Shanghai 200040, Tel: 6279 8082. Open Monday– Friday 9am–5pm, Saturday 9am–noon.
Xiamen, Rm 27, 2/F Holiday Inn Crowne Plaza Harbour View, 12-8 Zhen Hai Rd. Xiamen 361001, Tel: 212 0268, Fax: 212 0270.

Airline Offices

Beijing:

Air China, 15 Xi Changan Jie, Xicheng district, Tel: 6601 7755 (info) 6601 3336 (domestic), 6601 6667 (international).

Air France, Rm 2716, China World Trade Centre, Tel: 6505 1818.

Alitalia, Rm 139/140 Jianguo Hotel, Tel: 6591 8471.

All Nippon Airways, 1st Fl, China World Trade Centre, Tel: 6505 3311.

Asiana Airlines, Rm 134, Jianguo Hotel, Tel: 6468 1118.

British Airways, Rm 210, Scitech Tower, Tel: 6512 4070.

Canadian Airlines, Lufhansa Centre, Tel: 6463 7901.

China Eastern Airlines, Tel: 6017 589.

China Northwest Airlines, Air China Building, Tel: 6601 7755 x 2200.

China Sichuan Airlines, Air China Building, Tel: 6601 7755 x 2265.

China Southern Airlines, 227 Chaoyangmenwai Dajie, Tel: 6595 3622.

Dragonair, Rm L107, China World Trade Centre, Tel: 6505 4343.

Japan Airlines, Hotel New Otani Changfugong, Tel: 6513 0888.

Lufthansa, Beijing Lufthansa Centre, Tel: 6465 4488.

Malaysian Airlines, Rm 115A, West Wing, China World Trade Centre, Tel: 6505 2681.

MIAT (Mongolian), 1st Fl, Golden Bridge Plaza, Tel: 6506 4466 x 6052/6503.

Northwest Airlines, Rm 104, China World Trade Centre, Tel: 6505 3505.

Philippines Airlines, 12-53 Jianguomenwai Dajie, Tel: 6532 3992.

Qantas, Rm 102, Lufthansa Centre, Tel: 6467 4794.

SAS, 1st Fl, Scitech Tower, Tel: 6518 3738.

Singapore Airlines, Rm L109, China World Trade Centre, Tel: 6505 2233.

Swissair, 2nd Fl, Scitech Tower, Tel: 6512 3355.

Thai International, Rm 207-209, Scitech Tower, Tel: 6460 8899.

United Airlines, 1st Fl, Office Bldg, Lufthansa Centre, Tel: 6463 1111.

Hong Kong:

Air Canada, 10F, Wheelock House, 20 Pedder St, Central. Tel: 2522 1001 (res & flight info.); 2596 2299 (gen office).

Air France, 25/F Jardine House, Connaight Road, Central. Tel: 2524 8145 (res.); 25019590 (info).

Air New Zealand, 17/F Li Po Chun Chambers, 189 Des Voeux Road, Central. Tel: 2524 9041 (res.); 2842 3642 (flight info.).

Ansett, 17/F Li Po Chun Chambers, 189 Des Voeux Road, Central. Tel: 2527 7883 (res.); 2842 3642 (flight info.).

British Airways, 30F, Alexandra House, Chater Rd, Central, Tel: 2868 0303 (res); 2868 0768 (info.).

Canadian, Room 1608, New World Tower, Tower 1, 18 Queen's Road, Central. Tel: 2867 8111 (res.); 2769 7113 (flight info.).

Cathay Pacific, Peninsula Office Tower 10/F, 18 Middle Road, Kowloon. Tel: 2747 1888 (res.); 2747 1234 (flight info).

China, 3rd Fl, St George's Bldg, 2 Ice House St, Central, Tel: 2868 2299 (res.); 2769 8391 (info.).

Delta, Room 2503A Caroline Centre, 28 Yun Ping Road, Causeway Bay. Tel: 2526 5875.

Dragonair, 46/F Cosco Tower, 183 Queen's Road, Central Tel: 2590 1188 (res. & flight info.).

KLM Royal Dutch, 22nd Fl, World Trade Centre, 280 Gloucester Rd, Causeway Bay. Tel: 2808 2111 (res.); 2116 8730 (flight info.).

Lufthansa, 1109–10, wing Shan Tower, 193 Des Voeux Road, Central. Tel: 2868 2313 (res.); 2769 6560 (flight info.).

Northwest, 29F, Alexandra House, Chater Rd, Central, Tel: 2810 4288.

Qantas Airways, 37/F Jardine House, Central. Tel: 2842 1438 (res.); 2842 1400 (flight info.).

SAS, 14F, Harcourt House, 39 Gloucester Rd, Wan Chai, Tel: 2865 1370 (res.).

Singapore, 17F, United Ctr, 95 Queensway, Admiralty, Tel: 2520 2233 (res.); 2769 6387 (info.).

Swissair, 8F, Tower Two, Admiralty Ctr, 18 Harcourt Rd, Central, Tel: 2529 3670 (res.); 2769 6031 (flight info.).

United, 29F, Gloucester Tower, The Landmark, Central, Tel: 2810 4888 (res.); 2769 7279 (info.).

Virgin Atlantic, 41F Lippo Tower Lippo Ctr, 89 Queensway, Tel: 2532 6060 (res.); 2769 7017 (flight info.).

Shanghai:

Air China, 600 Huashan Lu, Tel: 6327 2676.

Air France, Shanghai Hilton, 250 Huashan Lu, Tel: 6248 0000.

All Nippon Airways, Shanghai Centre, 1376 Nanjing Xi Lu, Tel: 6279 7000.

Austrian Airlines, Equatorial Hotel, 65 Yanan Xi Lu, Tel: 6249 1202.

Canadian Airlines, Jin Jiang Tower, 161 Changle Lu, Tel: 6415 3091.

China Eastern Airlines, 200 Yanan Xi Lu, Tel: 6247 5953 (domestic), 6247 2255 (international).

Dragon Airlines, Shanghai Centre, 1376 Nanjing Xi Lu, Tel: 6279 8099.

Japan Airlines, Ruijin Dasha, 205 Maoming Nan Lu, Tel: 6472 3000.

Korean Airlines, Equatorial Hotel, 65 Yanan Xi Lu, Tel: 6248 1555.

Lufthansa, Shanghai Hilton, 250 Huashan Lu, Tel: 6248 1100.

Northwest Airlines, Shanghai Centre, 1376 Nanjing Xi Lu, Tel: 6279 8088.

SAS, Jin Jiang Hotel, 59 Maoming Nan Lu, Tel: 6472 3131.

Singapore Airlines, Shanghai Centre, 1376 Nanjing Xi Lu, Tel: 6279 8000.

Swiss Air, Shanghai Centre, 1376 Nanjing Xi Lu, Tel: 6279 7381.

United Airlines, Shanghai Centre, 1376 Nanjing Xi Lu, Tel: 6279 8009.

Qantas, Shanghai Centre, 1376 Nanjing Xi Lu, Tel: 6279 8660.

Practical Tips

Photography

Taking photographs or videos of military installations is prohibited. As in other countries, some museums, palaces, or temples will not allow photographs to be taken, or will charge a fee. Other times, photography is allowed, but without using flash.

Cameras must be declared when arriving in China. No special permit is necessary for video or movie cameras, as long as it is clearly not for professional use.

Emergencies

SECURITY & CRIME

There is still less crime in China than in many other countries, but as vigorous crime crackdowns by the government attest – thousands of executions per year – crime is increasingly a problem.

Take the same precautions applicable anywhere, on the street and with valuables in hotels and on public transportation. Pickpockets and bag-slashers can be a problem, especially on crowded trains and buses, and in stations. Because of migrant workers, cities such as Guangzhou have more crime than elsewhere. Still, one needn't worry in most towns and cities.

The **Public Security Bureau** (*Gongan Ju*) is the ever-present police force responsible for everything – chasing murderers, quenching dissent, issuing visa extensions. They are usually friendly towards foreigners, even if the rules that they are strictly enforcing seem illogical at times. Also, with serious travel-related disputes – for example, with taxi drivers or hotels

– they are usually able to resolve the problem. To stay on their friendly side, don't be caught trying to travel in restricted areas or on an expired visa.

LOSS OR THEFT OF BELONGINGS

If you've lost something, do what one would do anywhere else: Notify the hotel, tour group leader or transportation authorities, and the police, who will usually make a serious effort to recover items. Then, most likely, you might start considering how to replace the lost or stolen items.

LUGGAGE

Forget designer luggage with fine leather trim, useful only for posturing in a hotel lobby. Likewise with shiny aluminium cases which plead to be stolen. Take sturdy, strong luggage. This is especially recommended if travelling independently or away from the catered tourist venues. Luggage should be lockable, sometimes a requirement for transport.

Medical Services

There is a big difference in China between urban and rural medical services. If travelling in the countryside, there may be no appropriate medical services beyond primary health care, which is good in China. Some hospitals in cities have special sections for foreigners and where English is spoken.

Many of the large hotels have their own doctors. Payment must be made on the spot for treatment, medicine and transport. If planning to visit areas outside of Beijing, Shanghai, Guangzhou and Hong Kong, consider emergency evacuation insurance.
International SOS Assistance, 507 Kai Tak Commercial Bldg, 317 Des Voeux Road, Central, Hong Kong, Tel: 2541 6483, Fax: 2528 9933.
Asia Emergency Assistance (AEA),

Allied Resources Bldg 9F, 32 Ice House St, Central, Hong Kong, Tel: 2810 8898, Fax: 2845 0395. Beijing: 6462 9100.

BEIJING

Emergency/Evacuation:
MEDEX Assistance Corporation, Beijing Lufthansa Centre, Regus Office 19, Tel: 6465 1264, Fax: 6465 1269.
SOS Assistance, Suite 433, Kunlun Hotel, Xinyuan Nanlu, Tel: 6500 3419, Fax: 6501 6048.
Emergency/General:
Asia Emergency Assistance Centre, 2-1-1 Tayuan Diplomatic Office Bldg, 14 Liangmahe Nanlu, Tel clinic: 6462 9112; emergency: 6462 9100; admin/fax: 6462 9111.
International Medical Clinic, Rm 106, Regus Office Bldg, Lufthansa Centre, Tel: 6465 1561/62/63, Fax: 6465 1961.
General:
Sino-German Polyclinic, Rm B1, Landmark Tower, Tel: 6501 1983, Fax: 6501 1944.
Peking Union Medical Hospital, 53 Dongdanbei Dajie, Tel: 6529 5269, emergency: 6529 5284.
Beijing United Family Hospital, 2 Jiangjui Lu, tel: 6433-3960, fax: 6433-3963. Family health care and gyneocological facilities; 24-hr pharmacy.

CHONGQING

People's Hospital (Renmin Hospital), 256 Xinhua Lu, Tel: 6370 8624

GUANGZHOU

Emergencies:
Red Cross Hospital, Tel: 8444 6411, in English.
Children's Hospital, Tel: 8188 6239.
Heart Centre, Tel: 8384 5357.
Guangzhou No. 1 People's Hospital, 602 Renmin Beilu, Tel: 8333 3090.

Provincial Hospital, No. 1, Foreigners' Dept., 123 Huifu Xilu, Tel: 8777 7812.

HONG KONG

Though many Chinese people still prefer traditional cures for minor ills, modern Western practices dominate the field, and most doctors did much of their training overseas. There are also numerous expatriate doctors and dentists. Private physicians' fees tend to be internationally scaled.

Hospitals:
None are cheap, but all are comfortable and offer highest quality specialists and facilities. The most notable private hospitals (in descending price order) are: **Matilda** 41 Mt Kellett Road, The Peak. Tel: 2849-0111, **Canossa** 1 Old Peak Road, Mid Levels. Tel: 2522-0181. **The Baptist Hospital** 222 Waterloo Road, Kowloon. Tel: 2337-4141 **Hong Kong Adventist Hospital**, 40 Stubbs Road, Happy Valley. Tel: 2574-6211. Operates an expat-staff out-patient department Sun–Fri noon, and also has a good **dental clinic** with 24-hour emergency service.

Central Medical Practice, 1501 Prince's Building, Central, Tel: 2521 2567.
Hong Kong Central, 1B Lower Albert Rd, Central, Tel: 2522 3141.

Clinics:
Clinics are a practical and economical alternative. The **Anderson & Partners** tel: 2523-8166, **Vio & Partners** tel: 2521-3302 and **Dr Oram & Partners**, tel: 2525-1730, all have clinics on both sides of the harbour.

KAIFENG

Kaifeng No. 1 Hospital, Caizhengting Jie, Tel: 55 6602.

KASHI (KASHGAR)

People's Hospital (Renmin Hospital), Jichang Lu, Tel: 282 2338.

LANZHOU

Gansu Province People's Hospital, 96 Donggang East Road, Tel: 841 6801.

LUOYANG

Luoyang People's Hospital No. 1, Dongxinglong Jie, Tel: 395 1279.

INGDAO

Qingdao Hospital, Jiaozhou Lu, Tel: 282 7971.

SHANGHAI

Emergency/Evacuation:
SOS International Assistance, Tel: 6248 4344.
Emergency/General:
Shanghai Emergency Centre, 68 Haining Lu, Tel: 6324 4010.
Shanghai Medical Area Intl, 2606 Shartex Plaza, 88 Zunyi Road, tel: 021-6295 0099 (24-hr hotline).
Huashan Hospital, 12 Wulumuqi Zhonglu, 19th floor Foreigners' Clinic tel: 6248-9999, Ext 1921/6248-3986.
New Pioneer Intl, 2/F, 3/F, Ge Ru Bldg, 910 Hen Shan Lu, tel: 021-6469 7259, 6469 4884, 6469 3898 (24-hr hotline).
World Link Medical Centre, Shanghai Centre, 1376 Nanjing Xi Lu, Tel: 6279 7688.

ÜRÜMQI

Xinjiang People's Hospital, 91 Tianchi Lu, Tel: 282 2927.
Ürümqi Chinese Medical Hospital, 60 Youhao Nanlu, Tel: 452 0963.
XI'AN
Shaanxi Province People's

Hospital, 214 Youyi Xilu, Tel: 525 1331 ext. 2283/2284.

ZHENGZHOU

Hospital No. 1, Henan Medical University, Daxue Lu, Tel: 696 4992.

Weights & Measures

Both the local and international standards for weights and measures are used in China:

feet	chi	metre
3.28	03.00	1.00
1.09	01.00	0.33
1.00	00.91	0.31
acre	**mu**	**hectare**
0.62	15.00	1.00
0.31	01.00	0.51
1.00	03.22	1.61
pound	**jin**	**kilo**
2.20	02.00	1.00
1.10	01.00	0.50
1.00	00.91	0.45
gallon	**sheng**	**litre**
0.22	11.00	1.00
1.00	14.55	4.55

Business Hours

Shops are open everyday, including public holidays. Opening hours are usually from 8.30am or 9am to 8pm. Government offices and banks are usually open from Monday to Friday, 8.30am to 5.30pm, with a lunch break from noon to 1.30pm. Times are approximate; allow for local variations. In western China, for example, offices often open later – they are on Beijing time, but it's before dawn when it's bright daylight in Beijing.

Tipping

Officially, it is still illegal to accept tips in China. Moreover, for a long time, it was considered patronising. Tourists and visitors in recent years, however, have changed attitudes in areas such as Guangzhou and Shanghai. It's also become the custom for travel groups to give a tip to the Chinese travel guides and bus drivers. If you are travelling with a group, ask the guide, who is responsible for the "official" contacts of the group, whether a tip is appropriate and how much.

Tipping is still not common in most restaurants and hotels, although it is accepted in the top-class hotels and restaurants. Note that as part of the ritual any gift or tip will, at first, be firmly rejected.

Religious Services

Officially, the People's Republic encourages atheism. However, the dominant religion in China is Buddhism, with Buddhist temples and places of worship throughout the country. Daoist temples can also be found, as are mosques in the Muslim areas and in all large cities, which have regular prayers at the prescribed times. Catholic and Protestant churches can also be found in most big cities.

Media

An English-language newspaper, the *China Daily*, is published in China daily except on Sundays. It is informative and sometimes even a bit bold, depending upon the climate at the moment. Often obtainable from the big hotels for free, it contains the television schedule and a diary of cultural events in Beijing. The sports section is good. Unfortunately, same-day editions are available only in large cities; elsewhere, it'll probably be several days late.

Overseas editions of the *China Daily* are published in Hong Kong and the United States. In Shanghai, two other English-language publications, the *Shanghai Star* and *Shanghai Talk*, are free.

Most large hotels sell foreign language newspapers and journals, including the *International Herald Tribune*, *The Times*, *Asian Wall Street Journal*, *Time*, *Newsweek*, *Far Eastern Economic Review*, and many more. The overseas edition of the party newspaper *Renmin Ribao* (*People's Daily*) is sold in hotels.

Telecommunications

TELEPHONE

Domestic long-distance calls are cheap, international calls are expensive. Local calls in China, including in the hotels, are usually free of charge. International calls made from hotels typically have high surcharges added to China's already high IDD rates. Increasingly common are card phones, with cards available in Y20, 50, 100 and 200. There are also street stalls where you can make calls, for about Y20–30 a minute. China has also announced that the international rate is coming down to prepare for opening up to foreign competition.

Like many nations expanding their domestic telephone networks, China's telephone numbers can change without too much fanfare. If you hear a funny ringing sound on the line and can't get through, the number may have changed.

E-MAIL

Beijing

Many hotels have facilities in their business centres. Some, such as the **Twenty-First Century Hotel**, 40 Liangmaqiao Lu, tel: 6466-3311, have separate Internet centres. Beijing also has several internet cafes, including the **Unicom Sparkice Internet Cafe** at the China World Trade Centre, tel: 6505-2288 x8209 (www.sparkice.com.cn). Other Sparkice Internet cafes are at the Capital Stadium, West Wing, Baoshiqiao Lu, Haidian District, tel: 6833-5335; B1810 Wantong New World Plaza, 2 Fuchengmenwai Dajie, Xicheng District, tel: 6857-8794; and the Parkson department store, 101 Fuxingmennei Dajie (west of Changan Avenue, close to Fuxingmen underground stop), tel: 6205-2650.

Hong Kong

A number of cyber cafés operate in Hong Kong. Some of the best are: **Xyberia Interactive**, China Bear Mui Wo Centre, 3 Ngan Wan Road, Mui

Dialling Codes

Country code for China: 86
Direct-dial international calls: dial 00, then the country code and telephone number.
Home country direct-dial: dial 108, then the country's international area code. For example, to call Britain, dial 108-44, then the domestic area code and number. For the United States and Canada, dial 108-1. (For AT&T, 108-11; MCI, 108-12; Sprint, 108-13.

Wo, Lantau Island, e-mail: sahr@xyberia.com. HK$40 per hour. **Cyber-X Multimedia Fun Pub Café**, G/F Empress Plaza 17–19 Chatham Road, Kowloon, tel: 2367-2399; fax: 2367-9678; daily 11am–2am; e-mail: webmaster@cyber-x.com.hk. HK$1 per minute. **Kublai's** 3/F Capital Place, 18 Luard Rd, Wan Chai, tel: 2529-9117; daily 12.30am–10.30pm; e-mail: webmaster@kublais.com www.kublais.com. HK$48 per half hour (but this can be used towards purchase of food and drink as well). All branches of the Pacific Coffee Company grant free access for the price of a cup of coffee (www.pacificcoffee.com).

FAX AND TELEX

Most of the big hotels have telex and fax facilities to help business people. Alternatively, central telegraph and post offices offer telex and fax services.

TELEGRAMS

Sending telegrams abroad is relatively expensive. Express telegrams are double the price. There is usually a telegram counter at the hotel; otherwise, go to the central telegraph or post office.

Domestic Area Codes

Add 0 to the codes below if
dialling from within China:

Beijing	10
Chengdu	28
Chongqing	811
Guangzhou	20
Guilin	773
Hangzhou	571
Harbin	451
Jilin	432
Kunming	871
Luoyang	379
Nanjing	25
Shanghai	21
Shenyang	24
Shenzhen	755
Suzhou	512
Taiyuan	351
Tianjin	22
Urumqi	991
Wuhan	27
Wuxi	510
Xi'an	29
Xiamen	592
Xinxiang	373
Zhengzhou	371

The international dialling code for
Hong Kong is 852; for Macau it
is 853.

Courier/Postal Services

Domestic mail delivery is
exceedingly fast and cheap, and it
puts most Western postal services
to shame. Within some cities, there
is often same-day delivery; between
large cities, delivery is usually
overnight. International mail, too, is
efficient.

Express mail (EMS) is available
to most international destinations,
as are private international courier
services. Large parcels must be
packed and sealed at the post
office, but for smaller parcels there
are more comprehensive mail
services.

For general delivery or post
restante services, visit the central
post office in each city. Card
members can also use American
Express offices for receiving mail.

COURIER SERVICES

Beijing
DHL: Tel: 6466 2211, Fax: 6462
9490.
Federal Express: Tel: 6462 3188,
Fax: 6467 6952.
TNT: Tel: 6465 2227, Fax: 6462
4018.
UPS: Tel: 6593 2932, Fax: 6593
2941.

Shanghai
DHL: Tel: 6279 8664.
Federal Express: Tel: 6472 3060.
UPS: Tel: 6248 6060.

Xi'an
DHL: Tel: 731 8313.
Federal Express: Tel: 328 2754,
322 7713.
UPS: Tel: 742 0830, 742 0141.

Embassies & Consulates

Beijing
Australia, 21 Dongzhimenwai Dajie,
Tel: 532 2331.
Canada, 19 Dongzhimenwai Dajie,
Chaoyangqu, Tel: 532 3536, Tlx:
222445 CANAD CN.
Ireland, 3 Ritan Donglu, Tel: 532
2691.
Mongolia, 2 Xiushui Bei Jie,
Jianguomenwai, Tel: 532 1203.
Nepal, Sanlitunlu, Xiliujie, Tel: 532
1795.
Netherlands, 4 Liangmahe Nanlu,
Tel: 532 1131.
New Zealand, Ritanlu Dong erjie,
Tel: 532 2731.
Russia, Dongzhimen Beizhongjie,
Tel: 532 2051 (visa section: 532
1267)
Singapore, 1 Xiushuibeijie,
Jianguomenwai, Tel: 532 3926.
United Kingdom, 11 Guanghualu,
Jianguomenwai, Tel: 532 1961,
Fax: 532 1939.
United States, Jianwai Xiushui
Beijie No. 3, Tel: 532 3831, Fax:
532 3178, Tlx: 22701 AMEMB CN.

Shanghai
Australia, 14 Fuxing Xi Lu, Tel:
6433 4604, Fax: 6437 6669.
Canada, Shanghai Centre, Suite
604, 1376 Nanjing Xi Lu, Tel: 6279
8400, Fax: 6279 8401.
Great Britain, Shanghai Ctr, Suite
301, 1376 Nanjing Xi Lu, Tel: 6279
7650, Fax: 6279 7651.
Japan, 1517 Huaihai Zhong Lu, Tel:
6433 2726, 6433 6639, Fax: 6433
1008.
Korea, Shanghai International Trade
Centre, Suite 402, 2200 Yanan Xi
Lu, Tel: 6219 6417, 6219 6420,
Fax: 6219 6918.
New Zealand, Qihua Tower, 15B,
1375 Huaihai Zhong Lu, Tel: 6433
2230, Fax: 6433 3533.
Singapore, 400 Wulumuqi Lu, Tel:
6437 0776, 6433 1362, Fax: 6433
4150.
United States, 1469 Huaihai Zhong
Lu, Tel: 6433 6880, Fax: 6433
4122.

Hong Kong
Australia, 24th Fl, Harbour Ctr, 25
Harbour Rd, Wan Chai, Tel: 2827
8881.
Austria, 22nd Fl, Emperor House,
34-37 Connaught Rd, Central, Tel:
2522 8086.
Belgium, 9th Fl, St. John's Bldg, 33
Garden Rd, Central, Tel: 2524
3111.
Canada, 12th Fl, Tower One,
Exchange Square, 8 Connaught
Place, Central, Tel: 2810 4321.
Great Britain, c/o Hong Kong
Immigration Department,
Immigration Tower, 7 Gloucester Rd,
Tel: 2824 6111.
Japan, 46th Fl, Tower One,
Exchange Square, Central, Tel:
2526 1483/0796.
Korea (South), 5th Fl, Far East
Finance Ctr, 16 Harcourt Rd,
Central, Tel: 2529 4141.
New Zealand, Rm 2705, Jardine
House, Connaught Place, Central,
Tel: 2877 4488.
Singapore, 9th Fl, Tower One,
Admiralty Ctr, 18 Harcourt Rd,
Central, Tel: 2527 2212.
South Africa, 27th Fl, Sunning
Plaza, 10 Hysan Ave, Causeway
Bay, Tel: 2577 3279.
United States, 26 Garden Rd,
Central, Tel: 2523 9011.

Getting Around

All main cities can be reached by plane and train. railways, buses and airplanes. In the regions along the big rivers, boats play an important part. The road network has been improved in recent years but is still very poor in many areas.

ROAD NAMES

Street names are determined by the traditional checkerboard of Chinese urban design. The most important traffic arteries are divided into sectors and laid out in a grid typically based upon the compass points.

Suffixes are added to the primary name to indicate north, south, east or west, and, additionally, to indicate the middle section. The middle section is called *zhong*; *nan* means south; *bei*, north; *dong*, east; and *xi*, west. A main road is *lu*, smaller is *dajie* or *jie*. A small lane is named *long*.

On Arrival

You will have to fill in a customs declaration listing all items of value, such as camera, tape recorder, watches, and money. Another form asks for details of your health. A third requirement is the entry card, on which you fill in details about the length of your stay in China. It will be put with your passport. Keep the customs declaration safe, because you need to hand it in at the end of the trip. When you hand in your customs declaration, customs officers may check whether you are taking out all the items you

declared. The loss of the customs declaration can incur a high fine.

There are exchange bureaux at the arrival halls of airports, railway stations and ports where you can change money. You can also find taxis to your hotel. The Chinese airlines provide buses that will take travellers from the airport, which is often a long way outside the city, to the airline offices in town. The fare is modest.

Be wary of people offering taxis before you reach taxi ranks. Before setting off in a taxi, agree on a price for the journey, or ensure that the driver agrees to use the meter.

Domestic Travel

RAILWAYS

The Chinese rail network covers 53,400 km (32,500 miles), of which 2,700 miles (4,400 km) are electrified. Average train speed is not very high, mainly due to poor construction. There is no first or second class on Chinese trains, but four categories or classes: *ruanwo* or soft-sleeper; *ruanzuo* or soft-seat; *yingwo* or hard-sleeper, and *yingzuo* or hard-seat. The soft-seat class is usually only available for short journeys. Long-distance trains normally only have soft-sleeper or hard-sleeper facilities. The soft-sleeper class has 4-bed compartments with soft beds. It is to be recommended particularly for long journeys. The hard-sleeper class has open, 6-bed compartments. The beds are not really hard, but are not very comfortable either. While you can reserve a place for the first three classes (you always buy a ticket with a place number), this is not always essential for the lowest class.

There is always boiled water available on the trains. There are washrooms in the soft-sleeper and hard-sleeper classes. The toilets, regardless of which class, are usually not very hygienic, and it is a good idea to bring your own toilet paper. There are dining cars on long-distance trains.

Trains are usually fully booked and it is advisable to get a ticket well in advance. This is particularly so during the main travel season. There are special ticket counters for foreigners at railway stations. Fares are higher for foreigners than for the Chinese. The price also depends on both the class and the speed of the train; there are slow trains, fast trains, express trains and inter-city trains. Reservations can be made at ticket offices in the town centre or through travel agencies. Be on time, as trains tend to be punctual.

LONG-DISTANCE BUSES

Overland buses are the most important means of transport in many parts of China, especially where there is no railway line. In most towns and settlements, there are main bus stations for overland buses. They are the cheapest means of transport, but are also correspondingly slow. There are regular breaks during bus journeys; on journeys lasting several days you will usually find simple restaurants and overnight accommodation near the bus stations. Many overland buses have numbered seats and it is advisable to book a ticket and seat well in advance. Modern buses with air conditioning are frequently available in the tourist centres.

WATER TRANSPORT

There are regular ferry and boat connections between the large coastal cities in China. The same is true for some of the big rivers, particularly the Chang Jiang (Yangzi) and the Zhu Jiang (Pearl River), but not the Huang He (Yellow River). Both the ocean liners and the inland river boats have several classes. You can find out the exact timetable from travel agents or the shipping agencies.

TOWN TRANSPORT

The visitor can choose between taxis, buses, or bicycles for transport in the cities. In Beijing, Hong Kong, Guangzhou and Shanghai there is also the underground.

Taxis are certainly the most comfortable form of transport, and can be hired for excursions.

Buses in Chinese towns are always overcrowded. The fare depends on distance, and should be paid to the conductor. Buses are usually easy to use, and timetables or town maps are available everywhere. In some Chinese cities such as Beijing, there are also minibuses for certain routes. They carry a maximum of 16 people. They are a bit more expensive but will stop at any point you want along the route. Drivers will pack in as many people as they can and you may end up standing or sitting next to the driver.

You can hire bicycles in many Chinese towns, either at the hotels or at special hiring shops. It is advisable to park the bicycle at

Air Times

The following list shows the time needed for flight connections from Beijing to other domestic destinations.

From Beijing to	hrs/min
Chengdu	2.35
Chongqing	2.30
Dalian	1.10
Guangzhou	2.40
Guilin	2.35
Hangzhou	1.50
Harbin	1.40
Hohhot	1.15
Kunming	2.55
Lanzhou	2.10
Nanjing	1.50
Qingdao	1.15
Shanghai	1.50
Taiyuan	1.35
Ürümqi	3.55
Wuhan	1.45
Xi'an	2.00

guarded parking spaces for a small fee. China has bicycle thieves and there is a fine for illegal parking.

Rail Times

By Rail: The distance and time needed to travel from Beijing to other domestic destinations are as below:

Beijing Time to:	Distance km (mi)	hrs
Chengdu	1,273 (2,048)	34
Chongqing	1,586 (2,552)	40
Datong	249 (400)	8
Dalian	770 (1,239)	19
Guangzhou	1,437 (2,313)	33
Guilin	1,326 (2,134)	31
Hangzhou	1,026 (1,651)	26
Harbin	862 (1,388)	17
Hohhot	423 (680)	14
Kunming	1,975 (3,179)	59
Lanzhou	1,169 (1,882)	33
Luoyang	509 (819)	12
Nanjing	719 (1,157)	15
Qingdao	551 (887)	17
Shanghai	908 (1,462)	17
Suzhou	855 (1,376)	21
Taiyuan	319 (514)	9
Ürümqi	2,345 (3,774)	73
Wuhan	764 (1,229)	16
Wuxi	829 (1,334)	17
Xi'an	724 (1,165)	17

Group Travel

The simplest and most comfortable way of travelling to China at a reasonable price is in a group. Participants will have their passage, hotel accommodation and meals, and sightseeing program booked in advance. There are hardly any additional costs apart from drinks and shopping. Sometimes, additional excursions may be on offer once you have arrived, but they are generally not too costly. Some places charge for taking photographs.

The local tour guide is supplied by the Chinese tourist office and is in charge of taking you to the sights.

Specialists will have better knowledge of places of special

interest when planning a particular route. Also, the pitfalls of a journey through China have increased rather than diminished in recent years; an experienced tour operator can avoid many difficulties.

Another decisive factor for a successful group trip is the tour guide. While each group with more than ten participants is allocated a permanent Chinese guide in addition to the local guides, their qualifications vary considerably, both in terms of organising the trip and in their knowledge of the country and its sights, and their ability to communicate. The importance of the guide employed by the tour operator shouldn't be underestimated.

A number of tour operators now offer trips around a theme as well as the traditional routes. A few offer courses in shadow boxing, calligraphy, or acupuncture. Some even offer language courses.

Individual Travel

There are three ways of travelling in China for the individual traveller. The most comfortable, and of course, most expensive way, is to book a full package tour through an experienced travel agent. Everything is pre-booked, including flights and journeys, accommodation, meals, and transfers, with the difference that the traveller can choose a route according to preference. The same is the case for sightseeing: a guide from a China travel agency is available in each town and will help with putting together and arranging a sightseeing program.

The second possibility is booking a mini-package tour. The agent pre-books the flights, accommodation with breakfast, transfers, and transport of luggage in China while the traveller is responsible for organising sightseeing. The traveller is met at the airport or railway station on arrival at each town and taken to the hotel. Each hotel has a travel agency counter, where you can discuss your plans for sightseeing and have them arranged for a fee.

The individual tourist may have the most pleasant travel. The most essential bookings have been made (to make them yourself requires a lot of time and strong nerves), and with thorough preparation, you have a good chance of getting to know China beyond the usual tourist routes. You should get a definite booking with an experienced travel agent three months before departure at the latest.

Then there is completely independent travel, without any pre-booking. This form of travelling in China has increased in recent years. The Chinese travel bureaus have partially adapted to it and can help, in the large towns, with buying air and train tickets. You have to arrange your own air and train tickets at each place you visit; unless you speak Chinese, you will probably find it easiest to do this through a travel agency, where it is more likely you will find English-speaking staff. At airports and stations, you will often find that information about destinations is given in pinyin, or sometimes only in Chinese characters. You shouldn't expect last-minute plans to come through; it can easily happen that you have to wait several days for your railway or air ticket, or abandon your chosen destination and choose a different town for your next visit. Try and reserve air or rail tickets as soon as you arrive. Tickets cost more for foreigners than for Chinese, and only in rare cases might you succeed in getting a ticket at the cost that overseas Chinese pay.

Travel agencies will book hotels for a small fee, though only with high-class hotels.

Where to Stay

Choosing a Hotel

China's large cities have seen the sprouting of numerous new hotels, most of them at the high end of the market, including many of world-class calibre. Many belong to international hotel chains, or else to international marketing associations, and their management and staff have been trained abroad. Usually the prices of these better hotels are in line with hotel prices in the West.

Tour groups are usually accommodated in good tourist hotels, which are well-appointed. Except in the first-class hotels, take caution with laundry service, particularly with delicate clothes.

Bookings with hotels in the middle and lower price ranges sometimes can be difficult, particularly during the main seasons in May, September and October, when they are hopelessly booked. Fortunately, if you have confirmed reservations, your room will be waiting, as hotels rarely overbook.

Worth mentioning are a few well-preserved hotels built by the colonial powers in some cities. They include the Peace Hotel (Heping) in Shanghai, the People's Hotel (Renmin Dasha) in Xi'an and the Friendship Hotel (Youyibinguan) in Beijing. Interiors have been modernised, of course.

Luxury hotels abound in the largest cities. Hong Kong is saturated with them. Rates at all but the cheapest hotels are subject to 10 to 15 percent service surcharge Rates for each price category are shown in the yellow boxes in the listings and are for a standard room.

Beijing

$$$$$
China World Hotel
1 Jianguomen Dajie
Tel: 6505 2266
Fax: 6505 3167.
Top service and accommodation, with health club, swimming pool, shopping and business centres, plus several Western and Asian restaurants. Part of the China World Trade Centre business complex.
Guangdong Regency Hotel
2 Wangfujing Dajie
Tel: 6513 6666.
Comfortable atmosphere and deluxe environment in prime location.
Hilton Hotel
1 Dongfang Lu
Dongsanhuan Beilu
Tel: 6466 2288
Fax: 6464 3052.
Next to the airport expressway and convenient to several business centres. All the conveniences that business travellers expect.

Price Cateories

$$$$$	=	US$200 and up
$$$$	=	US$150–US$200
$$$	=	US$100–US$150
$$	=	US$50–US$100
$	=	below US$50

Kempinski Hotel
Beijing Lufthansa Centre
50 Liangmaqiao Lu
Tel: 6465 3388
Fax: 6465 3366.
Attached to Youyi (Friendship) Shopping City, this hotel has all facilities, including health club, restaurants and Paulaner Brauhaus.
Palace Hotel
8 Jinyu Hutong
Wangfujing Dajie
Tel: 6512 8899
Fax: 6512 9050.
Modern, functional construction combines with Chinese imperial architecture. Located in a lively alley, ideal for shopping and Tiananmen.
Shangri-La Hotel
29 Zizhuyuan Lu

Haidian District
Tel: 6841 2211
Fax: 6841 8002.
On the western edge of the city, the Shangri-La provides a shuttle-bus service to downtown areas.
Swissotel Beijing
Hong Kong – Macau Centre
Dongsishiqiao Lu
Tel: 6501 2288
Fax: 6501 2501.
A semicircular, mirrored facade dominates one of Beijing's busy intersections. Popular with business travellers.

$$$$
Holiday Inn Crowne Plaza
48 Wangfujing Dajie
Dengshikou
Tel: 6513 3388
Fax: 6513 2513.
Located on one of central Beijing's busiest shopping streets, close to the Imperial Palace. Health club and swimming pool.
Holiday Inn Lido
Jichang Lu
Jiangtai Lu
Tel: 6437 6688
Fax: 6437 6237.
A kind of haven for foreigners, the Lido has shops, including a deli and a bakery, supermarket, offices and apartments. Just 20 minutes from the airport.
Hotel New Otani Changfugong
26 Jianguomenwai Dajie
Tel: 6512 5555
Fax: 6512 5346
Japanese joint venture to the east of the city centre and close to the embassy district.
Jinglun Hotel (Beijing-Toronto)
3 Jianguomenwai Dajie
Tel: 6500 2266
Fax: 6500 2022.
Next to the Jianguo and known for its cuisine, the Jinglun is another business favourite.
Radisson SAS Royal Hotel
6A Dongsanhuan Beilu
Tel: 6466 3388
Fax: 6465 3186.
Complete facilities, and CITS office, Scandinavian cuisine, wine garden, tennis courts.
Traders' Hotel
(China World Trade Centre) 1

Jianguomenwai Dajie
Tel: 6505 2277
Fax: 6505 0818.
Solid service, food and accommodation. Well located for business in the east of the city.

$$$
Beijing International Hotel
19 Jianguomenwai Dajie
Tel: 6512 6688
Fax: 6513 7842.
Good location near Beijing Railway Station, with full facilities including booking offices for international flights and trains.
Jianguo Hotel
5 Jianguomenwai Dajie
Tel: 6500 2233
Fax: 6500 2871.
Convenient for the Friendship Store, silk market and most embassies, this is a favourite with long-term business visitors.
Novotel Beijing
88 Dengshikou
Dongcheng district
Tel: 6513 8822
Fax: 6513 9088.
Clean and functional, a bargain for central Beijing.
Peace Hotel
3 Jinyu Hutong
Wangfujing Dajie
Tel: 6512 8833
Fax: 6512 6863.
In the same lively alley as the Palace Hotel, close to Tiananmen and the Imperial Palace.
Prime Hotel Beijing
2 Wangfujing Dajie
Tel: 6513-6666
Fax: 6513-4248
Relaxing atmosphere and de-luxe accommodation in a prime location.
Scitech Hotel
22 Jianguomenwai Dajie
Tel: 6512 3388
Fax: 6512 3543.
Formerly the CVIK Hotel, behind the Scitech Plaza shopping centre.

$$
Beijing Bamboo Garden Hotel
24 Xiaoshiqiao Lane
Jiugulou Dajie
Tel: 6403 2229
Fax: 6401 2633.
Simple, clean rooms that open onto

a classical Chinese garden. Close to the Drum Tower and Deshengmen gate in the old city wall.

Price Cateories

Rates are for standard rooms.

$$$$$	=	US$200 and up
$$$$	=	US$150–US$200
$$$	=	US$100–US$150
$$	=	US$50–US$100
$	=	below US$50

Fragrant Hills Hotel
inside Fragrant Hills Park
Tel: 6259 1166
Fax: 6259 1762.
Modern sanctuary from urban noise, in the lush hills northwest of Beijing, beyond the Summer Palace. There is a swimming pool, and Chinese and Western restaurants.
Friendship Hotel
3 Baishiqiao Lu
Haidian district
Tel: 6849 8888
Fax: 6849 8866.
Huge state-run hotel spread out in pleasant grounds close to the Summer Palace and university district. Home to many long-term foreign residents.
Qianmen Hotel
175 Yongan Lu
Tel: 6301 6688
Fax: 6301 3883.
Standard accommodation in old outer city, near Tiantan. Nightly Beijing opera performances.
Ritan Hotel
1 Ritan Lu
Jianguomenwai
Tel: 6512 5588
Fax: 6512 8671.
Intimate little hotel inside Ritan Park, near the main embassy area. Peaceful and reasonably priced for basic accommodation.
Xinqiao Hotel
2 Dong Jiaomin Xiang
Dongcheng District
Tel: 6513 3366
Fax: 6512 5126.
Elegant old-style hotel in the former Legation Quarter, close to Tiananmen Square.

Chengdu

$$$$ – $$$
JinJiang Hotel
180 Renmin Lu (People's Road) at
the intersection with the JinJiang
River
Tel: 558 2158
Fax: 558 1849.
Remodelled in 1994, this is one of
Chengdu's classiest hotels, with 500
rooms and a real cosmopolitan feel.

$$
Tibet Hotel
Peoples Road North
Tel: 333 3988
Fax: 333 3526.
A three-star hotel sponsored by the
government of Tibet has a good
range of accommodations, as well
as several restaurants, business,
travel, health and shopping centres.

$
Traffic Hotel
Tel: 555 1017
Fax: 558 2777.
On the JinJiang (Golden River), next
to the Xinnanmen intercity bus
station is both economical and
enjoys a good reputation amongst
travellers for its convenient, no-
nonsense services, cleanliness,
helpful staff and overall value, 170
rooms, which can be rented by the
bed (dormitory style) or by the
room.

Chongqing

$$$$
Holiday Inn Yangtze
15 Nan Ping Beilu
Tel: 6280 3380
Fax: 6280 0884.
This lively 4-star hotel offers all the
standard comforts and amenities
associated with its name, including
Chinese, Japanese, French, and
German restaurants. Its relatively
inconvenient location south of the
city centre across the Chang Jiang,
however, has not deterred many
international guests.

$$$
Chongqing Guest House
235 Minsheng Road

Tel: 6384 5888
Fax: 6383 0643.
This recently-renovated 4-star hotel,
somewhat on the tacky side, is
done in a Chinese motif complete
with rockeries in the lobby and a
separate entertainment building
from which booms the ubiquitous
karaoke. Separate VIP wing.
Centrally located near the city's
commercial centre.
Chung King Hotel
41-43 Xin Hua Road
Tel: 6383 8888
Fax: 6384 3085.
Located near the Chaotianmen
Docks, this 3-star hotel,
reminiscent of dull, old Soviet-style
monoliths, offers standard mid-
range rooms and facilities including
banking, tour and travel bookings.
Popular with foreigners.
Golden Mountain Hotel
97 Zhongshan 1st Road
Tel: 6353 8888
Fax: 6353 8889.
Hoping to lure away some of
Holiday Inn's guests, this new 4-
star hotel, opened since 1997, is
modern, elegant, and centrally
located. Full facilities, comfortable
rooms, friendly staff, and
competitive rates.
Huixian Lou Hotel
186 Minzu Road
Tel: 6383 7495
Fax: 6384 4034.
Centrally located near Jiefang Bei
and within walking distance of the
docks, this is one of the few
examples of budget accommodation
in town. However, it is still
overpriced.
Renmin Hotel
173 Renmin Road
Tel: 6385 1421
Fax: 6385 2076.
Housed in ornate, traditional
Chinese-style buildings evoking a
bygone era, this 4-star hotel is
located on the northwestern end of
the main peninsula and offers a
range of Western and Asian
restaurants, and full facilities
including the capacity to book
hotels anywhere in the world. CITS
is located on its premises.
Shipin Binguan
72 Shaanxi Lu

Tel: 6384 7300
Fax: 6384 6725.
This budget hotel in a tired grey
building offers better value for
money than Huixian Lou, but here
too the rooms are spartan and
dark. The staff are friendly and
courteous, though. Located
within minutes of the Chaotianmen
Docks.
Yu Du Hotel
168 Ba Yi Road
Tel: 6383 5215
Fax: 6381 8168.
Other than its central location in the
heart of the city's commercial
centre and its proximity to some
excellent restaurants, this hotel is
unremarkable and overpriced for the
quality of its rather bland
accommodations. Foreigners are
charged 30 percent extra.

Price Categories

$$$$$	=	over US$200
$$$$	=	US$150–US$200
$$$	=	US$100–US$150
$$	=	US$50–US$100
$	=	below US$50

Dali

Dali Guesthouse (No. 1)
Fuxinglu, Dali City.
Still the nicest location in the old
town, with local Bai-style
embellishments in the architecture
and furnishings. Set back from the
street, so rather quiet, yet still
close to the action.
Xichou Villa
Xichou (17 km north of Dali).
Converted Bai mansion, outfitted
with modern furnishings, but still in
the traditional style. Lots of
woodcarved art. On the outskirts of
a pleasant, Bai-majority village that
used to be an important trading
stop on the Tea and Horses Road
to Tibet.

Guangzhou

$$$$
China Hotel
Liuhua Lu, Guangzhou

Tel: 8666 6888
Fax: 8667 7014.
5-star hotel managed by the New
World Group of Hong Kong.
Restaurants include the Hard Rock
Cafe and the famous Food Street. A
small shopping gallery is attached.
Centrally located across the street
from the Guangzhou Trade Fair
grounds.

Dongfang Hotel
120 Liuhua Lu
Guangzhou
Tel: 8666 9900
Fax: 8666 2775.
This five-star hotel was built in the
1950s by the Soviets and a new
wing added in the 1970s. Has
managed to retain a lot of charm.
Centrally-located and convenient for
businessmen, as the China Trade
Fair grounds are just opposite.

Garden Hotel
368 Huangshi Donglu
Guangzhou
Tel: 8333-8989
Fax: 8335-0467.
Five-star hotel located across the
street from the largest Friendship
Department Store.

White Swan Hotel
1 Shamian Nanlu, Guangzhou
Tel: 8188 6968
Fax: 8186 1188.
One of the finest hotels in China
and a member of the Leading
Hotels of the World network. The
843-room hotel sits by itself on
Shamian island with a gallery of
high class boutiques and
restaurants.

$$$
Gitic Riverside Hotel
298 Yan Jiang Lu C
Guangzhou
Tel: 8383 9888
Fax: 8381 4508.
On the banks of the Pearl River, this
four-star hotel features spacious
rooms, full facilities, and decent
restaurants. Close to Beijing Lu
shopping area.

**Holiday Inn City Centre Overseas
Chinese Village**
Huanshi Dong, 28 Guangmin Lu
Tel: 8776 6999
Fax: 8775-3126.
A 430-room hotel which opened in

1990, it is known for its friendly
service.

Landmark Hotel
2 Nanhu Lu
Shenzhen
Tel: 217-2288
Fax: 229-0473.
A Cathay International hotel. The
hotel has restaurants, coffee shop,
bar and night club, and health club
with swimming pool.

Ramada Pearl Hotel
9 Mingyue Yilu
Tel: 8777-2988
Fax: 8776-7481.
This 400-room hotel is located in
the eastern part of the city.

Shangri-La
East Side, Railway Station Jianshe
Lu, Shenzhen
Tel: 223-0888
Fax: 223-9878
Luxuriously appointed 553-room
hotel, with extensive food and drink
outlets.

$$
Airlines Hotel
130 Shennan Dong Lu
Shenzhen
Tel: 223-7999
Fax: 233-7866.
Recently redecorated, now clean
and comfortable.

Century Plaza
Cunfeng Lu
Shenzhen
Tel: 8222-0888
Fax: 8223-4060
Luxury hotel situated in the hub of
Shenzhen. Five restaurants, pool,
and health and business centres.

China Merchants Hotel
8-111 Liu Hua Lu, Guangzhou
Tel: 8668 1988
Fax: 8666 2680.
240 rooms, 14 floors, one Western
and one Chinese restaurant,
karaoke, business centre, laundry
service.

Equatorial Hotel
931 Renmin Lu, Guangzhou
Tel: 8667 2888
Fax: 8667 2583.
Range of food and beverage
outlets, business centre, health
club and discotheque.

Forum
67 Heping Lu

Shenzhen
Tel: 8558-6333
Fax: 8556-1700.
Opened in 1990, the Forum is
located just west of the railway
station. A member of the Inter-
Continental hotel and resorts
chain.

Oriental Regent
Financial Centre Bldg
Shenan Zhonglu
Shenzhen
Tel: 8224-7000
Fax: 8224-7290.
Centrally located, four-star hotel.
Close to nightlife area.

Overseas Chinese Hotel
90 Zhanqian Lu
Guangzhou
Tel: 8666-3488
Fax: 8666-3230.
A 400-room hotel with two
restaurants, a coffee house
and disco.

Shenzhen Bay Hotel
Overseas Chinese Town
Shenzhen
Tel: 8660-0111
Fax: 8660-0139.
Facing Deep Water Bay and a short
walk from attractions like Splendid
China, China Folk Culture Village and
Windows of the World. This resort-
style hotel on the beach offers a full
range of recreational facilities.

Victory Hotel
54 Shamian Sijie
Guangzhou
Tel: 8186-2622
Fax: 8186-1062.
Located on the former concession
island of Shamian, near the old
town. This was one of Guangzhou's
top hotels in the 1930s.

$
Guangdong Hotel
294 The Bund, Guangzhou
Tel: 8188 3601.
Down the street from the Dong Ya,
the Guangdong hotel is of the same
2-star quality. Chinese restaurant
and karaoke. Cheap single rooms
with shared bathroom.

Guangzhou Youth Hostel
2 Shamian Sijie, Guangzhou
Tel: 8188 4298.
Cheap rooms can be found at this
hostelry, nicknamed the "Black
Duck", as it faces the luxury White

Swan Hotel. A favourite with backpackers for its cleanliness and key location.

Xin Xing Hotel
1115 Jiefang Bei Lu, Guangzhou
Tel: 8668 3288
Fax: 8666 2032.
2-star hotel located in Sanyuanli by the train station. Clean rooms, business centre, laundry service and popular Chinese restaurants.

Guilin

$$$
Guilin Osmanthus Hotel
451 Zhongshannanlu
Tel: 383 4300
Fax: 383 5316.
In the heart of the city on Peach Blossom River, a short walk from Elephant Trunk Hill, 1 km north of railway station. Range of facilities includes water massage pond.

Guilin Park Hotel
1 Luosi Hill
Tel: 282 8899
Fax: 282 2296.
On Guihu Lake, at the foot of Old Man Hill. Beautifully designed, with white walls, green tiles, Chinese pagoda-style roofs. Set in one of the most scenic parts of the city, with pool, Chinese and Western restaurants.

Lijiang Hotel
1 Shanhubeilu
Tel: 22 2881
Fax: 22 2891.
Centrally located, overlooking Cedar Lake and facing nearby Elephant Trunk Hill. Big rooms, modern facilities, including sauna and gymnasium. The local rolling-skating rink is around the corner, plus Binjianglu, along the river, especially pretty at night.

$$
Guishan Hotel
Chuanshan Road
Tel: 581 3388
Fax: 581 4851.
Across the Li River from Elephant Trunk Hill with a good view of the port area at night. A short walk from Seven Star Park. The usual modern facilities in a less congested neighbourhood.

In Xishuangbanna

Tai Garden Hotel
8 Nonglinnanlu, Jinghong
Tel: 212 3888
Fax: 212 6060.
Nicely sited beside the Liusha River. 3-star facilities with Dai-influenced architecture. Pool and nearby lake and minorities' park. Cantonese and Western restaurants, also Yunnanese and Dai cuisine in the Peacock Flavour Restaurant, with Dai dance show.

Xishuangbanna Hotel
11 Honggazhonglu
Tel: 212 3679
Fax: 212 3368.
Quiet location on the west bank of the Lancangjiang (Upper Mekong). Dai-style architecture, decor and staff dress. Lots of oil palms and coconut trees in the vicinity. Peacock Dance and other Dai performances in the local flavour restaurant.

Hong Kong

$$$$$
Conrad International
Pacific Place, 88 Queensway
Tel: 2521 3838
Fax: 2521 3888.
A European-style deluxe boutique hotel. Understated elegance; spacious rooms and good location adjacent to Pacific Place shopping, Admiralty MTR and tramlines.

Grand Hyatt
1 Harbour Rd, Wan Chai
Tel: 2588 1234
Fax: 2802 0677.
Probably the most expensive and glitziest hotel in Hong Kong. Luxury on a truly palatial level; overlooking the harbour and only a short walk to Hong Kong Convention and Exhibition Centre and the Hong Kong Arts Centre.

The Hongkong Hotel
3 Canton Rd, Tsim Sha Tsui
Tel: 2113 0088
Fax: 2113 0011.
Many rooms with magnificent harbour views. Deluxe facilities include an outdoor pool and five restaurants. Shopping opportunities are unparalleled as it's inside the enormous shopping complex stretching from Ocean Terminal up to the Gateway.

Island Shangri-La
Pacific Place, Supreme Court Rd, Central
Tel: 2877 3838
Fax: 2521 8742.
This gracious oasis lives up to its name. Elegant decor, helpful staff and beautiful, spacious rooms with stunning panoramic views of the harbour or Peak. Adjacent to Hong Kong Park, Pacific Place shopping and Admiralty MTR and tramlines.

Price Categories

$$$$$	=	over US$200
$$$$	=	US$150–US$200
$$$	=	US$100–US$150
$$	=	US$50–US$100
$	=	below US$50

Kowloon Shangri-La
64 Mody Rd, Tsim Sha Tsui East
Tel: 2721 2111
Fax: 2723 8686.
Opulence and great harbour views. Full range of deluxe facilities including indoor pool and highly rated restaurants. Across from Tsim Sha Tsui East waterfront with easy hoverferry access to Central.

Mandarin Oriental
5 Connaught Rd, Central
Tel: 2522 0111
Fax: 2810 6190.
Classy hotel established in 1963 and consistently rated among the world's best. Impeccable service and quality. Full range of facilities including a indoor pool and some of the finest hotel F&B establishments in town. Convenient location.

The Peninsula
Salisbury Rd, Tsim Sha Tsui
Tel: 2366 6251
Fax: 2722 4170.
Hong Kong's oldest and most prestigious hotel has been a byword for impeccable service and colonial-style grandeur since it opened in 1928. Extensively refurbished, with a new 30-storey extension tower. Eight top restaurants and superb location in the heart of Kowloon's shopping, restaurant and

entertainment area; close to Tsim Sha Tsui MTR.

The Regent
Salisbury Rd, Tsim Sha Tsui
Tel: 2721 1211
Fax: 2739 4546.
Elegant with breathtaking views across Victoria Harbour. Full range of facilities, including a poolside spa, the 1930s-style Club Shanghai nightclub, and top-notch Lai Ching Heen and Plume restaurants. Superb location on the waterfront; convenient to the Star Ferry and Kowloon's prime entertainment district.

Ritz-Carlton
3 Connaught Rd, Central
Tel: 2877 6666
Fax: 2877 6778.
Post-modernist exterior gives way to classy traditionalist interior decorated with period art and antiques. Facilities include outdoor pool and good Italian and Japanese restaurants. Convenient location close to Star Ferry, and Admiralty and Central business and commercial districts.

Sheraton Hong Kong
20 Nathan Rd, Tsim Sha Tsui
Tel: 2369 1111
Fax: 2739 8707.
Swish hotel on corner of Nathan and Salisbury roads with full range of deluxe facilities, including an outdoor pool and 5 top-notch restaurants. Good location close to museums, MTR, and Kowloon's prime entertainment district.

$$$$
Century Hong Kong Hotel
238 Jaffe Rd, Wan Chai
Tel: 2598 8888
Fax: 2598 8866.
Modern hotel with good facilities including an outdoor pool, health club and Lao Ching Hing, one of oldest and best Shanghai restaurants in town. Convenient for HK Exhibition and Convention Centre and Wan Chai's commercial district.

The Excelsior
281 Gloucester Rd, Causeway Bay
Tel: 2894 8888
Fax: 2895 6459.
Overlooking the colourful Causeway

Bay typhoon shelter. Managed by the Mandarin Oriental group, the hotel offers efficient service and a pleasant environment. Close to Causeway Bay's shopping and commercial district and MTR.

Furama
1 Connaught Rd, Central
Tel: 2525-5111
Fax: 2845-9339.
Quietly plush business hotel. Good value considering its convenient location to Central MTR, Star Ferry, and Admiralty and Central district.

Grand Plaza
2 Kornhill Rd, Quarry Bay
Tel: 2886 0011
Fax: 2886 1738.
Modern business hotel with good facilities including golf-putting green, tennis courts, indoor pool and gym. Close to Tai Koo MTR.

The Kowloon Hotel
19–21 Nathan Rd, Tsim Sha Tsui
Tel: 2369 8698
Fax: 2739 9811.
Smart, modern business hotel tucked in behind The Pen, in the heart of Kowloon's commercial and entertainment district. Convenient for the MTR.

Majestic
348 Nathan Rd, Yau Ma Tei
Tel: 2781 1333
Fax: 2781 1773.
Well-appointed business hotel. Close to Temple Street night market, shops, cinema and Jordan MTR; also well-served by buses.

Marco Polo
Harbour City, Canton Rd,
Tsim Sha Tsui
Tel: 2113-0888
Fax: 2113-0022.
Elegant, Continental-style hotel in the middle of Harbour City complex; marginally cheaper than its sister-property, the Hong Kong Hotel, but lacking views and pool.

Nikko
72 Mody Rd, Tsim Sha Tsui East
Tel: 2739-1111
Fax: 2311-3122.
Japanese business hotel with impeccable service and panoramic harbour views. Outdoor pool and good Cantonese, French and Japanese restaurants. Convenient location just across from Tsim Sha Tsui East waterfront promenade.

Prince
Canton Rd, Harbour City
Tsim Sha Tsui
Tel: 2113-1888
Fax: 2113-0066.
Similar standard to Marco Polo; outdoor pool; convenient for China Ferry Terminal and Kowloon Park.

Regal Airport
Chek Lap Kok, Lantau
Tel: 2286-8888
Fax: 2286-8686.
Five minutes by covered walkway from the international airport, this light and airy hotel makes the most of its location with views over the runway.

Wharney Hotel
57–73 Lockhart Rd, Wan Chai
Tel: 2861 1000
Fax: 2865 6023.
Smart modern hotel with good facilities including indoor pool. Located in the heart of Wan Chai's commercial and nightlife district, close to HK Convention Centre, MTR and trams.

$$$
Concourse
22 Lai Chi Kok Rd, Mong Kok
Tel: 2397 6683
Fax: 2381 3768.
Well-appointed modern hotel popular with Asian business travellers. Bargain shopping nearby in Fa Yuen St factory-outlets. Close to MTR.

Harbour View International House
4 Harbour Rd, Wan Chai
Tel: 2802 0111
Fax: 2802 9063.
Worth paying the extra HK$200 for a harbour-view room, but book early at this upscale YMCA, next door to Arts Centre and across the road from the Convention and Exhibition Centre.

Hotel New Harbour
41–49 Hennessy Rd, Wan Chai
Tel: 2861 1166
Fax: 2865 6111.
One of the cheapest deals for a centrally-located hotel on Hong Kong Island. Convenient for HK Convention and Exhibition Centre, Wan Chai's commercial and entertainment districts, MTR and tramlines.

Imperial Hotel
30–34 Nathan Rd, Tsim Sha Tsui
Tel: 2366 2201
Fax: 2311 2360.
Pleasant rooms. Good value at the bottom end of this price category. Convenient location on Tsim Sha Tsui's 'Golden Mile', close to shops, restaurants, MTR.

Nathan Hotel
378 Nathan Rd, Yau Ma Tei
Tel: 2388 5141
Fax: 2770 4262.
Close to Temple Street night market, Yue Hwa Chinese merchandise emporium, restaurants and shops, cinema and Jordan MTR.

New Cathay Hotel
17 Tung Lo Wan Rd, Causeway Bay
Tel: 2577 8211
Fax: 2576 9365.
Good option for single travellers. Close to tramlines, Hong Kong Stadium, Victoria Park and Causeway Bay commercial, dining and shopping districts.

The Salisbury (YMCA)
41 Salisbury Rd, Tsim Sha Tsui
Tel: 2369 2211
Fax: 2739 9315.
Book ahead to be sure of a room at this very upscale YMCA. All rooms are well-equipped and many enjoy panoramic views of the harbour. Large indoor pool and other sports facilities. As conveniently located as The Pen but a fraction of the cost.

$$
Bangkok Royal
2–12 Pilkem St, Yau Ma Tei
Tel: 2735 9181
Fax: 2730 2209.
Bottom end of this price category. A good option for single travellers and small groups. Good Thai restaurant. Jordan MTR is nearby.

Caritas Bianchi Lodge
4 Cliff Rd, Yau Ma Tei
Tel: 2388 1111
Fax: 2770 6669.
Clean, spacious rooms in well-run Roman Catholic hostel between Nathan Road and the Meteorological Station. Close to Temple Street night market, shops, restaurants, and Yau Ma Tei MTR.
Eaton Hotel, 380 Nathan Rd, Yau Ma Tei
Tel: 2782 1818
Fax: 2782 5563.
Well-equipped rooms; good value restaurants with regular clientele. Close to Temple Street night market, shops, cinema and Jordan MTR.

Evergreen Hotel
42–52 Woo Sung St, Yau Ma Tei
Tel: 2780 4222
Fax: 2385 8584.
Clean, tidy rooms. Triples and 4-bed rooms are good value for small groups. Near Temple Street night market, Yue Hwa Chinese emporium and Jordan MTR.

South China Hotel
67–75 Java Rd, North Point
Tel: 2503 1168
Fax: 2512 8698.
Well-appointed with modern decor. Cantonese restaurant. Close to MTR and ferry piers.

$
Anne Black Guest House (YWCA)
5 Man Fuk Rd, Ho Man Tin
Tel: 2713 9211
Fax: 2761 1269.
Clean, simple rooms for women and couples. A short walk away from the Ladies' Market, Mong Kok KCR and MTR stations.

Chungking House
4–5 Fl, Block A, Chungking Mansions, 40 Nathan Rd
Tel: 2366 5362
Fax: 2721 3570.
There are cheaper deals in the area but Chungking House is the only establishment to win the HKTA's seal of approval. Steps away from MTR.

Ma Wui Hall Youth Hostel
Mt Davis Path, Victoria Rd
Tel: 2817 5715.
Spartan dormitory accommodation but superb views from mountain-top location above Kennedy Town. Advance booking advised as these beds fill up quickly.

Kaifeng

$$
Dongjing Hotel
Yingbin Lu
Tel: 398 9388.
Large, modern hotel with four separate wings.

Kaifeng Guesthouse
Ziyou Lu
Tel: 55 5589.
xtensively renovated, Russian-style building. Centrally located.

Kashi (Kashgar)

$$$
Kashgar Hotel
7 Tawuguzi Road
Tel: 282 2367, 282 2368
Fax: 282 4679.
Located somewhat inconveniently on the outskirts of town, this 2-star hotel, complete with the usual facilities, is more popular with tour groups than with individuals. However, its quiet and pleasant surroundings which include courtyards, gardens and fountains, make it an ideal escape from the noise and bustle of the city.

Qinibagh Hotel
93 Seman Road
Tel: 282 4173, 282 2084
Fax: 282 3842.
In this centrally located compound are now 2 hotels laying claim to the same name but which are separately administered. The old wing, formerly the British consulate, is popular with Pakistani traders. If you don't mind the raucous ambience and the occasional incidences of harassment, the rooms here are adequate and cheap. The new wing, hoping to attract different clientele, has only standard rooms and suites.

Seman Hotel
170 Seman Road
Tel: 282 2147, 282 2001
Fax: 282 2861.
Not quite up to the standard set forth in its self-proclaimed moniker

as "one of the top ten hotels in the world based on service and facilities", the 2-star Seman is nevertheless one of only 3 real options in Kashi. Occupying the premises of the former Russian embassy, this hotel offers basic rooms, relatively clean dorms, friendly Uighur staff. Has a not-to-be-missed swimming pool.

Kunming

Camellia Hotel
154 Dongfengdonglu
Tel: 316 3000.
More moderately priced, quiet yet close to the heart of the city. Comfortable new wing, ticketing services, breakfast buffet, fancy adjoining restaurant with floor show. The old wing houses the Laos and Myanmar consulates.
King World Hotel
28 Beijinglu
Tel: 313 8888
Fax: 313 1910.
Near the train station, main inter-city bus station and a short distance from the airport, this is Kunming's swankiest. 4-star accommodation, a revolving restaurant on top, elegantly dressed pianist in the lobby lounge and modern facilities. The Thai Consulate is also housed here.
Kunming Hotel
145 Dongfengdonglu
Tel: 312 2063.
Opposite Holiday Inn and Sakura Department Store, near the junction with Baitalu, where lie the city's fashionable, up-market boutiques. Slightly ritzier than the Camellia, with discotheques in a separate building. The city's first micro-brewery is next door.

Lanzhou

$$$$
Lanzhou Legend Hotel
599 Tianshui Road
Tel: 888 2876
Fax: 888 7876.
Plush, elegant, and expensive, this is the nicest and only 4-star hotel in Lanzhou. Full facilities and

services. Even if they don't stay here, travellers who have been too long in the desert find themselves coming for the orange juice and fresh coffee.

$$$
Jincheng Hotel
601 Tianshui Road
Tel: 841 6638
Fax: 841 8438.
Billing itself as the first 3-star foreign-funded modern hotel in Lanzhou, this place offers unspectacular but comfortable rooms, the central wing having recently been renovated. Service is efficient. The hotel offers 14 western and Asian restaurants, an entertainment centre, gym, and business centre. Located right next to the food alley Nongmin Xiang.

Price Categories

$$$$$	=	over US$200
$$$$	=	US$150–US$200
$$$	=	US$100–US$150
$$	=	US$50–US$100
$	=	below US$50

Lanzhou Hotel
434 Donggang Xilu
Tel: 841 6321
Fax: 841 8608.
A sprawling grey Soviet-style edifice, this 3-star hotel is very popular for its standard, no frills accommodations and convenient location between the railway station and points west. The hotel also houses several independent travel agencies and offers adequate dorm rooms.
Ningwozhuang Hotel
366 Tianshui Road
Tel: 841 6221
Fax: 841 7639.
As the "official designated state guesthouse of Gansu Province", this sleepy hotel has since 1995 been open to common people, and now features a modern VIP wing that's separately managed, though distinguished guests still seem to prefer the garish opulence of the old wing. The hotel is in its own secluded compound, and rather

quiet, away from the main road, and features fountains, gardens and Chinese pavilions.

Lijiang

Jade Spring Hotel
Red Sun Square
Tel: 512 3522
Fax: 512 3926. Conventionally modern hotel, moderately priced and comfortable. Next to the Mao statue and close to several tour services and an inter-city bus terminal. Halfway between the old town and picturesque Black Dragon Pool Park.
Lijiang Grand Hotel
Xinyi Street, Dayan
Tel: 512 8888
Fax: 512 7878.
Thai-managed luxury hotel just opposite the top end of the old town. Excellent restaurants plus a marvellous variety of dishes (Chinese, American, European, and Thai) at the breakfast buffet. Television movies, and several Chinese and two Thai stations.
Sanhe Jiujia
Xinyi Street, Dayan
Tel: 522 1018
Fax: 522 8797.
Just inside the old town, a rebuilt traditional Naxi compound. Common baths and toilets, but all rooms in local style, giving it a very Naxi atmosphere. Excellent Naxi and Chinese food at the hotel restaurant. Occasional music and dance shows.

Luoyang

$$$
Peony Plaza
2 Nanchang Lu
Tel: 493 1111
Fax: 493 2514.
Luxury hotel with revolving restaurant, food street, swimming pool and a piano bar in its vast marble foyer.

$$
New Friendship Hotel
6 Xiyuan Lu
Tel: 419 201
Fax: 419 702.

Joint venture with eight restaurants, classical-style courtyard garden, and simple elegance in guest rooms.

Macau

INTERNATIONAL CLASS
Westin Resort
1918 Entrada de Hac Sá
Coloane Island
Tel: 871111
Fax: 871122.
Peaceful seclusion at the southeast tip of Coloane Island. Eight-storey resort hotel with 208 spacious rooms each with private outdoor terraces overlooking the beach. Adjacent 18-hole golf course.

SUPERIOR CLASS
Hyatt Regency Macau
2 Estrada Almirante Marques Esparteiro, Taipa Island
Tel: 831234
Fax: 830195.
All mod cons, including an attractive landscaped pool, tennis courts and restaurant offering Macanese cuisine in a relaxed setting,
Mandarin Oriental Macau
956–1110 Avenida de Amizade
Tel: 567888
Fax: 594589.
Five-star comfort and facilities, including the excellent Mezzaluna restaurant and a casino. A new resort area between the hotel and the new Cultural Centre has now added a full range of resort-style facilities.
Pousada de São Tiago
Avenida de Republica
Tel: 378111
Fax: 552170.
Macau's most romantic hotel, an elegant Portuguese-style inn built within the walls of the 17th-century Barra fort. Only 23 rooms, so book ahead.

STANDARD CLASS
Hotel Royal
2–4 Estrada de Vitoria
Tel: 552222
Fax: 563008.
Value-for-money hotel located in the citycentre hotel; facilities include an indoor pool.

Nanning

Yongjiang Hotel
41 Jiangbindong Lu
Tel: 20 8123
Fax: 20 0535.
Attractive modern building near the central bridge over the Yong River. Several restaurants and a complimentary Chinese-style breakfast. Taxis waiting at the gate.

Qingdao

$$$
Huiquan Dynasty Hotel
9 Nanhai Lu
Tel: 287 3366.
Across the street from Qingdao's trendiest beach.

Guesthouses

Individual travellers may find accommodation in guesthouses in smaller towns off the tourist track. They usually have rooms with two or more beds, and often dormitories are available; there are usually shower and washing facilities, as well. Recommended as cheap accommodation for backpackers.
Some guesthouses or simple hotels refuse to take foreign guests, usually because of the rules of Chinese travel agencies or the local police, who often determine where foreigners may stay.

$$
Haitian Hotel
39 Zhanshan Dalu
Tel: 387 1888.
Quiet location opposite the No. 3 Beach.

Qufu

$$
Queli Hotel
1 Queli Jie
Tel: 441 1300
Fax: 441 2022.
Traditional courtyard building with modern facilities, close to most of Qufu's tourist sites.

$
Gold Mansion Hotel
1 Beimen Dajie
Tel: 441 3469
Fax: 441 3209.
Taiwanese-funded hotel next to the town's north gate.

Shanghai

$$$$$
Garden Hotel
58 Maoming Nan Lu
Tel: 6415 1111
Fax: 6415 8866.
This beautiful 33-story five-star hotel in the old French Concession is managed by the Japanese Okura Group and built atop the former French Club of old Shanghai. The hotel is beautifully appointed but presents luxury with a sort of Japanese coldness.
Holiday Inn Crowne Plaza
400 Panyu Lu
Tel: 6280 8888
Fax: 6280 2788.
Email: hicpsha@uninet.com.cn
This 496-room, four-star property in the western side of the French Concession is known for its friendly service, quality facilities and good food outlets.
Portman Ritz-Carlton/Shangri-La
Shanghai Cantre
1376 Nanjing Xi Lu
Tel: 6279 8888
Fax: 6279 8800
Email: portman@public.sta.net.cn
Shanghai's most popular hotel due to its quality facilities and great location. Situated in the Shanghai Centre, it seems to be in the midst of everything – an American office and housing complex including Western shopping, airline offices, foreign restaurants and active theatre. 600 rooms are well-appointed; the gym is the most comprehensive in town.
Shanghai Hilton
250 Huashan Lu
Tel: 6248 0000
Fax: 6248 3868.
The beautifully-appointed five-star 43-story hotel boasts some of the best dining in town, top-rate, luxurious accommodation, and a great location in the city centre.

Shanghai JC Mandarin
1225 Nanjing Xi Lu
Tel: 6279 1888
Fax: 6279 1822.
Situated in a perfect location in the heart of the city centre, the five-star 30-story hotel is Singapore-managed with all the fixings and good Southeast Asian food.

Westin Tai Ping Yang
5 Zunyi Nan Lu
Tel: 6275 8888
Fax: 6275 5420.
Email: westin@uninet.com.cn
This luxurious five-star Japanese-managed high-rise hotel located in Hongqiao is extremely formal, and everything is done with a flourish, down to the "welcome" gauntlet that meets you at the front entrance.

$$$$
Grand Hyatt Shanghai
Jinmao Building
177 Lujiazui Lu, Pudong
Tel: 5049 1234
Fax: 5049 1111.
Decadent Art-Deco luxury hotel, high above Pudong, featuring gorgeous, comfortable rooms, a spectacular atrium patio, indoor pool, six restaurants and business facilities.

Hotel Sofitel Hyland
505 Nanjing Dong Lu
Tel: 6351 5888
Fax: 6351 4088.
Located smack in the middle of the downtown chaos, the French-owned four-star hotel is managed by Accor. The 34-story hotel has 400 tastefully decorated rooms and comprehensive facilities and is convenient for walking on Nanjing Lu and the Bund.

Jinjiang Hotel
59 Maoming Lu
Tel: 6285 2582
Fax: 6427 5588.
Built before 1935, its buildings were some of the old French Concession's most popular addresses. Rooms are comfortable, traditionally furnished, and homey but not luxurious, with the exception of the Grosvenor House which offers the most decadent suites at the most decadent prices.

Yangtze New World Hotel
2099 Yanan Xi Lu
Tel: 6275 0000
Fax: 6275 0750.
Email: gm_ynwh@online.sh.cn
This four-star hotel in Hongqiao is especially noted for its excellent Chinese restaurants. 553 rooms are modern and comfortably furnished, and facilities are comprehensive.

$$$
Jinjiang Hotel
59 Maoming Nan Lu
Tel: 6258 2582
Fax: 6472 5588.
Formerly some of the nicest residential apartments in the French Concession. The north building has been renovated to five-star status. Good dining choices and a shopping gallery.

Pudong Shangri-La
33 Fucheng Lu
Tel: 6882 8888
Fax: 6882 6688.
Elegant hotel directly opposite the Bund in Pudong. Friendly staff and well-appointed facilities. Popular with business travellers.

$$
City Hotel
5–7 Shaanxi Nan Lu
Tel: 6255 1133
Fax: 6255 0211.
Three-star hotel with great location, business facilities, Chinese and Western cuisine and a disco.

Hengshan Hotel
534 Hengshan Lu
Tel: 6437 7050
Fax: 6433 5732.
Formerly the Picardie Mansions, this Art Deco-style hotel is located on fahionable Hengshan Lu. Adequate rooms, Western and Chinese restaurants, a business centre and a health club.

Longhua Hotel
2787 Longhua Lu
Tel: 6439 9399
Fax: 6439 2964.
Connected to the Longhua Temple, the modern Longhua Hotel caters to Buddhist guests, but accepts secular travellers as well.

Ocean Hotel
1171 Dongdaming Lu
Tel: 6545 8888
Fax: 6545 8993.
Located in Hogkou, this four-star hotel has modern facilities and a revolving restaurant with excellent views of the city. Popular with tour groups.

Pacific Hotel
104 Nanjing Lu
Tel: 6327-6226
Fax: 6326-9620.
One of Shanghai's older establishments, the hotel is sagging and somewhat Gothic in ambience. The granite structure is architecturally interesting: a gold-plated dome with a clock tower crowns the roof, and a classically-robust entrance leads into an Art Deco lobby.

Park Hotel
170 Nanjing Xi Lu
Tel: 6327 5225
Fax: 6327 6958.
This historic structure overlooking People's Park was once the tallest hotel in Shanghai. Today the 208-room state-run hotel isn't as glamorous, but the rooms have been tastefully refurbished.

Peace Hotel
20 Nanjing Donlu
Tel: 6321 6888
Fax: 6329 0300.
Email: peacehtl@public.sta.net.cn
Shanghai's most famous hotel has been called the most romantic in Asia, and is probably Shanghai's most treasured historic building. Its Art Deco fixtures are still intact, and the rooms retain their old Shanghai feel. Even if not staying here, drop by the bar in the evening to hear the Old Jazz Band.

Ruijin Guesthouse
118 Ruijin Erlu
Tel: 6472 5222
Fax: 6473 2277.
The Morris Estate, now Ruijin Guesthouse, was built by a western newspaper magnate during pre-Liberation times. Today, five state-run villas in the old French Concession house 47 rooms among huge green lawns and trees. Chinese and Western cuisine served.

Shanghai Mansions
20 Suzhou Beilu
Tel: 6324 6260
Fax: 6306 5147
Email: shds@publicl.sta.net.cn
This old Art Deco building located on the Bund right on Suzhou Creek is state-run and has simple but comfortable rooms with great views of the river.

Taiyuan Guest House
160 Taiyuan Lu
Tel: 6471 6688
Fax: 6471 2618.
Previous occupants include George Marshall and Mme. Mao. Now a charming guesthouse with fireplace, wood paneling, seven rooms and two suites. Chinese and Western cuisine is served.

Xingguo Guesthouse
72 Xingguo
Tel: 6212 9998
Fax: 6251 2145.
This collection of quaint old Shanghai villas in the former French Concession is situated around a huge green lawn. Rooms are old and simple, but traditionally furnished.

$
Metropole Hotel
180 Jiangxi Zhonglu
Tel: 6321 7365.
Over 60 years old, this hotel has seen better days, but offers reasonably priced rooms close to the Bund, as well as a Chinese restaurant, health club and bar.

Pujiang Hotel
15 Huangpu Lu
Tel: 6324 6388
Fax: 6324 3179.
One of the oldest hotels in Shanghai and today one of the cheapest alternatives. Located just north of the Bund. Dorm beds available.

Ürümqi

$$$$
Holiday Inn
168 North Xinhua Road
Tel: 281 8788
Fax: 281 7422.
As the city's first international and four-star hotel, this staple offers all the standard conveniences and comforts, and is also located in the heart of the city. Has Western, Asian, and Muslim restaurants, as well as the full range of business and entertainment facilities, including airport pick-up service.

Price Categories

$$$$$	=	over US$200
$$$$	=	US$150–US$200
$$$	=	US$100–US$150
$$	=	US$50–US$100
$	=	below US$50

Islam Grand Hotel
22 Zhongshan Road
Tel: 281 1017
Fax: 281 1513.
Located in a busy part of town with good access to transportation and shopping, this rather tired looking 3-star hotel is nevertheless popular with Western tourists. Muslim flavour permeates everything from the architecture and the staff's uniforms, to the whole roast sheep you can order for dinner. With serviceable rooms, the usual business and entertainment centres, and a tacky dance hall.

Yin Du Hotel
39 Xibei Road
Tel: 453 6688
Fax: 451 7166.
Opened in 1996, this modern hotel is a gem, if a slightly garish rainbow-coloured one on the outside. Even though it has all the conveniences and facilities of any large 4-star hotel, the plush, comfortable rooms, the friendly and efficient service, and the warm and courteous staff make a stay here a surprisingly cosy one.

$$$
City Hotel
119 Hongqi Road
Tel: 230 9911
Fax: 230 1818.
Looking a like a building out of Lego-land, this hotel provides solid no frills accommodation backed up by friendly, earnest staff. There is a good variety of restaurants located nearby.

Hongshan Hotel
108 Xinhua Beilu
Tel: 282 4761
Fax: 281 1378.
This hotel is popular with budget travellers for its central location and the many travel agencies in the hotel offering services from day tours to purchasing plane and train tickets. It is often full during the peak summer months. Spartan but clean rooms.

Xinjiang Hotel
107 Changjiang Lu
Tel: 585 2511.
Located far from the centre of town, staying here makes sense only if you want to be based near the railway station. Accommodations range from dorms to suites though the place appears to be more popular with budget travellers.

Xi'an

$$$$$
ANA Grand Castle Hotel
12 Xi Duan Huan Cheng Nan Lu
Tel: 723 1800
Fax: 723 1500.
Spacious, modern, 5-star hotel located just outside the South Gate of the old city. The roof of the hotel is modeled after the Great Wild Goose Pagoda. Full facilities including Western, Chinese and Japanese restaurants.

Hyatt Regency Xian
158 Dongda Jie
Tel: 723 1234
Fax: 721 6799.
Top of the line accommodation in an elegant setting. Conveniently located within the old city wall near the heart of the shopping district on Dong Dajie. Business centre, conference rooms, health club and various Western and Asian restaurants.

Shangri-La Golden Flower
8 Changle Road West
Tel: 323 2981
Fax: 323 5477.
Located 3 km (2 miles) to the east of the historic city centre in an unremarkable neighbourhood, this posh and pleasant 5-star hotel also has apartments with kitchens for long- and short-term rental.

$$$$
Grand New World Hotel
48 Lian Hu Lu
Tel: 721 6868
Fax: 721 9754.
A cavernous hotel with friendly, efficient service. It is just inside the western city wall and is a short walk from the night market and the Muslim quarters. The hotel also offers a Tang dynasty cultural show.
Xi'an Garden Hotel
Tang Hua, 4 Yan Yin Lu, Dayan Ta
Tel: 526 1111
Fax: 526 1998.
Constructed in the style of a Chinese garden with lakes, willow trees, and pavilions, this popular four-star hotel is located 6 km outside of the old city, right next to the Dayan Ta. It offers Western and Asian restaurants, and even a set dinner featuring Chinese herbal health cuisine.

$$$
Bell Tower Hotel
Southwest Corner of Bell Tower
Tel: 727 9200
Fax: 721 8767.
Managed by Holiday Inn, this friendly, functional, 3-star hotel is popular for being directly in the centre of town. Good solid service. It offers a business centre, a mini-mart, and a CYTS office.
JieFang Hotel
321 Jie Fang Road
Tel: 742 8946
Fax: 742 2617.
Drab, no frills budget accommodation located right across from the railway station. It is also near the northeastern entrance to the old city wall. Offers standard rooms as well as triples and quads. Ticket booking and money changing services available.
May First Hotel (WuYi Hotel)
351 Dongda Jie
Tel: 723 1844
Fax: 721 3824.
A former budget traveller's paradise, this hotel was renovated in 1997, and is now a mid-range hotel with full facilities. Still popular with travellers, it offers clean and comfortable rooms, and a great location right in the city centre.

People's Hotel (Renmin Dasha)
319 DongXin Jie
Tel: 721 5111
Fax: 721 8152.
A large, sprawling hotel, it is dark and somewhat run-down, although the East Tower was renovated in the mid-1990s. Located near the city centre, the hotel offers 600 rooms, over 20 restaurants, a business and commercial centre, gym, shops, and an entertainment and recreation centre.

Price Categories

$$$$$	=	over US$200
$$$$	=	US$150–US$200
$$$	=	US$100–US$150
$$	=	US$50–US$100
$	=	below US$50

Zhengzhou

$$
Novotel International Hotel
Henan, 114 Jinshui Lu
Tel: 595 6600
Fax: 599 7818.
Plush surroundings and full facilities in eastern suburbs.

$
Friendship Guesthouse
Xintongqiao
Tel: 622 8807.
Close to Renmin Park and city Centre shops and restaurants.

Zhongdian

Gyalthang Dzong Hotel
Tel: 822 7610
Fax: 822 3620.
Up-market hotel 2 km east of the old town. Decor and architecture are Tibetan, including interior murals. Excellent dining facilities.
Tibet Hotel (Yongsheng Lüguan)
106 Cangfang Road
Tel: 822 2448
Fax: 822 3863.
Long a favourite with backpackers, it now has a fancy new wing with Tibetan decor, plus electric blankets for those cold nights on the Plateau. Located at the top of the old town.

Others

It is practically impossible for foreigners to find accommodation outside of hotels and guesthouses. Private lodgings are unknown because of crowded living conditions. At times, some universities and institutes have guesthouses where foreign visitors can find good, cheap accommodation. Advance booking is not possible.

If going on a long trip or hike in the countryside, especially in Tibet or in areas around the sacred mountains of China, you will come across various types of "long-distance travellers' lodgings". It is advisable to carry a sleeping bag.

Where to Eat

For Westerners, the single identifying symbol of Chinese cuisine is the use of chopsticks, which are practical as the food is cut into small pieces. Due to the short supply of fuel over the centuries, it has been necessary to prepare food using a minimum of cooking – small pieces cook quicker.

Only about 10 percent of China's land area is suitable for agriculture. Thus, beef is not a significant source of food; the need to cultivate intensively means grazing is neither possible nor common, except in the extreme north and northwest. Thus, until recently, milk and dairy products were not widely known. In place of animal protein, soybeans have often been a primary source of protein.

Traditionally, food should not only be filling, but it should also have a healing effect. A Chinese meal is based on balance, even at the largest and most extravagant banquets.

There are roughly four main styles of Chinese cuisine. (This does not take into account the often completely different cooking and eating traditions of the national minorities).

Northern cuisine is centred around Beijing, where the soil is fairly poor: thus the food it produces is unvaried. In contrast to the south, where rice is preferred, noodles dishes predominate here. The main vegetable is Chinese cabbage: boiled, steamed, fried, preserved, with a variety of spices. Special mention should be made of Peking Duck and the Mongolian hotpot, feasts not to be missed if in Beijing.

Haiyang, from the eastern coastal areas around Shanghai, specialises in fish (particularly freshwater) and shellfish. There is a greater choice of vegetables here than in the north.

Cantonese, the southern cuisine, is the most familiar to Westerners, and the most common in Chinese restaurants around the world.

Sichuan cuisine is famous for its highly-spiced foods, good for keeping warm through the cold, damp Sichuan winters.

Macau: Over the centuries Macau has developed a unique cuisine blending influences from Portugal's African and Indian colonies. For many, one of the highlights of a visit involves the sampling of signature Macanese dishes such as African chicken or spicy prawns. Portions tend to be large and prices low. More traditional Portuguese food is also good, with excellent Portuguese wine available at a fraction of the price you'd pay elsewhere in the region.

The Chinese tend to eat quite early; lunch is often served in Chinese restaurants from 11am. (Hotels and restaurants for foreigners have, of course, adjusted to preferences.) In the evenings, you won't easily find a meal after 8pm, though this is different in the south, where social life continues until the late evening.

Chinese meals are best eaten in a group, with diners sharing a variety of different dishes; Chinese restaurants are often not suited to individual diners.

The individual traveller is more likely to frequent one of the typical Chinese roadside eateries. Make sure the restaurant is clean and the food has been freshly prepared and is hot.

Bringing one's own chopsticks isn't considered an insult at all. Chinese restaurants are often not heated even during winter (nor are theatres or concert halls), so it is advisable to dress warmly.

Beijing

PEKING DUCK

Qianmen Quanjude Roast Duck Restaurant
32 Qianmen Dajie
Tel: 6701 1379.
Beijing's most famous. The restaurant is arranged so you can watch the duck being prepared. **$$**

Zhengyangmen Quanjude Roast Duck Restaurant
East side of Tiananmen Square, opposite War Heroes Monument
Tel: 6512 2265.
Clean and well-run, with more than 300 different duck dishes. **$**

SHANDONG

Dishes from neighbouring Shandong Province are the main element in what Beijingers refer to as home cooking. The number of restaurants serving this fare outnumber any other kind. Because Shandong is a coastal province, its dishes feature seafood such as jumbo shrimp, eel, shark's fin and sea cucumber.

Confucian Heritage Restaurant
3 West Liulichang Jie
Tel: 6303 0689.
An inviting two-storey teahouse in the historical Liulichang area. **$–$$**

Special Flavours Restaurant
7/F Beijing Hotel, Old West Wing, 33 East Chang'an Ave
Tel: 6513 7766 ext 374.
Dine in a classic Chinese banquet room. **$$**

SICHUAN

Sichuan Restaurant
51 Xi Rongxian Hutong
Tel: 6603 3291.
Frequented by some of Beijing's leaders. Located in what was the mansion of a Qing dynasty prince. **$**

Yidairen Home Made Food
181 Xi'anmen Dajie (opposite the Honglou Cinema)
Tel: 6601 5097.
Cosy and clean, privately-owned restaurant with cooks from Sichuan Province. **$**

Yuyuan Restaurant
Northeast corner of Ritan Park
Tel: 6502 5985.
Indoor and courtyard dining in the
Temple of the Sun Park.
Reservations usually necessary. **$**

CANTONESE

Four Seasons
1/F Jianguo Hotel Jianguomenwai
Dajie
Tel: 6500 2233 ext 8041.
Quiet, classical setting enhances
the fine food. **$$**
Hong Kong Food City
18 Dong'anmen Dajie
Tel: 6513 6668.
Fresh seafood served in a lively
dining hall. **$$**
Windows On The World
28/F, CITIC Bldg 19 Jianguomenwai
Dajie
Tel: 6500 3335.
Excellent dim sum dishes served in
a pleasant dining room on the 28th
floor, overlooking the city. **$$**

OTHER CHINESE

Bamboo Garden Hotel Restaurant
24 Xiaoshiqiao Jiugulou St
Tel: 6403 2229.
Hearty Chinese dishes served in a
classical garden restaurant.
Formerly the home of a shadowy
secret security chief, Kang Sheng. **$**
Donglaishun Restaurant
(2 branches), 16 Jinyu Hutong and
198 Wangfujing Dajie
Tel: 6552 2092, 6550 069,
6556 465.
Mongolian hotpot. **$**
Duyichu Dumplings
36 Qianmen Dajie
Tel: 6511 2094.
Beijing tradition. **$**
Fangshan Canting
Qionghua Dao Beihai Park
Tel: 6401 1889. Garden setting at
Beihai Park. **$$**
Kaorouji Restaurant
14 Qianhai Dongyan
Tel: 6401 2170, 445 921.
Muslim-style grill on Qianhai Lake. **$**
Li Family Restaurant
11 Yongfang Hutong, Denei Dajie

Tel: 6601 1915.
Serves four tables of up to 12 each
day – two at lunch and two at dinner
in the home of the chef, who has a
story for each dish. Book ahead. **$$**
Xinjiang Restaurants
Weiguncun Uyghur Village off
Baishiqiao Rd.
Pick any restaurant in this three-
block area for noodles and grilled
mutton made by Uighur people.
While the food is great, wear old
clothes. **$**

OTHER ASIAN

Go Nin Nyakushou
2/F Beijing Hotel, East Chang'an
Ave
Tel: 6513 7766 ext 666.
Japanese food and posh ambience.
$$$
Liyuan Restaurant
8 Xi Huangchenggen
Tel: 6601 5234.
Thai and Chinese food. **$$**
Omar Khayyam
Asia Pacific Bldg, 8 Yabao Lu
Tel: 6513 9988 ext 20188.
Tasty Indian cuisine in pleasant
surroundings. **$$**
Sakura
2F Changfugong, New Otani Hotel,
Jianguomenwai Dajie
Tel: 6512 5555 ext 1226.
Japanese. Light and sunny
atmosphere. **$$**

WESTERN

Frank's Place
Gongrentiyuguan Donglu (next to
Chains City Hotel)
Tel: 6507 2617.
The best burger and chilli in town.
Darts and re-runs of football add to
the fun. **$**
Maxim's
2 Chongwenmennei Dajie
Tel: 6512 1992.
French restaurant, modelled after
Maxim's of Paris. Owned by
couturier Pierre Cardin. **$$$**
Metro Cafe
No 6 Gong Ti Xi Lu
Tel: 6591 7828.
A variety of pastas and sauces. **$**

Paulaner Brauhaus
Beijing Lufthansa Ctr, 50
Liangmaqiao Lu
Tel: 6465 3388 ext 5734.
Friendly pub serving tasty German
fare. The beer is brewed in-house.
$$
Peppino's Shangri-La Hotel
29 Zizhuyuan Lu
Tel: 841 2211.
Italian restaurant. Candlelight and a
roving guitarist. **$$**
T.G.I. Friday
No 19 Dongsanhuanbei, Lu Hua
Peng Da Sha
Tel: 6595 1386.
Chain well known in the States. **$**

Guangzhou

CANTONESE

Banxi
151 Longjin Xilu
Tel: 8181 5718.
Established more than a century
ago, this is one of the oldest
restaurants in Guangzhou. Located
on the shore of Liwan Lake, there is
an old pavilion where the dining
room is entirely wood-paneled and
decorated with antique porcelain.
Regular concerts of Beijing opera
and Chinese classical music are
held for diners. **$$**
Dansanyuan
260 Changdi Lu
Tel: 8188 3277.
A popular restaurant that has been
opened for 30 years, Dansanyuan is
known for its stewed shark's fin
soup, chicken feet and tea chicken.
A very noisy and energetic spot. **$$**
Datong Restaurant
63 Yanjiangxi Lu
Tel: 8188 8441.
Serving over a thousand dishes
with crispy skin chicken, roast
suckling pig, Xi Shi duck and cactus
with chicken wings as the
favourites. Eight floors overlooking
the Pearl River. **$$**
Dongjiang Restaurant
337 Zhongshansi Lu
Tel: 8333 5568.
Another bustling popular Cantonese
spot with over 1000 dishes. Ask for
salt roasted chicken, stuffed
beancurd, steamed pork with

pickled cabbage and eight treasure duck. **$$**

Fo Si Jie
Niunai Changjie, off Tongfu Zhonglu
Tel: 8444 0726.
Located south of the Pearl River near the small Hai Tong Si temple, this is one of the few restaurants in Guangzhou that serves Buddhist vegetarian food. **$**

Food Street
Ground Fl, China Hotel Liuhua Lu
Tel: 8666 3888.
The concept of Food Street was so successful, it has been copied by other hotels. A variety of open kitchens serve dim sum, hot pot, Cantonese and a combination of regional foods. Good Shanghainese xiao long bao buns. **$**

Guangzhou Restaurant
2 Wenchang Lu
Tel: 8109 9839.
The largest in Guangzhou, serving 10,000 a day, with branches south of the city, and also in Hong Kong and Los Angeles. The restaurant is famous for its sharks' fin soup and abalone sprinkled with 24K gold flakes. **$$$**

Imperial Garden
Gitic Plaza Hotel, 339 Huanshi Lu
Tel: 8331 1888.
Specialising in seafood dishes and Cantonese favourites. Designed like a garden with pavilions around an artificial pond. **$$$**

Jade River
White Swan Hotel, Shamian Island
Tel: 8188 6968.
A luxurious restaurant with superb Cantonese dining and seafood specialties. Try the fresh steamed fish. **$$$**

Jade Palace
Dong Fang Hotel, 120 Liu Hua Lu
Tel: 8666 9900.
One of the most popular restaurants in Guangzhou with a wide selection of seafood, dim sum, soups and Cantonese favourites. **$$**

Ming Ji Seafood City
171 Xingang Xi Lu
Tel: 8445 6189.
Located South of the Pearl River by the gates of Zhongshan University, this large restaurant features outdoor seating with seafood in

buckets for customers to choose from. Snakes, insects, rabbits and other unusual meats are also available. A Guangzhou eating extravaganza at a reasonable price. **$$**

Ocean Palace
330 Zhong Shan Ci Lu
Tel: 8183 3877.
Eight stories make up the Ocean Palace with seafood galore on the bottom floors and private dining, karaoke and live entertainment on the top floors. Extremely popular. **$$**

She Can Guan
43 Jianglan Lu
Tel: 8188 3811.
For a taste of the exotic. This restaurant has been specialising in snake meat for the past 80 years. Try longhufeng soup, a dish prepared with snake, cat and chicken meat. **$**

Xin Jia Lu
383 Renmin Zhonglu
Tel: 8188 7992.
Another restaurant serving unusual dishes. The house speciality of country rat meat is delicately called Super Deer. **$**

OTHER ASIAN

Banana Leaf
8 Lu Hu Lu
Tel: 8359 1288.
A popular Thai restaurant, large portions at reasonable prices. Spicy noodle dishes and seafood soups. **$**

Hirata
Mezzanine fl, White Swan Hotel, 1 Shamian Nanlu
Tel: 8188 6968.
The only genuine Japanese restaurant in Guangzhou, according to local Japanese residents. Food prepared by well-trained Cantonese cooks and supervised by a Japanese ma'tre d. **$$$**

Dong Nam Ya Canting
105 Haoxian Lu
Tel: 8335 1654.
Serves food from Cambodia, Indonesia, Laos, Thailand and Vietnam, prepared by overseas Chinese returnees from Southeast

Asia. Located near the Pearl River, not far from the end of Beijing Lu. **$**

Hong Kong

CHINESE

Carrianna Chiu Chow
151 Gloucester Rd, Wan Chai
Tel: 2511 1282; also at
Hilton Tower
Tsim Sha Tsui East
Tel: 2724 4828.
Some of the best value Chiu Chow food in town, except luxury items like shark's fin. Go for staples like fried e-fu noodles and pomfret fish. **$$–$$$**

Dim Sum
63 Sing Woo Rd, Happy Valley
Tel: 2834 8893.
Wonderful dim sum in a retro-nostalgia setting, away from the tourist circuit. **$–$$**

Great Shanghai
26 Prat Ave, Tsim Sha Tsui
Tel: 2366 8158.
This massive eatery with a 400-item menu lives up to its name. Tasty traditional home-style cooking from Shanghai and the Yangtze River region. **$–$$**

Han Lok Yuen Restaurant
16-17 Hung Shing Ye, Yung Shue Wan, Lamma Island
Tel: 2982 0608/0680.
Relaxed family-run restaurant with a terrace overlooking Hung Shing Ye beach. Minced quail in lettuce and roast pigeon are the house specialties but seafood dishes are also good. Closed Monday. **$**

Jumbo Floating Restaurant
Shum Wan, Wong Chuk Hang Aberdeen Harbour
Tel: 2553 9111.
A theatrically-decorated palace of twinkling lights in the middle of a junk and yacht-choked waterway. The food's only so-so but the kitschy setting is memorable. **$–$$**

Kung Tak Lam Shanghai Vegetarian Restaurant
31 Yee Wo St, Causeway Bay
Tel: 2890 3127.
Imaginative and, if requested, MSG-free vegetarian fare from a renowned family enterprise established a century ago. **$$**

Luk Yu Tea House
24-26 Stanley St, Central
Tel: 2523 5464.
A 1930s tea house with an atmosphere that is classic: dark wooden booths, marble-backed chairs, brass spittoons and surly waiters. Some of the best dim sum in town. **$$**

Man Wah
25th Fl, Mandarin Oriental Hotel
5 Connaught Rd, Central
Tel: 2522 0111.
Gracious service combined with stunning harbour views and elegant surroundings make this one hard to beat. Mouthwatering Cantonese food complemented by Imperial dishes and a superb wine list. Smart dress, reservations essential. **$$$$**

High Tea

High tea is an institution in Hong Kong, and the best-known milieu for the past half century has been the colonnaded lobby of the Peninsula Hotel. Taking high tea there offers a good opportunity to watch the world go by.

The Luk Yu Tea House located at 26–42 Stanley Street, Central, Hong Kong, tel: 2523-5463 offers high-tea in a classic Cantonese atmosphere.

One Harbour Road
8th Fl, Grand Hyatt Hotel, 1 Harbour Rd, Wan Chai
Tel: 2588 1234.
The classic Cantonese menu, wine list and service are all top-notch. The setting is stunning, complete with trees and lily pond and spectacular harbour views. Smart dress, reservations essential. **$$$–$$$$**

Peking Garden Alexandra House
6 Ice House St, Central (and other locations)
Tel: 2526 6456.
This restaurant provides an enjoyable introduction to northern Chinese cuisine, including the famous Peking duck; order beggar's chicken and join in the clay-breaking ceremony. **$$–$$$**

Red Pepper
7 Lan Fong Rd, Causeway Bay
Tel: 2577 3811.
The spicy hot Sichuan food is a perennial favourite with expats and tourists but the service can be a bit brusque. **$$–$$$**

Steam & Stew Inn
21-23 Tai Wong St E, Wan Chai
Tel: 2529 3913.
Tasty casseroles and other homely, MSG-free Cantonese and Shanghainese fare served with unusual nutty red rice. Frequented by local political luminaries and often packed. **$**

Tai Woo
17–19 Wellington St, Central
Tel: 2524 5618 (and other locations).
Seafood is the forte of this highly-rated Cantonese restaurant. Set menus are a boon to the uninitiated. **$$**

Tin Tin Seafood Harbour
4th Fl, Elizabeth House, 250 Gloucester Rd, Causeway Bay
Tel: 2833 6683 (and other locations).
Boisterous Cantonese seafood palace where staff communicate by walkie-talkie. Select your fish and crustaceans from the tanks. **$$**

Yung Kee
32-40 Wellington St, Central
Tel: 2523 1624/2343.
A local dining institution for over 50 years, this Cantonese restaurant is famous for its specialty, roast goose. Its four floors accommodate as many as 1,000 diners at one sitting. **$$**

OTHER ASIAN

Banana Leaf Curry House
440 Jaffe Rd, Wan Chai
Tel: 2537 8187 (and other locations).
Popular Malaysian restaurant serving a delectable medley of Malay, Indian and Straits Chinese favourites on banana leaves instead of plates. **$–$$**

East-West Cafe Deco Bar & Grill
Level 1 & 2, Peak Galleria, 118 Peak Rd, The Peak
Tel: 2849 5111.
Eclectic menu strong on pizza, tandoori and Thai. Spectacular city views and live jazz each evening. Dinner reservations advised, especially for a window table. **$$–$$$**

Gaylord
1st Fl, Ashley Centre, 23-25 Ashley Rd, Tsim Sha Tsui
Tel: 2376 1001/1991.
One of the oldest, plushest Indian restaurants in town. **$$**

Gu Gu Jang Korean Barbecue
3rd Fl, Caroline Ctr, 28 Yun Ping Rd, Causeway Bay,
Tel: 2577 2021.
Nibble on spring onion pancakes while you watch marinated meat and fish sizzle to perfection on a table-top hotplate. **$$**

Her Thai
Tower 1, China Hong Kong City Canton Rd, Tsim Sha Tsui
Tel: 2735 8898.
Excellent Thai food with added panoramic views. **$$**

Indochine 1929
California Tower, 30-32 D'Aguilar St, Lan Kwai Fong, Central
Tel: 2869 7399.
Designer-chic recreation of yesteryear Vietnam. Excellent food and the verandah-style interior evokes images of bygone French colonial elegance. **$$$**

Koh-I-Noor
California Entertainment Bldg, 34 D'Aguilar St, Central
Tel: 2877 9706 (and other locations).
Delicately spiced Mughlai, tandoori and other delicious fare from northern India. **$–$$**

Kublai's
3rd Fl, One Capital Place, 18 Luard Rd, Wan Chai
Tel: 2529 9117 (and other locations).
All-you-can-eat Mongolian barbecue restaurant. Excellent value for money. **$**

Lee Kam Kee Vietnamese Restaurant
53 Pilkem St, Yau Ma Tei
Tel: 2735 7703 (and other locations).
Authentic traditional Vietnamese food at rock bottom prices. Specialties include crispy stuffed

pancakes (bánh xèo) and meat stew with vermicelli (bún bò Hué). **$**

Nadaman Island Shangri-La Hotel
Pacific Place, 88 Queensway, Admiralty
Tel: 2820 8570.
Gracious service and elegant surroundings heighten the gastronomic pleasure of fine Japanese cuisine. **$$$$**

Peak Cafe
121 Peak Rd, The Peak
Tel: 2849 7868.
Good Mediterranean and pan-Asian fare in a picturesque old colonial building with a vaulted ceiling. The leafy terrace is perfect for romantic dinners. High on charm and very popular so book ahead.
$$–$$$

Rangoon Hoi Kung Building
265 Gloucester Rd, Causeway Bay
Tel: 2893 2281.
Warm, friendly little place offering a rare chance to sample Burmese food outside of Myanmar. **$**

Tokio Joe
16 Lan Kwai Fong, Central
Tel: 2525 1889.
Pleasantly avant garde sushi bar and Japanese restaurant with good value set lunches. **$$$**

Woodlands International
Ground Fl, Mirror Tower, 61 Mody Rd, Tsim Sha Tsui East
Tel: 2369 3718.
Good Indian vegetarian food in a relaxed environment. Try the crispy dosai pancakes and thali appetisers. **$**

Wyndham Street Thai
38 Wyndham St, Central
Tel: 2869 2616.
Inspired Thai food with an Australian slant in a designer-chic setting. Good wine list. Reservations advised.
$$$–$$$$

WESTERN

American Pie California Entertainment Building
34-36 D'Aguilar St, Central
Tel: 2877 9779.
New England eatery famous for its sublime desserts. The Mississippi mud and banana cream pies, and

New York cheesecake are positively sinful; salads and main dishes are good too. **$$**

Casa Lisboa
20 Staunton St, Central
Tel: 2869 9631.
Traditional Portuguese fare, enthusiastic young staff and a warm, southern European ambience. **$$**

Dan Ryan's Chicago Grill
114 The Mall, Pacific Place, 88 Queensway, Admiralty
Tel: 2845 4600; also at 200 Ocean Terminal, Harbour City, Tsim Sha Tsui
Tel: 2735 6111.
Bustling, 1950s-style American brasserie serving the biggest and best burgers in town. **$$–$$$**

Fat Angelo's
G/F 414 Jaffe Road, Causeway Bay
Tel: 2574 6263,
A recessionary success story, opened in the depths of the economic crisis. The cheap and cheerful Italian fare (huge portions) struck a chord with Hong Kong's impoverished night-outers. Ideal for groups. **$**

Gaddi's
1st Fl, The Peninsula Hotel, Salisbury Rd, Tsim Sha Tsui
Tel: 2366 6251 ext 3171.
Superlatively classy restaurant that deserves every one of the accolades it receives for its classic French cooking, fine wines, impeccable service and elegant setting. Reservations, smart dress essential. **$$$$**

Grissini
2nd Fl, The Grand Hyatt Hotel, 1 Harbour Rd, Wan Chai
Tel: 2588 1234 ext 7313.
Mouthwateringly delicious Milanese food, charming service, striking modern interior and spectacular harbour views add up to one chic, very classy yet pleasantly relaxed Italian hotel restaurant.
$$$–$$$$

Harry Ramsden's
213 Queen's Rd East, Wan Chai
Tel: 2832 9626.
A cheery retro-nostalgia fish 'n chips restaurant from Yorkshire. Great family-dining with generous portions, and friendly staff. **$**

Michelle's at the Fringe
1st Fl, South Block 2, Lower Albert Rd, Central
Tel: 2877 4000.
Good Continental menu, well-chosen wine list, pleasant service, lovely arty dining room and an aura of romantic intimacy. **$$$**

Post 97
9-11 Lan Kwai Fong, Central
Tel: 2810 9333.
Trendy European cafe-restaurant with a welcoming ambience and imaginative menu. Tasty vegetarian options and herb teas for the health-conscious. **$$**

Shanghai

CHINESE

Chang An Dumpling Restaurant
2 Yunnan Lu
Tel: 6328 5156/0695; also at 1588 Pudong Lu, Pudong
Tel: 6885 8416/4917.
The city's most famous dumpling house claims to have over 100 types of dumplings. Open 24 hours.
$

Dragon and Phoenix Room
Peace Hotel, 20 Nanjing Donglu
Tel: 6321 6888.
The food here is good, but the real reason to come here is for the restaurant's historic significance and atmosphere. Located on the 8th floor of the Peace Hotel, it offers spectacular views of the Oriental Pearl TV Tower, the Huangpu River and the Bund. **$$$**

Quan Ju De
786 Hauihai Zhonglu
Tel: 6433 7286.
Serves traditional Beijing duck. **$$**

The Grape
55 Xinle Lu
Tel: 6472 0486.
A Shanghai stalwart. Two outlets have a bustling business of foreign and Chinese clientele, friendly service, great food and even better prices. **$**

Meilongzhen
1081 Nanjing Xilu
Tel: 6256 6688.
Probably Shanghai's most famous restaurant, the traditional Meilongzhen is one of the oldest

establishments in town and dates to 1938. Serves regional and Sichuanese specialities. **$$**

Park Hotel
170 Nanjing Xi Lu
Tel: 6327 5225.
A large and loud Chinese establishment with great Beijing Duck. **$$**

Revolving 28
Ocean Hotel, 1171 Dong Daming Lu
Tel: 6545 8888.
On the east side of the river and at a height of 28 stories, this revolving restaurant offers dizzying views of the Bund and the surrounding area. **$$$**

Soho
2077 Yanan Xi Lu
Tel: 6219 2948.
A chic restaurant with a Western-style atmosphere, an attentive, professionally trained wait staff, and a menu that is Chinese but with a Western twist. **$$**

Tian Tian Wang Hotpot Restaurant,
975 Huaihai Zhonglu
Tel: 6415 7559.
Popular with late night crowd, this lively eatery offers tasty food in a no-frills environment.

Yunnan Lu food Street
Yunnan nanlu and Yanan Zhonglu.
Two rows of restaurants offering tasty food at rock-bottom prices. Particularly lively at night. **$**

CANTONESE

The Dynasty
Yangtze New World Hotel, 2099 Yanan Xi Lu
Tel: 6275 0000.
Once known as the best Cantonese restaurant in Shanghai. **$$$**

The Forum Palace
188 Huaihai Zhong Lu
Tel: 6386 2608.
Designed in the typical Hong Kong style with great food and dim sum. **$$$**

Fu Lin Xuan
37 Sinan Lu
Tel: 6358 3699.
Located in the former French Concession, serves seafood Cantonese-style. *Dim sum* brunch at weekends. **$$**

Xian Yuee hien
Ding Huayuan, 853 Huashan Lu
Tel: 6251 1166.
Quality Cantonese and Shanghainese cuisine in a pretty garden setting. **$$**

CHAOZHOU

Chaozhou Garden
Yangtze New World Hotel, 2099 Yanan Xi Lu
Tel: 6275 0000.
Chaozhou cuisine in an elegant Chinese setting with excellent service. **$$$**

Chaozhou Restaurant
New Asia Tomson hotel, 777 Zhangyang Lu, Pudong
Tel: 5831 8888.
Mouth-watering cuisine to enjoy high above Pudong. **$$$**

SHANGHAINESE

Henry
8 Linle Lu
Tel: 6473 3448.
Background jazz selection is more impressive than the food, which is of varying quality. **$$**

Lubolang Restaurant
115 Yuyuan Lu
Tel: 328 0602.
A well established and popular restaurant serving such specialities as Shanghai *dim sum* and shark fin. **$$**

Lulu
69 Shimen Yi Lu
Tel: 6258 5645.
A small, crowded, smoke-filled restaurant which has become the hip, late-night place to go for Shanghai's young fashionable crowd. Great for seafood. **$$**

Nanxiang Dumpling Restaurant
87 Yuyuan Old Street
Tel: 6355 5156 4206.
The best place in town for Shanghainese *xiaolongbao* (dumplings). **$**

The Big Fan
1440 Hongqiao Lu
Tel: 6275 9131 ext. 268.
Shanghainese food in an old-Shanghai setting. **$$**

The Gap Salon
127 Maoming Nan Lu
Tel: 6433 9028.
One in a chain of six restaurants serving reliable Shanghainese fare. This one also has a band and dancing. **$$**

1221
1221 Yanan Xi Lu
Tel: 62136585; also at
The Village, 137 Tianping Lu
Tel: 62828018.
Run by a mother-daughter team from Hong Kong, these two restaurants serve Shanghainese food. The Village is more homey, 1221 more chic. Excellent food and service. **$$**

1931 Café and Pub
112 Maoming Nanlu
Tel: 6472 5264.
Dine in the atmosphere of old Shanghai. This lovely place serves simple but delicious Shanghainese fare. **$**

SICHUANESE

Sichuan Court
250 Huashan Lu
Tel: 6248 0000.
The sleek, sky-high eatery at the top of the Hilton serves Sichuanese dinners with views overlooking the city. **$$$**

Sichuan Restaurant
1733 Yanan Xi Lu
Tel: 6259 4583.
Great Sichuanese food in a colourful setting on the outskirts of Tianshan Park. **$$**

VEGETARIAN

Gongdelin
445 Nanjing Xi Lu
Tel: 6327 1532.
The Gongdelin has been serving vegetarian specialties for over 50 years. Mock duck and mock beef made from tofu. **$**

Jue Lin Shu Shi Chu
250 Jinling Lu
Tel: 6326 0115.
Vegetarian cuisine in a Buddhist-inspired setting. **$**

WESTERN

Buon Appetito
Sheraton Huating Hotel, 2nd Floor
Tel: 6439 6000.
Excellent Italian cuisine. $$$
Continental Room
Garden Hotel, 58 Maoming Nan Lu
Tel: 6415 1111.
High-class French cuisine served in
an elegant atmosphere. $$$
Dublin Exchange
Senmao Building, 101 Yincheng
Dong Lu, Pudong
Tel: 6847 2052.
Irish stews, breads and seafood in
a bander's club setting. Of course
the Guinness flows – on tap. $$
Hard Rock Café
Shanghai Centre, 1376 Nanjing Xi Lu
Tel: 6279 8133.
Typical American fare, some of the
best salads in town. $$
Johnny Moo
Vanke Plaza, 37 Shuicheng Lu,
Gubei
Tel: 6270 8686.
Arguably the best cheeseburgers
and milkshakes in Shanghai. $
M on the Bund
5 Guangdong Lu, 7th Floor
Tel: 6350 9988.
World class international cuisine.
Spectacular views of the Bund. $$$
Malone's
255 Tongren Lu
Tel: 6247 2400.
This American sports bar and grill
serves American favourites such as
Philly cheese steaks, buffalo wings,
burgers, and pizza. $$
Park 97/Lava
2 Gao Lan Lu
Tel: 6318 0785.
Extra-trendy Tapas bar. Good
cappuccinos. $$
Tony Roma's A Place for Ribs
Shanghai Centre, 1376 Nanjing Xi Lu
Tel: 6279 7129.
U.S. chain known for its ribs. $$

INDIAN

The Tandoor
Jinjiang Hotel, 58 Maoming Nan Lu
Tel: 6472 5494.
Beautifully-appointed with excellent

food it's not surprising that many
people call this restaurant the
best in Shanghai. The Indian
presentation here is superb, from
the food down to the service. $$$

JAPANESE

Da Jiang Hu
30 Donghu Lu
Tel: 6467 3332.
All-you-can-eat buffet, offering the
usual Japanese fare of sushi,
noodles, sake and more. $$
Ganki Sushi
29 Dongping Lu
Tel: 6466 9419.
Incredibly good-value, all-you-can-eat
buffet. $
Hana Yoshi
160 Fumin Lu
Tel: 6247 3077.
A cute little establishment with
sushi bar that has excellent *negi
toro* rolls. $$$
Sakura
Garden Hotel, 58 Maoming Nan Lu
Tel: 6415 1111.
The Japanese mecca of Shanghai
serves great sushi at outrageous
prices. $$$$
Sushi and Bowl
136 Maoming Nan Lu
Tel: 6466 1763.
Not the best sushi in town, but
some of the most affordable. $$

KOREAN

Alilang
28 Jiangsu Bei Lu
Tel: 6252 7146.
One of Shanghai's stalwarts in
Korean food, Alilang serves typical
Korean barbecue and cold dishes.
$$
Gao Li
181 Wuyuan Lu
Tel: 6431 5236.
Delicious Korean food. Open late.

SOUTHEAST ASIAN

Frankie's
118 Changde Lu
Tel: 6247 0886.

Serves up great Singaporean food.
$
Irene's Thai
263 Tongren Lu
Tel: 6247 3579.
Tasty authentic Thai food at
reasonable prices. $$

Macau

CHINESE

456 (Shanghai Restaurant)
Lisboa Hotel, New Wing, Avenida do
Infante D. Henrique, Macau
Tel: 377 666.
One of the region's best
Shanghainese food restaurants,
Macau or Hong Kong. Open till
1am.
Canton Tea House
Hyatt Regency Hotel, Taipa Is.
Tel: 831 234 ext. 1930 or 1937.
Cantonese style, serves Dim Sum
at lunch time. Open 8am–3pm,
6.30–11pm.
Cidade Chiu Chow
Av. Conselheiro F. de Almeida, Pak
Wai Bldg., Macau
Tel: 312 213.
Cantonese style, serves Dim Sum
at lunch time. Open
Monday–Saturday 11am– midnight,
Sunday 10am–midnight.
Dynasty
Mandarin Oriental Hotel, Avenida de
Amizade, 2F, Macau
Tel: 567 888 ext. 3821 or 3876.
Another very up-market, top of the
line Cantonese restaurants, serves
Dim Sum at lunch time. Open
8am–3pm, 6–11pm.
East Garden
11-13 Rua do Dr. Pedro Jose Lobo,
Macau
Tel: 562 328.
Cantonese style, serves Dim Sum
at lunch time. Open 8am–11.30pm.
Federal
19-21 Av. do Dr. Rodrigo Rodrigues,
5F, Macau
Tel: 313 313.
Another of Macau's favourite
eateries. Open 8am–11pm.
Fok Lam Moon
63A Avenida de Amizade, Macau,
Tel: 786 622.
Cantonese style, serves Dim Sum
for lunch. Open 7.30am–11.30pm.

Jade Garden
35-39 Rua do Dr. Pedro Jose Lobo, Macau
Tel: 710 203.
Cantonese style, serves Dim Sum at lunch time. Open 8am–midnight.

Long Kei
7B Largo do Senado (on the city's main square)
Tel: 573 970.
By reputation one of the best Chinese restaurants in town. Prices moderate and above. Open 11am–11pm.

New Ocean
1-3 Rua do Dr. Pedro Jose Lobo, 4 & 5F, Macau
Tel: 371 533.
The spot for seafood. Open 7:30am–11.30pm.

Pep'n Chilli
9-13 Rua Gago Coutinho, Macau
Tel: 515 151.
Macau's best Sichuan style restaurant. Open weekdays 10am–midnight, weekends 9am–midnight.

Tak Heng Hoi Sin Fo Vo (2 outlets)
10E Rua de Ribeira do Patane, Macau
Tel: 517 970; also at
16 Rua das Lorchas, Macau
Tel: 572 092.
Both considered among Macau's better Chinese restaurants and the best places for late night dinning. Open (both) 3pm–4am.

MACANESE/PORTUGUESE

1999
Parque de Coloane (Coloane Country Park), Coloane Is.
Tel: 328 295.
Named after the year Macau reverted to China, it serves a wide range of Portuguese dishes, plus others such as veal sausages, pig's knuckles and spaghetti. Open noon–3pm, 7–10.30pm.

Afonso's
Hyatt Regency Hotel, Taipa Is.
Tel: 831 234 ext. 1921 or 1922.
One of the top Portuguese restaurants in Macau. Beautiful seafood. Lovely Portuguese breads. Portuguese buffets on Sundays. Open noon–3pm, 7–11pm (closed on Tuesdays).

A Lorcha
289A Rua Almirante Sergio, G/F, Macau
Tel: 313 193.
A small unpretentious eatery on the Inner Harbour specialising in Portuguese food. Its Chinese dishes are good too as they have a distinct Portuguese flavour. Open 1–3pm, 7–11pm.

Barra Nova
287A Rua do Almirante Sergio, G/F, Macau
Tel: 512 287.
Small restaurant featuring Portuguese and Macanese cuisine on the Inner Harbour, located just near the A-Ma Temple. Open noon–4pm, 6–11pm.

Bee Vee
Rotunda de Leonel da Sousa, Praca da Portagem, Taipa Is.
Tel: 812 288.
A great spot for Portuguese and Macanese specialties. Open noon–midnight.

Caracola
8 Rua das Gaivotas, Coloane Village, Coloane Is.
Tel: 882 226.
This is a restaurant popular with many locals. Bright and cosy, and located in an older Mediterranean-style house, the restaurant serves Portuguese food in large portions. Try the rabbit stew, and for dessert, the Nun's Belly. Open 12.30–3pm, 7–11pm.

Fernando's
9 Praia Hac Sa, Hac Sa Beach, Coloane Is.
Tel: 882 264.
Large menu with both Portuguese and Chinese dishes. Seafood, especially clams, and rabbit specialities. Wonderful place to while away an afternoon when you are tired of the beach. Open noon–9:30pm.

Flamingo
Hyatt Regency, Taipa Is.
Tel: 831 234 ext. 1834 or 1874.
Authentic Portuguese and Macanese food served in the open air in a pavilion over a man-made lake. Marvellous atmosphere. Open noon–2.30pm, 7–10.30pm.

Galo
45 Rua dos Clerigos, G/F and 1st

Fl, Taipa Is.
Tel: 827 318.
This is the place to go for African Chicken though the other Portuguese and Macanese dishes are also on the menu. Open 11am–3pm, 6–10.30pm.

O-Manel
90 Rua Ferao Mendes Pinto, Taipa Is.
Tel: 827 571.
A local favourite in a quaint setting. Open 2–3pm, 6.30–10pm.

Panda
4-8 Rua Carlos Eugenio, G/F, Taipa village, Taipa Is.
Tel: 827 646.
One of the many Portuguese restaurants located around Taipa village, this restaurant has a large seating area behind a deceptively small storefront. Open weekdays noon–10.30pm, weekends 11.30am–10.30pm.

Pinocchio's
4 Rua do Sol, Taipa Is.
Tel: 827 128.
Spicy fish and fowl in a tree-shaded courtyard. Open noon–10pm.

Portuguese
16 Rua do Campo
Tel: 375 445.
Real home cooking and no-nonsense red wine. Very cheap. Open 11am–1am.

Praia Grande
10A Praca de Lobo de Avila, G/F, Macau
Tel: 973 022.
One of Macau's older and better restaurants. Open noon–3pm, 7–11pm.

Riquexo (means rickshaw)
69 Avenida Sidonia Pais, Macau
Tel: 565 655.
Everything is literally home-cooked because many of the dishes are prepared at home by Macanese housewives and brought here daily. Open 12.30–9pm.

Santos
20 Rua do Cunha, Taipa Is.
Tel: 827 508.
This is a small restaurant with a gritty, authentic feel. Often overlooked (and it seems the owner and customers prefer it that way), this restaurant has excellent fish dishes and is a good place for a

cosy lunch. Open noon–3pm, 6–10pm.
Solmar
11 Rua da Praia Grande, Macau
Tel: 574 391.
Boulevard cafe and bistro, a local favourite. Moderate prices. Open 11am–10.30pm.

ASIAN

Tee Jei (Indian)
Estrada Nova, Va Fai Un Bldg., Taipa Is.
Tel: 827 103.
Macau's best Indian eatery. Open noon–3pm, 6–10.30pm.
Thai (Thai)
27E Rua Abreu Nunes, Macau
Tel: 573 288.
For the unsuspecting, the Thai cuisine here is some of the hottest in Asia. The tom yam is a good test of your endurance. Open noon–3pm, 6pm–6am.
Rasa Sayang (Malaysian)
Estrada Noroeste da Taipa, Ocean Garden, B1.12, D, E & F, Taipa Is.
Tel: 810 187.
Macau's only Malaysian eatery. Open noon–10.30pm.

Drinking Notes

In most hotel rooms there are thermos flasks with hot and cold water, and bags with green or black tea (hong, or red). A cup of hot tea, or just "white" tea (hot water), as the Chinese usually drink it, is the most effective way of quenching your thirst. At meal times, Chinese beer, which contain less alcohol than European counterparts, mineral water or lemonade (often very sweet) are offered in addition to the ubiquitous green tea.

While being drunk in public is considered unacceptable in China (unlike in Japan, for example), there is a surprisingly large choice of Chinese spirits on offer. The most famous are *maotai jiu*, a 55-percent spirit made of wheat and sorghum that, for centuries, has been produced in Maotai, in Guizhou Province, and *wuliangye jiu*, a spirit

made from five different grains. You'll either take to it immediately or not in a lifetime. Chinese wines, both red and white, tend to be very sweet, tasting a bit like sherry. Try the *huang jiu*, warmed and with a slice of ginger!

Several foreign joint-venture wineries are now producing a variety of drinkable red and white table wines. Dozens of international and local name beers are being brewed across China. Imported wines and spirits are commonly available in larger cities.

Culture

Museums

There are a great variety of museums in China. From the revolution to natural history, everything is captured in exhibitions at various places. Many Chinese museums are not very well administered and not easy for the visitor to appreciate. English labelling is the exception. Recommended below are mainly museums in the field of art and culture. Opening hours are usually between 9am and 5pm, and there is typically an admission fee.

BEIJING

Ancient Observatory (Gu Guanxiangtai)
2 Dongbiaobei Hutong, Jiangguomenwai Dajie
Tel: 6524 2202, 6524 2246.
An observatory was built here in 1422, on what was the old city wall. Replicas of several 17th-century astronomical instruments are displayed on the roof of the tower, and an exhibition on the ground floor shows how ancient Chinese astronomers developed their science.
Beijing Lu Xun Museum (Lu Xun Bowuguan)
Fuchengmennei Dajie
Tel: 6616 4169.
This traditional courtyard house, where Lu Xun lived from 1923–1925, contains photographs of, and manuscripts and letters by China's most famous 20th-century writer.
China National Art Gallery (Zhongguo Meishuguan)
1 Wusi Dajie, Chaoyangmennei
Tel: 6401 7076.
Permanent displays of some of the

finest traditional Chinese watercolours and calligraphy contrast with temporary exhibitions of modern oil paintings and sculpture.

Military Museum (Junshi Bowuguan)
9 Fuxingmenwai Dajie
Tel: 6851 4441.
Tanks and weapons, photographs of the young Mao, and an exhibition of the history of the People's Liberation Army are among the military highlights.

Museum of Chinese History (Zhongguo Lishi Bowuguan)
Tiananmen Square, east side
Tel: 6512 8986.
Covers the entire history of China, and has many precious cultural relics from across the country.

Museum of the Chinese Revolution (Zhongguo Geming Bowuguan)
Tiananmen Square, east side
Tel: 6526 3355.
Photographs, paintings, documents and relics represent the leading events and personalities that brought communism to China.

CHENGDU

Sichuan Museum
Renmin Nanlu (People's Road South)
Tel: 522 2158.
A large provincial museum where one may get an in-depth and detailed look at the rich background and identity of the region (closed Mondays).

CHONGQING

Chongqing Municipal Museum (Chongqing Shi Bowuguan)
72 Pipashan Zhengjie.
A comparatively small museum displaying some interesting brick reliefs from the Han dynasty, as well as pottery, sculptures, and Buddhist carvings from the Tang dynasty. Separate section displaying dinosaur fossils from Sichuan.

GUANGZHOU

Guangdong Folk Arts Museum,
Zhongshan Qi Lu
Tel: 8881 4559.
Housed in the Chen Family Temple, this museum is more a gallery of arts and crafts from various regions in China. Pottery, porcelain from Shiwan, stone and wood carvings, embroidery and stitchwork are displayed in the halls of the temple.

Museum of the Western Han Tomb of the Nanyue King
867 Jiefang Bei Lu.
The emperor Wen Di, who ruled southern China from 137 to 122 BC, was buried here. Today a museum houses the skeletons of the emperor and 15 courtiers who were buried alive with him. Funerary objects from jade armour to bronze music chimes are displayed.

HONG KONG

Hong Kong Museum of Art,
16 Salisbury Road, Tsim Sha Tsui (next to Hong Kong Cultural Centre)
Tel: 2721 0116.
A 5,800-square-metre exhibition space that displays Chinese fine arts and antiquities, as well as contemporary Hong Kong art. Open 10am–6pm, Mon–Sat, closed Thurs and Sun am. Admission fee.

Hong Kong Museum of History
100 Chatham Road South, Tsim Sha Tsui
Tel: 2724 9000.
The museum presents "The Story of Hong Kong", not just since the colonial era but drawing on historical relics from 6,000 years ago. Open 10am-6pm Mon–Sat; 1–6pm Sun and public holidays; closed Fri.

Hong Kong Racing Museum
Happy Valley Racecourse
Tel: 2966-8065.
This museum, which was only opened in 1996, highlights the phenomenal popularity of horse-racing in Hong Kong since its introduction in the 1840s.
Open 10am–5pm Tues–Sun.

Hong Kong Railway Museum
Tai Po, New Territories
Tel: 2653-3339.
A small picturesque homage to Hong Kong's railway history located at the 1913 former Tai Po Market railway station. Open daily 9am to 5pm except Tues`.

Hong Kong Science Museum,
Science Museum Road, Tsim Sha Tsui East
Tel: 273 23232.
The most popular museum in Hong Kong, it offers hundreds of interactive exhibits covering science and technology areas such as robotics, virtual reality, and transport. Don't miss the 20-metre-high energy machine that produces spectacular audio-visual representations of diverse energy forms. Open 1pm–9pm Tues–Fri and 10am–9pm Sat, Sun and most public holidays. Closed Mon.

Hong Kong Space Museum
Cultural Centre Complex, Kowloon, Tsim Sha Tsui
Tel: 2734-2722.
A planetarium and space technology exhibition with screenings several times a day. Open 1pm-9pm Mon–Fri and 10pm-9pm Sat, Sun and most public holidays. Closed Tues.

Museum of Tea Ware
Flagstaff House, Central
Tel: 2869-0690.
Originally the home of the Commander-in-Chief of the British Forces, Flagstaff House is now one of the world's most obscure museums, devoted to a collection of Chinese teaware. The museum is in Hong Kong Park, and admission is free. Open daily except Wed 10am-5pm.

Police Museum
Wan Chai
Tel: 2849-7019.
The former Wan Chai Gap Police Station showcases the history of Asia's finest and includes exhibitions on narcotics and the notorious Triad Societies. Open 9am-5pm Wed–Sun, 2pm-5pm Tues. Closed Mon and public holidays.

KUNMING

Yunnan Museum for the National Minorities
Haigang, next to Yunnan National Minorities Village.
Extensive collection of ethnic costumes, accessories, jewelry, art and artifacts, musical instruments, tools and utensils. Well-displayed and labelled, with additional exhibits on land use, past and present, plus a floor of one building devoted to Yunnan's minerals and semi-precious stones.

LANZHOU

Gansu Provincial Museum (Gansu Sheng Bowuguan)
3 Xijing West Road.
Though inconveniently located on the western edge of town, this museum features an impressive exhibition of select cultural artifacts from Gansu and the Silk Road, starting from the Dadiwan cultures of 8000 BC up through the Yuan dynasty. The museum also houses a replica of the famous bronze flying horse (the original is in Beijing), cultural artifacts up through the Yuan dynasty, and a giant fossil of a mammoth, tusks still intact.

LIJIANG

The Dongba Research Centre
Black Dragon Pool Park
A massive collection of *dongba* manuscripts, the religious texts used by Naxi ritual specialists, written in a unique pictographic script. Another building exhibits various paraphernalia and ritual layouts used in ceremonies. The most eye-catching is the 20-metre-long painted scroll used in the funerals of dongbas.

LUOYANG

Luoyang Museum (Luoyang Bowuguan)
Zhongzhou Zhonglu
Tel: 491 3770.
It houses four special collections of bronzeware, ceramics, gold and silver artifacts, and jadeware. Some items date back to the Xia dynasty, 4,000 years ago.

NANJING

Nanjing Museum
321 Zhongshan Donglu.
The most precious exhibit, in addition to pottery, porcelain (including some from the Ming dynasty), bronzes, tortoise shells and jewelry from various dynasties, is a 2,000-year-old burial shroud made of 26,000 jade pieces.

NANNING

Guangxi Provincial Museum
Minzudadao.
Impressive collection of ancient bronze drums, used by non-Han aboriginals as part of a cult that spread to Yunnan and the northern rim of Southeast Asia. Also costumes of the eleven ethnic minorities of Guangxi, including several examples from Yao and Miao branches. Wooden houses of these people, plus the Zhuang, as well as Dong architectural examples, stand outside in an adjacent park.

SHANGHAI

Shanghai Art Museum (Shanghai Meishuguan)
456 Nanjing Xi Lu
Tel: 6327 0557.
At present, this state-run museum is fairly unimpressive, but when it moves to its new location in the former Shanghai Library, things will hopefully change. The government is planning to put more money into the establishment so that it can truly showcase the country's modern art.
Shanghai History Museum (Shanghai Lishi Bowuguan)
1286 Hongqiao Lu
Tel: 6275 5595.
The small museum chronicles Old Shanghai. It features the famous bronze lions that once graced the front of the former Hong Kong and Shanghai Bank Building.
Shanghai Museum (Shanghai Bowuguan)
People's Square, 201 Renmin Da Dao
Tel: 6372 3500.
The Shanghai Museum moved to its new location in the centre of People's Square in 1997. Truly one of Shanghai's treasures, this urn-shaped museum is by far the best showcase of relics and artifacts in the country. Its 11 state-of-the-art galleries are beautifully appointed and house China's first international-standard exhibits of paintings, bronzes, sculpture, ceramics, calligraphy, jade, Ming and Qing dynasty furniture, coins, seals, and minority art. The bronze collection is said to be the best in the world. Don't miss the audio tour.

ÜRÜMQI

Xinjiang Provincial Museum (Xinjiang Bowuguan)
132 Xibei Lu
Tel: 481 1453.
Contains an archaeological exhibition about the Silk Road, and an exhibition about the different minorities in Xinjiang, as well as a fascinating exhibition of 4000-year-old corpses of European and Asian ancestry.

XI'AN

Museum of the Terracotta Soldiers of the First Qin Emperor
This famous museum is in Lintong county near the tomb of Emperor Qin Shi Huangdi.
Shaanxi History Museum
This modern museum, opened in 1991, is in the south of the city near the Dayan Pagoda. It has five exhibition halls displaying cultural and historical artifacts from the surrounding areas from the

Paleolithic Age up to the Qing dynasty, including terracotta soldiers and horses.

Xi'an Beilin Bowuguan (Forest of Steles Museum)
This museum, formerly the provincial museum, is located in a former Confucian temple near the south gate of the city wall. It has three main departments: the history of Xi'an and its surroundings to the end of the Tang dynasty, Stele forest with over 1000 steles, and stone sculptures of animals.

ZHENGZHOU

Henan Provincial Museum (Henan Sheng Bowuguan)
11 Renmin Lu.
Ancient relics from around Henan form the main exhibitions, with a display to commemorate the February 7 (er qi) railway workers' revolt marked by the Erqi Pagoda in the city centre.

Acrobatics

Acrobatics are popular throughout China. Almost every large town has its own troupe of acrobats, many of which tour the country. You can get details of time and place of performances locally. In big cities such as Beijing, Shanghai and Guangzhou, there are permanent performances. In China, acrobatics means a mixture of proper acrobatics, magic and animal acts, and of course clowns.

Chaoyang Theatre
36 Dongsanhuan Beilu
Tel: 6507-2421.
Performances daily at 7.15pm.

Huaxia Cultural and Martial Arts Centre (National Children's Arts Theatre)
64 Donganmendajie
Tel: 6513-4115. (9am–8pm).

Shanghai Acrobatic Troupe
1376 Nanjing Xi Lu
Tel: 6279 8663
Shanghai is home to China's best acrobatic troupe, which performs at the Shanghai Centre Theatre daily at 7.15pm.

Chinese Opera

There are more than 300 types of opera in China. You can attend performances of traditional opera in virtually every town.

The most famous one is Beijing opera. The address of the opera and theatre is available from your hotel or from travel agencies. A visit to the Chinese opera is a relaxed affair and occasionally quite noisy. You can leave your evening dress and tie at home; normal day clothes are quite acceptable.

BEIJING

Guanghe Theatre
46 Qianmenroushi Jie, Qianmen Dajie
Tel: 6701 8216.
Phone to check, as the theatre stages plays and films as well as operas.

Lao She Teahouse
3rd Fl, 3 Qianmenxi Dajie
Tel: 6303 6830
Fax: 6301 7529.
Performances vary, but usually include Beijing opera and other folk arts such as acrobatics, magic or comedy.

Liyuan Theatre
Qianmen Hotel, 175 Yongan Lu
Tel: 6301 6688 x 8860.
Nightly performances in the most popular Beijing opera venue for tourists.

Zhengyici Theatre
220 Xiheyuan Dajie, Xuanwu district
Tel: 6318 9454.
This authentic wood-built theatre holds nightly performances in a traditional setting.

Zheng Yi Ci Theatre
The only surviving Peking Opera Theatre, built entirely of wood. Re-opened in 1995 after extensive renovation. Tea and snacks are included with the entrance fee, or you can pay extra and enjoy a Peking Duck dinner while you watch the opera. Perfomances are nightly at 7.30pm. Tel: 6303-3104 for reservations.

SHANGHAI

Yifu Theatre
701 Fuzhou Lu
Tel: 6322 6478.
Regular performances of Beijing opera, as well as the regional operas Huju, Kunju and Shaoxing.

Concerts

There are regular concerts of Western classical or traditional Chinese music in various cities. Indigenous or foreign songs and musical performances are often part of the programme. Dance performances are also common. In many areas – particularly in those of the national minorities – you can see performances of local dances and songs on the stage. Ballet is also performed. Young people are very keen on concerts by various pop stars, whether from the PR of China, Hong Kong or even Taiwan. You can find out about time and place of performances in each town from the hotel or through travel agencies.

Festivals

Holidays such as **National Day** and **International Labour Day** are fixed on the modern calendar, but most traditional festivals and events are determined by the lunar calendar, which means the date varies a little from year to year.

JANUARY/FEBRUARY

The most important festival time is the **Lunar New Year**, or **Spring Festival**, which falls in late January or early February. Public buildings are festooned with coloured lights, people from all over China travel to reunite with families, debts are settled, and there is food consumed – lots of it. On the first days of the lunar year, the Chinese visit family and friends. In recent years, a more relaxed atmosphere has brought the revival of old Spring Festival traditions, such as giving *hongbao* – small, red envelopes containing money – to children and young adults. Temple fairs feature martial arts demonstrations, stand-up comedy, home-made toys and, of course, food.

Northerners, who have amazing resilience to the bitterly cold winters, partake with gusto in ice-sculpting competitions and winter swimming. The time and duration of the festivals depends on the weather. Both Beijing and Harbin are noted for their ice-sculpting festivals.

APRIL

On the 12th day of the third lunar month, in the beginning of April, the Chinese honour their deceased ancestors by observing **Qingming**, sometimes referred to as the "grave-sweeping" day. It is much less impressive nowadays, as people are cremated instead of being buried. Qingming is a time for remembering ancestors, but also for revelling on a warm spring day.

MAY/JUNE

International Labour Day is a one-day public holiday. Following hot on its heels is **Youth Day**, a commemoration of the May 4th Movement of 1919, reflected by large editorials and government hoopla in the official press.

International Children's Day is celebrated in earnest on 1 June by letting classes out early and treating children to outings at public parks.

Hong Kong Holidays

In Hong Kong, the Christian **Good Friday** and **Easter Monday** are public holidays, as are **Christmas** and **Boxing Day**. There are also days off for the Chinese ancestor-worshipping festivals of **Qing Ming** (April) and **Chung Yeung** (October), as well as **Buddha's Birthday** (May) and **SAR Establishment Day** (July 1)

JULY/AUGUST

1 July is the **Anniversary of the Communist Party**, which was founded in Shanghai in 1921. This means very little to the average citizen but plenty of fun for high-level Party members.

The fifth day of the fifth lunar month – usually late July – brings the **Dragon Boat Festival**, marked by dragon boat races in many cities, sometimes involving teams from around the world. It commemorates the memory of Qu Yuan (340–278BC), a poet in the days of the Kingdom of Chu, who, rather than submit to political pressure, drowned himself in the Miluo River, in Hunan. To prevent the fishes from eating his body, the people threw glutinous rice cakes into the river. Nowadays, these *zongzi* are simply eaten to mark the occasion.

1 August is the **Anniversary of the People's Liberation Army**. Inaugurated in 1927 and formerly marked by enormous parades, it is now celebrated mainly in the media.

SEPTEMBER/OCTOBER

The **Mid-Autumn Festival** again depends on when the moon reaches its fullest, usually around mid-September. The shops do great business in 'moon cakes' – pastries filled with gooey sesame paste, red-bean and walnut filling. *Tang yuan*, glutinous rice flour balls with sweet fillings in sugar syrup, and *yue bing*, a cake baked specifically for this occasion, are eaten. In the tradition of poets, this is the time to drink a bit of wine and toast the moon.

Late September is normally the time when Chinese communities celebrate the memory of **Confucius**.

1 October is the PRC's birthday, **National Day**, celebrated with a two-day public holiday. Government buildings, road intersections and hotels are decked out in lights, and flower arrangements and Sun Yatsen's portrait are displayed in Tiananmen Square. Tens of thousands turn out on the square for picture-taking and general merry-making.

NOVEMBER/DECEMBER

November and December are quiet months in China, but **Christmas** is gaining momentum as a consumer's celebration. Christian churches hold special services that draw thousands of spectators. In Beijing, for example, it is trendy to exchange greeting cards and presents, while Santa Claus makes the odd shop appearance.

Nightlife

Bars, Discos & Karaoke

Nightlife is not particularly widespread in China, except in Hong Kong, Shanghai and Guangzhou, and increasingly in Beijing. Most restaurants close early, and theatres and concerts generally finish before 10pm. In southern Chinese towns, there is more life at night, with restaurants, bars, and cafes open till midnight or even later. The *China Daily* and some English language city newspapers have an adequate listing of cultural life in cities such as Beijing and Shanghai.

In the larger cities, many bars and pubs have opened, and are meeting places for affluent youths. Far more common, however, are karaoke bars. The Japanese-style singalong bars have swept China, increasing the planet's off-key harmonies considerably. Most are easily recognised by the letters "OK" amongst the characters for their names. Some of these are pricey, with the clientele being rich businessmen. Also, some of these bars are fronts for prostitution; such hostess-style bars are illegal, and can fleece customers.

Discotheques are popular throughout China and can be found in a number of towns. Many hotels have their own discos, which are frequented by well-off local youths. The most fashionable dances are as well-known here as anywhere else in the world. Many discos – particularly in the hotels – are often open until after midnight.

Shopping

What To Buy

Typically "Chinese" goods such as silk, jade and porcelain are still cheaper and of a better quality in Hong Kong than elsewhere. The choice varies – if you are lucky, the shelves are well stocked and you can find excellent and well-cut silk articles being sold cheaply; if the supply has dried up, you will only find meagre remnants even in Hangzhou, the centre of silk production.

You will usually find quality goods which are produced for export. These are mostly sold in the "Friendship Stores" (Youyi Shangdian) and in hotel shops.

Until recently, it was not usual to bargain It is still not advisable in the state-owned shops and warehouses. But at the many souvenir stands, it is a good idea to bargain because of the greatly overpriced goods on offer. It is also worth comparing prices in the free markets (if you can read them) and watch how much Chinese customers pay.

When buying antiques, it is essential to check that the official red seal of the shop is on the product.

Buying and exporting of antiques is only permitted with this official stamp, otherwise you could meet with great difficulties when leaving the country.

It is worth looking for local products in the smaller towns or in the places where ethnic minorities live. These will be difficult to find anywhere else in China. The most usual articles are craft objects for everyday use or specially worked or embroidered garments.

Import and Export

Antiques that date from before 1795 may not be legally exported. Those that can be taken out of China must carry a small red seal or have one affixed by the Cultural Relics Bureau. All other antiques are the property of the Peoples' Republic of China and, without the seal, will be confiscated without compensation. Beware of fakes; producing new 'antiques' (and the seal) is a thriving industry.

Foreign currency can be imported and exported without restrictions. You may not export more foreign currency than you imported, except with a special permit.

You should not export, nor even buy in the first place, objects made from wild animals, especially from ivory. Most Western countries ban the import of ivory objects, and will confiscate them without compensation.

Bargaining

Forget any notions about an austere workers' paradise. Consumerism is the only meaningful "-ism" around China these days.

The number of *dakuan* – the fat cats with portable phones – is increasing. New markets and stores are sprouting up everywhere.

It's advisable to check prices first at state-operated stores, such as the Friendship Store, before buying a similar item in a hotel shop or on the free market. And in the free market, bargain, and be stubborn – but friendly – if interested in an item. Avoid drawn out dickering just for the sport.

Bargaining usually begins with the shopkeeper suggesting a price and the buyer responding with a lower one. In Beijing, the starting price is generally 30 to 50 percent higher than the price that shopkeepers will eventually accept. Be persistent. Look for missing buttons, stains and other flaws, keep smiling, and walk away if you find the price unacceptable.

Where to Buy

Department stores: In every town there is a department store selling products for everyday use, from toothpaste to bicycles. However, the quality of clothing fabric (artificial), the cut and the sizes are usually not up to expectation.

The big department stores are state-owned institutions, but many small shops and street stalls – privately owned – have sprung up as well. Here you will often find products from Hong Kong, including higher-quality clothing.

Friendship Stores: A visit to the Friendship Store (Youyi Shangdian) is an essential part of the program of all tour groups. These stores usually offer a good selection of wares for export: silk fabric, craft articles, electronic devices, clothing and books. Often, there is a whole department offering both traditional and modern medical products and equipment. Individual travellers, too, should take the opportunity to look round these stores from time to time. The Friendship Store in Beijing, for instance, has an excellent food department. A visit to the antiques department in the Friendship Store in Shanghai is also worthwhile.

Some large Friendship Stores have a delivery section that will send purchases to one's home country. Shops and department stores generally open around 9am and close at 6pm or 7pm.

Markets: Food items such as fruit, vegetables, fish and meat are sold at markets. In the free markets, where prices are more flexible, and sometimes more expensive (off-setting higher quality and availability), there are often additional items, such as wicker baskets, metal and iron bits, and clothes; tailors are sometimes found. In the big towns, numerous street traders offer their wares well into the evening; one can often find jeans or silk blouses from Hong Kong at such places.

Watch how much the Chinese themselves pay. All too often, traders in free markets will happily fleece unwary foreign customers.

Beijing

SPECIALTY MARKETS

Silk Alley (Xiushui Shichang) – on Xuishiu Jie and intersecting with Chang'an Lu about 800 m east of the Friendship Store, has been growing in the past few years. As the name implies, vendors flog silk in all shapes and sizes – ties and boxer shorts, dresses and slinky nightgowns – at prices about half of those found in Hong Kong. Kong. This market has also recently become the place to buy goods that are made in China for export only. You can buy well known Western brands of clothing and footwear here at very low prices.

Just a few blocks away is **Yabaolu Market**, commonly known as the Russian market (open daily 9am–6pm) and on Ritan Lu, opposite Ritan Park. It is a huge clothing market specialising in cotton and wool garments, and also goose-down jackets.

A few blocks straight north of Yabaolu Market is the **Chaowai Flea Market** (open daily 10am–6pm), a favourite shopping ground for resident diplomats and journalists. The front building is filled with antique and classical-style furniture. In the rear building are curios: snuff bottles, ceramics and Mao memorabilia. **Hongqiao Farmers' Market**, on Tiantan Lu (open daily 7am–5.30pm), has the best collection of antique clocks and Mao statues, and freshwater pearls.

For traditional Chinese paintings, calligraphy supplies and rare books, poke around at **Liulichang** (open daily 9am–5.30pm), just west of Qianmen district. A bit further afield, but considered to be the most reliable source of antique porcelain in Beijing, is **Jingsong Market** (open daily 9am–6pm) located at East Third Ring Road at the Jingsong east intersection.

Tucked under the southeast corner of the Xizhimen overpass, the **Bird Market** (open daily 7.30am–sunset) is hardly an extension of nature, but it has a wonderful array of feathered creatures. At least as important are the elegant handmade cages, ceramic feeders and other avian paraphernalia sold here.

There are three lively shopping streets in the city centre that cater to local customers. **Wangfujing, Xidan** and **Dongdan**, which run perpendicular to Chang'an Lu, have mostly inexpensive local goods, with bargains on leather and furs. At 192 Wangfujing Dajie, check out the **Jianhua Leather Goods Company** (open daily 8am–8.30pm). Further north, along the east side of Wangfujing is the **Foreign Languages Bookstore**, run by the China News Agency. The first floor has a wide range of books on

Birds and Flowers

Jiangyin Bird and Flower Market, at Huangpi between Nanjing Xi Lu and Weihai Lu is the largest bird market in town. Fish, turtles, flowers, plants and teapots are also on offer here.

China. The upper floors have everything from Chinese art and language tapes to computers and a music store. All three streets are undergoing radical transformation, with more and more boutiques, watch stores and ice-cream shops replacing the old standbys. Xidan and Wangfujing are both undergoing massive rebuilding, which will expand the shopping greatly.

Among the most popular department stores for Chinese products is **Longfu Dasha** (No 95 Longfusi Jie, Chaoyang District; open daily 8.30am–8.30pm). This is the spot to buy China's most famous brands of household products – Flying Pigeon bicycles and Butterfly sewing machines.

ONE-STOP SHOPPING

Capitalism's answer for one-stop shoppers is the glossy, new joint-venture shopping centres that draw China's *nouveau riche*, as well as tourists and mobs of window shoppers. Directly across the street from the Friendship Store is the CIVIC-Yaohan (No 22 Jianguomenwai Dajie, open daily 9am–9pm), a Japanese department store full of luxury, trendy imports.

The **Youyi Shopping City** in the Beijing Lufthansa Centre (No 52 Liangmaqiao Lu, Chaoyang District; open daily 9am–9pm) carries products with a broader price range. The city's best silk selection – sold by the yard – is offered at reasonable prices.

Stock up on all the beautiful things that China produces – traditional paper cuttings (cheap and easy to pack), jade carvings, kites and chopsticks – at the state-run **Friendship Store** (No 17 Jianguomenwai Dajie; open daily 9am–9pm). The store is also good for getting an estimate of what things outside should cost, and for last-minute gifts.

Guangzhou

Don't expect the glitz and variety of goods available in Hong Kong. Still, Guangzhou offers interesting shopping and good bargains. Among Chinese cities, Guangzhou is considered to have the widest range of goods, many of which are imported from other parts of the country. The main shopping areas in Guangzhou are Zhongshan Wulu, Beijing Lu, Renmin Nanlu, Zhongshan Silu and Xiajiu Lu-Shangjiu Lu. The main open-air market is at Qingping Lu, near Shamian Island.

There are several large department stores in Guangzhou worth a visit for their wide array of foreign merchandise, at prices lower than in Hong Kong.

Nanfang Dasha (49 Yanjiang Xilu) offers a good choice of local products. Xihu Lu Baihuo Dasha, on Xihu Lu, has a huge choice, especially foreign goods, at amazing prices.

Xin Da Xin, at the corner of Beijing Lu and Zhongshan Wulu,

offers a good range of Chinese goods, including silk (and the rare Guangdong black-mud silk), and a large musical instrument department. The Guangzhou Foreign Trade Centre at the Guangzhou Fair Building, on Renmin Beilu, has a large arts and crafts department and a good choice of silk merchandise.

The government-owned Friendship Store, on the ground floor of the China Hotel, and the Kwangchow Friendship Store, at 369 Huanshi Donglu, opposite the Garden Hotel, offer a wide selection of goods.

ANTIQUES

The largest private market for antiques is the **Daihe Lu Market**, which sprawls over several lanes. Enter by the first lane on the right after entering Daihe Lu from Changshou Xilu. There are smaller antique markets nearby; one at the middle lane of the Qingping Market and the other at the Jade Market. Do not buy antiques that the vendor claims are over 100 years old, as they are probably fake.

Even if not trying to rip you off (and most are), a genuine antique that is over a century old cannot be exported if it doesn't carry an official red-wax seal.

Beware of fakes, as new "antiques" with the official seal is now a thriving industry in China. Despite the difficulties, there is still much to buy: *kam muk* (gilded sculptured wood panels), vintage watches, tiny embroidered shoes for Chinese women with bound feet, and a range of beautiful Shiwan porcelain.

For serious collectors, antiques with authentic red-wax seals authorising export can be bought from government shops. Try the **Guangzhou Antique Shop** (146/162/170 Wende Beilu, Tel: 8333 0175, Fax: 8335 0085) for *kam muk*, calligraphy works, jewelry boxes, paintings, porcelain and silver jewellery.

CLOTHING AND TEXTILES

Guangdong Province is a major production centre for ready-to-wear clothes and shoes. The biggest variety is to be found at the government-owned **Friendship Stores**. These stores are your best bet for down jackets (one-fifth the price you would pay elsewhere) and cashmere sweaters and scarves. The **Bingfen Fashion Market** on Haizhu Square, **Gong Lu Fashion Market** on Zhongshan Erlu in Dongshan District, the night market under the Quzhuang Overbridge, and the Xihu Lu night market are also good hunting grounds for apparel.

Of special interest is Guangdong black-mud silk, which is painstakingly hand-made and dyed as many as 30 times, using the red extract of the gambier root and the iron-rich river mud from the Pearl River. The material stays cool and dry in humid weather. The silk is available from the **Xin Da Xin** department store, at the corner of Beijing Lu and Zhongshan Wulu.

HANDICRAFTS

Paper Cuts
The Renshou Temple in Foshan, previously famous for its paper cuts of scenes from the Cultural Revolution, has remained the major production centre for this delicate craft. However, its production nowadays focuses on farm scenes.

Bird cages
The Chinese love songbirds and show them off in splendidly-decorated cages at public parks. Antique cages cost from 100 to 700 yuan; newer ones can be bought at the Bird Market, located at the Dongfeng Lu entrance of Liuhua Park.

Seals
You can have your name engraved in Chinese characters on a seal, called a chop in colonial English, at the basement floor of the White

Swan Hotel. When selecting your Chinese name, choose auspicious characters and limit yourself to two or three. If you need assistance, the staff at the shop will help you to choose the right combination. The material used can be hard wood, soapstone, crystal or agate. The shop will also sell you the special red ink (*hong yau*) that goes with the seal. Do not buy from side street sellers, as the seals they sell are made of bakelite and resin imitations of stone.

JADE AND PEARLS

Jade
Jade holds a greater fascination for the Chinese than any other stone. Traditionally, it is worn for good luck, as a protection against sickness and as an amulet for travellers. There are several types of jade: nephrite, jadeite, and a local variety, *nanyu* jade. Do not buy from open-air private markets, as there are plenty of imitations in the market. Buy from established shops like the **Jade Shop** (12–14 Zhongshan Wulu), Baoli Yuqi Hang (220 Zhongshan Silu), **Guangzhou Antique Shop** (696 Wende Lu), and the jewellery shops of the China, Garden and White Swan hotels.

Pearls
For centuries, pearls have been the indispensable ornament of the nobility, especially emperors. Most of the pearls on sale in Guangzhou are saltwater southern pearls called *hepu*, cultured in silver-lipped oysters. The largest of these lustrous pearls can have a diameter of 1.2–1.6 cm. Recommended shops: **Guangzhou Gold and Silver Jewellery Centre** (109 Dade Lu) and **Sun Moon Hall** (Equatorial Hotel, Renmin Beilu).

MAO MEMORABILIA

In celebration of Mao's 100th birthday in 1993, centennial souvenirs appeared, such as commemorative watches and musical cigarette lighters playing revolutionary ditties. The **Daihe Lu** antique market has a reasonable variety of Mao artifacts, while the Friendship Stores sell 24K, diamond-studded medals. For badges, the stamp market in People's Park has the best pieces. Prices can be steep.

Hong Kong

Hong Kong has frequently been called a shopper's paradise and it is certainly true that Hong Kong people are insatiable shoppers. Shopping places range from colourful night markets to glitzy malls, multi-storey department stores to bustling narrow streets of antiques and bric-a-brac. These days, Hong Kong is no longer the bargain-buy basement it once was for luxury goods, but the economic recession has helped bring prices back down to earth.

Tourists have clout in Hong Kong. If you run into significant problems with merchants that you cannot resolve, call the HKTA's multilingual hotline: 2807 6177. If the offending shop is a HKTA member, the tourist board will try to resolve the matter. Otherwise, it can recommend cases to the Hong Kong Consumer Council (Tel: 2929 2222).

Shopping guide

Before browsing, pick up a copy of the HKTA's official shopping guide – available at the HKTA Information Centres in Central and Tsim Sha Tsui – an invaluable free booklet with many useful tips. An important thing to note about shopping in Hong Kong is that goods purchased are not normally returnable or refundable; don't make expensive purchases if not certain.

WHERE TO SHOP

The "prime" shopping centres are Central, Admiralty and Causeway Bay on Hong Kong island and Tsim Sha Tsui and Mong Kok in Kowloon. Shopping hours vary, but the good news is that shopping basically goes on till late seven days a week. Even during public holidays, shops are almost always open, except during the annual lunar new year holiday. As a guide, shops in Central close earlier, around 6pm, but the other main areas tend to stay open until 9.30pm, sometimes later.

Malls
Hong Kong has some of the world's most glitzy and glamorous shopping malls. These may not seem as colourful to tourists as outdoor markets, but they are certainly more comfortable than traipsing around the streets during the hot and humid summers.

The best-known shopping malls on Hong Kong Island are Landmark in Central, Pacific Place in Admiralty, Times Square in Causeway Bay, and City Plaza in Taikoo Shing. In Kowloon, the linked Ocean Terminal and Harbour Centre complexes can keep you busy for a long time.

Bargaining
Contrary to popular belief, the practice of bargaining for goods in Hong Kong is very much on the way out. Price differences are usually so marginal that it is hardly worth the energy trying to bargain. Shopkeepers that are not used to bargaining will probably react rather impatiently to your efforts. If you settle by cash you may get a slightly better deal than by using credit cards. In many cases, shops will add an extra few percent to the price if you use credit cards.

WHAT TO BUY

Fashion
Hong Kong tailors are as skilled as ever, at both classic tailoring and copying existing garments. Prices vary according to the work involved, as well as the quality and quantity of cloth and trimmings. A good custom-tailored shirt starts at

around US$35, and a suit from about US$350. Quality tailors prefer several fittings; the so-called 24-hour suit, at rock-bottom prices, is rarely the bargain it sounds. Tailor Kwan (314, Worldwide Plaza, Central), Sam's Tailor (Burlington Arcade K, 92-94 Nathan Road, Tsim Sha Tsui), Yuen's Tailors (233, Escalator Link Alley, Central Market) and William Cheng & Son (8th Floor, 38 Hankow Road, Tsim Sha Tsui) are recommended.

Designer boutiques invaded Hong Kong during the 1980s, primarily to serve locals and Japanese tourists. All the big names are here – Armani, Chanel, DKNY, Issey Miyake and dozens more. They cluster in The Landmark, Pacific Place, Prince's Building and Times Square Galleria on Hong Kong-side; the top-flight hotel arcades – New World Centre and Harbour City complex – and along Canton Road in Tsim Sha Tsui. Don't expect lower prices than in Europe or US.

Inspiring work by up-and-coming Hong Kong designers can be found in the TDC's Design Gallery (Level 1, Convention Plaza, Harbour Road, Wan Chai). More unusual still are quintessential Chinese *cheongsam*, Mao suits and Tang jackets available off-the-peg, or custom-tailored, from Shanghai Tang (Pedder Building).

For real bargains, head for the street markets and factory outlets in Wan Chai, Tsim Sha Tsui, and Mong Kok. For a fraction of the price back home, these sell over-runs and slightly damaged 'seconds" of locally-manufactured clothes designed for the export market. As a general guide, bargain-priced women's wear, men's wear, T-shirts and jeans, and children's clothes can be found in the factory outlets along Haiphong and Granville roads, in Tsim Sha Tsui; Spring Garden Lane and Johnston Road in Wan Chai; Stanley Market and Jardine's Bazaar in Causeway Bay; and Tung Choi Street Ladies' Market and Fa Yuen Street in Mong Kok. The shops in Pedder Building, Central, are good places for quality women's wear, and the Temple

Custom Tailors

Having your own suit made to measure is still a popular luxury for visitors to Hong Kong. The territory has some of the legendary tailors of old Shanghai who have passed on their skills to the next generation. The speed and quality of craftsmanship and the range of fabrics are all excellent. It is no longer a sensational bargain, but still worthwhile.

A few places continue to offer the 24-hour suit, but these are not usually the best. Expect your tailor to take about a week if you want a high-quality garment worth paying for. There are plenty of tailors in Tsim Sha Tsui and a few in Wan Chai and Causeway Bay. The Shanghai Tang store in Central also offers a Shanghainese tailoring service for either Western- or Mandarin-style suits.

Street night market has cheap men's wear. The Chinese Products emporia, such as the CRC Department Stores have excellent bargains on silks.

Leather Goods
Many shops stock a wide range of leather shoes, bags, wallets and luggage. There are top-quality, brand-name goods as well as inexpensive wallets and bags from discount stores in the main shopping areas of Tsim Sha Tsui and Causeway Bay.

Sportswear
Hong Kong has many shops selling inexpensive sportswear. In Mong Kok there are several streets consisting of almost nothing but sports stores.

Computers
Hong Kong is a major exporter of computers, components, and accessories and you will find the most up-to-date models at bargain prices. There are a number of arcades solely devoted to selling

computers and accessories. The best are Star House in Tsim Sha Tsui near the Star Ferry, Windsor House in Causeway Bay, and Whampoa Gardens in Hung Hom, Kowloon.

Computer equipment can be found at the Computer Mall in Windsor House, Causeway Bay; Star Computer City in Star House and the Silvercord Centre in Tsim Sha Tsui; Mong Kok Computer Centre; New Capital Computer Plaza and Golden Shopping Centre in Sham Shui Po (the latter is renowned for pirated software). Prices for genuine PCs and programs are about the same as in Europe and North America.

Cameras and Electronic goods
If prepared to shop around, these are still good buys in Hong Kong. Shops selling televisions, video cameras and recorders, laser-disc and VCD players, stereo systems, and portable tape and CD players cluster in Causeway Bay and Tsim Sha Tsui, especially along Nathan, Peking, Mody and Carnarvon roads. Merchants can spot a sucker at fifty paces, so bargain hard; the fixed-price retail chains Broadway Photo Supply and Fortress are good alternatives.

The streets around Nathan Road are also full of camera shops. Most resident ex-pats buy their film and equipment in the shops in Stanley Street, Central. Beware of being ripped off in camera shops. Most camera and electronics stores are in Causeway Bay, Tsim Sha Tsui, and Mong Kok. They seldom have price tags on the items, so bargain, compare prices, and beware. There is not such a range in these areas, but they are friendly, reasonably priced, and there are few reports of cheating.

With electronic goods, remember to check for correct voltage, adaptors etc. Hand-held electronic games are particularly advanced in Hong Kong and make great gifts for teenagers. Hong Kong also has some of the best prices in the world for compact discs.

Art, Antiques & Crafts

Hong Kong is a centre for Asian arts and crafts, with museum-quality antique furniture, ceramics, sculptures, textiles and traditional paintings from China, Tibet, Japan, and Southeast Asia. More affordable are modern Chinese and Vietnamese paintings, Oriental rugs, reproduction Korean chests, 'antique' Chinese furniture and ceramics, Thai Buddha figurines, Balinese woodwork, Chinese folk paintings and other ethnic handicrafts.

The greatest concentration of antique and carpet dealers is along Hollywood Road and Wyndham Street in Central, but there are also a number of top-quality shops in Pacific Place, and at Harbour City and New World Centre on Kowloon-side. Fine-art galleries are considerably spread out, so it's best to check under exhibition listings in the newspapers, the free *HK* and *BC* magazines or HKTA's diary pages.

The Chinese Arts & Crafts and other PRC department stores are great places to look for Chinese arts and crafts. Shops like Amazing Grace Elephant Co. (Harbour City, Tsim Sha Tsui), The Banyan Tree (Prince's Building, Central and Harbour City), Tequila Kola (Prince's Building and United Centre, Admiralty), Vincent Sum Collection (Lyndhurst Terrace, Central) and Mountain Folkcraft (Wo On Lane, Central) stock furniture and craft items from elsewhere in Asia. Welfare Handicrafts in Jardine House and the HK Museum of Art shop are good places to pick up smaller gift items and cards.

Wan Chai is the best place for customised rattan and reproduction rosewood furniture, but Luk's Furniture warehouse in Aberdeen also has a good range of reproduction "antiques" and Korean chests.

Your best bet for Chinese ceramics is a local factory, like Wah Tung China in Aberdeen (which also has a small outlet on Hollywood Road) and Overjoy Porcelain Factory in Kwai Chung, New Territories.

Jewellery, Watches & Gemstones

Hong Kong is the world's fourth largest exporter of jewellery. Hong Kong is the world's largest jade market, the third-largest diamond trading centre (after New York and Antwerp), one of the largest gold brokers, and a magnet for precious stones from all over Asia and pearls from the Pacific Rim. Many finished items are manufactured in Hong Kong, ranging from simple gold bangles to exquisite diamond necklaces. There is a wide range of jewellery available in retail outlets. Because Hong Kong is a free port and there is no tax on the import or export of precious metals, prices are good.

A lot of people think they get the best buys on gold and jewellery at factory outlets in Hung Hom. But these have been flooded with bus loads of Japanese tourists in recent years and prices have risen accordingly. Better bargains, in fact, can be found in the jewellery and gold shops along Queen's Road Central. Chinese Arts & Crafts and other PRC department stores offer good deals on gold and jade, with a written guarantee. Top-flight hotel shopping arcades are another place to find quality jewellers. It's a good idea to get a professional gemologist to certify diamonds or other gemstones. Contact the HK Gemological Society at Tel: 2366 6006.

Designer watch shops selling the top brands cluster along the lower end of Nathan Road in Kowloon – which is equally famous for 'copy-watch' salesmen – and in the malls of Central. City Chain is a reasonably-priced watch retailer, with more than 40 branches in Hong Kong. Lots of watches are for sale at the Temple Street market. Be warned: they are fakes.

Particularly popular jewellery includes jade items (though you should avoid buying expensive items without expert advice) and bright yellow 24-kt gold, called *chuk kam* in Cantonese. Jewellery stores specialising in *chuk kam* are usually very crowded and the atmosphere resembles a betting shop more than an exclusive store. These items are sold by the weight of the gold only, so you pay no premium for the design. There are, of course, many fine jewellery stores selling gem set jewellery in a huge range of classical and stylish designs where you pay for the craftsmanship as well as the materials. Another good buy in Hong Kong is pearls, which come in all shapes, sizes and colours. The practice of bargaining is much less common in jewellery stores now, but you can try your luck by asking for a discount.

DEPARTMENT STORES

Hong Kong's oldest department store, Lane Crawford, and the upmarket Japanese store Seibu, in Pacific Place, are the local equivalents of Bloomingdale's or Harrods – classy and very expensive. For more down-to-earth prices, try long-established local department stores like Sincere and Wing On, where local people shop.

The popular Japanese department stores in Causeway Bay were largely decimated by the recession. However, the several branches of Marks & Spencer are a little piece of England in the tropics, although pricier than in the UK.

However, it's the mainland Chinese department stores that are most worthy of exploration, even if you don't intend to buy. Chinese Arts & Crafts is the most upmarket of all and concentrates on high-quality handicrafts, antiques, clothing and jewellery. Yue Hwa and Chung Kiu Chinese Products Emporiums stock arts and crafts, and a whole range of consumer items produced across the border. PRC department stores sell Chinese foodstuffs as well as inexpensive household items, ceramics and handicrafts. And finally, don't miss out on the Hong Kong-owned designer-chic 1930s-style Shanghai Tang department store (Pedder Building, Central), which has great retro-nostalgia Chinese fashions and gift items.

Shanghai

Shanghai is one of China's commercial capitals, and the number of both foreign and domestic goods available to the consumer has skyrocketed in the last few years. The best streets to shop on are Nanjing Lu and Huaihai Lu. Nanjing Lu is mobbed by local and out-of-town Chinese shoppers on the weekends, while Huaihai Lu offers a more quaint, upscale experience that attracts foreigners and Shanghai's *nouveau riche*.

DEPARTMENT STORES AND MALLS

Shanghai is full of Western-style malls and departments stores selling everything from local goods to foreign name brands.

The **Shanghai No. 1 Department Store**, 800–830 Nanjing Dong Lu, is the largest and most famous state-owned store in town, and specialises in domestic goods. The **Dickson Centre**, 400 Changle Lu, Tel: 6472 6888 and **Maison Mode**, 1312 Huaihai Zhong Lu, Tel: 6431 0100 offers high-level brand names like Ralph Lauren, Salvatore Ferragamo, Christian Dior, Nina Ricci, and Guy Laroche. The ritzy French-run **Printemps**, 939–947 Huaihai Zhong Lu, Tel: 6431 0118 also features upscale shopping and foreign name brands.

Middle- to high-level shopping can be found at the **Hongqiao Friendship Shopping Centre**, 6 Zunyi Lu, Tel: 6270 0000, and the huge **Yaohan Department Store**, 501 Zhangyang Lu, Pudong, Tel: 5830 1111, supposedly Asia's largest, which sell everything from groceries to clothing to furniture, both domestic and imported. The Japanese-run **Isetan**, 527 Huaihai Zhong Lu, Tel: 6375 1111; Nanjing Lu at Jiangning Lu is one of the most fashionable in Shanghai and has a good selection of mid- to up-scale boutiques such as Isetan, Episode and Benetton. **Jusco**, 218 Tianmu Xi Lu, Tel: 6354 1110, a true mall in the American sense, also contains a large department store and foreign boutiques.

On a more upscale, but still local, level is the **Orient Shopping Centre**, 8 Caoxi Bei Lu, Tel: 6407 1947, located in the bustling Gotham City-like area of Xujiahui. It sells everything from clothing to appliances.

ANTIQUES

Antique goods and furniture markets, shops and warehouses are plentiful in Shanghai, but prices have greatly increased over the last few years. Antique buying is made interesting at the **Fuyou Lu Sunday Market** off Henan Lu. Hawkers gather their goods on the sidewalks of this tiny alley early in the morning. You must come before 9am to find the best goods. The daily **Dongtai Lu Market** located off Xizang Lu also has a good selection of antiques, but goods are presented in stalls rather than on the ground. The **Haobao Building** in Yuyuan Garden, 265 Fangbang Lu, Tel: 6355 9999, has an entire floor of booths selling antiques.

For antique furniture, there are several warehouses in town that include renovation in the sale of any piece. They are located at: 1970 Hongqiao Lu, Tel: 6242 8734, 1220 Hongmei Lu, Tel: 6436 1500 ext. 195, 9100 7152, 307 Shunchang Lu, Tel: 6320 3812, and 1430 Hongqiao Lu.

ARTS AND CRAFTS

The famous state-owned department store, the **Friendship Store**, 40 Beijing Dong Lu, Tel: 6329 4600, sells foreign and domestic goods, primarily Chinese arts and crafts and silk. You can watch Shanghai artisans create traditional arts and crafts at the **Arts and Crafts Research Institute**, 79 Fenyang Lu, Tel: 6437 0509.

Porcelain and other wares can be purchased at the Shanghai **Jingdezhen Porcelain Store**, 1175 Nanjing Xi Lu, Tel: 6253 3178, while tea and Yixing pots are plentiful at the **Shanghai Huangshan Tea Company**, 853 Huaihai Zhong Lu, Tel: 6545 4919.

CLOTHING, FABRICS AND TAILORS

Shanghai has many professional tailors, such as Taylor Lee, 2018 Huaihai Lu (open Wednesday and Saturday only) , Hansheng, Shanghai Centre, 1376 Nanjing Xi Lu, Tel: 6279 8600, Wing's and Sakurai Yofuku, Friendship Shopping Centre, 6 Zunyi Lu, Tel: 6270 0000, and Ascot Chang, Dickson Centre, 400 Changle Lu, Room 211, Tel: 6472 6888.

A few tailors specialise in making Chinese qipaos (cheongsams). One shop at 258 Shimen Yi Lu does good work. Inexpensive street-side tailors can be found at Tailor Lane, which is a small alley leading to Hunan Lodge on Wuyuan Lu near Maison Mode Department Store. It's best if you bring in a garment to copy rather than commission more complicated work.

Shop for silk at the Golden Dragon Silk and Wool Company, 816 Huaihai Zhong Lu, Tel: 6473 6691, which has the widest selection in town. Quality fabrics can also be purchased at the Shanghai Silk and Wool Company, 816 Huaihai Zhonglu. You can buy ready-made silk clothing at the Friendship Store.

Sometimes you can find good knockoffs and seconds at the Huating Lu outdoor clothing market off Huaihai Lu just to the east of Changshu Lu. Bargaining is encouraged.

Macau

Macau is a good place to buy Chinese antiques and artifacts. The main street, Avenida Almeida Ribeiro, has a few antique shops on both sides of the street as you walk from the Outer Harbour (near the Lisboa and Sintra Hotels), and towards the Inner Harbour (near the Floating casino).

Otherwise, Macau is rarely thought of as a shopping mart, except for its magnificently-priced wines, brandies and ports (which are restricted upon return to Hong Kong). Though it is a duty-free port like Hong Kong, the array of goods available is not nearly so elaborate. Some items, such as cameras or stereo systems, are more expensive in Macau because of the smaller number sold. And like Hong Kong, Macau is a clothing manufacturing centre, especially of knitwear, though whatever little that is displayed is apparently not very fashionable.

Language

General

English is increasingly being used in the People's Republic of China, but on the whole, you will still find it difficult to meet people away from the big hotels and business and tourist centres who speak English, not to mention German or French. It is therefore advisable – especially for individual travellers – to learn some Chinese. Some people joke that, apart from *meiyou* ("it doesn't exist"), the most common words in China are "change money?", in English.

More than a billion people in China, and many other Chinese in Southeast Asia and North America, speak Chinese. In the People's Republic of China, other languages in addition to Chinese – the language of the Han people, the original Chinese – are spoken in the regions where the national minorities are settled, including Tibetan, Mongolian, Zhuang or Uighur. But everywhere in the People's Republic today, standard Chinese, also called Mandarin, is more or less understood or spoken. Regardless of whether you are in Guangzhou or in Heilongjiang, in Tibet or in Xinjiang, you can get along with standard Chinese.

The Chinese language is divided into several groups of dialect. For instance, a native of Guangzhou or Hong Kong cannot understand someone from Beijing or vice versa, unless both speak standard Chinese. The different dialects have, however, the same grammar and vocabulary; the writing is the same, it's the pronunciation that differs. The pronunciation may differ, but the written symbols can

be understood by all literate Chinese. Thus, a native of Guangzhou and a Beijing citizen can understand each other by simply writing the symbols.

Since the 1950s, all schools in the People's Republic of China teach standard Chinese or Mandarin – also called *putonghua* or common language. It is also used on radio and television. Young Chinese people, particularly, know standard Chinese. Consequently, one can manage throughout the People 's Republic – including in Guangzhou – by using standard Chinese. You will immediately notice the difference when you go from Guangzhou to Hong Kong: in Hong Kong, the official language amongst the Chinese is Cantonese.

The transcription of Chinese symbols: Standard Chinese is based on the pronunciation of the northern dialects, particularly the Beijing dialect. There is an officially approved roman writing of standard Chinese, called Hanyu Pinyin (the phonetic transcription of the language of the Han people). Pinyin is used throughout the People's Republic; many public transportation facilities show name places and street names both in symbols and in the romanised transcription.

Most modern dictionaries use the pinyin system. (Taiwan, however, usually uses the older Wade-Giles transliteration system.) This transcription may at first appear confusing if one doesn't see the words as they are pronounced. The city of Qingdao, for example, is pronounced *chingdow*. It would definitely be useful to familiarise yourself a little with the pronunciation of pinyin. Even when asking for a place or street name, you need to know how it is pronounced, otherwise you won't be understood. This guide uses the pinyin system throughout for Chinese names and expressions on occasion.

The pronunciation of Chinese: The pronunciation of the consonants is similar to those in English: b, p, d, t, g, k are all voiceless; p, t, k are aspirated, b, d, g are not aspirated. The i after the consonants ch, c, r, sh, s, z, zh is not pronounced, it indicates that the preceding sound is lengthened.

Pinyin/Phonetic/Sound

a/a/**far**
an/un/r**un**
ang/ung/l**ung**
ao/ou/l**oud**
b/b/**b**ath
c/ts/ra**ts**
ch/ch/**ch**ange
d/d/**d**ay
e/er/d**ir**t
e (after i,u,y)/a/t**ra**m
ei/ay/m**ay**
en/en/wh**en**
eng/eong/**ng** has a nasal sound
er/or/h**o**nour
f/f/**f**ast
g/g/**g**o
h/ch/lo**ch**
i/ee/k**ee**n
j/j/**j**eep
k/k/**c**ake
l/l/**l**ittle
m/m/**m**onth
n/n/**n**ame
o/o/b**o**nd
p/p/tra**pp**ed
q/ch/**ch**eer
r/r/**r**ight
s/s/me**ss**
sh/sh/**sh**ade
t/t/**t**on
u/oo/sh**oo**t
u (after j,q,x,y)/as German
u+/mu+de
w/w/**w**ater
x/ch/as in Scottish lo**ch**, followed by s
y/y/**y**ogi
z/ds/re**ds**
zh/dj/**j**ungle

It is often said that the Chinese language is monosyllabic. At first sight this may seem the case since, generally, each symbol is one word. However, in modern Chinese, most words are made up of two or three syllable symbols, sometimes more.

Chinese generally lacks syllables, there are only 420 in Mandarin to represent all symbols in sounds or tones. The tones are used to differentiate – a specifically Chinese practice which often makes it very difficult for foreigners when first learning the Chinese language. Each syllable has a specific sound. These sounds often represent different meanings. For instance, if one pronounces the syllable *mai* with a falling fourth sound (*mài*) it means to sell; if it is pronounced with a falling-rising third sound, it means to buy. When one reads the symbols carefully this is always clearly shown.

Mandarin has four tones and a fifth, 'soundless' sound: The first tone is spoken high pitched and even, the second rising, the third falling and then rising, and the fourth sound falling.

first sound *ma:* **mother**
second sound *má:* **hemp**
third sound *ma:* **horse**
fourth sound *mà:* **to complain**

The Chinese sentence structure is simple: subject, predicate, object. The simplest way of forming a question is to add the question particle 'ma'' to a sentence in ordinary word sequence. It is usually not possible to note from a Chinese word whether it is a noun, adjective or another form, singular or plural: it depends on the context.

The Chinese language is a language of symbols or images. Each symbol represents a one-syllable word. There are in total more than 47,000 symbols, though modern Chinese only use a part of these. For a daily newspaper, between 3,000 and 4,000 symbols are sufficient. Scholars know between 5,000 and 6,000. Many symbols used to be quite complicated. After 1949, several reforms in the written language were introduced in the People's Republic in order to simplify the written language. Today, the simplified symbols are used throughout mainland China, though in Hong Kong and Taiwan, the complex ones are still used.

Many Chinese words are composed of two or more symbols or single-syllable words. For instance, the Chinese word for film is *dian-ying*, and is made up of the two words: *dian* for electricity and *ying* for shadow. To make reading easier, the pinyin system joins syllables which, together, form words. Group travellers generally have translators with them in case of communication problems. But if you are travelling on your own, it is worth taking a dictionary.

Other Insight Guides

Looking for more on China? More detailed information on Beijing? In-depth information on Hong Kong? Consider, then, these other Apa Publications guides:

ART & PHOTO CREDITS

INSIGHT GUIDE
CHINA

Cartographic Editor **Zoë Goodwin**
Production **Mohammed Dar, Caroline Low**
Design Consultants **Klaus Geisler, Graham Mitchener**
Picture Research **Hilary Genin**

Index

Numbers in italics refer to photographs